Literature and Religious Experience

Literature and Religious Experience

Beyond Belief and Unbelief

Edited by
Matthew J. Smith and Caleb D. Spencer

BLOOMSBURY ACADEMIC
LONDON · NEW YORK · OXFORD · NEW DELHI · SYDNEY

BLOOMSBURY ACADEMIC
Bloomsbury Publishing Plc
50 Bedford Square, London, WC1B 3DP, UK
1385 Broadway, New York, NY 10018, USA
29 Earlsfort Terrace, Dublin 2, Ireland

BLOOMSBURY, BLOOMSBURY ACADEMIC and the Diana logo are
trademarks of Bloomsbury Publishing Plc

First published in Great Britain 2022
This paperback edition published 2023

Copyright © Matthew J. Smith, Caleb D. Spencer and contributors, 2022

Matthew J. Smith, Caleb D. Spencer and contributors have asserted their right under the
Copyright, Designs and Patents Act, 1988, to be identified as Authors of this work.

For legal purposes the Acknowledgments on pp. viii–ix constitute an
extension of this copyright page.

Cover design: Eleanor Rose
Cover image: *Square in a Circle*, 1928 (w/c on paper) by Wassily Kandinsky,
(1866–1944) / Russian. Photo © Christie's Images / Bridgeman Images

All rights reserved. No part of this publication may be reproduced or transmitted
in any form or by any means, electronic or mechanical, including photocopying,
recording, or any information storage or retrieval system, without prior
permission in writing from the publishers.

Bloomsbury Publishing Plc does not have any control over, or responsibility for, any
third-party websites referred to or in this book. All internet addresses given in this
book were correct at the time of going to press. The author and publisher regret any
inconvenience caused if addresses have changed or sites have ceased to exist, but
can accept no responsibility for any such changes.

A catalogue record for this book is available from the British Library.

A catalog record for this book is available from the Library of Congress.

ISBN: HB: 978-1-3501-9391-8
PB: 978-1-3501-9402-1
ePDF: 978-1-3501-9392-5
eBook: 978-1-3501-9393-2

Typeset by Newgen KnowledgeWorks Pvt. Ltd., Chennai, India

To find out more about our authors and books visit www.bloomsbury.com
and sign up for our newsletters.

Contents

Notes on Contributors	vii
Reflections and Acknowledgments	xi

Introduction: "The data of our feelings": Beyond Belief and Unbelief   1
  Matthew J. Smith and Caleb D. Spencer

Overture: Prayer: I Will Love You in the Summertime   11
  Christian Wiman

1 Revelation: Mallarmé and the Negativity of Prophetic Revelation in
  Modern Literature   21
  William Franke

2 Blessing: Shakespeare's Benedictional Designs   39
  Julia Reinhard Lupton

3 Longing: Young Geoffrey Hill and the Problem of Religious Poetry   55
  Kevin Hart

4 Interruption: Conversion as an Event in Paul of Tarsus and
  Paul of Burgos   73
  Ryan Szpiech

5 Vision: Building into the Blue   91
  Gavin Hopps

6 *Metanoia*: Tales of Transformation in Harriet Beecher Stowe and
  Wendell Berry   109
  John Gatta

7 Belief: Marilynne Robinson's *Gilead* and James Wood's *The Book
  Against God*   125
  Lori Branch

8 Turning: Alabaster's Wager and the Experience of Conversion   141
  James Kearney

9 Guidance: Understanding Providence in George MacDonald's Fiction   161
  Mark Knight

10 Silence: Kidnapping, Abuse, and Murder in Early-Twenty-First-
  Century White Evangelical Fiction   177
  Christopher Douglas

vi   *Contents*

11 One: Poetic Love in Ibn ʿArabī *Jeff Sacks*	193

12 Humankindness: *King Lear* and the Suffering, Wisdom, and
   Compassion within Buddhist Interbeing
   Unhae Park Langis
	209

13 Gift: The (Im)possible Conditions of Grace in Herman Melville *Tae Sung*	227
14 Fantasy: Magical Experiences and Postsecular Fiction *Zhange Ni*	241

15 Idolatry: Meaning, Power, and "Ideas" of Idolatry in *Heart of*
   Darkness and *Demian*
   Larry D. Bouchard
	259

Afterword *Terry Eagleton*	279
Index	287

Contributors

Larry Bouchard is Professor in the Department of Religious Studies at the University of Virginia. He is the author of *Tragic Method and Tragic Theology: Evil in Contemporary Drama and Religious Thought* (1989) and *Theater and Integrity: Emptying Selves in Drama, Ethics, and Religion* (2011). He is also coeditor of *Interpreting Disciples: Practical Theology in the Disciples of Christ* (1987).

Lori Branch is Associate Professor of English at the University of Iowa. She is the author of *Rituals of Spontaneity: Sentiment and Secularism from Free Prayer to Wordsworth* (2006) and is the editor of the book series "Literature, Religion, and Postsecular Studies" at Ohio State University Press.

Christopher Douglas is Professor of English at the University of Victoria. His books include *Reciting America: Culture and Cliche in Contemporary U.S. Fiction* (2001), *A Genealogy of Literary Multiculturalism* (2009), and *If God Meant to Interfere: American Literature and the Rise of the Christian Right* (2016). He is also the editor of the forthcoming special issue, "Literature and the Religious Right," in *Christianity & Literature.*

Terry Eagleton is Distinguished Professor in the Department of English Literature and Creative Writing at Lancaster University. He has published over forty books, including *The Ideology of the Aesthetic* (1991), *The Illusions of Postmodernism* (1996), *Culture and the Death of God* (2014), *Hope without Optimism* (2019), *Humour* (2019), and the forthcoming *Radical Sacrifice* (2020). He has held the positions of John Edward Taylor Professor of English Literature at the University of Manchester and Thomas Warton Professor of English Literature at the University of Oxford.

William Franke is Professor of Comparative Literature and Religious Studies at Vanderbilt University and a research fellow of the Alexander von Humboldt-Stiftung. His books include *A Philosophy of the Unsayable* (2014), *The Revelation of Imagination: From the Bible and Homer through Virgil and Augustine to Dante* (2015), *A Theology of Literature: The Bible as Revelation in the Tradition of the*

viii   *Contributors*

Humanities (2017), and *Apophatic Paths from Europe to China: Regions without Borders* (2018).

John Gatta is William B. Kenan Jr. Professor of English Emeritus at Sewanee, University of the South. His books include *Gracious Laughter: The Meditative Wit of Edward Taylor* (1989), *American Madonna: Images of the Divine Woman in Literary Culture* (1998), *Making Nature Sacred: Literature, Religion, and Environment in America from the Puritans to the Present* (2004), *The Transfiguration of Christ and Creation* (2011), and *Spirits of Place in American Literary Culture* (2018).

Kevin Hart is Edwin B Kyle Professor of Christian Studies at the University of Virginia. His critical books include *The Trespass of the Sign* (1989), *A. D. Hope* (1992), *Samuel Johnson and the Culture of Property* (1999), *The Dark Gaze: Maurice Blanchot and the Sacred* (2004), *Postmodernism* (2004), *Kingdoms of God* (2014), *Poetry and Revelation* (2017), *Contemplation and Kingdom* (2021), and *L'image vulnérable* (2021). His recent books of poetry include *Morning Knowledge* (2011), *Wild Track: New and Selected Poems* (2015), and *Barefoot* (2018). He coedits the book series "Thresholds: Philosophy and Theology" for Bloomsbury and is currently giving the Gifford Lectures at the University of Glasgow.

Gavin Hopps is Director of the Institute for Theology, Imagination and the Arts (ITIA) and Senior Lecturer in Literature and Theology at the University of St Andrews. He is the author of *Morrissey: The Pageant of His Bleeding Heart* (2009) and *The Extravagance of Music* (2018). He is the editor of *Byron's Ghosts: The Spectral, the Spiritual and the Supernatural* (2013), and with Jane Stabler he is the coeditor of *Romanticism and Religion from William Cowper to Wallace Stevens* (2006).

James Kearney is Associate Professor of English at the University of California, Santa Barbara. He is the author of *The Incarnate Text: Imagining the Book in Reformation England* (2009) and coeditor, with Kevin Curran, of "Shakespeare and Phenomenology," a special issue of *Criticism* (2012).

Mark Knight is Professor in Literature, Religion, and Victorian Studies at Lancaster University. His books include *Chesterton and Evil* (2004), *Nineteenth-Century Religion and Literature*, coauthored with Emma Mason (2006), *An*

Introduction to Religion and Literature (2009), and Good Words: Evangelicalism and the Victorian Novel (2019). Among his editorial projects is The Routledge Companion to Literature and Religion (2016). He is also the editor of the journal Literature & Theology (Oxford) and coedits the book series "New Directions in Religion and Literature" for Bloomsbury.

Unhae Park Langis, a teacher of twenty years, is now a visiting researcher at New Swan Shakespeare Center at the University of California, Irvine. She has authored Passion, Prudence, and Virtue in Shakespearean Drama (2011) and numerous essays in ethical criticism (recently, from Stoic, Buddhist, and Sufi perspectives) in collections and journals including Shakespeare Studies, EMLS, Upstart Crow, and Literature Compass. She is presently collaborating with Julia Reinhard Lupton on a collection on Shakespeare and wisdom literature.

Zhange Ni is Associate Professor in the Department of Religion and Culture at Virginia Tech. She is the author of The Pagan Writes Back: When World Religion Meets World Literature (2015).

Julia Reinhard Lupton is Professor of English at the University of California, Irvine. Her books include Citizen-Saints: Shakespeare and Political Theology (2005), Thinking with Shakespeare: Essays on Politics and Life (2011), and Shakespeare Dwelling: Designs for the Theater of Life (2018). Her editorial projects include A Critical Guide to Romeo and Juliet (2016), Shakespeare and Hospitality: Politics, Ethics, Exchange, with David Goldstein (2016), Face to Face in Shakespearean Drama: Ethics, Performance Philosophy, with Matthew Smith (2019), and Shakespeare and Virtue: A Handbook, with Donovan Sherman (2022).

Jeff Sacks is Chair and Associate Professor of Comparative Literature and Arabic at the University of California, Riverside. He is the author of Iterations of Loss: Mutilation and Aesthetic Form, al-Shidyaq to Darwish (2015) and translator of Mahmoud Darwish, Why Did You Leave the Horse Alone? (2006).

Matthew J. Smith is Associate Professor of English at Azusa Pacific University. He is the author of Performance and Religion in Early Modern England: Stage, Cathedral, Wagon, Street (2018) and coeditor, with Julia Reinhard Lupton, of Face to Face in Shakespearean Drama (2019). He is the guest editor of two special issues of *Christianity & Literature: The Sacramental Text Reconsidered* (2016) and *Sincerity* (2017).

Caleb D. Spencer is Associate Professor of English at Azusa Pacific University. His essays appear in *Religion & Literature, Journal of the Religion and Popular Culture,* and *Christianity & Literature.* He coedited "Sincerity," a special issue of *Christianity & Literature* (2017). He also serves as Associate Editor of the journal *Christianity & Literature.*

Tae Sung is Associate Professor of English and Director of the University Writing Center at California Baptist University. His essays appear in *William James Studies, Books and Culture,* and *The Princeton Encyclopedia of Poetry and Poetics.*

Ryan Szpiech is Associate Professor in the Departments of Romance Languages and Literatures and Judaic Studies and an affiliate of the Department of Comparative Literature at the University of Michigan. He is the author of *Conversion and Narrative: Reading and Religious Authority in Medieval Polemic* (2012), editor of *Medieval Exegesis and Religious Difference: Commentary, Conflict, and Community in the Premodern Mediterranean* (2015), and coeditor of *Astrolabes in Medieval Culture* (2019). He also serves as Editor of the journal *Medieval Encounters.*

Christian Wiman is Professor of the Practice of Religion and Literature at Yale Divinity School. His books include *Stolen Air: Selected Poems of Osip Mandelstam* (2012), *My Bright Abyss: Meditation of a Modern Believer* (2013), *Hammer is the Prayer: Selected Poems* (2016), and *He Held Radical Light: The Art of Faith, the Faith of Art* (2018). From 2003 to 2013 he served as Editor of *Poetry Magazine.*

Reflections and Acknowledgments

This volume began in an intellectual friendship that itself grew within a peculiar place and time: a historically religious university in the pluralistic and ethnically diverse atmosphere of greater Los Angeles. What it means in the twenty-first century for a university to be aligned with a faith tradition and yet also to encourage academic freedom and student action is unclear. "Methinks the ground is even," says one. "Horrible steep," says the other. The year 2020 has exacerbated the vertigo in similar terrains of higher education across the world, but many have found hidden sanctuaries buried beneath isolation, media saturation, and political unrest. Religion is one such space. As a term, "religion," as opposed to belief or even practice, captures the strange negotiations that characterize acts of self-transcendent devotion. Piety and confession may not exist at all if it were not for ulterior motives—and not just pieties of creedal confession but also of rites of doubt and renunciation, giving and receiving, refusing and acknowledging. Religions are full of ceremonies and intermediations. As a category, the religious announces the non-immediacy of salvation. This sequence of need and fulfillment has made many modern philosophers and theorists suspicious, since it is vulnerable to abuse and primed to promote self-delusion. Yet the search for salvation is also so historically ubiquitous, even in professedly secular contexts, that it seems sometimes to be a familiar friend or home comfort. It is through the religious concepts of the numinous, affective, apophatic, and epiphanic that we can collect disparate traditions under the same banner of the religious, and it is through these same aesthetic and experiential concepts that we discover the meanings of pluralism, atheism, and secularism. Such observations led us to invite scholars to contribute to a volume about literature and *religious* experience. Some might find this choice unusual, since religion carries negative connotations in many faith circles today because it seems to denote mere practice—rites without faith. The flesh profits nothing, they say. But the examples featured in the following pages show that the opposite is also true: faith without rites is dead.

First acknowledgment belongs to the authors who wrote for this volume. It is the blessing of an editor to receive such gifts of time, creativity, and intellectual rigor. Our gratitude extends also to our colleagues and friends at Azusa Pacific

University and beyond, particular to the Faculty Research Council for their support. Special thanks to Alexis Cox who helped with the preparation of the manuscript as well as J. Eliot Reasoner for some transcription work. Finally, we recognize the many students whose intellectual curiosity spurred our work on the phenomenology and anthropology of religion as it relates to literary texts and performances. Their company, wit, and sometimes also their faith were encouragements to think more carefully.

Introduction: "The data of our feelings": Beyond Belief and Unbelief

Matthew J. Smith and Caleb D. Spencer

In 1950 the editors of *Partisan Review* ran the first of four symposia entitled "Religion and the Intellectuals."[1] They opined in their Editorial Statement that one "of the most significant tendencies of our time, especially in this decade, has been the new turn toward religion among intellectuals" (5). The editors enlisted their usual phalanx of midcentury commentators to discuss "the growing disfavor with which secular attitudes and perspectives" were "now regarded in not a few circles that lay claim to the leadership of culture." But it is the "turn" they go on to describe that makes this symposium so interesting. For the editors are not indicating a purely intellectual interest in religion—which was already well established by structuralist critics such as Northrop Frye—nor simply a growth in individual adherence, conviction, and practice. Rather, the turn is toward an appreciation for the experience of religion. Thus, in his essay, the critic Clement Greenberg reflects that "science has told us nothing about the absolute ground of being" and argues, by contrast, that, for the poet, Christianity allows one to "to believe once more in the data of our feelings." Greenberg suggests that the solution to T. S. Eliot's "disassociation of sensibility"—his sense that subjective experience conflicted with the objective representation—is the religious (69).

But it was not just Eliot who thought that religion was a solution to the poet's problem of a "divergence between thought and feeling." Religion helps to mend a kind of "schizophrenia" that severs the mind from its life in body and world. His protégé W. H. Auden writes as eloquently in the volume as Greenberg does of the limits of "naturalism" for the poet, averring that religion reorders the dissonance

---

[1] *Partisan Review*, "Religion and the Intellectuals."

between the material truths being championed by science and the secular age and the "data of feeling." Auden claims that all people, religious and otherwise, "share with everyone else in our civilization the experience of 'alienation,'" the condition of being disconnected from one's source or oneself: "Our dominant religious experience … is of our distance from God" (25). Accordingly, he views the return of intellectuals to religion, specifically Christianity, as caused by the way "Christianity … attaches a unique importance to history." History here is not just the aggregate of human agency or a Hegelian march of the dialectic but instead what Auden identifies in Augustine's *Confessions* as the convert's "personal historical situation" (23). Religion, for Auden, Greenberg, Eliot, and many other respondents in the *Partisan Review* symposia, put the person, the experiencer, back into the equation. Empirical data includes that of feeling, sensing, and coming to know, and at that point in European and North American history, religion presented itself as a potential bridge between knowledge and the one who discovers it.

Soon it wasn't just the New York intelligentsia championing religion in exclusive magazines. *TIME* would feature Reinhold Niebuhr and Paul Tillich on its covers as the 1950s saw an explosion of popular interest in religion. Likewise, shortly after, the academy witnessed the establishment of programs focused on the intersections of religion and literature at institutions like Boston University and the University of Chicago. Under the influence of writers like Nathan Scott and Paul Tillich, such programs understood religion in experiential terms, as embodying the paradox of the universal particular.

Yet the *Partisan Review* examples notwithstanding, the relationship between art and religion has only recently been figured as a history of separation, or secularization. This is partly due to the interdependence of art and religion in anthropology and to the relative prominence of anthropological methodology in midcentury literary and art criticism. The history of secularization in the west is in part the telling of the story of *poiesis* and its liberation from religion, and, while it is true that there have long been scholars (e.g., Christian Smith, Peter Berger, Paul Tillich) who would argue that all cultural objects imply an aspect of the religious, it has become common academic practice to assume that you can study works of art without studying religion and study religion without studying works of art. A principal reason for this practice is the removal of experience— enacted at different moments in intellectual history and for different reasons— as an essential component of religion, focusing instead on dogma, institutional structure, or ideology. So if it is true that in recent decades religion and art have often been considered separable analytic valences, it is probably also not surprising that experience has been separated from religion, even as more

Introduction

and more people over the last two centuries have grown interested in religious experience.

The present volume therefore engages with the historical conversation about religious experience that extends back at least as far as Friedrich Schleiermacher's *On Religion* and its historic formulation of a *sui generis*—that is, in a class of its own—conception of religious experience described by Wayne Proudfoot as the production of an "autonomous moment in human experience."[2] Schleiermacher's work influences William James's *The Varieties of Religious Experience*, which in many ways is as much a work of literary criticism as a study of religion. Simultaneous with James's book are the writings of Emile Durkheim, Max Weber, and Rudolf Otto who each rely on the *sui generis* conception of Schleiermacher to articulate accounts of religions in which experience is one of the key constitutive parts. Aldous Huxley in his *The Perennial Philosophy* systematizes this conception and makes possible mid-twentieth-century classical works of religious sociology, including Peter Berger's *The Sacred Canopy* and Mircea Eliade's *The Sacred and the Profane*, which separately argue for the centrality of designations of the sacred and the profane in experience and literary production. Throughout the middle decades of the twentieth century, literary critics looked to the sociology and anthropology of religion to produce readings of fiction, poetry, and drama. Scholars like Nathan Scott, Colin Still, Robert Deitweiler, Thomas Altizer, and William Lynch applied the interrogative potential of religion across time and tradition and discovered an understanding of religious experience, whether sacred or profane, within what Scott calls "traditions of sensibility" in literature.[3] Though such writers were later criticized for homogenizing patterns in religious practice, this was a time when literary criticism expanded the salience of religion to literary texts. Yet with the opponents of New Criticism came a challenge to sociological and anthropological readings of religion in literature, as theorists like Jacques Derrida, Michel Foucault, and Rudolf Steiner drew attention to the extent to which such structuralist views of human experience were not only descriptive but also prescriptive. "Experience" came to be seen as a product and function of language and culture. But in the last decade in Religious Studies, for instance, Anne Taves and Donovan Schaefer[4] have each criticized this linguistic and grammatical turn in the work of Proudfoot and others in the "ascriptive" field of Religious Studies revealing a renewed interest in religious experience.

---

[2] Proudfoot, *Religious Experience*.
[3] Scott Jr., *Rehearsals of Discompospure*; Still, *Shakespeare's Mystery Play*; Detweiler, *Four Spiritual Crises in Mid-Century American Fiction*; Altizer, *The New Apocalypse*; Lynch, *Christ and Apollo*.
[4] Taves, *Religious Experience Reconsidered*; Schaefer, *Religious Affects*.

4   *Literature and Religious Experience*

We are now seeing a return to the *sui generis* and perennialist tradition, on the one hand, and an adoption of affect and animal studies, on the other hand.

When religion charged back onto the literary critical scene in the last decade of the twentieth century, religious experience was still largely eschewed from focus. By 2005 the religious turn in literary studies was already being called "the religious turn." The decade preceding it witnessed the publication of Barbara Newman's *God and the Goddesses*, Stephen Greenblatt's *Hamlet in Purgatory*, Amy Hungerford's *Postmodern Belief*, and Stanley Fish's *How Milton Works*.[5] All of such work cannot be lumped together, of course, but one common interest that emerges is in the materialism of religion in literary studies. Themes under this banner include studies of heresy, vernacular theology, political theology, iconoclasm, and sectarianism. One can see how these topics, though diverse and innovative, nonetheless adhere to a historical view of Religion with a capital "R," identifying deviations from the institutional orthodoxy. The goal of much of this work was to locate outliers, exceptions to the institutional rule, and to show how these religious outliers were, in fact, part of the religious establishment more broadly conceived, challenging narratives of natural progress and the tidy dissemination of belief. Thus, the groundbreaking work of the recent religious turn has emphasized hyper-specific historical moments, the idiosyncrasies of particular doctrines, religious materialisms, and movements of secularity. New Historicist criticism played a particularly prominent role in the earlier years of the contemporary turn to religion. And as Ken Jackson and Arthur Marotti observe, such criticism "organizes itself around a claim to respect alterity, otherness, and difference, whether that be a marginalized group in a culture or the distant past itself."[6] The religious turn in literary studies might be characterized by a paradoxical expansion and limiting of religion's influence. While it excavated religion's material foundations in specific historical moments, it also confined religion to certain rules of excavation, redistributing Scott's "sensibility" among an array of worldly motivations and conditions.

There is discontinuity between the scholarship of the religious turn and the mythic, formalist, and structuralist work that preceded it, but more recent developments in literature and religion have begun to close the loop. Earlier interests of the religious turn in material history have evolved into new emphases on the body, ethnicity, conversion, doubt, affect, sacrament, and poetics. In a

---

[5] Newman, *God and the Goddesses*; Greenblatt, *Hamlet in Purgatory*; Hungerford, *Postmodern Belief*; Fish, *How Milton Works*.
[6] Jackson and Marotti, "The Turn to Religion in Early Modern English Studies."

Introduction

word, the religious turn has made a second turn toward religious experience. For instance, recent work on narratives of conversions to and from Judaism and Islam ("turning Turk") in Christian societies sheds light on the economic, sexual, and racial anxieties that are bound up with acts of confession and belief.[7] The return of religious experience to literary studies is signaled also by increased interest in poetics—poetics of belief, silence, and sacrament.[8] Peter Jaeger, for instance, has explored how the artist, John Cage, used a poetics of illegibility to intimate an ecological perspective inspired by Buddhism.[9] The worry to avoid universalizing across history and geography is still present but is internalized in such a way that enables us to consider concepts like revelation, blessing, silence, and prayer as they have existed in the dialectics between belief and practice.

The religious turn in literary studies is one example among many of how religion has, in fact, grown in scholarly interest even as sociological studies have prophesied the growth of a population with no religious affiliation (the "nones"). Reasons and etiologies for this growth abound. One explanation is scientific, where scholars simply follow the presence of religiously significant material in the works they study, unrelated to their own religious or anti-religious motives or yearnings. Another explanation for the continued growth of religious scholarship in the humanities is through the study of the alleged decline of religious practice, namely, the question of the secularity hypothesis. It is now possible for scholars to proclaim that the "secularity hypothesis is dead." And yet, even as secularity of some type might be in decline, much debate remains about the nature of religious commitment and practice that typifies and corresponds with this decline in secularity.

Understandings of religious psychology and sociology have expanded to include the "secular" under the label of the "postsecular." Postsecularism proposes an end to the secularity hypothesis, but not necessarily a turn, or return, to full-blown religious commitment. Instead scholars have tended to look at what might be called "partial faiths" and "new spiritualities." Such adapted, noninstitutional religious behaviors operate within this crack between full-blown religious adherence and secular doubt. John McClure defines the "postsecular" as a "mode of being and seeing that is at once critical of secular

---

[7] Vitkus, *Turning Turk*.

[8] See Johnson, *Poetics / Praxis*; Esmail, *The Poetics of Religious Experience*; Langdell, *Thomas Hoccleve*; Ricoeur, *Poetics and Religion*; Domestico, *Poetry and Theology in the Modernist Period*; and Schwartz, *Sacramental Poetics at the Dawn of Secularism*.

[9] Jaeger, *John Cage and Buddhist Ecopoetics*.

constructions of reality and of dogmatic religiosity."[10] Similarly, Amy Hungerford argues that many authors of the post-1945 generation reject immanent frames of secularity without wholly embracing a traditional religious point of view. Postmodern fiction represents a third way between religious dogmatism and Comte's secularization hypothesis.

The notion of the postsecular in contemporary fiction incidentally recenters faith on experience, but some may argue that it overcorrects its heading. Writing from the field of Religious Studies, Tracy Fessenden argues that the "Problem of the Postsecular" is that it hides acts of faith too far away from doctrine and belief. In place of doctrine, postsecular critics and the texts they champion seem to Fessenden to privilege "religious experience" and a confrontation with the sacred "of Being, Presence, Transcendence, Ultimacy, the Really Real, the Wholly Other, the *Mysterium Tremendum*, and so on."[11] While several of the essays in this book discuss the postsecular, we hope to show that this third way, the non-confessional confession of the postsecular, is and has long been part of religion's influence upon literary creation. Moreover, we argue that it is through the literary performance that experience and belief are on display in their ever-complicated dances. The intersection of literature and religious experience, in other words, defines a field that has long existed in theology and religious studies, lying dormant and going by different names in previous decades.

Our authors enhance the dialogue between literary studies and religious studies, including scholars from both disciplines. And while our focus is on literary texts and performances as sites of religious experience, we hope to demonstrate how literature shapes conceptions of religious experience as well as how religious experiences shape literary texts. These essays consider ways that competing accounts of religious experience have influenced distinct strands of literary analysis. Conversely, they also discuss how literary representation and criticism have influenced conceptions of religious experience within the area of religious studies. To this end, we reflect on how critical attention to environment, materiality, and race, for example, respectively contribute to new ways of verifying an individual experience or social practice as "religious," corresponding perhaps to attributive, epistemological, or phenomenological accounts of religious experience.

This volume uses the tools of several critical religious turnings to renovate the notion of religious experience in literary studies. Beyond the binaries of

---

[10] McClure, *Partial Faiths*, xi.
[11] Fessenden, "Problem of the Postsecular," 160.

Introduction 7

orthodoxy and heresy, secular and sacred, and homogeneity and pluralism, we seek to identify religion's phenomenological, sociological, and anthropological dimensions as they appear in literary texts and performances. Together, these essays re-enfranchize the data of feeling, living, and becoming. This is not to make a claim about the existential or moral primacy of experience over intention, belief, form, history, or incarnation. Rather, it is, in part, to give a name to the current drive among scholars to return religion to something that looks and feels more like its acts of faith—love, conversion, blessing, doubt, and the other experiences on which these shorts essays focus. As Mark Knight has commented in the Introduction to the recent *Routledge Companion to Literature and Religion*, the "disciplines of literature and religion are now so voluminous … that it is difficult to fix the lines that define them and their interdisciplinary subset."[12] Moreover, the very adjective, "religious," as Kevin Hart has argued, "bespeaks irruptions of modernity going on around it."[13] Just as at one time the multivalent capacities of literature were at risk of being suppressed by Religion (capital "R"), today religion as a category of continuity, comparison, and practice risks dissolving into so many disconnected acts of critical isolation. Might literary studies play a part in sustaining the tension between praxis and belief that characterizes lived religion through the prism of religious experience and its representations?

While a variety of religious traditions are represented in this book—including Islam, Buddhism, Greco-Roman polytheism, and practices of "magic"—it is important to acknowledge that studies of Christian and Jewish religious experience are the most prevalent. As fellow editors know, there are derivative as well as inductive factors involved in gathering contributions to collections. While our efforts to promote on a wide variety of religions and ethnic and cultural traditions produced some fruit, the inductive phenomenon of being Jewish- and Christian-centered is worth reflecting on. It prompts us to ask what it is about the notion of religious experience specifically, both as an ideal concept and as a historically emergent construction within a primarily Protestant and Jewish context in European and American Sociology and Religious Studies, that seems inviting to some scholars and unfamiliar to others. One way we attend to the causes that underlie this question is by encouraging our contributors to adopt a dialectical perspective on the relationship between religious belief or doctrine and experience. Instead of assuming a normative and uniform definition of

---

[12] Knight, *The Routledge Companion to Literature and Religion*, 4.
[13] Hart, *Poetry and Revelation*, 3.

religion and religious experience given to subjects from the outside, we explore the dual potential of devotional acts as both expressions and revelations of spiritual realities. The essays in this book are historically and theoretically self-critical about the genealogy of religion and its relationships to "religious experiences" understood in such categories as the heirophanic, numinous, sacred, revelatory, perennial, theophanic, affective, apophatic, sublime, and epiphanic. A category like "the sacred," for instance, when viewed through experiences of the sacred and formulated within the tradition from Weber and Durkheim to Otto and James, does not limit its analysis of religion to forms that fit within institutional hierarchies and dogmas. As an experience, the sacred is both constructed and iterated. It may be constructed in reaction to conditions of culture and economics. At the same time, we can view experiences of the sacred as iterations of a theme that runs through many or all of these cultural examples.

A similar acknowledgment could be made about the inclusion and presence of literary authors of color. The editors of this volume are also two of the editors of the journal, *Christianity & Literature*. It is our observation that approximately one third of the journal's submissions are essays about the same seven or eight authors. They include Robinson, O'Connor, McCarthy, Waugh, Eliot, Tolkien, Milton, and Shakespeare, all of whom are white. Which authors of color are nearest this group in submission data? Toni Morrison, Ralph Ellison, and Shūsaku Endō, and perhaps Augustine and the authors of the Hebrew and Christian scriptures, but the latter are controversial. In concert with this pattern, studies on authors of color were encouraged for the present volume but are nevertheless underrepresented in its final form. Although our strides here are short, we hope to contribute to a precedent for studying religious experience, as opposed to theology and institutional history, which will in turn open easier access to analysis of religious experiences in the works of authors outside the conventional canons. For it is not difficult to anticipate how themes like Fantasy, Interruption, and Silence can illuminate religion from the critical perspectives of race and ethnicity.

The studies that follow foreground keywords of religious experience, and they locate these phenomena in literary texts, defined within the circumstances of contributors' historical and theoretical areas of research. The result is not a polemic for experience over confession but a web of intersections between the abstract and concrete, revealed and hidden, believed and doubted. A concept of religious experience, such as "guilt," may appear in a distinct aspect, for example, in the vernacular practice of late medieval morality theater, and at the same time, the unique dramaturgy of medieval theater may reveal qualities of religious guilt that were previously unseen by theological writers. Alternately, religious experience might be of the numinous presence variety, as narrated in many novels and memoirs of the post-45 period, and at the same time such novels serve to show us new ostensions of numinous religious sensibilities. The circularity of this critical logic is characteristic of many anthropological accounts of religious experiences—in Durkheim's terms, "collective representations that express collective realities."[14]

Literature and Religious Experience is an attempt to answer some of the same questions that were posed by the editors of *Partisan Review* some seventy years ago. We are interested in the ways that experiences which are not reducible to material conditions are both created by and conveyed through literary works, and we are intrigued by the prospect of transcendence that has been seen as latent in *poiesis* since at least Plato's *Republic* and *Ion*. At the least, the authors in this volume aim to take seriously the possibility that literature might be a conduit for religious experience and the argument that literary scholarship does not dissolve that experience but, by giving it words, might enrich it.

Bibliography

Altizer, Thomas. *The New Apocalypse: The Radical Christian Vision of William Blake*. Lansing: Michigan State University Press, 1967.

Detweiler, Robert. *Four Spiritual Crises in Mid-Century American Fiction*. Gainesville: Florida University Press, 1964.

Domestico, Anthony. *Poetry and Theology in the Modernist Period*. Baltimore, MD: Johns Hopkins University Press, 2017.

Durkheim, Èmile. *The Elementary Forms of Religious Life*. Translated by Carol Cosman. Oxford: Oxford University Press, 2001.

Esmail, Aziz. *The Poetics of Religious Experience: The Islamic Context*. London: I.B. Tauris, 1998.

Fessenden, Tracy. "Problem of the Postsecular." *American Literary History* 26, no. 1 (2014): 154–67.

Fish, Stanley. *How Milton Works*. Cambridge, MA: Harvard University Press, 2001.

Greenblatt, Stephen. *Hamlet in Purgatory*. Princeton, NJ: Princeton University Press, 2002.

Hart, Kevin. *Poetry and Revelation: For a Phenomenology of Religious Poetry*. London: Bloomsbury, 2017.

Hungerford, Amy. *Postmodern Belief*. Princeton, NJ: Princeton University Press, 2004.

---

[14] Durkheim, *Elementary Forms*, 11.

Jackson, Ken, and Arthur F. Marotti. "The Turn to Religion in Early Modern English Studies." *Criticism* 46 (2004): 167–90.

Jaeger, Peter. *John Cage and Buddhist Ecopoetics*. London: Bloomsbury, 2013.

Jager, Colin. "The Secular and the Literary." *Christianity & Literature* 67, no. 3 (2018): 411–18.

Johnson, Kimberly, ed. *Poetics / Praxis*, a special issue of *Christianity & Literature* 68, no. 3 (2019).

Knight, Mark ed. *The Routledge Companion to Literature and Religion*. London: Routledge, 2016.

Langdell, Sebastian J. *Thomas Hoccleve: Religious Reform, Transnational Poetics, and the Invention of Chaucer*. Liverpool: Liverpool University Press, 2018.

Lynch, William. *Christ and Apollo: The Dimensions of the Literary Imagination*. London: Sheed and Ward, 1960.

Newman, Barbara. *God and the Goddesses*. Philadelphia: University of Pennsylvania Press, 2003.

Partisan Review. "Religion and the Intellectuals." No. Three. A Symposium by James Agee and others. New York, 1950.

Proudfoot, Wayne. *Religious Experience*. Berkeley: University of California Press, 1987.

Ricoeur, Paul. *Poetics and Religion*. Leuven: Uitgeverij Peeters, 2011.

Schaefer, Donovan O. *Religious Affects: Animality, Evolution, and Power*. Durham, NC: Duke University Press, 2015.

Schwartz, Regina. *Sacramental Poetics at the Dawn of Secularism*. Palo Alto, CA: Stanford University Press, 2008.

Scott, Nathan, Jr. *Rehearsals of Discomposure: Alienation and Reconciliation in Modern Literature: Franz Kafka, Ignazio Silone, D. H. Lawrence, and T. S. Eliot*. New York: King's Crown, 1952.

Still, Colin. *Shakespeare's Mystery Play: A Study of The Tempest*. London: C. Palmer, 1921.

Taves, Anne. *Religious Experience Reconsidered: A Building-Block Approach to the Study of Religion and Other Special Things*. Princeton, NJ: Princeton University Press, 2011.

Vitkus, Daniel. *Turning Turk: English Theater and the Multicultural Mediterranean*. London: Palgrave Macmillan, 2003.

Overture: Prayer: I Will Love You in the Summertime

Christian Wiman

Twenty years ago, watching some television report about depression and religion—I forget the relationship but apparently there was one—a friend who was entirely secular asked me with genuine curiosity and concern: "Why do they believe in something that doesn't make them happy?" I was an ambivalent atheist at that point, beset with an inchoate loneliness and endless anxieties, contemptuous of Christianity but addicted to its aspirations and art. I was also chained fast to the rock of poetry, having my liver pecked out by the bird of a harrowing and apparently absurd ambition—and thus had some sense of what to say. One doesn't follow God in hope of happiness but because one senses— miserable flimsy little word for that beak in your bowels—a truth that renders ordinary contentment irrelevant. There are some hungers that only an endless commitment to emptiness can feed, and the only true antidote to the plague of modern despair is an absolute—and perhaps even annihilating—awe. "I asked for wonders instead of happiness, Lord," writes the great Jewish theologian Abraham Joshua Heschel, "And you gave them to me."

I thought of this moment not long ago when one of my twin four-year-old daughters walked wide-eyed and trembly into my room at midnight. My wife was traveling. The girls are accustomed to me being gone and have learned to allay their anxieties with the prospect of airport presents, but they are less sanguine about the absence of their mother. Still, I thought we were managing pretty well. There had been a vociferous territorial dispute at the kiddie pool, and then a principled aesthetic disagreement (over the length of my hair in a chalk drawing) was decided by a bite. But dinner was lively, the ice-cream bribery effective, and after story-time, poem-time, I-love-you time, I slipped out of their room without a fuss. About an hour later though I looked up to find my blond-haired, blue-eyed, scarily intelligent sprite of a child Eliza standing in the doorway.

"Daddy," she said, "I can't sleep. Every time I close my eyes I'm seeing terrible things."

I am a lifelong insomniac. I used to freak my own parents out when I was a small child by creeping quietly into their room and opening up their eyelids with my fingers in an effort—so the story goes—to see what they were dreaming, and in fact I began this very essay between two and four one morning when "my thoughts were all a case of knives," to quote the great seventeenth-century poet and priest George Herbert. So I was sympathetic to my daughter's plight.

I suggested she pray to God. This was either a moment of great grace or brazen hypocrisy (not that the two can't coincide), as I am not a great pray-er myself and tend to be either undermined by irony or overwhelmed by my own chaotic consciousness. Nevertheless, I suggested that my little girl get down on her knees and bow her head and ask God to give her good thoughts, like the old family house in Tennessee that we'd gone to just a couple of weeks earlier, for example, the huge green yard with its warlock willows and mystery thickets, the river with its Pleistocene snapping turtles and water-bearded cattle, the buckets of just-picked blueberries and the fried Krispy Kremes, and the fireflies smearing their strange radiance through the humid Tennessee twilight. I told her to hold that image in her head and ask God to preserve it for her. I suggested she let the force of her longing and the fact of God's love coalesce into a form as intact and atomic as matter itself, to attend to memory with the painstaking attentiveness of a poet, the abraded patience of the saint, the visionary innocence of the child whose unwilled wonder erases any distinction between her days and her dreams. I said all this—underneath my actual words, as it were—and waited while all that blond-haired blue-eyed intelligence took it in.

"Oh, I don't think so Daddy." She looked me right in the eyes.

"What do you mean, Eliza, why not?"

"Because in Tennessee I asked God to turn me into a unicorn and"—she spread her arms wide in a disconcertingly adult and ironic shrug—"look how that's worked out."

What exactly does that mean: *to pray*? And is it something one ought to be teaching a child to do? And if we assume for a moment that it is indeed an essential thing to "learn," then what exactly ought one to pray for? A parking space? To be cured of some dread disease? For the emotional and

Overture 13

spiritual well-being of a beloved child? To be a unicorn? For one night of untroubled sleep?

The Polish poet Anna Kamienska died in 1986, at the age of sixty-six. She had converted to Christianity decades earlier, in her thirties, after the unexpected death of her beloved husband, the poet Jan Spiewak. People who have been away from God tend to come back by one of two ways: destitution or abundance, an overmastering sorrow or a strangely disabling joy. Either the world is not enough for the hole that has opened in you, or it is too much. The two impulses are intimately related and it may be that the most authentic spiritual existence inheres in being able to perceive one state when you are squarely in the midst of the other. The mortal sorrow that shadows even the most intense joy. The immortal joy that can give even the darkest sorrow a fugitive gleam.

Anna Kamienska, then. A devoted and tormented Catholic, her faith brought her great comfort and great anguish, often at the same time. No doubt this is precisely the quality that attracted me to her when I first came across a couple of passages from her diaries, high in the air above downtown Chicago in Northwestern Memorial Hospital, blood in my tubes and blades in my veins. I had—have—cancer. I have been living with it—dying with it—for so long now that it bores me, or baffles me, or drives me into the furthest crannies of literature and theology in search of something that will both speak and spare my own pain. Were it not for my daughters I think by this point I would be at peace with any outcome, which is, I have come to believe, one reason why they are here.

Not long before her death, Anna Kamienska wrote what I think is her best poem (available in English, at any rate), a stark, haunting, and insidiously hopeful little gem called "A Prayer That Will Be Answered." The title is worth some stress, in both senses of that word: "A Prayer that *Will Be Answered.*"

Lord let me suffer much
and then die

Let me walk through silence
and leave nothing behind not even fear

Make the world continue
let the ocean kiss the sand just as before

Let the grass stay green
so that the frogs can hide in it

so that someone can bury his face in it
and sob out his love

Make the day rise brightly
as if there were no more pain

And let my poem stand clear as a windowpane
bumped by a bumblebee's head

translated by Clare Cavanagh and Stanislaw Baranczak

This is an uncanny poem. It gives God all power (the continuance of the world) and no power (it was going to continue anyway). It is implicitly apophatic, you might say. That is, it erases what it asserts: it is a prayer to be reconciled to a world in which prayer *does not work*. "O Lord let me not love thee, if I love thee not," wrote George Herbert at the end of one of his own greatest poems ("Affliction I"). "We pray God to be free of God," says the thirteenth-century mystic Meister Eckhart. Behind Kamienska's poem, infusing it with an ancient and awful power, is the most wonderful and terrible prayer one can pray: "Not my will, Lord, but yours." That's Jesus in the Garden of Gethsemane before the Roman soldiers come to take him to his death, just after he has sweated blood, begged God to let the cup of suffering pass him by, and wept to leave this world that he has come to love so completely and, it seems, helplessly. And then: Not my will, Lord, but yours. It's difficult enough to pray a prayer like this when you're thinking of making some big life decision. It's damn near impossible when your actual life is on the line, or the life of someone you love, when all you want to pray is *help, help, help*.

Not my will, Lord, but yours.

Kamienska's poem is uncanny in another way too—and triumphant. "If you want me again," writes Walt Whitman near the end of "Song of Myself," "look for me under your boot soles," and this poem has a similar ghosting effect, givings its author a kind of posthumous presence. "Let my poem stand clear as a windowpane / bumped by a bumblebee's head." This, it turns out, has happened. The poem is indeed as clear as a windowpane, and we the readers, all these decades after Kamienska's death, are bumping our heads upon it. The prayer has been answered, and to feel the full effect of this poem is to feel a little ripple of spirit going right through the stark indifferent reality to which the poet sought to be reconciled.

***

For a long time I tried to write a poem that had as its first line "Are you only my childhood?" By *childhood* I meant not only the encompassing bubble of Baptist religiosity in which I was raised but also that universally animate energy, that primal permeability of mind and matter that children both intuit and inhabit ("The park lives outside," as one of my little girls said to the other when they were going to sleep), that clear and endlessly creative existence that a word like "faith" can only stain. By you I meant You. I took dozens of different tacks for the poem, but it was all will, and thus all wasted. Years passed. Then recently, in a half-dreaming state in the middle of the night, I heard myself ask the question again: "Are you only my childhood?" And from deep within the dream a voice— it was me, but the voice was not mine—said, with what seemed to be genuine interest and puzzlement: "Why do you say *only*?"

> Ah, my dear angry Lord,
> since thou dost love yet strike,
> cast down, yet help afford,
> sure I will do the like.
>
> I will complain, yet praise.
> I will bewail, approve.
> And all my sour-sweet days
> I will lament and love.

George Herbert again. It's likely he wrote the poem—"Bitter-Sweet," it's called— between the ages of thirty-seven and forty, when he had just swerved from a disappointing political career into parish ministry, was newly and very happily married, and obviously dying of tuberculosis. "All my sour-sweet days / I will lament and love." Destitution and abundance. Submission to God and aggression against God. What might it mean to pray an honest prayer? Well, maybe it means, like Meister Eckhart, praying to be free of the need for prayer. Maybe it means praying to be fit for, worthy of, capable of living up to the only reality that we know, which is this physical world around us, the severest of whose terms is death. Maybe it means resisting this constriction with the little ripple of spirit that cries otherwise, as all art, even the most apparently despairing, ultimately does. And maybe, just maybe, it even means praying for a parking spot in the faith that there is no permutation of reality too minute or trivial for God to be altogether absent from it. If Jesus's first miracle can be a kind of pointless party trick—he turns water into wine! Voila!—maybe the lesson that believers are meant to learn from this is that we have to turn *everything* over to God, including those niggling feelings and hesitations we have that the whole rigmarole of sifting scripture like bird's entrails, bowing one's suddenly brainless head, and "believing" in something more than matter—this is all just a

16   *Literature and Religious Experience*

little ridiculous, isn't it? An embarrassment even. The province, perhaps, of little children.

***

I can't tell a story of one daughter without including the other. Fiona, then. The olive-skinned and night-eyed child, the lithe and little trickster sister: Fiona.

When our girls were just two years old we spent a summer in Seattle, where I had lived for a while many years earlier. It was the first break I had managed to take from my editing job in a decade, and it was only eight months after I had undergone a bone marrow transplant. Time had a texture that summer, an hourly reality that we could taste and see. The girls went to a wonderful little daycare in the mornings so my wife and I could write, and then we all came together in the afternoons to do something fun in the city. We had the same nightly ritual that we do now. I'd read to the girls and tuck them in before my wife took over, and the last thing I'd say every night was "I love you," and they would always reply promptly, "I love you too, Daddy."

But then one night after my declaration Fiona was silent. She just kept staring at the ceiling.

"Do you love me too, Fiona?" I asked, foolishly.
A long moment passed.
"No, Daddy, I don't."
"Oh, Fiona sweetie, I bet you do," I said.
Nothing.
"Well," I said finally, "I love you, Finn, and I'll see you in the morning."

And then as I started to get up, I felt her small hand on my arm and she said dreamily, without looking at me, like a little Lauren Bacall, "I will love you in the summertime, Daddy. I will love you … in the summertime."

I have told this to a couple of people who thought it was heartbreaking, but I was so proud I thought my heart would burst. *I will love you in the summertime.* What a piercing poetic thing to say—at two years old. And for weeks I thought about it. A year later, just after that dream I related above, I even wrote a poem about it. *I will love you in the summertime.* Which is to say, given the charmed life we were living there in Seattle and all the grace and grief that my wife and I felt ourselves moving through at every second: I will love you in the time where there is time for everything, which is now and always. I will love you in the time when time is no more.

Now, do I think that's what my Athena-eyed and mysteriously interior two-year-old daughter meant by that expression? No, I do not. But do I think that sometimes life and language break each other open to change, that a rupture in one can be a rapture in the other, that sometimes there are, as it were, words underneath the words—even the very Word underneath the words. Yes, I do.

***

When Jesus says that you must become as little children in order to enter the kingdom of Heaven, he is not suggesting that you must shuck all knowledge and revert to an innocence—or, worse, a state of helpless dependence—that you have lost or outgrown. The operative word in the injunction is *become*. (The Greek word is *strepho*, which is probably more accurately translated as "convert," a word that more explicitly suggests an element of will and maturation.) Spiritual innocence is not beyond knowledge but inclusive of it, just as it is of joy and love, despair and doubt. For the hardiest souls, even outright atheism may be an essential element. ("There are two atheisms of which one is a purification of the notion of God," says Simone Weil.) There is some way of ensuring that one's primary intuitions survive one's secondary self; or, to phrase it differently, ensuring that one's *soul* survives one's self; or, to phrase it differently, to ensure that one's self and one's soul are not terminally separate entities. To *ripen* into childhood, as Bruno Schulz puts it.

So perhaps one doesn't teach children about God so much as help them grow into what they already know, and perhaps "know" is precisely the wrong verb. "Trying to solve the problem of God is like trying to see your own eyeballs," wrote Thomas Merton. It has been my experience that most adults will either smile wryly at this and immediately agree, or roll their eyes and lament the existence of this benighted superstition that pretzels intelligence into these pointless knots, this zombie zeal that will not die. It has also been my experience that there are on this earth two little children who, if told this koan by a father inclined to linguistic experiments, will separately walk over to the mirror and declare that in fact, Daddy, they *can* see their own eyeballs.

"I want only with my whole self to reach the heart of obvious truths." Thus says Anna Kamienska near the end of the fractured, intense, diamond-like diaries that circle around and around the same obsessive concern: God. I know just what she means. The trouble, though, as her own life and mind illustrate, is that, just as there are simple and elegant equations that emerge only at the end of what seems like a maze of complicated mathematics, so there are truths that depend upon the very contortions they untangle. Every person has to *earn* the clarity of common sense, and every path to that one clearing is difficult, circuitous, and utterly, painfully individual.

18 *Literature and Religious Experience*

Here's an obvious truth: I am somewhat ambivalent about religion—and not simply the institutional manifestations, which even a saint could hate, but sometimes, too many times, all of it, the very meat of it, the whole goddamned shebang. Here's another: I believe that the question of faith—which is ultimately separable from the question of "religion"—is the single most important question that any person asks in and of her life, and that every life is an answer to this question, whether she has addressed it consciously or not.

As for myself, I have not found faith to be a comfort but a provocation to a life I never seem to live up to, an eruption of joy that evaporates the instant I recognize it as such, an agony of absence that assaults me like a psychic wound. As for my children, I would like them to be free of whatever particular kink there is in me that turns every spiritual impulse into anguish. Failing that, I would like them to be free to make of their anguish a means of peace, for themselves or others (or both), with art or action (or both). Failing that—and I suppose, ultimately, here in the ceaseless machinery of implacable matter, there is only failure—I would like them to be able to pray, keeping in mind the fact that, as St. Anthony of the Desert said, a true prayer is one that you do not understand.

Witness

Typically cryptic, God said three weasels
slipping electric over the rocks
one current conducting them up the tree
by the river in the woods of the country
into which I walked
away and away and away;
and a moon-blued, cloud-strewn night sky
like an x-ray
with here a mass and there a mass
and everywhere a mass;
and to the tune of a two-year-old
storm of atoms
elliptically, electrically alive—
I will love you in the summertime, Daddy.
I will love you ... in the summertime.

Once in the west I lay down dying
to see something other than the dying stars
so singularly clear, so unassailably there,
they made me reach for something other.

Overture   19

I said I will not bow down again
to the numinous ruins.
I said I will not violate my silence with prayer.
I said *Lord, Lord*
in the speechless way of things
that bear years, and hard weather, and witness.

1

Revelation: Mallarmé and the Negativity of Prophetic Revelation in Modern Literature

William Franke

1. From Dante to Mallarmé via Shakespeare's *Hamlet*

In the modern era, divine revelation encounters new possibilities for expression along the path of poetry.[1] Modern poets ply a revelatory poetic art self-consciously produced by human inventiveness and indelibly marked by individual talents. In doing so, they reconfigure that which since ancient times has been called "prophecy." Literature begins to recognize its capacity to mediate an event of the divine Word and even to contribute to its richness, although not without some risk of distortion and even of falsification of the supposedly divine revelation conferred. In any event, a theologically revealed Word cannot escape the mediation of profane words. Only through human language, thanks to some form of "sacramentality" in the mode of its employment, can such a theological Word of revelation be deployed and become incarnate.[2]

Dante Alighieri is the incomparable pathbreaker of a particular modality of prophetic poetry that convoys theological revelation, as it was known anciently, especially in classical epic and in the Bible, toward modernity. He already discovers certain subjective and auto-reflexive aspects of poetic representation as constitutive of theological revelation in the human work of art, at least when such artwork aims at the highest ends and purposes imaginable, signally

---

[1] The first section of the essay and some other segments were originally written in French for an International Symposium on "Dante and Shakespeare: Cosmology, Politics and Poetics" sponsored by the University of Poitiers, Centre d'Études Supérieures de Civilisation Médiévale, April 4–6, 2019. My thanks to Isabelle Battesti and Pascale Drouet for this invitation. A French version was published as "De Dante à Mallarmé à travers l'*Hamlet* de Shakespeare," 65–83.

[2] Among modern critics who have best foregrounded the aesthetic metamorphoses of theological revelation in modern poetry I have learned from Calasso, *La letteratura e gli dèi*; Guerne, *Le verbe nu*; and Scott, *The Poetics of Belief*.

universal salvation. Dante is, in this regard, the first of a long line of modern prophetic poets, as was recognized by certain German Romantic critics such as Friedrich Wilhelm Josef von Schelling and the Schlegel brothers, Friedrich and August Wilhelm. They newly appreciated the prophetic potential of the poetic act and tried to realize it in turn in their own texts, treating history as a kind of retrospective prophecy.[3]

The German Idealists added to the speculative philosophical project of self-reflection, such as Dante had already discovered it, an explicitly modern dimension of the autonomous subject, following the lead of Immanuel Kant. But they also remained aware of self-reflection's analogous relation with and even derivation from the Christian theology of the Trinity. The Trinitarian model for self-reflexivity of the subject is theorized in finely articulated ways by Georg Wilhelm Friedrich Hegel.[4] The Trinitarian analogy might have seemed simply a dogmatic reflex in Dante, but it is unveiled as a universal structure of consciousness by his Romantic successors, who are also architects and founders of the modern, secularized world. Even so, the role of theology is still far from obsolete, as Romanticism in particular made evident.

Victor Hugo took up the torch of prophetic poetry, carrying forward its miraculous aspect as revelation, especially in *La légende des siècles* (1859–83). In opening with "La vision d'où est sorti ce livre" and in concluding with "La pente de la reverie" as a sort of dream-vision frame for the whole, his work offers a project of epic proportions and prophetic tonalities. However differently, the poetry of Charles Baudelaire, as well as that of Arthur Rimbaud and the *symbolistes*, is characterized by the aspiration, if not the pretension, of being visionary ("voyante"). These are the vestiges of a tradition of prophetic poetry going back certainly to Dante and even further. The descent into hell is one of its indispensable recurrent themes. Rimbaud's "Une saison en enfer," as also Baudelaire's "Les fleurs du mal," with its urban degradations decked out in infernal imagery replete with litanies to Satan, are among the most flagrant testimonies of a self-consciously revelatory poetic.

However, the modern poet inhabits a different world determined by very different cultural and metaphysical presuppositions. This is dramatically illustrated by William Shakespeare's *Hamlet*, with all its archetypal value for the modern age. And already during the waning of the Middle Ages, Geoffrey

---

[3] For the figure of the historian as retrospective prophet, see Schlegel, *Der Historiker als rückwärts gekehrter Prophet*.
[4] Koslowski, "Hegel – 'der Philosoph der Trinität?.'"

Chaucer reverses Dante's inspiration from above. In parodying the human and social comedy, he discovers the means of revealing a vision of the world that completes and counterpoints—when it does not directly contradict—the latter's orientation to the unattainable height of a Truth presumed to be divine. In *The Canterbury Tales*, the poignancy of human reality is exposed nakedly, thanks to poetic imitation that creates a relation—even if only a negative relation—with the ultimate truth of the Holy Scriptures. This Truth is represented most explicitly at the end of the work in *The Parson's Tale*. Given that their doctrine can no longer be rationally demonstrated, nor even as such be known, the Holy Scriptures can no longer be believed except by taking recourse to an irrational faith and thus through a sort of fideism.

But Chaucer's fideism is only the beginning, a precursor of the Renaissance, which will usher in an erosion of all dogmatically assured prophecy and inaugurate its replacement by another sensibility. The "renaissance" sensibility manifest programmatically in *Hamlet* oversees the staging of a tragic drama pivoting on the loss of prophetic truth that characterized the preceding period. The medieval world is incarnated by the defunct King Hamlet, the prince's father, who has become a specter. The nascent scientific age that now propagates its outlook, emanating from university centers such as Wittenberg, where Hamlet and Horatio are students, brings on an irresistible current of religious skepticism that undermines the ancient, and especially the biblical, bases of belief in revelation. The new mentality strives, instead, to establish an experimental basis for knowledge. Still, the denouement of the play sets the scene for a new kind of faith, a blind faith in providence, a new and still groping kind of confidence in the good order of things.[5]

That prophecy turns from positive prediction to simply relating oneself to the unknowable, and even to unmasterable chance, with a certain degree of trust, as Stéphane Mallarmé (1842–1898), at the heart of his poetics, affirms is the measure of its becoming modern. We find this transformation acting in original ways in *Hamlet*. The prince comes not only to doubt but even to despise all supposed forms of predicting the future. By the time of the last Act, he declares, "We defy augury" (V. ii. 199). The word "augury" suggests a certain low, materialistic understanding of prophecy. Not the inspired interpretation of history in its ultimate ends and purposes, as with Virgil and Dante, but a crude pretense to foretelling facts is the degraded form of prophecy as it comes to

---

[5] Cutrofello, *All for Nothing*, explores Hamlet's "negative faith." This negativity has often dominated the play's reception history as recounted by Bevington, *Murder Most Foul*.

be understood in the age of the scientific paradigm of knowledge. However, a new practice consisting in a certain readiness to attune oneself to the inscrutable purpose of heaven also comes on the scene with Shakespeare's *Hamlet*. Devoid of determinate content regarding the future, nevertheless a faith in providence enables an embrace of the future, whatever it holds. This fundamentally reorients prophecy to *un*knowing. In a virtually delirious sort of rhapsody, Hamlet declares,

> There's a special providence in the fall of a sparrow. If it be now, 'tis not to come; if it be not to come, it will be now; if it be not now, yet it will come. The readiness is all. Since no man of aught he leaves knows, what is 't to leave betimes? Let be. (V. ii. 199–203)

The sparrow here is reminiscent of the imagery of the Gospels: "Are not two sparrows sold for a farthing? And one of them shall not fall on the ground without your Father" (Matt. 10:29).[6] The spirit of letting be and acceptance, of faith in a higher purpose and order controlling human life, can be based precisely on insuperable ignorance, just as it was once supposedly based on indubitable revelation. In this way, the reality of eternity is affirmed even as unrevealed—as concealed behind the veil of time.

The new possibilities for expressing theological revelation in poetry that are going to emerge paradoxically in a sort of visionary blindness are powerfully represented after Shakespeare by John Milton, among others, during the seventeenth century at the time of the rise of modern science. In Milton and more generally in baroque poetry, especially in England and Spain, the radical insufficiency of human words to describe or illustrate the divine results in the use, in a negative register, of a deliberately and ostentatiously subjective and emotional mode of expression. This leads, furthermore, to an iconoclastic and even self-subversive imagery—to what can be called a "self-consuming artifact" in the idiom made famous by Stanley Fish.[7]

Following Milton, certain Romantic poets like William Blake, whose spiritual and prophetic inclinations relaunch the ideal of theological inspiration for poetry, fashion new allegorical techniques of mythic symbolization and attempt once more to force open the gates of heaven. Nevertheless, "heaven" is now understood within a dimension immanent to human consciousness extended to infinity. For Blake, "all divinities reside in the human breast" ("The Marriage of

---

[6] Boitani starts his reading in *Il vangelo secondo Shakespeare* from this reference.
[7] Fish, *Self-Consuming Artifacts*.

Heaven and Hell"). If we can draw this conclusion concerning immanence, it is thanks to the new bases of prophecy that are announced by Shakespeare's *Hamlet* and then fleshed out as a consequence of developments rendered possible in its wake.

In a preceding work, I have studied the heirs of Dante as prophetic poet among modern secular poets in a lineage reaching from Chaucer, Shakespeare, Milton, and Blake to Giacomo Leopardi, Baudelaire, Emily Dickinson, and W. B. Yeats.[8] In the present essay, I propose to pursue this line in modern poetry understood as prophetic revelation along a different trajectory from Dante to Mallarmé. Of great importance for understanding the stakes of the poetry of Mallarmé as prophetic and perhaps as, in some ways, a revelation, yet secularized, is also its reception among contemporary French political philosophers.[9] These thinkers and critics interrogate the *revolutionary* as much as the revelatory, the political as much as the religious, potential of the poetic work of Mallarmé. Mallarmé emerges as offering the ultimate disclosure of the potency of poetic language for bearing—and transforming—religious significance in modern literature and in a secular society.

2. From Dante to Mallarmé's *Hamlet* via the Experience of Nothing

Revelation understood as positive dogma on the model of the authority of Holy Scripture is eclipsed, but a new dimension of negativity in language that is itself immanent to the speaking subject opens up. This dimension is already opened and exploited by Dante, especially in his *Paradiso*. His ascension to the *visio Dei* is accompanied always by avowing the ineffability of his divine object. The incomprehensible transcendence characterizing the phenomena he experiences in Paradise constrains him to dumb stuttering followed by metaphorical construction and invention in fantasy meant to correspond to an intimate experience that amounts to nothing in objective, expressible terms. Its object can hardly be distinguished from infinite emptiness and openness perceived via an interior void.

This sort of failed experience and expression of God is characteristic of negative theology. Dante's narrated experiences of ascension and transcendence

---

[8] *Secular Scriptures*, from which a few paragraphs above are loosely adapted.
[9] This territory is expertly mapped out by Boncardo, *Mallarmé and the Politics of Literature*.

alike constitute a setting to work of negative theology practiced both as mysticism and as poetics.[10] Certainly, Dante describes his experience as full to overflowing—as a "saturated phenomenon," if ever there was one. Nonetheless, this plenitude intimates and unveils something else, a mystery entirely beyond finite sensation and expression. It can be apprehended throughout modern literature in numerous religious poets such as George Herbert as a kind of "disincarnate" revelation.[11]

This genre of negative revelation in the experience of poetic language attains a certain apogee in the work of Mallarmé. But the pivot for the experience of Mallarmé is found precisely in the figure of Shakespeare's Hamlet, "le prince amer d'écueil" (the bitter prince of the reef). This figure occurs tellingly in *Un Coup de dés*, the definitive work of Mallarmé that arguably collapses sheer hazard together with providence or salvation. The nothing that determines chance is all that can save us from an arbitrary enslavement to time. Entering into and surrendering to the power not to be is necessary for this purpose. Hamlet, for Mallarmé, superlatively illustrates the condition of nonbeing as holding and conserving the latent power of being. This prescient power is expounded throughout the poetic texts of Mallarmé, the chief progenitor of *symboliste* poetry, as well as in his critical and occasional writings, which amply testify to his intellectual itinerary. The latter include an essay, "Hamlet," in "Crayonné au Théatre" (299–302). A histrionic "bad Hamlet" ("mauvais Hamlet") is evoked already in the early lyric "Le Pitre chatié."

Poetry as prophecy realizes the promise inherent in its very name to be a *making*, a *poiesis*, as the original Greek term says. Prophecy in its turn foretells or "pre-dicts," but in so doing gives things their form and contributes essentially to realizing that which it envisages. This is the principal purpose of what Mallarmé undertakes to achieve by his poetics of the Book. How different this seems from the aims of Dante, who counted on really influencing the history of events, starting from the descent of the Emperor Henry VII into Italy, the "garden" of the Empire. And yet, the revelation (and thereby in some sense the creation) of the other world, or of the world made other, by the power of the poetic word, remains the common goal of these two poets at opposite extremes of a certain trajectory of poetry in the modern European vernaculars that can be called prophetic or visionary.

---

[10] I read Dante's *Paradiso* in this negative theological key in *Dante and the Sense of Transgression*.
[11] This (anti)phenomenon is intriguingly theorized by Smith, "The Disincarnate Text," 363–84. Smith's essay introduces a wide range of samples drawn from medieval and early modern literature to the contemporary novel for a special issue on "The Sacramental Text Reconsidered."

Revelation 27

The work of Mallarmé, starting from *Igitur*, is obsessed with the example of Hamlet, who incarnates the eternal hesitation of the discourse and consciousness of the subject. Mallarmé's modern subject is haunted by an ancestral exigency driving it to the act of realizing itself definitively, something that Igitur can finally achieve only by suicide. Hamlet is raised by Mallarmé to the level of an archetype of literary discourse that through its *un*working ("désœuvrement," to use Maurice Blanchot's vocabulary) becomes a species of revelation of an other world, an aesthetic world that appears thanks to art's becoming, in effect, a prophetic revelation transfigured into an aesthetic work.

In his existential crisis and his fight against Nothing ("le Néant"), Mallarmé had declared that destruction was his Béatrice ("La Destruction fut ma Béatrice").[12] This clearly hinted at the association of his project with that of Dante, but for Mallarmé the reinvention of prophetic poetry in a modern guise is rendered possible above all by the process of doubt that is acted out by Shakespeare's Hamlet. Hamlet, by his penchant for doubt and for death ("To be, or not to be, that is the question," III. i), becomes the emblematic figure of the poetry of Mallarmé. The state of incertitude is essentially productive of art such as Mallarmé understands it. From the beginning of "L'après-midi d'un faune," the thoughts of the protagonist-speaker "complete themselves in myriad subtle doubts" ("s'achèvent en maints doutes subtiles"), and this multiplication of incertitude is one of the principal sources of the creativity of Mallarmé's poetry. It underwrites his poetics of allusion and "suggestion," which eschews all fixation by the positivity of things that are simply given ("Crise de vers").[13] This is a perfectly modern poetry, but also a poetry that takes up the originally Orphic task of art, namely, to reveal a world beyond the quotidian world accessible to the common view of mortals. Revelation of an other world (or of the world as other) in the immanence of art becomes the audacious bid of the *Grand' Œuvre* that Mallarmé sought to realize throughout his mature artistic life, producing a plethora of partial and preliminary versions of this ultimate, in principle impossible, work.

The personage of Shakespeare's Hamlet doubts the prophetic revelation received directly from the ghost of his father concerning his uncle unmasked as regicide. This doubt is the root of the tragedy that unfolds at Elsinore, as also

---

[12] Mallarmé, "Lettre à Eugène Lefébure." Mallarmé's correspondence is quoted from Mallarmé, *Oeuvres complètes*, 717.
[13] Mallarmé's criticism and poems are quoted from Mallarmé, *Oeuvres complètes*, 366.

at Elbehnon in Mallarmé's *Igitur*. The "et beh non" ("well, then, no") buried in this name echoes the name of the castle and at the same time expresses the hesitation of the prince. Hamlet lives in the age of the emergence of modern experimental science, which he is discovering through his studies at Wittenberg. As stated by his companion Horatio, he is enjoined to believe nothing but the veritable sensorial evidence of his own eyes—"the sensible and true avouch / Of mine own eyes" (I. i. 55–6). Nonetheless, deep down, Hamlet remains attached to other, older ideals. He is animated by a completely different vision of the world. He admonishes his bosom friend and confidant, "There are more things in heaven and earth, Horatio, / Than are dreamt of in your philosophy" (I. v. 165–7).

Looking well beyond the rationalized world of the new science, Hamlet remains viscerally connected to a universe of myths, including the myth of royalty, a universe in which prophecy opens a window upon another world. He internalizes it and is even haunted by it. Even before the apparition of the ghost, he already had an intimate premonition of his uncle's guilt, as it is unconcealed in the scenario laid out before him by the ghost. This enables him to exclaim, "O my prophetic soul" (I. v. 40) in response to the ghost's secret divulged.

Hamlet finds himself torn between two worlds and between two visions of the world. The play stages the crisis of the prophetic vision of the world inherited from the Middle Ages. It was incarnated by Hamlet's father up until his death, but from then on, alas, it has become nothing but a ghost. An entire world of nobility and stable order disappears for Hamlet with the death of his father. The father tries to reach his son by supernatural means of prophetic revelation, appearing to him as a ghost, but Hamlet can no longer immediately believe in such manifestations without subjecting them to verification procedures proper to the new scientific spirit, which dispenses with purportedly prophetic knowledge. Even the theater piece within the play, the "Mousetrap" is concocted as an experiment in empirical criminal psychology designed to make the truth spring forth in an uncontrollable reaction from the conscience of the king. "The play's the thing / wherein I'll catch the conscience of the king" (II. ii. 633–4). Hamlet deploys here his own rationally calculated mechanism and scheme in order to try to provoke the king to betray his guilt, even though the evidence that it might produce would still remain only circumstantial or "relative" (II. ii. 570), as Hamlet's own quest for "grounds" admits.

3. From Hamlet's Doubt to Mallarmé's Dice

This tragic doubt of Hamlet becomes productive of an apotheosis of poetic language for Mallarmé. The hesitation that refuses to fix itself in a univocal signification is the element of properly poetic expression as Mallarmé discovers it through his forging of a symbolist poetics of "suggestion." This poetic culminates in the "toss of the dice" ("Coup de dés") that dissolves authorial agency in a random play of signifiers. All this might seem very far from the incandescent faith of Dante. That symbolist poetic language should be a new form of prophetic revelation, thus a sort of reincarnation of Dante's project, is not at first evident. Nevertheless, radical doubt concerning oneself is not at all unfamiliar to Dante and to his dialectic of self-subversion. This is already patent in Dante's self-critical and self-deconstructive descent into hell.[14] But it is especially in the *Paradiso*, in the face of the ineffable (*l'ineffabile*), which escapes every linguistic expression, as well as every precise knowing, that ineluctable doubt becomes constitutive of Dante's path.[15]

The attempt by Mallarmé to invent a new religion has been much discussed in the "political" interpretations of this poet apparently so far removed from practical political engagements and so invested in art as a substitute for what is presumed to be real and even for life itself. The paradox of Mallarmé's *œuvre* resides in its capacity to render poetic language in itself an agent of revolution simply as pure language. If this opens a normally unsuspected dimension of experience, it is not inappropriate to speak of it as a sort of prophetic revelation. This dimension retrospectively illuminates the transformation of poetic language as a theological revelation unveiling another world, a world beyond the ordinary experience of mortals, that is in act programmatically in the work of Dante.

For Mallarmé, poetic language is the veritable revolution, as certain prose pieces ("Conflit," "Action Restreinte," "Le Livre. Instrument spirituel") touching obliquely on the subject suggest. Julia Kristeva has developed such a thesis in considerable detail in *La révolution du langage poétique – L'avant-garde à la fin du XIXe siècle: Lautréamont et Mallarmé* (1974). Writing often in reaction to her, a generation of philosophers historicize Mallarmé in different ways yet still place the accent finally on the political stakes of Mallarmé's language. Poetic language changes everything and nothing. Its comprehensive novelty, which

---

[14] See Chapter 5 of my *The Revelation of Imagination*.
[15] This doubt ("Zweifel") is the central axis of the interpretation of Dante's oeuvre as a whole by Stierle in *Das große Meer des Sinns*.

repeats the very origin of language, is the bearer of the veritably prophetic vocation of poetry. Yet this is a prophetic revelation immanent to the very language of poetry. Already for Hamlet, as we saw, revelation resituates itself on a plane of psychological immanence with his exclamation: "O my prophetic soul" (I. v. 40). The locus of immanence would become language itself with Mallarmé in anticipation of the "linguistic turn" (made famous in twentieth-century philosophy) already anticipated by Dante near the outset of modern vernacular literature.

Dante engages himself concretely in the attempt to bring about a radical historical-political transformation in his own times, saluting and encouraging the advent of the Emperor Henry VII for the purpose of subjugating the refractory city states of Italy, beginning with Florence. Still, the revolution in language effected by poetry is equally at the heart of his political vision and cultural program. In his *De vulgari eloquentia*, Dante outlines a cultural politics that gives precedence to language as key to the political foundation of a nation, to the moral transformation of society, and to the becoming noble of the human species as a whole.[16] This poetic-prophetic language is a revolutionary foundation that aims to renew everything, starting from the very foundations of the community and the original act of speech inaugurating humanity—the *primiloquium* of Adam, according to *De vulgari eloquentia*, I. 4. Thus, in some sense, Dante aims "to give a purer sense to the words of the tribe" ("donner un sens plus pur aux mots de la tribu"), in the resonant phrase from Mallarmé's tribute to Edgar Allen Poe in "Au tombeau d'Edgar Poe."

Mallarmé's *oeuvre* lends itself to being understood as the continuation of the trajectory launched by Dante and leading to a revolution in and by poetic language. The prophetic powers of poetic language are the only leaven that can effectively dynamize society and history in the image of the intrinsic order of the universe and of the inherent harmony of Creation, including the inventive capacity of the human spirit, which Dante discovers with a new sense of marvel. Such a vision axised on poetic language unites the Middle Ages of Dante with the modernity of Mallarmé by pivoting from Shakespeare's *Hamlet*. All three of these poetic geniuses envisage a revolutionary state of human existence starting from a revelation of the human in the world by means of language in its original creativity discovered anew through fundamental processes of poetic invention.

---

[16] Alighieri, *De Vulgari Eloquentia*.

4. The Negativity of Revelation in Dante and Mallarmé

Revolutionary in its essential import, poetic language overthrows the order of things understood as simply given and opens a depth perspective on the very origin of beings. On his visit to the poet at Valvins in Spring 1997, Paul Valéry, after being shown Mallarmé's draft of Un Coup de dés, remarked: "Was I not witnessing an event of universal order, and was this not in some sense the ideal spectacle of the Creation of Language?" ("N'assistais-je pas à un évènement de l'ordre universel et n'était-ce pas, en quelque manière le spectacle idéal de la Création du Langage?").[17] This experience of the origin of language and therewith of the universe constitutes what is most essentially at stake in Mallarmé's poetry. It makes poetry a means of entering into and revealing an absolute, creative act reaching beyond any specific authorial intentions. To this end, poetry must be liberated from serving any extrinsic functions and purposes, whence the talk about it as "pure." Simply in its own self-reflexive self-revelation, poetry becomes revealing of the whole universe from its very origins in the word and its poetic making.[18]

A memorable controversy broke out in the 1920s between Henri Brémond (author of Prière et poésie, 1926) and Albert Thibaudet (author of La poésie de Stéphane Mallarmé, 1926) over whether "pure poetry" is a matter of religious inspiration or rather of writerly technique. Both agreed, in any case, in connecting Mallarmé's insight into time and eternity gained through linguistic creation with Henri Bergon's "durée pure" ("pure duration") experienced by the "Moi profond" ("deep I") as opposed to all temporal progression by narration or logic in the classical, rhetorical construction of discourse.[19] Adopting Bergson's terms, both suggest that the power of intuition working together with intelligence and its techniques produces time creatively in a way that escapes merely "given time" ("le temp donné"). This poetic making through language as creative duration that itself gives time its form allows Mallarmé to surmount the typical opposition between the Classical and the Romantic and to reconcile Romantic inspiration with Symbolist craftsmanship. However, the usual rhetorical functions of narrating, teaching, describing ("narrer, enseigner, décrire"; "Crise de vers") are bracketed and held at a distance. The poetic verse, as Mallarmé rediscovers and reinvents it, taps into a deeper level of reality than

---

[17] Valéry, "Le Coup de dés," 624.
[18] In Dante's Paradiso and the Theological Origins of Modern Thought: Toward a Speculative Philosophy of Self-Reflection (New York: Routledge, 2021), I show this to be the original vocation of modern poetry ever since Dante.
[19] Combe, "L'idée de 'poésie pure'," 131–42.

that which can be narrated in linear time or be described or taught. It involves sacrifice of the poet's own sovereignty over the verse and even over his own subjectivity. It entails, furthermore, a relinquishing of "reality" as any kind of stable reference. In analogous terms, Hugo Friedrich defined "poésie pure" by "derealization" and "depersonalization."

Such poetry illuminates the essentially negative process of language inasmuch as language *is* not that which it names, not that which it, for this very reason, calls into being. The negativity of linguistic experience in general is deeply explored by Mallarmé as by Dante before him. Like Dante, with his negative poetics of the Ineffable, so Mallarmé, with his mysticism of Nothing, engages in a practice of prophetic revelation in and by language.

For Dante, negative theology, as for Mallarmé a metaphysics of Nothing, undergird their discoveries as poets with philosophical reflections informed by the most radical currents of thought of their respective ages. Mallarmé is informed by Hegelian dialectical negation, while Dante works in the wake of Scholastic negative theologies and their mystical expressions and applications.

The keystone of this prophetic revelation in poetic language consists paradoxically in its negativity. Already constitutive of language as such, which *is not* what it says or names, negativity is even more essentially constitutive of the theological, of which the object ("God"), by virtue its absolute transcendence, escapes every positive determination. Every theological concept ends up annulling itself in negations already within the millenary tradition of negative or mystic theology, which extends from Patristic authors to the Scholastics, who serve as intellectual foundations for Dante in his invention of a negative poetics of ineffability analogous to negative theology.

Dante stands as harbinger of one of the new ways in which poetics is going to become the privileged path for general exploration of the known in its entire extent. But even more than just the knowable, poetry probes the unknowable and, momentously, the Absolute, whether the latter is interpreted theologically or simply as Nothing. This dimension of negative theology declares itself already with forthrightness as an obsession omnipresent in the last work of Dante. And something like it becomes the essential task of the entire aesthetic and existential engagement and adventure of Mallarmé.

Already with Dante a negative way of renunciation of the pretension of being able adequately to say counts as validation of the authenticity of the poet as a prophet. It is by virtue of this negativity that experience opens itself up entirely and becomes penetrated by an in-depth vision that perceives not only objective things but also the causes and even the last causes of things. Yet this perception is not at all an objective knowing. It is rather an *un*knowing that leads to a recognition and acknowledgment of the divine cause as an incomprehensible mystery beyond every possible objective given. In this sense, in his essay "The Mystery in Letters" ("Le mystère dans les lettres"), Mallarmé interprets everything from the basis of something unknown, a mystery. He affirms, "There must be something occult, I decidedly believe in something absconding, a closed and hidden signifying, that inhabits the common" ("Il doit y avoir quelque chose d'occulte, je crois décidemment à quelque chose d'abscons, signifiant fermé et caché, qui habite le commun," 383).

Mallarmé and the Event *Manqué*

Negative theologian or not, Mallarmé is in any case a devotee of the Nothing and reveals the deep logic of negation as harboring a potential for a kind of prophetic revelation of the real. Reality cannot be deeply experienced and known except in this dimension of the negative in which Mallarmé encountered his "Béatrice." His understanding of poetry as an art of negation of ordinary language and of "revolution" as a negation of the reigning bourgeois society distinguishes what many interpreters, especially the political philosophers among them, have recognized as Mallarmé's "doctrine." In uniting the political and the poetic, or rather in grasping both at a level of depth where they are quite inseparable, Mallarmé is truly Dante's heir and on a trajectory of modern meditation based on doubt that we see opened up emblematically in Shakespeare with Hamlet.

Nonetheless, no particular political program is disclosed and blazoned by Mallarmé's poetry, and this lack would seem to make it opposite in tenor to Dante's work, given the latter's militant Ghibellinism, at least as it can be inferred from his insistently imperialist political ideology. Most significant for Mallarmé is, rather, the metaphysical status of poetic language as opening upon an infinite void. By exposing this originary void, poetry reveals a certain impossibility of being contemporary with oneself. The impossibility of the event is Mallarmé's constant lesson rendered definitive in his "*Un Coup de dés*," where nothing takes place but the place itself ("rien n'aura eu lieux que le lieu"). This pure, empty, nonevent upstages every actual, determinate event. It is "anarchic" (literally, "without beginning"), an ancient catastrophe that has always already occurred and is already withdrawn from view.

Structured in this way, poetic language reveals an antecedence to time, an eternal or prophetic dimension that determines a priori everything that can be described linguistically and therefore be apprehended subsequently as

34 *Literature and Religious Experience*

happening in time. The Nothing is revealed as the negative counterpart of the unaccountably intricate and serendipitous verbal structure that emerges in the Mallarméan poem. This miraculous construction bears witness to an invisible ordering principle that cannot be apprehended, except negatively. It is imaged typically as a primordial disaster in the poems of Mallarmé and is particularly designated as "the obscure disaster" ("le désastre obscure") in his funerary poem for Poe ("Le tombeau d'Edgar Poe").

Extraordinary about Mallarmé's poems is especially their sinuously perfect syntax in the way it manages to connect everything together in an articulable whole of reciprocally corresponding components. Mallarmé's syntax creates a connectedness much more complex than that of ordinary temporal succession. Breaking with the ordinary line of syntactical connection, Mallarmé opens multiple possible lines of connection that are reversible and infinitely repeatable and variable. The elements connected are so bizarrely incongruous and even contradictory that it seems impossible that they should have anything to do with one another. However, in the torturously yet perfectly completed syntax of the Mallarméan phrase, they become all mutually revealing, as if by miracle. A different and higher reality seems to be constituted—or rather to have enabled this remarkable verbal construction to come into being. The impression of unity created by syntax is based also on a necessary break because a phrase has to start from somewhere, from some element arbitrarily chosen out of the continuum of the real. An original gap of nonentity and nonevent, the "before" of every possible temporal structure, is thereby exposed.

Such a pre-event or nonevent exerts a retroactive force of evacuation on events, which are turned thereby into signs of something else quite beyond themselves. Just such a nonevent is repeated throughout Mallarmé's *Poésies* (1898) from the first ("Salut") to the last ("Ses bouquins refermés sur le nom de Paphos"). It appears as the foam left behind in the wake of a catastrophe that can never be seized as such, never as a present event, but only as the foamy and hypothetical antecedent of *every possible* event. In "Salut," "A ruin blessed by a thousand foamings" ("Une ruine, par mille écumes bénie") is never present except under erasure as "Nothing, this foam, virgin verse / To designate only the cup" ("Rien, cette écume, vierge vers / A ne désigner que la coupe").

Such an event *manqué* is fully operative again in the fourteen lines of the poem "Le vierge, le vivace, et le bel aujourd'hui." Everything revolves around "flights that never took wing" ("des vols qui n'ont pas fui"), around an event that is ardently desired again and again but that never takes place. Instead, it remains forever poised to happen—as if frozen in a glacier. This Mallarméan sonnet forms the point of departure for Jean-Claud Milner's interpretation of Mallarmé's thought and poetry in *Mallarmé au tombeau*. This would naturally issue in a sketch of the general philosophical problematic of an apophatic lack marking this universally consequential catastrophic event of Nothing in its diffusion throughout Mallarmé's *oeuvre*.

5. The Nothing of the Present and Its Political Implications

This line of thought, moreover, is embedded in a reflection about the crowd that hints at Mallarmé's position on the revolution of the masses: they alone, for him, could instigate a true revolution. After declaring that there is no present ("un présent n'existe pas"), Mallarmé registers a hypothetical exception, which would be the concerted revolutionary action of the people. No action is truly revolutionary *unless* it is the action of the masses, the crowd: "Failing the Crowd's declaring itself, failing—everything" ("Faute que se declare la Foule, faute—de tout"; "L'Action restreinte," 372). The last phrase seems to suggest that a truly popular movement of the crowd *would* be the condition of a true (revolutionary) event but that everything is lacking for this condition to be fulfilled.

The lack of such a concerted declaration from the people is the lack of everything that would make for a political and revolutionary present. That kind of action just does not happen, at least no longer in the nineteenth century. And in its absence, all that is left is the more restricted action of poetry that changes everything, but only on a plane of ideas and not directly of material facts. This is the "sacred" rite and mission of poetry, yet it takes place in isolation. In "L'Action restreinte," Mallarmé writes of "poetry, a sacred rite; it tries isolatedly in chaste crises, while another gestation is under way" ("La poésie, sacre; qui essaie, en de chastes crises isolément, pendant l'autre gestation en train," 372). While poetry may vainly aim at direct action to change things, a certain ferment or "gestation" is going on. We are left to infer that this may refer to the conditions for a future hypothetical revolution that will eventually erupt in its own time and place.

As a virtuous ("chaste") exercise, such poetry is more pure and virginal than it is fecund in really making things happen politically. Such, at least, is Mallarmé's assessment of the predicament of poetry in his age. His analysis concedes in advance W. H. Auden's point that "Poetry makes nothing happen" ("In Memory of W. B. Yeats"). Such poetry still retains its prophetic posture, albeit deprived of the historical efficacy ascribed to it by Dante. Nonetheless, piercing to a reality beyond time and its representations has been the most essential office of the poetry most appropriately termed "prophetic" ever since Dante and all throughout his tradition hailing from Virgil and the Bible. It should be remembered that even Dante's political position, notwithstanding the apparent positivity of his "Ghibellinism," is actually dialectical and turns on self-negation in order to open into genuine universality. Any apparently unilateral political positioning is retracted through the scathing critique also of the "Ghibellini" in *Paradiso* VI. 103–5.

Mallarmé comes to the prophetic insight that the present does not exist—certainly not the present of chronological time recorded by "universal reportage," the genre of journalism that Mallarmé so disdained and that was teeming so abundantly in the 1880s and 1890s under the Third Republic. Poetry accesses another completely different kind of temporal dimension, one from which time as we ordinarily experience it issues. Such is this poetry's capacity for prophetic insight, which cannot help but have revolutionary implications. This capacity enables envisioning a counter-time resistant to the determinism of history (that of the victors) and even a *palingenesis*, whereby history and even creation can start all over again. Indeed, twisting Auden's pronouncement in a paradoxically positive direction, Mallarmé's poetry makes the Nothing actually happen and take effect in a *form* of revolution.

Bibliography

Alighieri, Dante. *De Vulgari Eloquentia: Dante's Book of Exile*. Translated by Marianne Shapiro. Lincoln: University of Nebraska Press, 1990.

Bevington, David. *Murder Most Foul: Hamlet through the Ages*. Oxford: Oxford University Press, 2014.

Boitani, Piero. *Il vangelo secondo Shakespeare*. Bologna: Il Mulino, 2009.

Boncardo, Robert. *Mallarmé and the Politics of Literature: Sartre, Kristeva, Badiou, Rancière*. Edinburgh: Edinburgh University Press, 2018.

Calasso, Roberto. *La letteratura e gli dèi*. Milan: Adelphi, 2001.

Combe, Dominique. "Mallarmé et la genèse de l'idée de 'poésie pure.'" *Europe* 76, no. 825–6 (janvier-février 1998): 131–42.

Cutrofello, Andrew. *All for Nothing: Hamlet's Negativity*. Cambridge, MA: MIT Press, 2014.

Fish, Stanley. *Self-Consuming Artifacts: The Experience of Seventeenth-Century Literature*. Berkeley: University of California Press, 1972.

Franke, William. *Dante and the Sense of Transgression: "The Trespass of the Sign."* London: Continuum, 2013.

Franke, William. "De Dante à Mallarmé à travers l'*Hamlet* de Shakespeare: Négativité de la révélation poético-prophétique dans la modernité." In *Dante and Shakespeare: Cosmologie, politique, poétique*, edited by Pascale Drouet and Isabelle Battesti, 65–83. Paris: Garnier, 2020.

Franke, William. *Dante's* Paradiso *and the Theological Origins of Modern Thought: Toward a Speculative Philosophy of Self-Reflection*. New York: Routledge, 2021.

Franke, William. *The Revelation of Imagination: From Homer and the Bible through Virgil and Augustine to Dante*. Evanston, IL: Northwestern University Press, 2015.

Franke, William. *Secular Scriptures: Modern Theological Poetics in the Wake of Dante*. Columbus: Ohio State University Press, 2016.

Guerne, Armel. *Le verbe nu: Méditation pour la fin des temps*. Paris: Seuil, 2011.

Koslowski, Peter. "Hegel – 'der Philosoph der Trinität?' Zur Kontroverse um seine Trinitätslehre." *Theologische Quartalschrift* 162 (1982): 105–31.

Mallarmé, Stéphane. "Lettre à Eugène Lefébure." In *Oeuvres complètes*, edited by Bertrand Marchal. Paris: Pléiade, 1998.

Mallarmé, Stéphane. *Oeuvres complètes*. Edited by Henri Mondor and G. Jean-Aubrey. Paris: Pléiade, 1945.

Schlegel, Friedrich. *Der Historiker als rückwärts gekehrter Prophet: Aufsätze und Vorlesungen zur Literatur*. Leipzig: Reclam, 1991.

Scott, Nathan A., Jr. *The Poetics of Belief: Studies in Coleridge, Arnold, Pater, Santayana, Stevens, and Heidegger*. Chapel Hill: University of North Carolina Press, 1985.

Smith, Matthew. "The Disincarnate Text: Ritual Poetics in Herbert, Paul, Williams, and Levinas." *Christianity and Literature* 66, no. 3 (2017): 363–84.

Stierle, Karlheinz. *Das große Meer des Sinns: Hermeneutische Erkundungen in Dantes "Commedia."* Munich: Fink, 2007.

Valéry, Paul. "Le *Coup de dés*. Lettre au directeur des *Marges*." In *Œuvres* I, edited by J. Hytier. Paris: Gallimard, 1957.

2

Blessing: Shakespeare's Benedictional Designs

Julia Reinhard Lupton

May Adonai bless you, and guard you—
May Adonai make His face shine unto you, and be gracious to you—
May Adonai life up His face unto you, and give to you peace.

Priestly Blessing, Num. 6:24-26

Blessed shalt thou be when thou comest in, and blessed also when thou goest out.

Deut. 28:6

Bless thy sweet eyes, they bleed.

King Lear, 4.1.52

1. Greeting Blessing

Scenes of blessing abound in William Shakespeare. At the end of *The Winter's Tale*, dumbstruck Hermione finally finds her voice when her daughter kneels before her and asks her blessing. In Shakespeare, mothers deliver benedictions almost as frequently as fathers, and examples of maternal blessings directed to both sons and daughters survive from the period.[1] In *Hamlet* and *All's Well That Ends Well*, parents send their sons off with admonishments cast as benedictions, and in *The Tempest*, Prospero's wedding masque is a shower of blessings. Court performances may have ended with a blessing of the sovereign, with actors and guests joining in the final "Amen."[2] Everywhere in the plays, characters casually

---

[1] Young, "Parental Blessings," 181; Breton, *The Mother's Blessing*; Anonymous, "The Northern Mothers Blessing."

[2] See "To the Queen," a poem attributed to Shakespeare in *New Oxford Shakespeare: Modern Critical Edition*, ed. Gary Taylor, John Jowett, Terri Bourus, and Gabriel Egan, 2016. All citations from Shakespeare are from this edition.

40   *Literature and Religious Experience*

greet each other and exchange goodbyes upon entrance and exit, sometimes revealing the depths or shallows of the relationships at hand.[3]

"Farewell. My blessing season this in thee" (*Hamlet* 1.3.80): salutations and valedictions address the other as a person worthy of respect and a creature deserving of care in a shared setting of vulnerability and risk. In drama and in life, blessings prompt speech, tune ambience, share wisdom, express concern, and recognize others. Blessing is a dramaturgy that conscripts kneeling, bowing, bending, waving, and stretching into ritually heightened speech. Blessings scan the environment for its offerings, not in order to maximize resources but to receive gifts. Inculcating the virtues of gratitude, respect, care, trust, lovingkindness, and justice, blessings belong to what I call a virtue ecology: a dynamic ensemble of capacities shaped by social and physical factors that diversely influence the moral projects and realized potential of human beings and the communities they build together.

The Hebrew *baraka*, "blessing," may be linked to the Arabic root *brk*, "to kneel," signaling blessing's incorporation of gesture and movement into its supplicatory repertoire.[4] The Greek εὐχαριστία (Latin *eucharistia*) means thanksgiving, and the range of words in the New Testament for blessing, including *eulogein*, "to praise" or "bless," attach the particle "*eu-*" (meaning "well") to words indicating speech, gift, peace, or love, placing benediction's verbal formulas in affective scenarios of relationality, receptivity, and exchange. Blessing flows freely among divine and human actors, as explained by one sixteenth-century commentator:

> For God blesseth man, man blesseth God, and man blesseth man: howbeit diuerse and differing waies. When God is said to blesse man, the meaning is, That God in speaking the word, prospereth and dealeth well with him. For the worde of God is his worke: and what he saith, is done. Man is said to blesse God, when with a true faith he praiseth & glorifieth God for his benefits, through Iesus Christ, and that with the heart, & outward confession of the mouth. ... Man is said to blesse man, when he wisheth him prosperitie, and praiseth that all things may goe well with him.[5]

Blessings of all sorts—for rain and fertility, for God's justice and mercy, or simply for comfort in crisis—recur throughout Jewish and Christian Scriptures

---

[3] Hillman, "Ave Desdemona," 133–56. See also Hillman, "Salutation and Salvation in Early Modern Theology," 821–5.

[4] Mitchell, *The Meaning of BRK*, 10. On the dynamics of kneeling, see Whittington, *Renaissance Suppliants*. On prayer and performance, see Sterrett, *Prayer and Performance in Early Modern English Literature*.

[5] Hemmingsen, *Epistle of the Blessed Apostle*, 13.

Blessing 41

and in Islam.[6] The oldest part of the Hebrew Bible is the Priestly Blessing or *Birkat HaKohanim*, cited as an epigraph to this essay and found on silver amulets outside Jerusalem dating from the late Iron Age.[7] Upon creating Adam and Eve, "God blessed them, and God said unto them, Be fruitful and multiply" (Gen. 1:28 [Geneva]), a benediction that precedes the primal curse of exile from Eden. The stories of the patriarchs overflow with blessings, including God's promises to Abraham, the birthright stolen by Jacob from Esau at the bed of their father Isaac, and the prophesies that Jacob later delivers on his own deathbed to his twelve sons. Naomi blesses her Moabite daughters-in-law Ruth and Orpah by releasing them from obligation after the deaths of their Israelite husbands.

Blessings contribute to the phenomenology of theatrical and religious experience, which Matthew Smith defines as the tracking of "distinctive engagements with spiritual community and performative self-reflexivity" within dynamic environments of address and encounter.[8] Whether delivered at dinner table, doorway, or sickbed, blessings engage the senses and reframe phenomena into things shared and received. Blessings also lend themselves to phenomenological readings in the more Kantian, transcendental sense developed by Sanford Budick. In a powerful essay on secular benediction in *King Lear*, Budick argues that the radical reduction of Cordelia, Lear, Edgar, and Gloucester to the "nothing" of destitution, disability, and exile allows these subjects to rediscover each other as moral persons through acts of blessing.[9] In *King Lear*, blessing unfolds both experientially (honoring environments of flourishing) and existentially: bringing unaccommodated human beings into regenerative contact with each other. The phenomenology of blessing yields what I call *benedictional designs*, with "design" indicating both the orchestration of experiential affordances in ritualized speech and the affirmation of the conditions of coexistence in expressions of gratitude that acknowledge dependency in the presence of others.

King Lear begins with acts of cursing and failed or withheld blessing that ravage the domestic, social, and communicative worlds of the play, culminating in abandonment, torture, and storm before yielding to works of care and healing in Act Four.[10] Across *King Lear*, blessings repeatedly overflow their phatic, lyric, and valedictory functions to color the narrative scenes that house them. The play's

---

[6] Westermann, *Blessing in the Bible*; Anderson, *The Blessing*; Meri, "Aspects of Baraka," 46–60.
[7] Barkay et al., "Amulets from Ketef Hinnom," 41–71.
[8] Smith, *Performance and Religion*, 7.
[9] Budick, "Shakespeare's Secular Benediction," 330–1.
[10] Hartman, *Saving the Text*, 128–32; Quiring, *Shakespeare's Curse*.

42   *Literature and Religious Experience*

two major reconciliation scenes, between Lear and Cordelia and between Edgar and Gloucester, are composed out of casual, formal, and imagined blessings. By the end of the play, when Cordelia enters dead in Lear's arms, blessings appear stripped of divine promise, and trust in language must be restored by purely human means. Here and elsewhere in his plays, Shakespeare draws on the biblical resonances, gestural reach, and sensory appeal of benediction to craft a choreography of hope and healing in landscapes of shattered trust.

2. *King Lear's* Liturgy of Curses

The opening scene of *King Lear* stages a patriarchal blessing gone awry, on the model of the deathbed testaments of Isaac, Jacob, and Moses (Genesis 27, 49; Deuteronomy 33). In eighteenth- and nineteenth-century illustrations, Lear is often styled as an Old Testament prophet or patriarch, on the model of Michelangelo's Sistine Chapel lunettes. Yet, rather than dispensing wisdom or expressing gratitude and humility at the end of life (contrast with Gaunt in *Richard II*), Lear baldly asks his daughters to praise him in exchange for land and power: "Tell me, my daughters, / Which of you shall we say doth love us most, / That we our largest bounty may extend / Where merit doth most challenge it" (1.1.38–41). Compare Lear's preemptory bequests and requests to Jacob's blessing of Joseph:

> Joseph *shall be* a fruitful bough, *even* a fruitful bough by the well side: the small boughs shall turn upon the wall: And the archers grieved him, and shot *against him*, and hated him. But his bow abode strong, and the hands of his arms were strengthened, by the hands of the mighty *God* of Jacob, of whom *was* the feeder *appointed* by the stone of Israel, *Even* by the God of thy father, who shall help thee, and by the almighty, who shall bless thee with heavenly blessings from above, with blessings of the deep that lieth beneath, with blessings of the breasts, and of the womb. (Gen. 49:22-27 [Geneva])

The image of the fruitful bough supported by well and wall sketches a landscape of mutual support among features of the built and unbuilt environment.[11] The blessing links human initiative and valor to divine favor and plants human flourishing within a cosmic frame that reaches upwards to "heavenly blessings" and downwards to the "blessings of the deep." A father speaking to his sons, the

---

[11] In Hebrew, Joseph is a "wild ass," not a fruitful bough, yielding a different ecological scenario. Levenson, *Joseph*, 190.

Blessing 43

dying patriarch also reminds the assembled company of the fecundity of breasts and womb, evoking God's feminine aspect and recalling Jacob's reliance on his mother Rebecca to receive his own father's benediction.[12]

Jacob's blessing of Joseph provides a complete picture of human flourishing dependent on household cooperation, technical skill, respect for the natural world, and a sense of beholdenness and awe, a scene edged but not overwhelmed by the memory of fraternal rivalry and the threat of external aggression. Lear's map, on the other hand, depicts land as territory to be divided, and he sets the sisters against each other in a love contest that fans the antagonisms managed by Jacob's testament.[13] Lear depicts himself, not God or earth, as the source of "our largest bounty," a possessive and sovereign perspective that clashes with the divine amplitude of blessing expressed by the patriarchs.

Understanding her father's attempt at blessing as its perversion, Cordelia refuses to play the game. Geoffrey Hartman notes that "Cordelia's 'nothing' has, in its very flatness, the ring of a curse," to which Lear responds with his own terrible malediction.[14] If the division of the kingdoms is a failed patriarchal blessing, Lear's second major speech-act appropriates the liturgical cursing instituted in Deuteronomy 27–28, a ceremony that ratifies the covenant between God and Israel after the twelve tribes cross into the Promised Land. The Deuteronomic liturgy begins with twelve anathemas outlawing a set of clandestine transgressions, sins that are likely to escape human detection and justice and thus require divine punishment, in the form of curses affirmed by the people's choral "Amen." The second part of the ceremony consists of six blessings for those who obey the law followed by a much longer list of curses for those who fail to keep the covenant, including hunger, infertility, disease, defeat in war, frustration of worldly efforts, exile, infamy, servitude, and siege, the latter driving its victims to eat their young (Deut. 28: 53-7). Both the curses and the blessings revolve around creaturely well-being on the one hand and inclusion or exclusion from the community on the other, their litany offering a montage of the good life and its destruction in the ancient world. In an interconnected environment of fleeting abundance and encroaching dearth, survival depends upon human fairness and cooperation. The curses and blessings enumerated in the liturgy do not flow directly from God as punishment and reward but rather

---

[12] In the version of Joseph's blessing delivered by Moses at the end of Deuteronomy (33:13-17), Joseph's head is hallowed by "the favor of the Presence" [*shekinah*], God's feminine aspect. Levenson, *Joseph*, 193.

[13] On maps and territory in *King Lear*, see Elden, *Shakespearean Territories*.

[14] Hartman, *Saving the Text*, 129.

44 *Literature and Religious Experience*

issue from the forms of ethical life adopted by individuals and communities in their dealings with one another.

In the Church of England, the Deuteronomic recitation of anathemas became the liturgy of Commination (meaning denunciation), performed on Ash Wednesday as a call and response between priest and congregation. The second anathema may have resounded for Lear:

> *Minister.*   Cursed is he that curseth his father, and mother.
> *Answere.*   Amen.[15]

Lear receives Cordelia's answer as a monstrous affront to his dignity that requires an equally strong response:

> Well, let it be so. Thy truth then be thy dower;
> For by the sacred radiance of the sun,
> The mysteries of Hecate and the night,
> By all the operation of the orbs
> From whom we do exist and cease to be,
> Here I disclaim all my paternal care,
> Propinquity, and property of blood;
> And as a stranger to my heart and me
> Hold thee from this for ever. The barbarous Scythian,
> Or he that makes his generation
> Messes to gorge his appetite,
> Shall be as well neighboured, pitied, and relieved
> As thou my sometime daughter. (1.1.93–105)

Lear's "Let it be so" translates the Hebrew "amen" as he assumes the parts of both minister and congregant in the Commination service. Though expressed in pagan rather than Hebrew terms, the specter of "he that makes his generation / Messes to gorge his appetite" (1.1.102–3) recalls the graphic scenes of parental cannibalism described in Deut. 28:53-7, a set of images directly imitated in the scene of famine at Tarsus in *Pericles* (1.4.42–44), a play closely linked to *King Lear*. The biblical language of the rights of strangers to be "well neighbored, pitied, and relieved" (1.1.104) pushes through the pagan patina of the speech; these neighbors and strangers will reappear on the heath, in the form of the shivering Fool and unaccommodated Tom, as companions in Lear's sojourn from curse to blessing.[16]

---

[15] Cummings, *Book of Common Prayer*, 177. This line is a direct citation from the Geneva Bible translation of Deut. 27:16.

[16] On the Biblical allusion to love of neighbor and care for the stranger, see Schwartz, *Loving Justice*, 44–5.

Blessing   45

If Lear accuses Cordelia of cursing him through her refusal of praise, echoing Deut. 27:16 and the Commination liturgy, she speaks from another prooftext when she declares, "I love your majesty /According to my bond, nor more nor less" (1.1.76–7); "I return those duties back as are right fit:/ Obey you, love you, and most honour you" (1.1.81–2). Her words recall the Fifth Commandment, which enjoins not an infinite and unqualified love of parents, but rather, as the rabbis point out, the more sober and realistic injunction to *honor* one's parents, an attitude of respect realized in substantive duties and attitudes of care.[17] Her honoring of Lear is taken up by France when his love "kindles to inflamed respect" (1.1.250) at the sight of her abasement; both love and respect—love in its aspect as respect—are virtues cultivated by blessing.[18] "Honor," *kavod*, comes from *kaved*, "heavy"; in Hebrew, the corresponding anathema in Deuteronomy speaks of children holding their parents lightly (*makleh*), the sense captured in the King James translation: "Cursed be he that setteth light by his father or his mother" (Deut. 27:16).[19] This concern around light and heavy speech and action runs through Cordelia's response to her father: "I cannot heave / My heart into my mouth" (1.1.75–6), she says, presumably because it is too heavy to be lifted into words. Although Lear believes that his own sovereign speech carries the most weight—in the Trevor Nunn film, everyone but Cordelia crouches when McKellen's Lear hurls his curse at her—his curse in fact disturbs the fragile assemblage of words, meanings, affects, and intentions that supports trust. The impulsive and misdirected curse, spoken out of anger rather than justice, makes light of language, makes language light. In Giorgio Agamben's formulation, vengeful curses challenge "the relationship between words and facts (or actions)": "What the curse sanctions is the loosening of the correspondence between words and things."[20] Although Lear's words carry an immediate power, instantly transforming Cordelia's legal standing, his curse ultimately contributes to his divestiture and to the increasingly misdirected and uncalibrated efficacy of words in the play.[21]

> Lear makes his exit by snubbing his new son-in-law:
> Thou hast her, France; let her be thine, for we
> Have no such daughter, nor shall ever see
> That face of hers again. Therefore be gone
> Without our grace, our love, our benison.
> Come, noble Burgundy. (1.1.245–9)

---

[17] Lieber, *The Fifth Commandment*.
[18] On France's "inflamed respect" as "the passionately felt respect for another's moral being," see Budick, "Shakespeare's Secular Benediction," 339; and Budick, "Respect."
[19] Tigay, *Deuteronomy / Devarim*, 255. The Bishops Bible follows the Geneva Bible.
[20] Agamben, *The Sacrament of Language*, 36, 42.
[21] Quiring, *Shakespeare's Curse*, 180–3.

This refused valediction may echo the Priestly Blessing: "Our grace, our love, our benison" follows the same three-part structure, and the reference to Cordelia's face in the preceding line recalls the appearance of "face" and "countenance" in the prayer from Numbers. Turning away from France and exiting with Burgundy, Lear's refusal to say goodbye has its own body language, its own preemptory about-face. Everyday blessings cluster around greetings and farewells; Deuteronomy's liturgy promises to the obedient, "Blessed shalt thou be when thou comest in, and blessed also when thou goest out" (28:6), whereas the breakers of covenant shall be cursed "when thou comest in, and cursed also when thou goest out" (28:19). Salutation and valediction recognize real risks at threshold moments and in threshold spaces. Lear's refusal to bless the departing couple seals their excommunication and the larger crisis in communication itself that began with his curse.

In the opening scene of *King Lear*, failed, withheld, and anti-blessings loosen the bonds of trust and language to create a veritable landscape of curses, in which barren heaths provide little shelter to the denizens who wander beneath Deuteronomy's pestilent and climate-shaken skies. Deuteronomy's curses of infertility and frustrated labor spill over into Lear's invective against Goneril: "Into her womb convey sterility ... Create her child of spleen, that it may live / And be a thwart disnatured torment to her" [1.4.244–9]). The love test had removed the performance of gratitude from the substantive practices of recognition that Cordelia invokes in her "duties ... right fit." In his curse against Goneril, the accusation of ingratitude gnaws at the souls of both parties in a vicious circle of verbal violence, "sharper than a serpent's tooth" (1.4.255). Deuteronomic diseases ("the botch of Egypt ... the hemorrhoids ... the scab ... the itch" [28:27]) erupt as Lear's psychosomatic torment by his cursed daughter, whom he has expelled into the inflamed innards of his vexed being: "Thou art a boil, / A plague-sore, an embossèd carbuncle / In my corrupted blood" (2.2.369–70). The more legally ineffectual Lear's curses become, the more wounding and visceral is his language, aimed increasingly at the pregnant wellsprings of creaturely life, the blessings of breasts and womb that lend benediction its feminine graciousness: "Smite flat the thick rotundity of the world, / Crack nature's mould, all germens spill at once / That make ingrateful man" (3.2.7–9).

Kent glosses Lear's curse of Cordelia as a blessing denied: "His own unkindness / That stripped her from his benediction, turned her / To foreign casualties, gave her dear rights / To his dog-hearted daughters" (4.3.43–5). Blessings are often figured as shields against danger and curses as acts that strip the person of blessing's protections, exposing them to temptation, madness, disease, destitution, or death.[22] Yet *humiliation* by the curse is linked to the *humility* of the blessing, expressed in postures of bowing, kneeling, and prostration. As Budick and Regina Schwartz argue, Cordelia, Lear, Edgar, and Gloucester must become "nothing" in order to receive blessing from those they love and begin to recognize each other as moral persons and living beings by blessing them in turn.[23] When children bow or kneel for blessing, they humble themselves before their parents in order to be lifted up by recognition. When parents bless children, they speak not as sovereign sources of power but as hopeful well-wishers for insecure futures from which they themselves are destined to disappear. Humility and risk ripple in the extended hands of the parents as well as the bent knees of the children, who find the most provisional of shelters beneath the canopy of hands. In *King Lear*, blessing reveals itself as an *askesis*, a physical and spiritual exercise, that involves the humbling of pretensions in order to affirm the needs, rights, and identities of others in settings in which flourishing is suddenly, terribly, contingent and what matters is the affirmation of relationality, at whatever cost.

3. *King Lear*'s Benedictional Designs

Although the play's tragic action is set into motion by failed blessings and excommunicative curses, the play bends toward benediction, treated both inventively and reverentially by Shakespeare, in the two parallel scenes in which Edgar rejoins his father as his guide toward death and Cordelia and Lear learn to practice mutual forgiveness. The "benedictional designs" orchestrate space, time, gesture, movement, and sensory experience, unfolding the resources of blessing for theater and life. The Edgar–Gloucester and Cordelia–Lear sequences begin with unremarked blessings, swell into formal benediction, and then cede to narrated or anticipated blessing, practicing benediction as an *askesis* or exercise designed to remedy mental and spiritual damage and repair language through poetry.

Prologues: Beginning with blessings. Edgar's first direct words to his blinded father are "Bless thee, master" (4.1.38), followed soon after by the infinitely poignant "Bless thy sweet eyes; they bleed" (4.1.52). The English "bless" sounds like the French *blesser*, to wound, and may come from a Gothic word meaning to

---

[22] Little, "Separation of Religious Curses," 34.
[23] Budick, "Shakespeare's Secular Benediction," 337–8; Schwartz, *Loving Justice*, 45.

48   *Literature and Religious Experience*

sacrifice or consecrate with blood, resonances that color Edgar's aghast greeting at his father's bleeding rings.[24] Gloucester's blood, however, no longer flows freely from open sockets but rather blooms through the poultice applied by the unnamed servants in the house of Gloucester, a recipe signed with a blessing just as Edgar's greeting is: "Go thou; I'll fetch some flax and whites of eggs / To apply to his bleeding face. Now heaven help him!" (3.7.103–4). The Priestly Blessing glows with images of God's shining face and upturned countenance; here the divine presence is nowhere to be seen—except, that is, among the servants and beggars who send and accompany Gloucester on his long farewell and in the evidence of their work, which swathes a terrible nothing into a tender something. Framing the threshold actions of exits and entrances as existential comings and goings, blessing anoints a home economics of care that exercises the human art of lovingkindness in the shadow of that art's felt limitations.

In her conversation with the doctor in the field hospital, Cordelia calls upon "All blest secrets / All you unpublished virtues of the earth" to be "aidant and remediate" (4.4.15–18); expressed as a prayer, her words unfold the environmental dimensionality of blessing implicit in the servants' skilled nursing of Gloucester. In Carolyn Sale's gloss, "the idea here, of Earth as the repository of 'virtues' that have not been disclosed, released, or made public, is that of humans as remediating figures actively seeking the release of material and immaterial resources to one another."[25] Joseph's fruitful bough by well and wall becomes the temporary shelter of the field hospital, a provisional tent for the "untented woundings of a father's curse"(1.4.267), while Cordelia's "unpublished virtues of the earth" plumb Joseph's "blessings of the deep" for their healing powers. The view of life and labor from the imagined edge of Dover Cliff effects a parallel sounding of the deep, with Edgar's samphire gatherer echoing Cordelia's beneficent pharmacy. In both sequences, blessings prepare for the action to come by establishing an environment of care and an attitude of reverence in scenes of privation and danger.

Culminations: Blessing, divided. Before Gloucester falls upon the ground, he blesses Edgar *in absentia* and then says goodbye to Poor Tom: "If Edgar live, O bless him— / Now, fellow, fare thee well" (4.6.41–2). Overflowing from one line to the next, the two blessings alight on the single person of Edgar as Poor Tom. Gloucester speaks kneeling, as if receiving a blessing himself, and then falls forward, recalling radical forms of supplication such as full-body

[24] Hartman, *Saving the Text*, 132.
[25] Sale, "Cordelia's Fire."

Blessing 49

bowing on Yom Kippur, *sujūd al-shukr* or "thanksgiving prostration" in Muslim prayer, or the supplication of Jacob and his sons before Joseph in Egypt (Gen. 42: 6-9).[26] Prostration expresses humility and even humiliation, the reduction to nothing that Budick sees as the play's central repeated action, leading to the generation of a tragic community. The scene exploits the performativity and physical situatedness of blessing by calling attention to the flatness of the stage and the kinetics of kneeling and falling. Like Jacob's blessing by Isaac, Edgar's blessing by Gloucester is a blind benediction, executed without the full consent and knowledge of the father. In both Bible and play, the deception is anxiously authorized: the trickster Jacob is also God's elect who must grow into his stolen blessing through trial and sojourn, and the self-withholding Edgar is a healer and psychopomp wrestling with his own demon-angels.[27] Whereas Jacob is blessed in place of Esau, Edgar-as-Tom is blessed in place of Edgar-as-Edgar, so that Gloucester's double blessing both names and heals Edgar's division by disguise. Shakespeare had replayed this Biblical scene for its comedy in *Two Gentlemen of Verona* and *The Merchant of Venice*; here, he lifts comedy into several forms of irony: dramatic irony (Tom is really Edgar), generational irony (father kneeling to son), and moral irony (righteous deception). These ironies are suspended but not overcome in the power of benediction itself, which travels from the Bible through comedy to tragedy in order to be freshly rededicated by its Scriptural source.

As in the Edgar–Gloucester scene, the reunion between Cordelia and Lear develops the performance potential of blessing in a scene ripe with nonverbal expression: the healing kiss on the head, the Davidic playing of music to mend the mind, the use of a sick chair or bed to support the ailing body of the king, and the scripting of assisted entrances and exits to signal debility (Lear enters carried in his chair) and convalescence (Lear leaves supported by Cordelia). At the heart of this performance is the action of double kneeling, as each party attempts to receive rather than give blessing, an acceptance that becomes itself a kind of gift.[28] If in the Gloucester–Edgar scene doubleness yields a mounting irony held in check by benediction, the keynote in the Lear–Cordelia scene is more like mirroring, in which differences in age and gender are at once acknowledged and overcome in a solicitous mutuality that houses humility, reverence and "inflamed respect." Mehrdad Bidgoli suggests that Lear should

---

[26] Tottoli, "The Thanksgiving Prostration," 309–13. On rebuke and forgiveness in the Joseph story, see Schwartz, *Loving Justice*, 101–3.
[27] Palfrey, *Poor Tom*, 225–7.
[28] Young, "Parental Blessings," 204.

encounter Cordelia as a stranger, "with no pre-judgment and presupposition that might treat the Other as a phenomenon to be mastered and appropriated, or any recognition which reduces to kinship or servanthood."[29] Estranged by his curse in Act One, Cordelia reappears as a different kind of stranger in Act Four: as the neighbor who solicits and delivers care and blessing in Leviticus and Deuteronomy.

As if finding his way in the dark towards her shining countenance, Lear gropes towards recognition: "For, as I am a man, I think this lady / To be my child Cordelia" (4.7.71–2): the delivery of her proper name, the apex of recognition and itself a kind of blessing or baptism, comes at the end of a series of designations that affirm their common humanity while progressively articulating the nature of their relationship to each other. Humanity (*man*) becomes gender (*lady*) becomes generational (*child*) becomes the moral person, fully present, named, and acknowledged: *Cordelia*. Smith, following Paul Ricoeur, writes that scenes of anagnorisis in Shakespeare achieve a "'festive' quality, a celebration of recognition as a meaning-making act."[30] Blessing as ritualized speech draws out the festive, theatrical, and gracious character of recognition, requesting the audience's silent amen.

Epilogues: Blessing retold. When Edgar recounts the death of his father to Albany, he says,

> Not sure, though hoping of this good success,
> I asked his blessing, and from first to last
> Told him my pilgrimage; but his flawed heart—
> Alack too weak the conflict to support
> 'Twixt two extremes of passion, joy and grief—
> Burst smilingly. (5.3.191–6)

The shift from performed to narrated speech suggests the ongoing work of recollection in the practice of intergenerational blessing. "Not sure, though hoping of this good success," the retelling is fraught with the uncertainty that accompanies all of Edgar's decisions at Dover. Blessing is no assurance of God's providential reward: the revelation does kill Gloucester. Yet he dies of "joy and grief" together, not of despair alone, and the blessings enjoyed in their shared "pilgrimage" initiate a new moral relationship between father and son.

In his "Let's away to prison" speech, Lear imagines an endless loop of mutual blessing:

---

[29] Bidgoli, "On Cordelia's Defiance."
[30] Smith, "The Course of Recognition," 80.

Blessing 51

No, no. Come, let's away to prison.
We two alone will sing like birds i'th' cage.
When thou dost ask me blessing, I'll kneel down
And ask of thee forgiveness. (5.3.8–11)

Whereas Stanley Cavell sees Lear's lyric as the further avoidance of love and Janet Adelman accuses Lear of escaping into a fantasy of maternal plenitude, James Kuzner insists that Lear and Cordelia remain separate: one asks for blessing and the other for forgiveness, spiritual exercises both linked and distinguished at the end of *The Winter's Tale*.[31] Even if we allow that father and daughter remain morally autonomous, do repeated blessings lose energy and meaning? Again, Shakespeare acknowledges the insecurity of blessing, removing it from a providential frame and gifting it to humans, who are free to use, misuse, or abandon it, to reduce praisesong to singsong like birds in a cage. Yet the very nakedness and contingency of blessing strikes me as the bequest of both scenes, in which Shakespeare endows missed, anticipated, or remembered blessings with their own healing power, placing the responsibility to receive and renew blessing in the imaginative capacities and spiritual exercise of the audience.

With so much blessing bringing parents and children together, how, then, do we account for the play's devastating conclusion, with Cordelia dead in Lear's arms? In his study of blessing in the Bible, Claus Westermann suggests that the existential portions of Hebrew wisdom literature, including the book of Job and the darker Psalms, express a crisis in blessing, pointing beyond the economy of reward and punishment to acknowledge situations in which the good suffer and God seems absent or indifferent.[32] *King Lear*, Shakespeare's greatest contribution to wisdom literature, clearly participates in that more existential strain of scriptural thought. The play ends with Edgar's (or Albany's) effort at wisdom, a *sententia* often judged deficient by modern readers:

The weight of this sad time we must obey,
Speak what we feel, not what we ought to say. (5.3.319–22)

The "weight of this sad time" is carried into the injunction to "speak what we feel, not what we ought to say," lifted from the heaviness of suffering into the responsibility of *kavod*, honor or respect. This existential *kavod* frees speech from an externally imposed code of behavior and reclaims it for a deeper duty drawn from the endurance of loss, the humility of the nothing, and the painful

---

[31] James Kuzner summarizes the critical history of the passage and presents his own reparative reading in " 'Come, let's away': *King Lear*, Lyric, and Loving Reading," unpublished paper.
[32] Westermann, *Blessing in the Bible*, 62–3.

yet clarifying and even festive work of recognition. The sudden pressure of "this sad time" asks that we weigh our words, to heave them from our hearts to whomever will accept the risk of receiving them. *Benedicere* means "to speak well," to speak with the aim of supporting human flourishing by affirming relationships at the hazardous thresholds of coming and going. In *King Lear* and across his works, Shakespeare invites us to consider blessing in its fullest phenomenological dimensionality as physical and spiritual exercise. Let it be so.

Bibliography

Agamben, Giorgio. *The Sacrament of Language: An Archaeology of the Oath*. Stanford, CA: Stanford University Press, 2008.

Anderson, Jeff S. *The Blessing and the Curse: Trajectories in the Theology of the Old Testament*. Eugene, OR: Cascade Books, 2014.

Anonymous. "The Northern Mothers Blessing." In *Certaine Worthye Manuscript Poems of Great Antiquitie*. London: Robert Robinson for Robert Dexter, 1597.

Barkay, Gabriel, et al. "The Amulets from Ketef Hinnom." *Bulletin of the American Schools of Oriental Research* 334 (May 2004): 41–71.

Bidgoli, Mehrdad. "Ethics, Subjectivity, and Alterity in King Lear: On Cordelia's Defiance and Sacrifice." *Religion and the Arts* 25 (221): 385–420.

Breton, Nicholas. *The Mother's Blessing*. London: Thomas Creede for John Smethick, 1602.

Budick, Sanford. "Respect." In *Shakespeare and Virtue: A Handbook*, edited by Julia Reinhard Lupton and Donovan Sherman. Cambridge University Press, 2023.

Budick, Sanford. "Shakespeare's Secular Benediction: The Language of Tragic Community in *King Lear*." In *Religious Diversity and Early Modern English Texts: Catholic, Judaic, Feminist, and Secular Dimensions*, edited by Arthur F. Marotti and Chanita Goodblatt. Detroit, MI: Wayne State University Press, 2013.

Cummings, Brian, ed. *The Book of Common Prayer*, 1559. In *The Book of Common Prayer: The Texts of 1549, 1559, and 1662*. Oxford: Oxford University Press, 2011.

Elden, Stuart. *Shakespearean Territories*. Chicago: University of Chicago Press, 2018.

Hartman, Geoffrey. *Saving the Text: Literature/Derrida/Philosophy*. Baltimore, MD: Johns Hopkins University Press, 1981.

Hemmingsen, Niels. *Epistle of the Blessed Apostle Sainte Paule to the Ephesians*. London: Thomas East, 1580.

Hillman, David. "Ave Desdemona." In *Shakespeare and Hospitality*, edited by David Goldstein and Julia Reinhard Lupton, 133–56. New York: Routledge, 2016.

Hillman, David. "Salutation and Salvation in Early Modern Theology." *Renaissance Quarterly* 72 (2020): 821–5.

Levenson, Alan T. *Joseph: Portraits through the Ages*. Lincoln: University of Nebraska Press, Jewish Publication Society, 2016.

Lieber, Moshe. *The Fifth Commandment: Honoring Parents—Laws, Insights, Stories and Ideas*. Brooklyn: Mesorah/Artscroll, 1998.

Little, Lester K. "The Separation of Religious Curses from Blessings in the Latin West." *Memoirs of the American Academy in Rome* 51/52 (2006/7): 29–40.

Meri, Josef W. "Aspects of Baraka (Blessings) and Ritual Devotion among Medieval Muslims and Jews," *Medieval Encounters* 5, no. 1 (1999): 46–60.

Mitchell, Christopher Wright. *The Meaning of BRK "To Bless" in the Old Testament*. Atlanta, GA: Scholars Press, [1987] 1997.

Palfrey, Simon. *Poor Tom: Living King Lear*. Chicago: University of Chicago Press, 2014.

Quiring, Björn. *Shakespeare's Curse: The Aporias of Ritual Exclusion in Early Modern Drama*. Oxon: Routledge, 2014.

Sale, Carolyn. "Cordelia's Fire," Shakespeare Association of America seminar on Shakespeare and Virtue, 2020.

Schwartz, Regina Mara. *Loving Justice, Living Shakespeare*. Oxford: Oxford University Press, 2017.

Smith, Matthew James. *Performance and Religion in Early Modern England: Stage, Cathedral, Wagon, Street*. Notre Dame, IN: University of Notre Dame Press, 2019.

Smith, Matthew James. "The Course of Recognition in *Cymbeline*." In *Face-to-Face in Shakespearean Drama*, edited by Matthew James Smith and Julia Reinhard Lupton. Edinburgh: University of Edinburgh Press, 2019.

Sterrett, Joseph, ed. *Prayer and Performance in Early Modern English Literature: Gesture, Word, Devotion*. Cambridge: Cambridge University Press, 2018.

Tigay, Jeffrey H., trans. and ed. *Deuteronomy/Devarim*. Philadelphia: Jewish Publication Society, 1996.

Tottoli, Roberto. "The Thanksgiving Prostration ('sujūd al-shukr') in Muslim Traditions." *Bulletin of the School of Orientatal and African Studies* 61, no. 2 (1998): 309–13.

Westermann, Claus. *Blessing in the Bible and the Life of the Church*. Translated by Keith Crim. Philadelphia: Fortress Press, 1978.

Whittington, Leah. *Renaissance Suppliants: Poetry, Antiquity, Reconciliation*. Oxford: Oxford University Press, 2016.

Young, Bruce. "Parental Blessings in Shakespeare's Plays." *Studies in Philology* 89, no. 2 (Spring 1992): 179–210.

3

Longing: Young Geoffrey Hill and the Problem of Religious Poetry

Kevin Hart

In 1917, a year before the First World War would finally end, Mary Webb published her second novel, *Gone to Earth*. It is the story of Hazel Woodus, an unlettered girl, daughter of a gypsy and a harp player, who lives in the Callow, "a spinney of silver birches and larches that topped a round hill," apparently one of the Stiperstones bordering on Wales, in the sparsely populated southwest of Shropshire.[1] She lives flush with the hard, beautiful country of those parts, freeing trapped wild animals and looking after her fox cub, "Foxy." Without having any great desire to do so, she marries Edward Marston, a Non-Conforming minister. He lives "on a hill five miles from the Callow, called God's Little Mountain," where one finds a chapel and minister's house, "all in one—a long, low building of grey stone surrounded by the graveyard, where stones, flat, erect, and askew, took the place of a flower garden."[2] On the day he sees her for the first time, Marston hears Hazel singing to the accompaniment of her father, a song about singing to Christ accompanied by a "splintered harp without a string."[3] "Poor child!," Marston thinks to himself, "Is it mystical longing or a sense of sin that cries out in her voice?"[4]

It is neither of those things, the narrator tells us. "It was the grief of rainy forests and the moan of stormy water; the muffled complaint of driven leaves; the keening—wild and universal—of life for the perishing matter that it inhabits."[5] Certainly God's Little Mountain does not at first attract the earthy, pagan Hazel. Yet she listens to what the hills tell her.

[1] Webb, *Gone to Earth*, 13.
[2] Webb, *Gone to Earth*, 15, 63.
[3] Webb, *Gone to Earth*, 68.
[4] Webb, *Gone to Earth*, 69.
[5] Webb, *Gone to Earth*, 69.

They were of a cold and terrific color, neither purple nor black nor grey, but partaking of all. Kingly, mournful, threatening, they dominated the life below as the race dominates the individual. Hazel gazed up at them. She stood in the attitude of one listening, for in her ears was a voice that she had never heard before, a deep inflexible voice that urged her to do she knew not what. She looked up at the round wooded hill that hid God's Little Mountain so high, so cold for a poor child to climb. She felt that the life there would be too righteous, too well-mannered.[6]

Her intuitions are partly right: the marriage is not consummated. Beautiful and vital, Hazel soon finds herself the object of Jack Reddin's passion, whom she dislikes at first because he hunts foxes, and who is as sensual and narrow in his worldliness as Marston is spiritual and gentle in his otherworldliness. "Love that was abnegation was to his idea impossible," the narrator says of Reddin, yet that is the love affirmed and practiced on God's Little Mountain.[7]

Her sexual desires awakening, Hazel hastily interprets a blue petal on her path to be a sign to go to Reddin. And so she does. He rapes her, yet she is nonetheless drawn to him, even after that act. Indeed, the violence is figured as protection. "He caught her and flung her into the bracken, and suddenly it seemed to her that the whole world, the woods, herself, were all Reddin. He was her sky, her cloak."[8] Thereafter, Hazel lives with Reddin at Undern Hall, while also yearning for the love she has known on God's Little Mountain. Pulled in different directions by her sensual desire and spiritual longing, she is torn apart, while rural Shropshire broods in the background, sometimes flexing itself and becoming the foreground: pre-Christian, lyrical, almost suffocating its inhabitants with the intensity of its timeless presence. During a storm Hazel looks toward her former home: "Yet the Mountain shone in paradisal colors— her little garden; her knitting; the quiet Sundays; the nightly prayers; above all, Edward's presence, in the aura of which no harm could come—for all these things she passionately longed."[9] She goes back to Marston, who has now lost his faith precisely because he realizes that in introducing Hazel to Christianity he has given her a "mortal wound."[10] "He only knew he must care for Hazel as Christ cared for the lambs of His fold. And darkly on his dark mind loomed his new and bitter creed, 'There is no Christ.'"[11] There is to be no happiness for the injured couple, however, in this new Godless world: Hazel and Foxy are torn

[6] Webb, *Gone to Earth*, 130.
[7] Webb, *Gone to Earth*, 254.
[8] Webb, *Gone to Earth*, 215–16.
[9] Webb, *Gone to Earth*, 287.
[10] Webb, *Gone to Earth*, 313.
[11] Webb, *Gone to Earth*, 296.

Longing 57

in pieces by the hounds on one of Reddin's foxhunts. She has gone to earth, although her hiding place will be the grave, as it already is for so many British soldiers in the Great War. Nature and humankind respond alike: "There was silence on God's Little Mountain for a space."[12]

***

In 1952, the expression "God's Little Mountain" was doubled: the original remained in *Gone to Earth* while its copy became the title of a poem in Geoffrey Hill's first booklet of poems, the eleventh in Oscar Mellor's Fantasy Press series, and so took on a new life. At the time Hill was an undergraduate reading English at Keble College, twenty years of age, having come up to Oxford in 1950 from Bromsgrove, Worcestershire, southeast of the Shropshire countryside so densely and piercingly evoked by Webb. The booklet contained only five poems, the second one being "God's Little Mountain":

> Below, the river scrambled like a goat
> Dislodging stones. The mountain stamped its foot,
> Shaking, as from a trance. And I was shut
> With wads of sound into a sudden quiet.
>
> I thought the thunder had unsettled heaven;
> All was so still. And yet the sky was cloven
> By flame that left the air cold and engraven.
> I waited for the word that was not given,
>
> Pent up into a region of pure force,
> Made subject to the pressure of the stars;
> I saw the angels lifted like pale straws;
> I could not stand before those winnowing eyes
>
> And fell, until I found the world again.
> Now I lack grace to tell what I have seen;
> For though the head frames words the tongue has none.
> And who will prove the surgeon to this stone?[13]

Anyone opening up the Fantasy Press's *Geoffrey Hill* would have recognized the author to be a highly literary young poet. The first poem is entitled "To William Dunbar," the fifth, "For Isaac Rosenberg," while others pay homage to eighteenth-century poets: "Genesis: A Ballad of Christopher Smart" and "Holy

---

[12] Webb, *Gone to Earth*, 320.
[13] Hill, *Broken Hierarchies*, 5.

Thursday of William Blake."[14] Only the second poem, "God's Little Mountain," is not immediately recognizable as offering tribute to another writer unless, of course, one has read Webb's novel, and even if one knows *Gone to Earth*, the relations of the lyric to the novel are less than clear, if there are any in the first place. We know with hindsight that Hill has long meditated on the moral weight of the First World War, as registered in English poetry, and so the allegory of *Gone to Earth* would have lodged as firmly with him as the evocation of the countryside.[15] Neither landscape nor war is marked in the poem, though, and we are more likely to read "God's Little Mountain" as establishing a distance from the visionary Blake of *Songs of Innocence and Experience* (1794), perhaps by way of Alfred Edward Housman's *A Shropshire Lad* (1896), than as creating a space for itself inside the narrow world of *Gone to Earth*. Why, then, does Hill draw the title of his poem from Webb's novel?

Also on opening the booklet, the reader will sense that the poet admires from a studied distance different things in the semantics and rhetoric of several contemporary American poets: Allen Tate (a poem such as "The Traveller"), Richard Eberhart ("The Groundhog," in particular), and Robert Lowell ("The Quaker Graveyard in Nantucket," among others). The young Hill is a formal poet, and as he says in "The Poetry of Allen Tate" (1958), "the ideal of 'form' dismisses the legend of the 'mad' disruptive poet, and affirms the social value of the Respectable Artisan."[16] He is not a formal poet in search of smoothness, however; he is drawn to a "wanton roughness of form," apparent in his preference for slant rhymes.[17] He may not play a splintered harp, but his harp has splinters nonetheless. Yet what distinguishes Hill, even at this early stage of his writing, is less an interest in the formal possibilities of the modern lyric (an interest shared, after all, by a good many other English-speaking poets at the time) than a stress on the value of the letter of the poem. In the essay from which I have just quoted, Hill quotes with approval from Tate's essay "The Man of Letters in the Modern World" (1952). The task of the man of letters, Tate says,

> is to preserve the integrity, the purity and the reality of language wherever and for whatever purpose it may be used. He must approach his task through the letter—the letter of the poem, the letter of the politician's speech, the letter of the

---

[14] In *For the Unfallen* and later editions of his poetry, Hill dropped the subtitle of "Genesis" and the reference to Blake in "Holy Thursday." Hill did not reprint "To William Dunbar" and "For Isaac Rosenberg."

[15] See, e.g., Hill, *Collected Critical Writings*, essays 14, 25, and 26.

[16] Hill, "Poetry of Allen Tate," 11.

[17] See Hill, "Richard Eberhart," 31.

law; for the use of the letter is in the long run our one indispensable test of the actuality of our experience.[18]

"How splendid and how true this is!" Hill exclaims after quoting it.[19] And how well its lesson is taken to heart by the young poet, as we shall see.

Lastly, anyone opening up the thin booklet would have identified Hill as a religious poet and would have asked, as though with Marston, whether he speaks here out of mystical longing, or a sense of sin, or both. If he is a religious poet, he is one of a peculiar kind, someone for whom Christianity has been received as a blunt ache and a quiver of sharp questions, and a poet for whom "religious poetry" has become a problem more than a means of expressing immortal longings.[20] "Genesis," a highly condensed, postlapsarian hexameron, as powerful in its lyric way as the more orthodox homilies on the six days of Creation by St. Basil of Caesarea, St. Ambrose of Milan, and St. Bonaventure, concludes with stanzas that will disconcert believer and nonbeliever alike:[21]

On the sixth day, as I rode
In haste about the works of God,
With spurs I plucked the horse's blood.

By blood we live, the hot, the cold,
To ravage and redeem the world:
There is no bloodless myth will hold.

And by Christ's blood are men made free
Though in close shrouds their bodies lie
Under the rough pelt of the sea;

Though Earth has rolled beneath her weight
The bones that cannot bear the light.[22]

The speaker (call him Hill) reflects not on the creation of human beings on the sixth day but, rather, on a postlapsarian human act: he digs his spurs into the horse's sides in order to make it go faster.[23] Is Hill actually doing God's work

---

[18] Tate, "The Man of Letters," 20.
[19] Hill, "Poetry of Allen Tate," 11.
[20] This train of questioning is continued in Chapter 6 of this book.
[21] See St. Basil of Caeserea, *Exegetic Homilies*; St. Ambrose, *Hexameron, Paradise, and Cain and Abel*; and St. Bonaventure, *Collations on the Six Days*, in *The Works of Bonaventure*, V.
[22] Hill, *Broken Hierarchies*, 4.
[23] In choosing, for convenience, to call the speaker "Hill" one should be aware that the "I" of the early poems is not encumbered with personal details. A remark from one of Hill's early pieces of criticism is worth quoting: "When a writer seeks to create a work of art he must, indeed, have modesty and 'keep himself in the background'. That is the true modesty of the artist" ("A Writer's Craft," 14).

60   *Literature and Religious Experience*

or is he merely running around observing it? Either way, his attention to God leads him to cruelty. In turn, the horse's blood prompts him to ponder the Fall and the Atonement. And in a sense he has repeated the sin of Adam in the wake of Adam's sin, for he plucks the horse's blood as the first man plucked the fruit of the Tree of the Knowledge of Good and Evil, an act that quickly led to the spilling of blood in the murder of Abel.

His meditation is far from orthodox. We are likely to read the second stanza as saying that only blood-myths—those of infanticide, matricide, patricide, self-sacrifice, and war—have sustaining power, and that while they ravage us they also redeem us from insignificance. The thought rubs up against Blaise Pascal's *pensée* that "Man's greatness lies in his knowing himself to be wretched."[24] Other myths, such as the story of the Pleiades or that of Atlanta, do not have holding power; they explain something or entertain us but do not enter deeply into the mystery of being human. Things change with the third stanza. We are told in no uncertain terms that "And by Christ's blood are men made free," which catches on the earlier verb "redeem" as well as on 1 Pet. 1:18-19 ("ye were … redeemed … with the precious blood of Christ") (4). What are we to make of this? We seem to have two choices. First, we may fold the allusion to the Atonement back into the general claim about blood-myths, which makes the Atonement into a myth. The claim is certainly possible to make in a poem written in 1952: Rudolf Bultmann's controversial essay, "Neues Testament und Mythologie" (1941), with its sharp insistence that we must strip away myth from the New Testament in order to reveal its κήρυγμα, was already well known and widely discussed.[25] The speaker of this poem *needs* the myth of the Atonement, it seems, although one may well wonder whether one can need a myth when it is known to be a *myth*. Second, we may see the allusion to the Atonement as contrasting with what we have been told of blood-myths. The Christ-event bespeaks the truth and has genuine power to redeem us, unlike all blood-myths. For no myth, whether bloody or unbloody, can support belief because, being a myth, it is ultimately bloodless. Only the suffering and death of Christ can "ravage and redeem the world" (4).

If we accept this second interpretation the poem does not remain for long in the comfort of orthodox hope. For what is a Christian to make of the final statement, "Though Earth has rolled beneath her weight / The bones that cannot bear the light"? (4). Is it merely a conventional remark that the bodies of the

---

[24] Pascal, *Pensées*, 32.
[25] See Rudolf Bultmann, *The New Testament and Mythology and Other Basic Writings*, 1–43.

drowned sailors are dead (with the hope of the general resurrection being understood)? Or is it a more final statement, at odds with Christian doctrine about the last things, that some of the dead will not rise again? The ambiguity turns first on the verb "bear." It could be that the bones of the drowned cannot endure the light because they are in inky darkness on the ocean floor, or it could be because they cannot affirm the revelation of God in Christ. And the ambiguity turns, second, on how we read "Though." We might take it to be an adjective in which case the final couplet maintains that, in spite of the terrible pressure at the bottom of the ocean that crushes their bones, the drowned will be resurrected in the flesh. Or we might take it to be a conjunctive adverb that modifies what has been asserted so that the line says the drowned who have lost faith in Christ have been ground to nothing by the Earth and Ocean to which they have foolishly entrusted themselves.

As an undergraduate reading English at Oxford, Hill's education was regulated at a distance by, among others, J. R. R. Tolkien, then Merton Professor of English Language and Literature. Tolkien had worked on the Oxford English Dictionary after the First World War, and on his return to teach at Oxford in 1926 he was concerned to revise the curriculum of the School of English Language and Literature. He did so in 1932, and the new curriculum remained solidly in effect while Hill was at Keble. That revision was essentially to overcome the old (and sometimes bitter) divide between philology and literature at Oxford, requiring students to balance, if not always to interlace, philology and literature.[26] Hill grew up hearing lectures and participating in tutorials that presented the need for sound philology almost as a moral imperative, to which he added—in his poetic practice if not in his tutorial papers—elements of the formalism of the New Criticism with its emphasis on the letter, which leads readers to maintain a focus on ambiguity and paradox. Both were in the air, and had been since William Empson's *Seven Types of Ambiguity* (1930). Many critics of the day, Christian or not, read English poetry, confessional or not, in terms of the paradoxes inherent in the faith (Jesus as God-man, Mary as Mother of God, suffering as redemptive, weakness as strength, etc.), sometimes in a manner than can only seem reductive for poetry and faith alike. They did not do so for long with impunity.

After completing *The Structure of Complex Words* (1951), Empson turned from doubleness in literature to more ethical concerns, setting himself with fierce determination against the Christian faith, which he thought promoted a

---

[26] The details of the new division between Course I, II, and III may be found in the *Handbook to the University of Oxford* (Oxford: Clarendon Press, 1932), 157.

wicked view of God and life in general, and sideswiped those critics—"Neo-Christians" he called them—who reduced the complexities of moral experience to the paradoxes of the faith in the service of "Eng. Lit."[27] Helen Gardner, Hugh Kenner, Rosemond Tuve, and W. K. Wimsatt were readily caught within his sights. What seems particularly to have upset Empson is the ease with which critics would appeal to the interpretation of the Atonement known as "penal substitution" in order to explicate poets as different as John Donne, Andrew Marvell, and Samuel Taylor Coleridge. It is, as he put it in later life, "the belief that the Father could be bought off from torturing mankind eternally (or rather, a tiny remnant of mankind) in exchange for the specially intense pleasure of having his Son tortured to death."[28] It is hard to know who to credit with this blood theology when it is caricatured so freely. Empson associates Tertullian with the teaching on the basis of the theologian's idea of hell, but in fact Tertullian had very little to say about the Atonement.[29] Anselm's *Cur deus homo* is a case in point, as is Luther's 1535 commentary on Galatians, and in the *Institutes* Calvin speaks of the Atonement in terms of criminality.[30] No one, though, conceives the Father taking pleasure in the suffering of the Son. In their different ways, each speaks of the unity of love and justice. Empson's is a crude misunderstanding of the Atonement and of sacrifice in general, one that shows no awareness of κένωσις or of personal love as self-sacrifice.[31] Clearly, he liked his Christianity vulgar.

What one finds in "Genesis," however, is not something that would have given the Neo-Christians much satisfaction or given Empson cause to savage Hill.[32] We find there an abiding interest in the letter of the word, one that is fastened to what Tate calls the "actuality of our experience," which for Hill means that the

---

[27] See Haffenden, *William Empson*, ch. 14.

[28] Empson, "To Frank McMahon," 571. Empson's letter is dated August 21, 1973. His fury with Neo-Christianity reached a height in his memorable *Milton's God*. However, also see "Literary Criticism and the Christian Revival" (1966), in *Argufying*, 632–7.

[29] Empson, "The Satisfaction of the Father," in *Argufying*, 622. Tertullian uses the word *satisfacere* but not in the sense of "vicarious sacrifice." See Roberts, *The Theology of Tertullian*, 180. Tertullian evokes the fires of hell in his *Apology*, bound with *De Spectaculis*, trans. T. R. Glover, and Felix, *Octavius*, trans. W. C. A. Kerr, XLVIII, 13–15.

[30] See Luther, "Lectures on Galatians," 280; and Calvin, *Institutes of the Christian Religion*, Vol. I, Book II, ch. 16, section 1.

[31] As Empson indicates, his main source for his understanding of the Atonement is part of an article in *The Catholic Encyclopedia*. He seems not to have read the Fathers on the topic of the Atonement and bases much of his idea of the Atonement on Milton's sense of it.

[32] I should add that Empson was not an unreserved admirer of Hill's poetry, which he felt, rightly, could be "artificial" and could "harden into mere mannerism." See "To Christopher Ricks," June 30, 1978, in *Selected Letters of William Empson*, 645, 646. Similarly, Hill expresses reservations about Empson's poetry in his review of the special number of *The Review* devoted to Empson. See Hill, "The Dream of Reason," 91–101.

Longing 63

double nature of some words in his poem bespeaks an ambivalence to what they denote: in particular, an ambivalence to the claims of visionary experience and the Christian teachings that underwrite it.[33] If Hill would come highly to value certain martyrs and saints—St. Edmund Campion and St. Robert Southwell, in particular—he would also deepen his interest in the pathology of martyrdom and sainthood.[34] This ambivalence would be practiced at a high level in *Tenebræ* (1978), especially in "The Pentecost Castle" and "Lachrimæ," although the particular worry of those poems is already in evidence in Hill's first poems, in "Genesis," to some degree, though more clearly in "God's Little Mountain."

***

To which I turn, beginning with the title, which, taken from *Gone to Earth*, is left with the sixteen lines beneath it and an open set of references produced by the conjunction of "God" and "mountain" (not to mention the teasing qualification "little") to help make sense of it. Plainly, the speaker of the poem has climbed the mountain and failed to be worthy of a revelation at its summit, or even to be able to articulate what has been heard there. The questions remain, "Which mountain is it?" and "Why is it little?"

The poem begins with Hill high on the mountain. "Below," we are told, "the river scrambled like a goat / Dislodging stones" (5). This small disturbance pales to nothing when compared with what comes next. "The mountain stamped its foot, / Shaking, as from a trance" (5). The title constrains us to think of God, but the lines themselves suggest that a fairy tale giant, like the one that bothers Hop o' My Thumb, has been woken from a deep sleep. It is a far cry from the self-denying love one finds at the top of God's Little Mountain in *Gone to Earth*. We may well wonder if this great being is angry for good cause or is merely petulant. In an odd way Hill is protected by the sudden noise; it is the means by which he experiences "a sudden quiet" that blots out every other sound. The quiet, I take it, is wholly interior or entirely beyond the senses. The huge thunder may well have "unsettled heaven" if the stillness is any index.[35] What could have caused this catastrophe? Only, it seems, Hill's presumption in attempting as an impure man to climb the holy mountain. And how could this show of anger or petulance have rendered heaven no longer at ease?

That last question is engaged, if not fully answered, by a metaphor in the sixth line, "And yet the sky was cloven," that picks up the allusion to the goat in

---

[33] See Empson, *The Structure of Complex Words*.
[34] See Hill, "The Art of Poetry," LXXX, interview with Phillips, *The Paris Review*, 154 (2000): 281.
[35] See Hill's remarks on the "uneasy thunder" of the "Divine Voice" in his review of Blake's *Jerusalem*, *The Isis*, March 4, 1953, 22.

the first line and extends it, since the Devil is often represented as a goat.[36] The sky is not simply divided; it is demonically torn in two by flame. If we thought the good, great God rules heaven while the Devil is consigned to Hell, we must revise our judgment. For now we have no coercive reason to draw a strong clear line between God and the Devil, either because there is no such distinction in fact or because we cannot tell the difference between them in the first place. Hill protests that he waited "for the word that was not given," and yet something seems to be have been given to him: the flame leaves the air "cold and engraven" (5). Commenting on Deut. 33:2, Rashi observes in the Jerusalem Talmud that Torah existed before Creation. "It was written with letters of black fire upon a background of white fire" (*Shekalim*, 13b).[37] Rabbi Isaac the Blind, the father of Kabbalah, suggests that the mystical, written Torah is engraved in the white fire while the oral Torah is persevered in the black fire.[38] Mystical Torah is illegible and will remain so until the Messiah comes. Could it be that Hill expects the legible Torah and consequently misses the offer of the mystical Torah? If so, he is neither Moses, who receives biblical Torah and fully understands the mystical Torah, nor the Messiah, who will actually receive the mystical Torah.

Hill is "pent up into a region of pure force," and we may wonder whether this purity bespeaks raw, elemental power or a more elevated moral or spiritual strength (5). Either way, he is constrained by the divine will to remain on the mountain, and is subject to great cosmic powers. Also, he is strained by what is overfull within him. Is this his desire to receive the word? It would seem so. Equally, it could be that he is overfull with what he wants to say and is unable to express it, whether because it is forbidden or because he fears competing with the great poets of the past ("the stars"). The "pure force" may be outside him, confining him, or it may be what is deep within him, wanting to get out but blocked by what Harold Bloom calls "the anxiety of influence."[39] Certainly Hill

---

[36] Hill changed the line in his *Collected Poems* to read "And yet the sky was riven" (17). Following this edition, William Logan bases his interpretation of "God's Little Kingdom" on "riven" rather than "cloven" and thereby misses part of its theological point of the poem. See Logan, "The Absolute Unreasonableness of Geoffrey Hill," 43–4. It should at least be mentioned that the goat can be valued affirmatively in the Christian tradition. St. Gregory of Nyssa observes, in his fifteenth homily on the Song of Songs, "A goat is honored because its thick coat provides an image of beauty for the bride. Another reason for praise is that a goat can pass over rocks with a sure foot, agilely turn on mountain peaks, courageously pass through difficult, rough places, and can go safely on the road to virtue" (*Commentary on the Song of Songs*, 269). The image of the cloven hoof, however, surely overrides this positive image of the goat.

[37] Rabbi Isaac the Blind of Provence, "The Mystical Torah—Kabbalistic Creation," 74.

[38] See Rabbi Isaac the Blind of Provence, "The Mystical Torah—Kabbalistic Creation," 74.

[39] Bloom, *The Anxiety of Influence: A Theory of Poetry*.

Longing 65

sees poetry in visionary terms. As he writes in "Letter from Oxford" (1954), "the young student, the poet, maybe, hunched in his mackintosh on the top of the bus in the Banbury Road, sits apart from the crowd. Or he follows in the wake of a vision of life that goes before him and which he cannot grasp, a cloud by day and a pillar of fire by night."[40] And certainly Hill is not denied a vision in the poem: "I saw the angels lifted like pale straws" (5). The point is that the vision is too intense for him: "I could not stand before those winnowing eyes" (5). It is a biblical image of divine judgment. We think of Isaiah, "You shall winnow them, the wind shall carry them away, and the whirlwind shall scatter them," and Jeremiah, "And I will winnow them with a winnowing fan in the gates of the land."[41] In Hill's poem, though, the impure prophet or poet is winnowed, not the wayward children of Israel. He is not allowed to descend the mountain with dignity but falls and finds "the world" again.

Back in "the world," an expression slightly stained with a Pauline sense of distaste, Hill finds that he lacks "grace" to tell what he has seen. Reading this line with Christian mystical visions in mind, we recall St. Paul saying how someone he knew (himself, in all likelihood) "was caught up into paradise, and heard unspeakable words, which it is not lawful for a man to utter."[42] There is no grace given to Paul to repeat the holy words of paradise. Yet Hill has already told us what he has seen: "I saw the angels lifted like pale straws" and "those winnowing eyes." There must be more that he has seen but cannot report or express. At the same time, we may take "grace" to be elegance and charm, in which case the complaint is that he cannot write the visionary poem he has in mind for want of inspiration or refinement of poetic skill. "God's Little Mountain" would therefore be the workmanlike, fallback poem that can be written but that is composed without grace. And so the poem provides its own defense against criticism for some stiffness in its lines. The slightly arch question that remains, "And who will prove the surgeon to this stone?," asks both who will enable Hill to speak properly of his religious vision and who will help him to write the visionary poetry that is pent up within him or, if not that poetry, then another kind (5).

***

Hill has climbed part of the way up God's Little Mountain. Stripped of all particulars, it does not seem at all like the mountain in *Gone to Earth*. Except for the river at its base and the allusion to the Devil, it appears to be like a smaller

---

[40] Hill, "Letter from Oxford," 72. Anthony Thwaite calls Hill a "runic visionary" in his essay "Geoffrey Hill," 17.

[41] Isa. 41:16, Jer. 15:7.

[42] 2 Cor. 12:4.

66　　　　　　　　　　*Literature and Religious Experience*

version of Mt. Sinai. We have only to open the Bible to make the identification. "And mount Sinai was altogether on a smoke, because the LORD descended upon it in fire: and the smoke thereof ascended as the smoke of a furnace, and the whole mount quaked greatly."[43] Yet Hill is no favored prophet like Moses. "And the LORD came down upon mount Sinai, on the top of the mount: and the LORD called Moses *up* to the top of the mount; and Moses went up."[44] While Moses is on Mt. Sinai, the children of Israel urge Aaron to build an object of worship. Angered by His people's turn to idolatry, God sends Moses down to the people; the prophet smashes the tables of the Law that God has given him. After praying for the people, Moses returns to Mt. Sinai; God allows him to see his "back parts," and new tablets of the Law are made.[45]

Must we take God's Little Mountain to be another peak, not the great mountain of the Lawgiver? Not necessarily, for God did not choose Mt. Sinai because it was the tallest mountain in the area but because it was the most desolate and the most pure. The Talmud points us in the right direction. "R. Joseph said: Man should always learn from the mind of his Creator, for behold, the Holy One, blessed be He, ignored all the mountains and heights and caused His *Shechinah* to abide upon Mount Sinai" (*Sotah* 5a).[46] God overlooked mountains higher than Sinai, such as Mt. Tabor and Mt. Carmel, even though those peaks each thought it deserved the honor of hosting the Lord God. And He did so because idols had been placed upon them and had rendered them impure. Only Sinai was untainted, and so it became God's little mountain, its relative smallness being a sign of God's modesty and a challenge for us to be modest as well. Indeed, so unassuming is Mt. Sinai that we are told in *Midrash Tanhuma* that it had to be miraculously expanded in order to be able to receive the glory of God and the "thousands and thousands and a myriad of myriads" of angels and chariots that accompanied Him when He descended in order to give the Law to Moses.[47] "The Holy One said to it: Widen and lengthen yourself to receive the children of your Lord."[48]

Perhaps, though, there are other mountains that are qualitatively little in comparison to Mt. Sinai. One contender, with a plausible basis in the poem, is Mt. Parnassus in central Greece, the home of the muses and therefore the mountain sacred to poetry, music, and learning, three things that are very

---

[43] Exod. 19:18.
[44] Exod. 19:20.
[45] Exod. 33:23.
[46] Come and Hear, "Babylonian Talmud: Tractate Sotah."
[47] *Midrash Tanhuma*, 108. See "Tractate Bahodesh," in *Mekilta de-Rabbi Ishmael*, II, 224.
[48] *Midrash Tanhuma*, 224.

important to Hill. There are several possibilities here. One is that Hill tries to climb Mt. Parnassus and fails: the muses disregard him, or at least the one he especially wants to court shuns him (maybe Polyhymnia, the muse of sacred song). Yet the allusion to angels in the lyric cannot be decently accommodated by this interpretation. Another possibility is that Hill climbs Mt. Sinai but as a poet rather than as a prophet, thinking—with Eugenio Montale, among others—of poetry as a *scala a Dio*, which would mean that he wishes to use poetry as a means of ascending to God or that he proposes to make poetry out of "religious experience."[49] For climbing the sacred mountain in the wrong spirit or with impure motives he is inevitably judged by God and thrown back to "the world." The third possibility is the most complex. Here Hill climbs the sacred mountain, doubtless believing that he is called to do so, yet is judged unworthy of high prophetic calling. Falling back into the world, he turns his experience into poetry: not, to be sure, a religious poem but a poem that analyzes failed religious experience. He is no Moses, no Joannes Climacus, no Guigo II, no Dante, and neither a prophet nor a mystic.[50] Nor is he a visionary poet, let alone a mystical one. He is, rather, an artisan who examines the desire for vision and its consequences.

It is instructive to look sideways for a moment and to consider another twentieth-century poem, a far greater one, which is concerned with descending from on high. In "Tea at the Palaz of Hoon" (1921), Wallace Stevens introduces us to the spirit he will later call "that mountain-minded Hoon."[51] It is a memorable meeting. In his dignified descent, hearing hymns of his own composition, Hoon maintains his visionary intensity. He wears the purple and has been anointed with ointment: so he holds Episcopal office, or, better, is a priest-king. Despite his elevation he has not lost himself in ecstasy, as the implied questioner has presumably suggested before the poem begins, but rather has found his self in that high state. Where "God's Little Mountain" figures Hill as waking an angry or petulant deity, and being summarily dismissed by Him, Stevens's Hoon has consecrated himself as priest, prophet, or king (or all three) and speaks to us in tones of supreme self-confidence. "Out of my mind the golden ointment rained," he declares.[52] Where Hill asks for a surgeon to loosen his tongue, Hoon is sublimely indifferent to anyone other than himself, his ears making "the

---

[49] See Montale, "Siria," 240.
[50] See Climacus, *The Ladder of Divine Ascent*; and Guigo II, *The Ladder of Monks*. It should be noted that Hill is not a Zarathustra, either: this prophet descends the mountain with his hard words and does not fall from it. See Nietzsche, *Thus Spake Zarathustra*, 40.
[51] Stevens, "Sad Strains of a Gay Waltz," 51.
[52] Stevens, "Sad Strains of a Gay Waltz," 51.

68 *Literature and Religious Experience*

blowing hymns they heard."[53] And where Hoon finds himself, Hill merely finds "the world again" (5). In his fall from the mountain, Hill is unable to express himself properly. Yet in his stately descent Hoon finds himself "more truly." He does not find himself "more strangely," as we would expect from the grammar, since the poem ends more strongly if it places an emphasis not on *how* he finds himself but on *what* he finds: his irreducible strangeness.

That Hill ends his poem with a question rather than with the assurance of Hoon's self-discovery indicates a sharp division between the visionary Stevens and the Hill who must content himself with examining failure of religious vision.[54] At first, we might say that the question does not seem to be a stumper. The surgeon who can treat his wound—we think of the "mortal wound" that Hazel receives—and make him able to speak of what he has seen is God. T. S. Eliot, whose later poetry is not greatly admired by Hill, is nonetheless surely in the background here when Eliot writes in "East Coker" (1940), "The wounded surgeon plies the steel / That questions the distempered part," the surgeon being Christ.[55] And the surgeon who can help Hill speak with more elegance and charm is the muse, or perhaps none other than his true self. The reader of Hill's later books, especially *King Log* (1968), *Tenebræ* (1978), and *The Mystery of the Charity of Charles Péguy* (1983), recognizes that the surgeon has finally performed his operation, enabling Hill to say everything while using just a few words. A second look at the question, though, shows it to be more difficult. *Who* will prove to be the surgeon who can make me speak? That is the question on which the poem ends, and it is a genuine, urgent question: Is it God or is it the Muse? Is Hill's silence, his inability to write the poem that "God's Little Mountain" should be, due to a religious failure or an artistic one?

***

What is "the problem of religious poetry" for the young Geoffrey Hill? First of all, as "God's Little Mountain" makes plain, it is that he cannot write religious poetry (as Blake, Hopkins, Claudel, and Eliot can, despite their many differences of confession and style) but only a poetry that considers failed or flawed religious vision. Part of the reason that a more elevated poetry is out of reach for him is because, as he says in "The Bidden Guest" (1953), "The heart's tough shell is still

---

[53] Stevens, "Sad Strains of a Gay Waltz," 51.

[54] In "Tea at the Palaz of Hoon," Stevens is a visionary of a certain sort, although one would hesitate to generalize of all his poems, even those in *Harmonium*, that he is always a visionary. "The Snow Man," to name just one lyric, is as bleak a poem in terms of religious vision as one can imagine, and yet it is a visionary poem. Not all visions are comforting.

[55] Eliot, "East Coker," 201. See Hill, "Dividing Legacies," in *Collected Critical Writings*, 377–8.

to crack."[56] But hardheartedness is not all. In falling back into the world he has been unsettled far more than heaven has in his bid to be considered worthy. The problem is with him, at least in this early lyric: he is not a mountain (like Milton, like Blake) but a hill. Still an undergraduate poet, he is God's *little* mountain, Geoffrey *Hill*, using a pun that was waiting dormant for him in *Gone to Earth* ("a hill five miles from the Callow, called God's Little Mountain"). God's true little Mountain is actually south of Shropshire in Worcestershire: such is the hidden joke of the poem. Second, the problem is that Hill cannot decide whether he needs surgery from God or the Muse. Is his problem in writing visionary poetry to do with the state of his heart or with the state of his poetic skill?

In "God's Little Mountain" the problem is posed simply at the level of indecision, which tends to make the final question seem a little coy. It is a beginning, and only a beginning. With "Lachrimæ" the problem will be raised to a higher power, and Hill, no longer so little, will worry more deeply whether art is constitutively a distraction from authentic spirituality. Art, "this trade," will become identified with "Self-love," and the religious poet—Southwell or Hill— will come into focus as a "Self-seeking hunter of forms."[57] Are these poetic forms, which turn the poet into a martyr for his art, or are they the forms of martyrdom, which turn the martyr into an artist, perhaps distracting him from his or her religious vocation? That is the cruel ambiguity around which "Lachrimæ" is constructed. But for the Hill of "Genesis" and "God's Little Mountain" that was unimaginable. He must first address himself to "the unfallen," those who, unlike him, have not fallen from the mountain or fallen in the more recent Second World War, and he must also pass through the difficult years of *King Log* (1968) and *Mercian Hymns* (1971).

Bibliography

Bloom, Harold. *The Anxiety of Influence: A Theory of Poetry*. Oxford: Oxford University Press, 1973.

Bultmann, *The New Testament and Mythology and Other Basic Writings*. Philadelphia, PA: Fortress Press, 1984.

Calvin, John. *Institutes of the Christian Religion*, 2 vols. Edited by John T. McNeill, translated by Ford Lewis Battles. Philadelphia, PA: Westminster Press, 1960.

---

[56] Hill, "The Bidden Guest," 22.
[57] Hill, "Lachrimæ," 16, 19.

Climacus, John. *The Ladder of Divine Ascent*. Translated by Coim Luibheid and
Norman Russell, introduction by Kallistos Ware, preface by Colm Luibheid.
New York: Paulist Press, 1982.

Come and Hear. "Babylonian Talmud: Tractate Sotah." Available online: http://www.
come-and-hear.com/sotah/sotah_5.html (accessed September 8, 2008).

Eliot, T. S. "East Coker." In *Collected Poems 1909–1962*. London: Faber and Faber, 1963.

Empson, William. *Argufying: Essays on Literature and Culture*. Edited by John
Haffenden. Iowa City: University of Iowa Press, 1988.

Empson, William. "To Frank McMahon." In *Selected Letters of William Empson*, edited
by John Haffenden. Oxford: Oxford University Press, 2006.

Empson, William. *Milton's God*. London: Chatto and Windus, 1961.

Empson, William. *The Structure of Complex Words*. London: Chatto and Windus,
1951.

Felix, Minucius. *Octavius*. Translated by W. C. A. Kerr, Loeb Classical Library.
Cambridge, MA: Harvard University Press, 1966.

Guigo II. *The Ladder of Monks: A Letter on the Contemplative Life and Twelve
Manifestations*. Translated and introduction by Edmund Colledge and James Walsh.
Kalamazoo, MI: Cistercian Publications, 1978.

Haffenden, John. *William Empson: Against the Christians*. Oxford: Oxford University
Press, 2006.

Handbook to the University of Oxford. Oxford: Clarendon Press, 1932.

Hill, Geoffrey. "The Art of Poetry." LXXX, interview with Carl Phillips, *The Paris
Review*, 154 (2000): 281.

Hill, Geoffrey. "The Bidden Guest." In *For the Unfallen*. London: André Deutsch,
1959.

Hill, Geoffrey. *Broken Hierarchies: Poems 1952–2012*. Edited by Kenneth Haynes.
Oxford: Oxford University Press, 2013.

Hill, Geoffrey. *Collected Critical Writings*. Edited by Kenneth Haynes. Oxford: Oxford
University Press, 2008.

Hill, Geoffrey. *Collected Poems*. London: Penguin, 1985.

Hill, Geoffrey. "The Dream of Reason." *Essays in Criticism* 14, no. 1 (1964): 91–101.

Hill, Geoffrey. *For the Unfallen*. London: André Deutsch, 1959.

Hill, Geoffrey. "Lachrimæ." In *Tenebræ*. London: André Deutch, 1978.

Hill, Geoffrey. "Letter from Oxford." *London Magazine* 1, no. 4 (1954).

Hill, Geoffrey. "The Poetry of Allen Tate," *Geste* 3, no. 3 (1958).

Hill, Geoffrey. "Richard Eberhart." *The Isis*, November 25, 1953, 31.

Hill, Geoffrey. "A Writer's Craft." *The Isis*, February 17, 1954, 14.

Lauterbach, Jacob Z., trans. and ed. *Mekilta de-Rabbi Ishmael*, 3 vols. Philadelphia: The
Jewish Publication Society of America, 1933.

Logan, William. "The Absolute Unreasonableness of Geoffrey Hill." In *Conversant
Essays: Contemporary Poets on Poetry*, edited by James McCorkle. Detroit: Wayne
State University Press, 1990.

Luther, Martin. "Lectures on Galatians." In *Luther's Works*, edited by Jaroslav
Pelikan and Walter A. Hansen, 55 vols, XXVI: *Lectures on Galatians*, 1535.
St Louis: Concordia, 1963.

Montale, Eugenio. "Siria." In *Tutte le poesie*, edited by Giorgio Zampa. Milano: Arnoldo
Mondadori, 2005.

Nietzsche, Friedrich. *Thus Spake Zarathustra: A Book for Everyone and No One*.
Translated and introduction by R. J. Hollingdale. Harmondsworth: Penguin, 1969.

Pascal, Blaise. *Pensées*. Translated and edited by Roger Ariew. Indianapolis: Hackett,
2005.

Rabbi Isaac the Blind of Provence. "The Mystical Torah—Kabbalistic Creation." In *The
Early Kabbalah*, edited by Joseph Dan, translated by Ronald C. Keiner, preface by
Moshe Idel. New York: The Paulist Press, 1986.

Roberts, Robert. *The Theology of Tertullian*. London: Epworth, 1924.

St. Ambrose, *Hexameron, Paradise, and Cain and Abel*. Translated by John J. Savage, The
Fathers of the Church, vol. 42. New York: Fathers of the Church, 1961.

St. Basil of Caeserea, *Exegetic Homilies*. Translated by Agnes Clare Way, The Fathers of
the Church, vol. 46. Washington, DC: Catholic University of America Press, 1963.

St. Bonaventure, *Collations on the Six Days*, in *The Works of Bonaventure: Cardinal,
Seraphic Doctor, and Saint*. Paterson, NJ: St. Anthony Guild, 1970.

St. Gregory of Nyssa. *Commentary on the Song of Songs*. Translated and introduction
by Casimir McCambley, preface by Panagiotes Chrestou. Brookline, MA: Hellenic
College Press, 1987.

Stevens, Wallace. "Sad Strains of a Gay Waltz." In *Collected Poetry and Prose*, edited by
Frank Kermode and Joan Richardson. New York: Library of America, 1997.

Tate, Allen. "The Man of Letters in the Modern World." In *The Man of Letters in the
Modern World: Selected Essays: 1928–1955*. New York: Meridian Books, 1955.

Thwaite, Anthony. "Geoffrey Hill." *The Isis*, November 18, 1953, 17.

Townsend, John T., trans. *Midrash Tanhuma*. Hoboken, NJ: KTAV Publishing
House, 1997.

Webb, Mary. *Gone to Earth*. With an introduction by John Buchan. London: Jonathan
Cape, 1952.

4

Interruption: Conversion as an Event in Paul of Tarsus and Paul of Burgos

Ryan Szpiech

The last decade of the fourteenth century is infamous as the period of the most forced conversions to Christianity in Iberian history. In June 1391, riots broke out in Seville's Jewish quarter and quickly spread to nearby cities, interrupting daily life in the crowns of Castile and Aragon including Toledo, Valencia, Barcelona, and even beyond on the Mediterranean island of Mallorca. Hundreds, perhaps thousands, of Jews were killed, and many thousands were forced to convert to Christianity. Many of these *conversos* continued Jewish practice privately while maintaining Christian identities in public. A culture of suspicion emerged in Christian society in which *conversos* faced social discrimination, increased coercion, violence, and eventually, inquisition.[1]

Not all Jewish converts of the late fourteenth century were forced, however. In 1390 or 1391—the evidence is not clear—rabbi of the northern city of Burgos, Solomon Halevi, converted willingly to Christianity and took the name Pablo de Santa María (Paulus de Sancta Maria in Latin, d. 1435). His conversion was of a very different sort from the many forced conversions of his brethren, and his experience after conversion was also unique. As a Christian, Pablo rose to a high social standing, becoming tutor to the Castilian king Juan II, close friend of the Avignon pope (or "Antipope") Benedict XIII, and bishop of the city of Burgos. His name (often shortened in Latin to *Burgensis*, "the Burgosian," and often given in English as Paul of Burgos) came to be known all over Europe through his writing, which included an influential Jewish-Christian dialogue known as the *Scrutiny of Scriptures* (Scrutinium Scripturarum), as well as a set of biblical glosses, the *Additiones* (Additions), appended to the commentary

[1] For an overview of the events of 1391, see Baer, *A History of the Jews in Christian Spain*, 2: 95–117.

74   *Literature and Religious Experience*

of fourteenth-century Franciscan Nicholas of Lyra. Pablo's glosses were later included with Lyra's commentary in many early modern printed editions of the Bible, and in this way, they found their way "into hundreds of libraries across the Continent in scholastic, monastic, cathedral, and courtly settings."[2] Writers as diverse as Marsilio Ficino, Thomas More, and Martin Luther cited his work. Pablo is, without a doubt, the most illustrious convert from late medieval Iberia.[3]

Pablo recounted his experience of conversion in the prologue to his widely distributed biblical gloss. Pablo's conversion evoked the model most familiar to Christian readers, that of Paul (Saul) of Tarsus, as narrated in the Acts of the Apostles. While the influence of Paul is not surprising, Pablo's own narrative differs in many ways. His transformation of faith was not the result of a violent epiphany, nor was it the result of violent upheaval, such as the forced baptisms that took place around him in many Iberian cities. Rather, his was a gradual experience of grace and faith, a slow transformation premised on "rereading" Scripture and training his mind in a new understanding. Thus, despite the aesthetic parallel, considered side by side, the conversions of Paul of Tarsus and Pablo de Santa María seem dramatically different.

This chapter compares the conversions of Paul and Pablo in terms of the different experiences of religious change they represent. Unlike Paul of Tarsus, for whom a turn to Christianity signified a sudden interruption of the status quo that radically reconfigured his subsequent experience, Pablo describes a conversion that transformed his former Jewish identity, combining his "Levite" identity in dialectical fashion with his new Christian faith. Reading Paul through Pablo's example, this chapter proposes that the Pauline paradigm of conversion includes two very different, even incompatible, models of change, and that this contradictory duality has yielded and continues to yield opposed models of religious experience. The first model, suggested in Paul's own epistolary language, describes faith as a definitive interruption of the past through the revelation of a new reality. The other, employed in the narrative representation of Paul in the Acts of the Apostles, casts conversion as a climactic moment in a coherent, diachronic history, a present bridge between past and future. Pablo, modeling himself on Paul, invokes this double tradition of, on the one hand, a "theological" Paul who breaks with the past, combined with, on the other hand, a "narrative" Paul who sees the past as a foreshadowing of the present and future.

---

[2] Klepper, *The Insight of Unbelievers*, 6.
[3] For an overview of Pablo's writing, see Szpiech, *Conversion and Narrative*, 41–2, which is the basis of the following discussion.

Interruption 75

Pablo's model, bridging medieval and early modern perspectives, serves to highlight in part the medieval legacy of this dual model of conversion. At the same time, a reading of Pablo's narrative points to themes that are still relevant in present-day debates about Paul's conversion. Thus, before turning back to Pablo's reading of Paul, this chapter will begin by considering the place of Paul's conversion in contemporary thought, including both philosophical discourse that cites Paul's conversion in debates about the nature of historical "events" and also theological debates that invoke it as part of what Lieven Boeve calls a "theology of interruption." Moving backward in time from this debate to a similar dual reading of Paul in the late medieval example of Pablo de Santa María, it will argue that Paul's complex legacy serves to illustrate a broader methodological challenge in the dialogue between theology and religious studies about how to characterize religious experience.

1. A Theology of Interruption

The question of how to understand Paul's experience on the road to Damascus is, for many Christian thinkers, part of a broader debate about the nature of God's intervention in history itself, which has emerged as an acutely important issue for theologians in the second half of the twentieth century. Johann Baptist Metz (d. 2019) has asserted that "the shortest definition of religion is *interruption*."[4] Metz's dictum provides the foundation of what Lieven Boeve calls a "theology of interruption" in which "God interrupts history" first through the death and resurrection of Jesus, and thereafter by the indelible memory of that violent interruption. "The category of 'interruption' also stands at the very heart of the Christian faith," he affirms because it "takes on its ultimate shape in the resurrection of Jesus crucified on the cross."[5] While for Metz, writing in the shadow of Auschwitz, "interruption" was most palpable in the confrontation with suffering and evil, for Boeve, working in a postmodern context, it becomes a confrontation with secularized "otherness" and the loss of tradition more generally in the face of a plurality of religious traditions. Theologically, this can take the shape of the radical otherness of God, but ethically it can mean also the irreducible reality of human others and their differences. The contemporary opposition between secular and religious worldviews is, for Boeve, itself a

---

[4] Metz, *Faith in History and Society*, 158, on which, see Ashley, *Interruptions*.
[5] See Boeve, "The Shortest Definition," 19.

76   *Literature and Religious Experience*

manifestation of the interruption of "all grand identity-forming narratives (the Christian one included)" with otherness.[6]

For Boeve, this amounts to a challenge to but not a destruction of Christian identity. In his words, "Interruption ... should not be equated with rupture." Boeve's assertion seeks to rethink the core semantic sense of the word, which is in fact directly linked with "rupture" (Lat. *rumpo, -ere*, "to rupture, to break," the core of *interrumpo, -ere*, "to rupture between" or "break apart"). In this, "interruption" (unlike related terms with the prefix *inter-* such as "intermission," "intercession," or "interlude") denotes a break or division, and in a temporal sense, a stopping of the course of things, even though, as Boeve insists, "what is interrupted does not cease to exist." Taken in figurative terms, the biblical imagery of "rupture" and interruption serves some thinkers as a fitting description for God's interaction with the world and intervention in human history through Providence, theophany, and miracle.[7]

The appeal made by some thinkers to the resurrection as the prototype of interruption follows Paul's apocalyptic theology. As Kevin Hart observes, "one could argue that Paul, the earliest documenter of the resurrection, invites us to consider the gospel as a blow that comes from outside all human knowledge, including religious knowledge."[8] René Girard approaches interruption as an intervention that can stop or change cyclical behavior. He sees the crucifixion and resurrection as the ultimate interruption of sacral violence, the "mimetic cycle" of ritualized scapegoating. As he explains, "the sacrificial crisis is a mimetic escalation and it is of such a nature that it takes a tremendous shock, something tremendously violent itself, to interrupt the scapegoat mechanism."[9] Drawing on Girard, Sandler Willibald describes "interruption" as a key aspect not only of Jesus's passion but also of his pastoral mission, noting that "Jesus had to interrupt the inherent dynamics of the law as a moral system (with Paul: the law that took sin into its service)."[10] The emphasis in these readings is on interruption as rupture, an event with the power to break closed and repetitive systems of thought or behavior. For both, "Jesus interrupts the systems" (in Willibald's words), albeit in different ways. For Girard, that interruption enables a new freedom outside of

---

[6] Boeve, "The Shortest Definition," 21. See also his "The Interruption of Political Theology," 55–6.
[7] In the Vulgate, *interrumpere* is used for verbs of destruction or breaking, such as *paratz*, "to break through" (2 Kgs 14:13, Isa. 30:13), corresponding to *rhégnumi*, "to break asunder" or "burst" in the Septuagint; and *baqa'*, "to cleave, break through, divide" (2 Kgs 25:4 and Ps. 77(78):13-15), corresponding to *diarréssó*, "to rend"' in the Septuagint.
[8] Hart, "'Absolute Interruption': On Faith," 192.
[9] Müller, "Interview with René Girard."
[10] Willibald, "Systematische Theologie," 11.

Interruption 77

the mimetic cycle of sacral violence. For Willibald, it also provides a model for how grace, and religion itself, can break open "self-contained systems" of human relations that are defined by secular social sciences.

By contrast with this focus on the interruption of systems and cycles, the use of "interruption" in the theology of Metz and Boeve depends on the subjective "encounter" with suffering and otherness. Like Willibald, they see interruption as an ongoing process in the world, thus situating the events of Jesus's life within a broader, open-ended Christian history. Such a reading moves between two different poles of Paul's conversionary persona, that of a sudden and singular "calling" and that of a character in a developed story of blindness and insight. Boeve himself insists that the impulse to characterize "interruption" both as a single force from outside time, but also as an ongoing opportunity for encounter within it, moves between these two Pauline views. Despite the power of interruption to "break open" closed narratives, he also stresses that religious experience itself can be conceived of as a perpetual form of interruption.[11] Jürgen Moltmann emphasizes the importance of that ongoing process, because interruption alone is not something that can be meaningfully integrated into Christian salvation history. "Interruption is not an eschatological category. The eschatological category is conversion."[12] One might paraphrase this as suggesting that the singular interruption of Paul's experience only takes on meaning in Christian history when it is incorporated into a temporal narrative.[13]

The dual readings of Paul's conversion are not unique to theologians. Contemporary philosophers have similarly turned to Paul as a case study of religious experience, diverging sharply over how Paul's conversion might or might not represent a dialectical understanding of history. For example, Alain Badiou insists that Paul's thinking was not dialectical, in which the present and future would be premised on the past, but is based only on rupture and the possibilities of a new creation. He states unequivocally, "Paul's argument is foreign to all dialectics ... Paul is obviously not the dialectician he is sometimes taken to be ... Ultimately, for Paul, the Christ-event is nothing but the resurrection. It eradicates negativity."[14] Badiou turns to Paul to exemplify his ontological ideal of "the event," which he defines as that which is beyond

---

[11] Boeve, *God Interrupts History*, 82.

[12] Moltmann, *The Coming of God*, 22; quoted in Hart, "'Absolute Interruption,'" 193.

[13] In a similar but nontheological vein, Jack Miles elaborates this view in purely literary critical terms, seeing the crucifixion and resurrection—and one might extrapolate this to include Paul's conversion as well—as structuring points that acquire meaning within a longer narrative timeline. See Miles, *Christ*, 207.

[14] Badiou, *Saint Paul*, 70–3.

78 *Literature and Religious Experience*

ontology, an unthinkable multiplicity that suddenly "interrupts" the unity of the state of affairs (the "world") with something new and therefore "belongs to that-which-is-not-being-qua-being."[15] In contrast to Metz, he proposes that religion "supposes a continuity between truths and the circulation of sense"; philosophy "is subtractive, in that it ... interrupts ... the circulation of sense."[16] Interruption, indeed, is nothing less than "the possibility of philosophy."[17] By characterizing Paul as a "poet-thinker of the event," he invokes him as the very embodiment of philosophy itself. This reading not only depends on Badiou's peculiar ontology but also on his idea of Paul's conversion, asking, "Is the term 'conversion' appropriate to what happened on the road to Damascus? It was a thunderbolt, a caesura, and not a dialectical reversal. It was a conscription instituting a new subject."[18] By stressing this subjective "thunderbolt," Badiou can also affirm, "Paul emphasizes rupture rather than continuity with Judaism."[19]

Badiou's conception of the "event" as fully new can be contrasted to Gilles Deleuze and Félix Guattari's more dynamic ontology of the event as a process of becoming rather than a happening or interruption. Although Deleuze and Guattari do not engage Paul as Badiou does, they nevertheless invoke his legacy obliquely by advocating for "empiricist conversion" in the fact of "happening."[20] But Badiou's argument that Paul represents a form of pure rupture is countered even more strongly by Giorgio Agamben, who sees in Paul's thinking "an unusual dialecticism," and in fact attributes the development of the Hegelian dialectical *Aufhebung* to Luther's German rendering of Paul's messianic terminology.[21] Agamben affirms that Paul's idea of a "soteriological dialectic" characterizes time after the coming of the Messiah. This messianic and dialectical interpretation of Paul builds on earlier uses of Paul by Martin Heidegger and Walter Benjamin, and it parallels contemporary readings concerning Paul's Jewish identity by Emmanuel Levinas and Jacob Taubes.[22]

---

[15] Badiou, *Saint Paul*, 2; Also, *Being and Event*, 189.
[16] Badiou, *Infinite Thought*, 166.
[17] Badiou, *Infinite Thought*, 94.
[18] Badiou, *Saint Paul*, 17.
[19] Badiou, *Saint Paul*, 35. On Badiou's engagement with Paul, see Cimino, *Enactment, Politics, and Truth*, especially ch. 1; Stephen Fowl, "A Very Particular Universalism: Badiou and Paul," 119–34; and Depoortere, "Badiou's Paul: Founder of Universalism and Theoretician of the Militant," 143–64.
[20] Deleuze and Guattari, *What Is Philosophy?*, 75. See Brent Adkins, "Deleuze and Badiou on the Nature of Events," 507–16; and Clayton Crockett, "Radical Theology and the Event," 210–23.
[21] Agamben, *The Time That Remains*, 99.
[22] Agamben, *The Time That Remains*, 57. See Alain Gignac, "Agamben's Paul," 165–91; Griffiths, "The Cross as the Fulcrum of Politics," 179–97. On Heidegger, see Cimino, *Enactment, Politics, and Truth*; and Kerekes, "The Figure of the Apostle Paul in Contemporary Philosophy (Heidegger, Badiou, Agamben, Zizek)," 27–53. On Taubes's reading of Benjamin, see Taubes, *The Political Theology of Paul*, 70–5; and Gignac, "Taubes, Badiou, Agamben," 155–211. On Levinas, see Bettina Bergo, "The Time and Language of Messianism," 178–95.

Like Metz's reading, Badiou's and Agamben's use of Paul is also overtly political, offering a premise for enacting reform and change in society. Unlike Metz, however, their different ideas of political interruption are both revolutionary, albeit in dissimilar ways. A notably different philosophical reading—no less ethical but in no way messianic or militant—is offered by Paul Ricoeur, who argues that Paul's understanding of salvation is premised on a dialectical understanding of the Law itself.[23] Unlike other philosophers, Ricoeur insists above all on the irreducible and paradoxical multiplicity in Paul's thinking. While one might see a strand of Paul's thinking in Badiou's emphasis on rupture and "caesura," Ricoeur argues that one should not let this universalizing discourse predominate over other parts of Paul's view of time, including the genealogical and autobiographical. Rather than simply side with Agamben's dialectical reading, however, he insists that one must "respect the diversity of Pauline discourse," accepting without resolution the paradox of both a *kairos* and a *chronos* in Paul's vision.[24] Interruption, for Ricoeur, must always involve an ongoing combination of historical event and narrative memory.

2. A Tale of Two Pauls: Conversion in the Epistles and Acts

These different theological and philosophical readings of Paul as a thinker of "rupture" in messianic terms or a thinker of "dialectic" in historical terms are not unique to modern interpretations. In fact, they replay an interpretive debate that has persisted through the history of Christian interpretation of Paul, a dichotomy that has its origins in the varied representation of Paul's religious change in the New Testament itself. How does Paul describe his experience and how does this compare with the description of him by others? Looking at the little he says about himself, we find language describing not "conversion," "return," or "repentance," but rather sudden insight.[25] He claims his faith was "received … through a revelation (*apocalypseos*) of Jesus Christ" (Gal. 1:12), an unveiling that came to him from without. "Before faith came," he explains in Gal. 3:23, "we were imprisoned and guarded under the law until faith would be *revealed*." Paul's change, in his words, is one of vision, literally and metaphorically, making him

---

[23] Ricoeur, *The Symbolism of Evil*, 140–1.
[24] See Ricoeur, "Paul the Apostle," 77–8.
[25] On the authorship of Paul's Epistles, see Roetzel, *The Letters of Paul*.

80   *Literature and Religious Experience*

a witness to the risen Christ. The resurrection interrupts the world and augers a
new time in which "there is neither Jew nor Greek" (Gal. 3:28).

The word *apocalypsis* (revelation) with which Paul repeatedly describes his
witnessing of the risen Christ hardly appears in the Gospels or in Acts, which
instead describe conversion as a "turning," employing *epistrephō* (from the root
strephō, "to turn") and its derivatives, meaning "to turn or return."[26] Forms
of *strephō* (patterned on the Hebrew verb, *shuv*, and its derivative, *teshuvah*,
"return") appear frequently in the Gospels, often in citations of the Septuagint,
to convey the ideal of returning to a better moral condition, thus linking
"conversion" to repentance, *metanoia*.[27] At the same time, they are rarely found
in the undisputed Pauline Epistles, and Paul never uses them to describe his own
experience.[28] In fact, he never refers to himself in his Epistles as a "convert" of
any sort but instead identifies as a "servant" (*dolos*) and "apostle" (*apostolos*) who
was "set apart" for God (Rom. 1:1). What one reader calls the "seeming lack of
conversion language" in Paul's writing has led some scholars to claim that Paul
was merely "called" but not converted, and led others even to question "the formal
appropriateness here of the word 'conversion' itself."[29] In the few passages where
Paul mentions his change from being a Pharisee to being a witness of the risen
Christ (e.g., Gal. 1:13-17; 1 Cor. 9:1, 9:16-17, 15:8; 2 Cor. 4:6), he consistently
describes his new understanding as a revelation from without rather than an
internal change or "turn." Similarly, in other passages describing they who have
gained faith through a vision (1 Cor. 15:5-7; 2 Cor. 12:2-4; Rom. 7:4), he does
not characterize the following of Christ as a form of "return" or repentance but
rather in terms of revelation and witnessing.

To understand Paul's conception of the resurrection as an "interruption"
in history, it is helpful to consider his vocabulary not only for his experience
but also for time itself. The New Testament makes varying use of traditional
Greek conceptions of time, above all the basic distinction between chronological
time, *chronos*, and incidental or seasonal time, *kairos*. While *chronos* indicates
linear, quantitative time, the time measured by a clock and a calendar, *kairos*

---

[26] On the use of *epistrephō*, see Balz and Schneider, *Exegetical Dictionary of the New Testament*, 2: 40–1;
Beverly Gaventa, *From Darkness to Light* 40–4; Aubin, *Le problème de la "conversion*," 70-7.

[27] The terms are found together in Matt. 12:41-2; Lk. 17:4; Acts 3:19, 11:18-21, 20:21, and 26:20. See
Jacbo W. Heikkinen, "Notes on 'epistrepho' and 'metanoeo'," 313–16.

[28] While *epistrephō* and *metanoia* / *metanoeo* are used seven and fourteen times, respectively, in Luke,
and eleven times each in Acts, they are used but three and four times, respectively, in Paul's Epistles
(2 Cor. 3:16; Gal. 4:9, 1 Thess. 1:9; Rom. 2:4-5; and 2 Cor. 7:9-10, 12:21). *Apocalypsis*, which appears
ten times in the Epistles, is found only once in the Gospels (Luke) and not at all in Acts.

[29] See Segal, *Paul the Convert*, 19–20, and also 9–10; Stendahl, "The Apostle Paul," 204–5. See also
Taubes, *The Political Theology of Paul*, 13–14, 47; Fredriksen, "Paul and Augustine," 15–16.

Interruption

is understood as qualitative time, the "right" time or opportune moment, the season of ripeness or stylistic time of measure and decorum.[30] In the Epistles, *kairos* refers most often to the present moment, the moment of the resurrection, the moment of messianic time. Paul's *kairos* is a radical interruption in time in which the uniqueness of the incarnation and resurrection divides mundane *chronos* into separate ages, into historical time and messianic time, the time that passes and, in Agamben's words, the "time that remains" between resurrection and apocalypse. For Agamben, Paul's "messianic" time begins with the novel interruption of the resurrection, a "now" that is, properly speaking, outside of history but not eternal.[31] In the wake of the resurrection, time is nearing its completion and "the end of the ages (*aionon*) has come" (1 Cor. 10:11). "You know what time (*kairos*) it is," Paul insists (Rom. 13:11). "The present form of this world is passing away" (1 Cor. 7:31). In this messianic "time that remains," conversion means recognizing that a new time is at hand.

Paul's own description, however, was not the image most associated with his experience, which instead depended on the narrative in the book of the Acts, likely written as much as half a century after his vision of Jesus.[32] Because the "epistolary Paul" speaks so little about "conversion" as such, and because the character of Paul figures so prominently in the narrative of Acts—more than any other character, including the Apostle Peter or the risen Jesus—the medieval understanding of his experience as a paradigm for Christian conversion derives principally from the latter representation. This is complicated by the fact that in Acts, Paul's "conversion" is represented not once but three times, first in Acts 9:1-19 (in a third-person voice), then in Acts 22 (as a direct quotation of Paul in the act of retelling his experience to a hostile Jewish crowd), and finally in Acts 26:9-18 (again as a quotation of Paul recounting his experience yet again to King Agrippa). With each retelling, Paul's "apocalypse" becomes less abrupt. Acts 9:1-19 depicts a sudden rupture, paradigmatic of the "Damascus Road" experience associated with Paul in Christian tradition in which "suddenly a light from heaven flashed around him. He fell to the ground." This rapid action continues when Ananias later speaks to him and "immediately, something like

---

[30] On the *kairos/chronos* dichotomy, see the entries in the *Theological Dictionary of the New Testament*, 3: 833–39 (*kairos*) and 9: 581–93 (*chronos*).

[31] Agamben, *The Time That Remains*, 62. The contrast between the characterization of time in the Epistles and in the Gospels can be seen by reading the only example of *kairos* and *chronos* being used side by side in the Gospels, in Lk. 20:9-10, with the only such instance in Saul/Paul's letters, in 1 Thess. 5:1.

[32] Brown, *Introduction to the New Testament*, 3–19, and throughout. On what Brevard Childs calls "the canonical effect of Acts within the New Testament," see *The Church's Guide for Reading Paul*, 237; and Christopher Mount, *Pauline Christianity*, 11–58.

82   *Literature and Religious Experience*

scales fell from Saul's eyes." Acts 22, retelling this story from another perspective, provides more narrative context, situating the sudden events between preamble and aftermath. Paul "stood on the steps and motioned to the people for silence … saying: 'While I was on my way … a great light from heaven suddenly shone about me. I fell.'" When Ananias speaks, Paul says "in that very hour I regained my sight." Acts 22 embeds the immediate action of conversion within the frame of a quotation, locating the suddenness of Paul's blindness and insight within the past-tense speech of Paul's retelling. This narrative embedding takes on another aspect in Acts 26, when Paul retells the same story, in slightly different words, to King Agrippa.

Each retelling further narrativizes the action, developing brief moments in the past into longer scenes that are elaborated in each retelling. For example, Acts 9 emphasizes the suddenness of the events in the use of the words *exaiphnēs*, "suddenly," in Acts 9:3 when Saul loses his sight, and *eutheōs*, "immediately," in 9:18, when he regains it. This unfolds more slowly under an added narrative layer in Acts 22, and Paul's "immediate" regaining of sight now becomes only *autē tē ōra*, "in the same hour" (22:13). This rapid reversal disappears entirely in Acts 26, in which blindness and insight no longer appear. The change in language in Acts 26 is even more apparent in the shifting of Paul's future mission from the mouth of Ananias to that of Jesus, who tells Paul of his mission to the Gentiles, "to whom I am sending you to open their eyes so that they may turn (*epistrepsai*) from darkness to light and from the power of Satan to God." Acts 26 leaves behind the "sudden" imagery of blindness and vision reminiscent of Paul's own description of "revelation," adding in its place the new language of "turning" that was entirely foreign to Paul's words in the Epistles.

This narrativization of Paul has consequences for the meaning of his conversion. What was for the "epistolary Paul" a singular revelation becomes in Acts just one moment of a linear narrative, thus fusing back together the historical and messianic time that was interrupted by the resurrection. While the "epistolary Paul" writes of revelation and the division of time by the resurrection, the "narrative Paul" in Acts embodies a dialectic of blindness and insight and "turning" from darkness to light. From a narratological perspective, Paul's unrepeatable experience of revelation becomes a completed, past experience within a linear narrative of development, a retrospective moment retold by another, acquiring exemplary meaning within the parameters of its wider narration. Just as the history of God's unique revelation to the Israelites later becomes, in Christian understanding, a closed chapter encapsulated within the larger narrative of

Christian supersessionism, so Paul's *apocalypsis* is contained within the narrative evolution from blindness to insight imposed by Acts. Contrary to the traditional image of Paul's Damascus Road experience as a unique event, conversion now becomes a *kairos* within a *chronos*, a teleological drama of evolution that follows an inexorable sequence of conflict, climax, and resolution.

3. Paul Redux: Rereading and Return in Pablo de Santa María (d. 1435)

Fourteen centuries after Paul's Damascus Road experience, Bishop of Burgos Pablo de Santa María wrote of his own conversion and naturally patterned his story on that of his namesake. His text, which was directed to his son Alfonso de Cartagena, is revealing in its recapitulation of both, contrary aspects of the Pauline paradigm of religious experience. Pablo's evocation of Paul is explicit in his choice of baptismal name as well as in his use of "Saul" and "Paul" to name the Jewish and Christian interlocutors in his *Scrutiny of Scriptures*. Both Paul and Pablo speak of their former Jewish identity in describing their new faith. Paul calls himself a "Hebrew born of Hebrews" (Phil. 3:5), speaking "to the Jews as a Jew (1 Cor. 9:20), and Pablo stresses to Alfonso (who converted with his father as a child) to remember that they are both "descendants of Levi." Moreover, just as Paul's conversion interrupted his own campaign of persecutions of early Christian communities, so Pablo's conversion took place on the eve of widespread attacks on Iberian Jews.

References to Paul are clearly evident throughout Pablo's conversion narrative, which begins with a reference to his childhood education:

> Since I had not received this [truth] in my boyhood, but [rather] was born under the perfidy of Jewish blindness, I had not learned sacred letters from holy teachers but I extracted erroneous meanings from erroneous teachers, always busy to rashly enwrap the correct letters with incorrect sophistries, like the other leaders of that perfidy. But, truly, when it pleased Him whose mercy knows no measure to recall me from darkness to light, from the murky whirlpool to the clear air: somehow the scales fell from the eyes of my mind, and I began to reread Holy Scripture somewhat more assiduously, [and I began] to seek after the truth, not faithlessly any longer, but humbly.[33]

---

[33] *Patrologia Cursus Completus*, 113: 35B. My translation. On Pablo's text, see Szpiech, "A Father's Bequest," 177–98; and the overlapping discussion in Szpiech, *Conversion and Narrative*, 41–50.

84   *Literature and Religious Experience*

Pablo commented extensively on Paul's epistles in his biblical commentary, and it is not surprising that traces of Paul's epistolary language appear in Pablo's conversion story.[34] Yet unlike Paul, who stresses that his message came from God (Gal. 1:12), Pablo stresses first what mistakes he received from other humans ("I extracted erroneous meanings from erroneous teachers"). Paul does not criticize his past as a Pharisee in the law as "erroneous" but as something he has left behind, noting, "I regard everything as loss" (Phil. 3:8). Pablo inverts Paul's self-characterization in Phil. 3:5 ("a Hebrew born of Hebrews"), instead characterizing his Jewish past as "the perfidy of Jewish blindness." Overcoming such "perfidy" did not amount to exchanging present for past but of progressing from erroneous to correct understanding.

Despite these references to the epistles, however, Pablo's conversion narrative relies even more heavily on the narrative representation of Paul's experience in Acts. The most salient example of this is Pablo's emphasis on repetition and return rather than rupture and revolution. Pablo claims he is "recalled" and, as he says twice, begins to "reread." This language echoes Acts by describing how he was called back, "from darkness to light," (echoing Acts 26:18) and stating that "the scales fell from the eyes of my mind" (as in Acts 9:18). In finding this new sight, Pablo does not fight against God, as Paul does when he "kicks against the goads" (Acts 26:14) but instead presents himself as one hopeful and passive, noting, "Night and day I awaited His help. And so it happened that the desire for the catholic faith was more strongly enkindled in my mind from day to day, until I professed publicly that very faith I was carrying in my heart."[35] For Pablo, conversion is less an experience in the world than an internal change in perception (with the "eyes of my mind"), less an external event that interrupts than an internal understanding that returns him to the text. His baptism is the end point of a long, slow process of inner transformation, not of a sudden revelation.

Pablo's narrative of conversion as a return to the core meaning of the Bible—unlike those "erroneous teachers" who would "rashly enwrap the correct letters with incorrect sophistries"—points to the dominance of the "narrative Paul" over the "epistolary Paul" in Pablo's vision. The combination of Pablo's appeal to the former in some aspects and the latter in others exemplifies the way that medieval readers conflated the two different Pauline models, transforming the

---

[34] On Pablo's commentary on Paul's epistles, see Levy, "Nicholas of Lyra (and Paul of Burgos) on the Pauline Epistles," 283–91.

[35] *Patrologia*, 113: 35B.

conception of conversion as an "interruption" in time into a form of narrative climax, a point now followed by the denouement of a longer chronology.

4. Conclusion: Interrupting Religion

The personal narrative of late medieval convert Pablo de Santa María provides a valuable point of comparison with its model by responding not only to Paul's theology but even more to his narrative persona. Pablo's depiction of conversion is emblematic of the medieval conception of conversion in the Latin West and can stand in for a long tradition of readings that responded to the disparate models of conversion offered in Christian scriptures. Reading Pablo's narrative in light of present-day invocations of Paul's conversion further brings to light the enduring influence of Paul's double conversionary model in secular philosophical discourse. The legacy of Paul's multifaceted persona is not only a legacy of his own theology; it is also in part a result of the textual elements—both first-person and third-person, both testimonial and narrative—of the broader Pauline paradigm of conversion in Acts. The ongoing and robust debate about Paul's "dialectical" or apocalyptic thinking is indicative of a deeper question about how the shape of texts and the context of their presentation and reception affect their meaning over time.

The tension between rupture and dialectical return, interruption and continuity, that obtained in medieval Christian conversion narratives like Pablo's is still an integral part of our current epistemic formulations today. The multiple ways that Paul's and Pablo's models present conversion, both as a single and unique event in historical time and also as a climax in a broader narrative of faith, cannot be reduced to a single paradigm. The event of revelation—the *apocalypsis* that interrupts—gains new meaning when we turn again to reread its record with the new insight of historical context. This fraught tension between event and narrative provides a challenge to different disciplinary approaches to religious experience and thought—as Boeve notes, "The relation between theology and religious studies can ... be grasped in terms of interruption"[36]— and also underscores the value of approaching conversion in a comparative context that does not exclude a literary critical view. Reading Paul not only in his own words, nor only through Luke's eyes in Acts, but also through Pablo's eyes in his confession and commentary, it is clear that Paul's conversion ought not be

[36] Boeve, "Mutual Interruption," 14.

understood in only one way—as Badiou proposes—but rather that, as Ricoeur stresses, the paradoxical diversity of Pauline discourses must be respected and embraced.

In this way, the characterization of Paul's conversion might stand for the possible methodological and intellectual approaches to religious experience itself, whose multiplicity of discourses must likewise be maintained and recognized, not subsumed into any single totalizing model. Pablo's recapitulation of the Pauline paradigm can be read as a bridge between Paul as he appears in the biblical texts by and about him and Paul as he is invoked in contemporary theological and philosophical theories of history. As this reading of Pablo's narrative in the context of modern debates makes evident, our understanding of conversion, like that of religious experience of any kind, cannot rely on only one interpretive model but must always allow itself to be productively interrupted by the hermeneutics of a manifold and widening horizon of understanding.

Bibliography

Adkins, Brent. "Deleuze and Badiou on the Nature of Events." *Philosophy Compass* 7, no. 8 (2012): 507–16.

Agamben, Giorgio. *The Time That Remains: A Commentary on the Letter to the Romans.* Translated by Patricia Dailey. Stanford, CA: Stanford University Press, 2005.

Ashley, J. Matthew. *Interruptions: Mysticism, Politics, and Theology in the Work of Johann Baptist Metz.* South Bend: Notre Dame University Press, 1998.

Aubin, Paul. *Le problème de la "conversion."* Paris: Beauchesne et ses fils, 1963.

Badiou, Alain. *Being and Event.* Translated by Oliver Feltham. London: Continuum, 2005.

Badiou, Alain. *Infinite Thought: Truth and the Return to Philosophy.* Translated by Oliver Feltham and Justin Clemens. London: Continuum, 2003.

Badiou, Alain. *Saint Paul: The Foundation of Universalism.* Translated by Ray Brassier. Stanford, CA: Stanford University Press, 2003.

Baer, Yitzhak. *A History of the Jews in Christian Spain*, 2 vols. Philadelphia: Jewish Publication Society of America, 1961.

Balz, Horst, and Gerhard Schneider, eds. *Exegetical Dictionary of the New Testament*, 3 vols. Grand Rapids, MI: Eerdmans, 1990–3.

Bergo, Bettina. "The Time and Language of Messianism: Levinas and Saint Paul." In *Levinas and the Ancients*, edited by Brian Schroeder and Silvia Benso, 178–95. Bloomington: Indiana University Press, 2008.

Boeve, Lieven. *God Interrupts History: Theology in a Time of Upheaval.* London: Bloomsbury, 2007.

Boeve, Lieven. "The Interruption of Political Theology." In *The Future of Political Theology: Religious and Theological Perspectives*, edited by Péter Losonczi, Mika Luoma-aho, and Aakash Singh, 53–66. New York: Taylor and Francis, 2012.

Boeve, Lieven. "Mutual Interruption: Toward a Productive Tension between Theology and Religious Studies." *Louvain Studies* 34 (2009–10): 3–18.

Boeve, Lieven. "The Shortest Definition of Religion: Interruption." *The Pastoral Review* 5, nos. 3–5 (2009): 3: 4–9; 4: 4–9; 5: 18–25.

Brown, Raymond E. *An Introduction to the New Testament*. New York: Doubleday, 1997.

Childs, Brevard. *The Church's Guide for Reading Paul: The Canonical Shaping of the Pauline Corpus*. Grand Rapids, MI: Eerdmans, 2008.

Cimino, Antonio. *Enactment, Politics, and Truth: Pauline Themes in Agamben, Badiou, and Heidegger*. New York: Bloomsbury Academic, 2018.

Crockett, Clayton. "Radical Theology and the Event: Paul with Deleuze." In *Paul and the Philosophers*, edited by Ward Blanton and Hent de Vries, 210–23. New York: Fordham University Press, 2013.

Deleuze, Gilles, and Félix Guattari. *What Is Philosophy?* Translated by Hugh Tomlinson and Graham Burchell. New York: Columbia University Press, 1994.

Depoortere, Frederiek. "Badiou's Paul: Founder of Universalism and Theoretician of the Militant." In *Paul in the Grip of the Philosophers: The Apostle and Contemporary Continental Philosophy*, edited by Peter Frick, 143–64. Minneapolis, MN: Fortress, 2013.

Fowl, Stephen. "A Very Particular Universalism: Badiou and Paul." In *Paul, Philosophy, and the Theopolitical Vision: Critical Engagements with Agamben, Badiou, Žižek and Others*, edited by Douglas Harink, 119–34. Eugene, OR: Cascade, 2010.

Fredriksen, Paula. "Paul and Augustine: Conversion Narratives, Orthodox Traditions, and the Retrospective Self." *Journal of Theological Studies* 37 (1986): 3–34.

Gaventa, Beverly. *From Darkness to Light: Aspects of Conversion in the New Testament*. Philadelphia, PA: Fortress Press, 1986.

Gignac, Alain. "Agamben's Paul: Thinker of the Messianic." In *Paul in the Grip of the Philosophers: The Apostle and Contemporary Continental Philosophy*, edited by Peter Frick, 165–91. Minneapolis, MN: Fortress, 2013.

Gignac, Alain. "Taubes, Badiou, Agamben: Reception of Paul by Non-Christian Philosophers Today." In *Reading Romans with Contemporary Philosophers and Theologians*, edited by David Odell-Scott, 155–211. New York: T&T Clark, 2007.

Griffiths, Paul J. "The Cross as the Fulcrum of Politics: Expropriating Agamben on Paul." In *Paul, Philosophy, and the Theopolitical Vision: Critical Engagements with Agamben, Badiou, Žižek and Others*, edited by Douglas Harink, 179–97. Eugene, OR: Cascade, 2010.

Hart, Kevin. "'Absolute Interruption': On Faith." In *Questioning God*, edited by John D. Caputo, Mark Dooley, and Michael J. Scanlon, 186–208. Bloomington: Indiana University Press, 2001.

Heikkinen, Jacob W. "Notes on 'epistrepho' and 'metanoeo." *Ecumenical Review* 19, no. 3 (1967): 313–16.

Kerekes, Erzsébet. "The Figure of the Apostle Paul in Contemporary Philosophy (Heidegger, Badiou, Agamben, Žižek)." *Journal for the Study of Religions and Ideologies* 14, no. 42 (2015): 27–53.

Klepper, Deeana. *The Insight of Unbelievers: Nicholas of Lyra and Christian Reading of Jewish Text in the Later Middle Ages*. Philadelphia: University of Pennsylvania Press, 2007.

Levy, Ian Christopher. "Nicholas of Lyra (and Paul of Burgos) on the Pauline Epistles." In *A Companion to St. Paul in the Middle Ages*, edited by Steven R. Cartwright, 265–91. Leiden: Brill, 2013.

Metz, Johann Baptist. *Faith in History and Society: Toward a Practical Fundamental Theology*. Translated by J. Matthew Ashley. New York: Crossroad, 2007.

Miles, Jack. *Christ: A Crisis in the Life of God*. New York: Knopf, 2001.

Moltmann, Jürgen. *The Coming of God: Christian Eschatology*. Translated by Margaret Kohl. Minneapolis, MN: Fortress Press, 1996.

Mount, Christopher. *Pauline Christianity: Luke-Acts and the Legacy of Paul*. Leiden: Brill, 2002.

Müller, Markus. "Interview with René Girard." *Anthropoetics* 2, no. 1 (1996). Available online: http://anthropoetics.ucla.edu/ap0201/interv/Top of FormBottom of Form (accessed October 1, 2020).

Patrologia Cursus Completus, Series Latina. Edited by J. P. Migne. 221 vols. Paris, 1844–55.

Ricoeur, Paul. "Paul the Apostle: Proclamation and Argumentation." In *Paul and the Philosophers*, edited by Ward Blanton and Hent de Vries, 256–80. New York: Fordham University Press, 2013.

Ricoeur, Paul. *The Symbolism of Evil*. Translated by Emerson Buchanan. New York: Harper & Row, 1967.

Roetzel, Calvin J. *The Letters of Paul: Conversations in Context*, 4th ed. Louisville, KY: Westminster John Knox, 1998.

Segal, Alan F. *Paul the Convert: The Apostolate and Apostasy of Saul the Pharisee*. New Haven, CT: Yale University Press, 1990.

Stendahl, Krister. "The Apostle Paul and the Introspective Conscience of the West." *Harvard Theological Review* 56 (1963): 199–215.

Szpiech, Ryan. *Conversion and Narrative: Reading and Religious Authority in Medieval Polemic*. Philadelphia: University of Pennsylvania Press, 2013.

Szpiech, Ryan. "A Father's Bequest: Augustinian Typology and Personal Testimony in the Conversion Narrative of Solomon Halvei/Pablo de Santa María." In *The Hebrew Bible in Fifteenth-Century Spain: Exegesis, Literature, Philosophy, and the Arts*, edited by Jonathan Decter and Arturo Prats, 177–98. Leiden: Brill, 2012.

Taubes, Jacob. *The Political Theology of Paul*. Translated by Dana Hollander. Stanford, CA: Stanford University Press, 2004.

Theological Dictionary of the New Testament. Translated by Geoffrey W. Bromiley. 10 vols. Grand Rapids, MI: Eerdmans, 1964–76.

Willibald, Sandler. "Systematische Theologie als Wissenschaft der Unterbrechung von Systemen." In *Tage kommen: Zukunft der Theologie*, edited by C. Mathis, P. Oberhofer, and P. Schuchter, 109–21. Innsbruck: Studia Universitätsverlag, 2000.

5

Vision: Building into the Blue

Gavin Hopps

The possible's slow fuse is lit by the Imagination.

Emily Dickinson

Although John Keats consistently expressed an antipathy toward "the great Consolations of Religion"[1] and, among the Romantics, is usually considered to be the least interested in theological issues, his poetry is recurrently concerned with moments in which it seems that we have "burst our mortal bars" and "stept / Into a sort of oneness" (*Endymion*, 190 and 795–6). In "Ode to a Nightingale," for example, the reader is immediately drawn into a present-tense vision whose affective intensity, paradoxical interior impressions, and syntactic blurring of subject and object announce an altered state of being that is problematized even as it is dramatically staged:

> My heart aches, and a drowsy numbness pains
>   My sense, as though of hemlock I had drunk,
> Or emptied some dull opiate to the drains
>   One minute past, and Lethe-wards had sunk:
> 'Tis not through envy of thy happy lot,
>   But being too happy in thine happiness,—
>   That thou, light-winged Dryad of the trees
>   In some melodious plot
> Of beechen green, and shadows numberless,
>   Singest of summer in full-throated ease. (1–10)

---

[1] Letter to Bailey, November 1817; in Keats, *The Letters of John Keats*, 1: 179.

92   *Literature and Religious Experience*

During the course of this ecstatic vision, which precariously wavers between an optative and an indicative stance—that is, between something longed for and something accomplished—the speaker associates the sense of leaving the world unseen with deceptive fancy, "fairy lands," the forgetful reverie of inebriation and a death-like dissolution of self. Yet, instead of concluding with an outright disavowal, the poem leaves us with a couple of obstinate questions:

> Was is a vision or a waking dream?
> Fled is that music:—Do I wake or sleep? (79–80)

One way of answering these questions has been put forward by Jerome McGann in his hugely influential study *The Romantic Ideology*.[2] McGann's answer, which focuses attention on "self-troubled" works such as "Ode to a Nightingale"[3] and picks up on the speaker's anxious questioning of the moment of vision but leaves aside the conclusion's reflexive questioning of this questioning, is as dogmatic as it is simple: all intimations of transcendence are a matter of "false consciousness."[4]

McGann's "demystifying" materialist approach is of course itself a reaction against an earlier critical tendency to take Romanticism's transcendent visions at face value. Douglas Bush, for instance, describes *Endymion*'s intimations of transcendence as a "direct statement of Keats's—and other romantic poets'— central quest, the attaining, through the imagination, of supra-human or supra-rational intuitions of spiritual reality."[5] Similarly, Jack Stillinger claims that Keats's "significant poems center on a single basic problem, the mutability inherent in nature and human life, and openly or in disguise they debate the pros and cons of a single hypothetical solution, transcendence of earthly limitations by means of the visionary imagination."[6]

---

[2] McGann, *The Romantic Ideology*; hereafter *TRI*.
[3] McGann, *TRI*, 132–3.
[4] McGann, *TRI*, *passim*.
[5] Bush, *Keats: Selected Poems and Letters*, 310.
[6] Stillinger, "Imagination and Reality," 3. Stillinger also offers a "blackboard diagram" to illustrate the "Keatsian structure" of the Romantic lyric, which he explains as follows:

> Characteristically, the speaker in a Romantic lyric begins in the real world (A), takes off in mental flight to visit the ideal (B), and then—for a variety of reasons, but most often because he finds something wanting in the imagined ideal or because, being a native of the real world, he discovers that he does not or cannot belong permanently in the ideal—returns home to the real (A1). But he has not simply arrived back where he began ..., for he has acquired something—a better understanding of a situation, a change in attitude toward it—from the experience of the flight. ("Imagination and Reality," 3)

> While Stillinger's diagram usefully directs us toward a number of key Romantic concerns, its schematic separation of "the real world" and "the ideal" is, I suspect, a little too settled and clear-cut for Keats, since surely the questions with which the nightingale ode concludes bespeak a state of

Vision   93

What I wish to do in this chapter is to propose a third way that is open to *both* of these divergent options. More specifically, I want to offer a "Ricoeurian" alternative to McGann's pessimistic model of ideology critique, which doesn't let go of the latter's suspicions of the visionary imagination but which favors a wider range of interpretive possibilities that takes cognizance of its potential positive functions as well. To begin with, it may be helpful to remind ourselves in a little more detail of McGann's construal of Romantic ideology.

1. The Evaporation of Disagreeables

Broadly speaking, *TRI* puts forward what Paul Keen describes as "a two-pronged critique of [the] 'dramas of displacement and idealization' which characterize both Romantic poetry and modern critics who remain trapped within the theoretical limits of Romanticism."[7] Undergirding the first of these is the assumption that Romantic works "carried out under utopian or transcendental signs" are "a body of illusions."[8] This assumption, as McGann makes clear, is based on a Marxist view of the world and so is defined as a form of thought or social practice that distorts in presenting us with "an upside-down view of" the world's realities.[9] It is, he explains, "a system of illusions" that "helps to maintain the status quo and to conceal the truth about social relations."[10] Taking issue with other Marxist critics, such as Louis Althusser and Pierre Macherey, McGann argues that poetry and art should not be exempted from the insidious dissimulative workings of ideology. Instead, he insists, art and poetry are "products at the ideological level, where a culture's ideas and self-representations are maintained."[11] Thus, he claims that Romanticism is "everywhere marked by extreme forms of displacement and poetic conceptualization whereby the actual human issues with which the poetry is concerned are resituated in a variety of idealized localities" and that a "socio-historical method pursued within the Critical tradition helps to expose these dramas of displacement and idealization."[12] Hence, for McGann, the realm of the ideal in Romantic writing is a pejoratively conceived utopia, which is to

---

epistemological puzzlement that problematizes this neat division in challenging our ability to draw such distinctions.

[7] Keen, *The Crisis of Literature*, 16.
[8] McGann, *The Beauty of Inflections*, 334; *TRI*, 12.
[9] See especially the Introduction and Afterword of *TRI*.
[10] *TRI*, 8.
[11] *TRI*, 3.
[12] *TRI*, 1.

94   *Literature and Religious Experience*

say a "nowhere" place that lures us into an escapist flight from reality. The second prong of McGann's critique then widens the compass of supposed delusion by including academic writing on Romanticism too, whose "priests and clerics"—in McGann's recurring ecclesial idiom—are similarly guilty of an "uncritical absorption" in the mystificatory discourse of the artists they study.[13]

Before comparing this model of ideology critique with the approach espoused by Paul Ricoeur, it is worth pausing to note that there are a number of problems with McGann's simplistic association of the visionary imagination with delusion. There isn't space to address all of these in detail here, though it might be helpful to highlight a few.[14]

Perhaps the most problematical aspect of McGann's critique concerns the claim that Romantic literature's transcendent visions are, *tout court*, a "body of illusions."[15] The pesky question that this all-determining claim provokes is, How does he know? McGann may well be right of course, but his unquestioned claim might equally be a nihilistic form of wishful thinking. Either way, the problem is that it is sheer assertion. As they used to say in Mathematics at school, he doesn't show his working out, which leaves one wondering how it was possible to get behind the curtain of things to establish such a momentous fact.[16]

In the second place, McGann seems to take for granted that truth in art is necessarily a matter of realist correspondence and that any idealized or enhanced description is a culpable departure from how the world is. What this neglects is the shyness of the real and the possibility that it may at times be necessary to embellish or distort how things appear in order paradoxically to disclose what is.[17] One thinks, for example, of the non-realist forms of Pablo Picasso, Salvador Dalí, Francis Bacon, or Peter Howson and the non-naturalistic figurations of Orthodox icons. In such cases, it would seem to

---

[13] *TRI*, 1.

[14] A more extensive consideration of McGann's work is offered in *Romantic Enchantment*.

[15] In *The Beauty of Inflections*, McGann concedes that *TRI* seems to "deny poetry and criticism its positive utopian functions" (334). Yet while these later concluding reflections acknowledge the possibility of a "positive utopianism" in Romantic writing, McGann continues to see such visions as "longed-for lies" and a form of displacement in a way that does little, if anything, to modify his earlier negative stance.

[16] In her discussion of "Ode to a Nightingale," Sonia Sikka calls attention to the posture of skeptical openness with which the poem ends and notes that this depends on the eschewal of opposing certitudes: "that the poet not conclude the intimation [of immortality] is true simply because he wants it to be, as that would involve a fallacious proof from pleasure" and "that he also not conclude the intimation is false because he does not want it to be," as that would commit "the nihilistic fallacy, which argues that if a belief is disenchanting and disconsoling, it is *ipso facto* true" ("On the Truth of Beauty," 259). Whether or not McGann falls prey to the nihilistic fallacy, the point of importance is that the critic closes off what the poet opens up.

[17] For an illuminating discussion of this, see Flannery O'Connor's essay "Novelist and Believer," in which she speaks about distortion as an instrument that reveals. *Mystery and Manners*, 162.

Vision 95

be missing the point to describe their departures from conventional realism as illusory. Manifestly, such figurative or catachrestic strategies become even more important if one is open to the possibility that there are more things in heaven and earth than are recognized by a materialist philosophy. For how else can one attempt to represent infinite or otherworldly forms by means of the finite? This issue has been recursively pondered by John Ruskin, whose theory of the "symbolical grotesque" recognizes the need for "fancy or tangible signs to set forth an otherwise less expressible truth,"[18] and who elsewhere insists that certain things can *only* be catachrestically evoked, observing that "what revelations have been made to humanity inspired, or caught up to heaven, of things to the heavenly region belonging, have been either by unspeakable words, or else by their very nature incommunicable, except in types and shadows."[19] One might, of course, continue to consider such visionary forms to be illusory. Yet, since not all the data are in, would it not be more accurate agnostically to describe them as aspiring to a sort of "transcendental realism"?[20]

In the third place, McGann's negative reading of the visionary imagination is the result of an exclusive reliance on retrospective or synchronic models of mimesis—that is, theories of representation in which reference is a matter of correspondence with a state of affairs that preexists or is concurrent with its signification. This is, to be sure, a conventional understanding of mimesis. Still, there are other "anachronic" models of signification that recognize the paradoxical possibility that a text may precede, and even elicit, the state of affairs to which it refers. According to such models, the utopian vision "is not only a dream but a dream that wants to be realized," which encourages a venturing beyond the actual not as an analgesic sojourn but in the interests of emancipation, by putting into question "what presently exists" and by shaping "new realities" *in front of* the text.[21]

Finally, McGann's model of ideology critique appears to assume that visionary literature is always and only concerned with representation. Its evaluation is therefore entirely dependent on the existence of an extratextual correlate. But what if representation isn't the only or primary function of such literature? What if it is intended to serve another more affective purpose? For example, might not such literature's disclosive capacities have less to do with signification and more

---

[18] Ruskin, *Modern Painters*, 3: 101.
[19] Ruskin, *Modern Painters*, 2: 142.
[20] Williams, *Grace and Necessity*, 21.
[21] Ricoeur, *Lectures on Ideology and Utopia*, 289 and 309; hereafter *LIU*.

to do with cognitive utility—such as its ability, in Percy Bysshe Shelley's phrasing, to awaken and enlarge the mind or transfigure the way we look at the world?[22] Alternatively, one might well wonder if it is always morally or psychologically harmful to allow oneself to be "carried away" by a work of art. Might not aesthetically engendered experiences of escapism, in which all disagreeables momentarily evaporate,[23] offer us a holiday from our quotidian concerns and in doing so contribute to our mental and emotional well-being?[24] Either way, if literature serves an affective purpose, the existence of an extratextual correlate becomes less important as an evaluative criterion, for what matters primarily from this point of view is not the "content" that such literature gives us but what the giving of the "content" does.

Recognizing the catachrestic, prophetic, and affective dimensions of visionary literature that are left aside in McGann's critique does not invalidate his reading of Romanticism. It does, however, limit its scope and reveal the possibility of other more constructive readings. In order to illustrate something of these alternative possibilities, I want to turn now to Ricoeur's more "ambidextrous" conception of ideological and utopian modes.

2. The Leap Outside

Ricoeur's work on ideology, which he addresses most systematically in his 1986 *Lectures on Ideology and Utopia*, though the central ideas of this aspect of his philosophy were sketched out ten years earlier in "Ideology and Utopia as Cultural Imagination," coincides in important respects with McGann's, most obviously in its debt to *The German Ideology* (the first five chapters of Ricoeur's *Lectures* are devoted to Marx) and in its conjunction of sociopolitical critique with reflections upon a literary genre (utopian fiction). In contrast to McGann's approach, however, with its univocally pejorative conception of ideology, which assimilates the utopian mode into itself without remainder, Ricoeur also considers the positive possibilities opened up by these interrelated phenomena,

---

[22] Shelley, *A Defence of Poetry*, in *Shelley's Poetry and Prose*, passim.
[23] John Keats, letter to George and Thomas Keats, December 28, 1817, in Keats, *The Letters of John Keats*, 1: 179.
[24] Thankfully, the puritanical disparagement of escapism has recently been challenged by thinkers in various fields who have defended experiences of aesthetic absorption (see, e.g., Scarry, *On Beauty and Being Just*, and Felski, *The Uses of Literature*). In addition, the practice of art therapy has helped to restore the dignity of these experiences by highlighting the emotional and psychological benefits of self-transcendence.

Vision

both of which, he suggests, have "wholesome" as well as "pathological" forms and can serve "constitutive" as well as a "distorting" role.[25] In what sense is this so?

Briefly, Ricoeur agrees with McGann, on the basis of his Marxist critique, that ideology and utopia are "figures of non-congruence" in relation to reality, and that "the first trait of ideology" is the gap between its "unactual representations" (religious, political, juridical, ethical, aesthetic, etc.) and "the actuality of the life process."[26] Additionally, he concurs with McGann that this becoming-autonomous of conscious representations—which Marx and Engels refer to as consciousness's emancipation of itself from the world[27]—may engender illusions or "false consciousness." With McGann, therefore, he endorses the Marxist critique of ideology as a "dissimulation and distortion" of reality, the main function of which is to preserve the power of a particular class and to "reinforce the belief in the legitimacy of the given systems of authority."[28]

If we turn then to the utopian mode, we find an initial convergence of views. So, for example, Ricoeur maintains with McGann that the "pathological" tendency of utopian discourse is toward "escapism" and a sort of "schizophrenia," in that its "flight into writing" involves an "eclipse of praxis" and a leap to an "elsewhere" beyond the given, which serves as an "alibi for the consolidation of the repressive powers that be."[29] Yet there is also a significant divergence of views, as Ricoeur refuses to accept McGann's totalitarian conception of ideology and argues that these "pathological" tendencies do not exhaust the possible functions utopian discourse. What other purposes might these two forms of imaginative practice serve?

With reference to ideology, Ricoeur argues that, although it disguises the real nature of things, it may also serve a *constructive* role, in helping to constitute identities and integrate social groups. The more interesting contention for our purposes though relates to the utopian mode, which, in addition to its "pathological" tendencies, may serve a more liberating and subversive purpose. This is so because, according to Ricoeur, one of the principal functions of utopia is "to open the possible."[30] Here is how he describes the two contrasting polarities:

> Every society possesses ... a socio-political *imaginaire*—that is, an ensemble of symbolic discourses that can function as a rupture or a reaffirmation. As

---

[25] Ricoeur, "Ideology and Utopia as Cultural Imagination," 17; hereafter "IUCI."
[26] "IUCI," 18.
[27] *The German Ideology*, 159.
[28] "IUCI," 23.
[29] Ricoeur, "The Creativity of Language," 30.
[30] *LIU*, 182.

98 *Literature and Religious Experience*

reaffirmation, the *imaginaire* operates as an "ideology" which can positively repeat and represent the founding discourse of a society, ... thus preserving its sense of identity. After all, cultures create themselves by telling stories of their past. The danger is, of course, that this reaffirmation can be perverted, usually by monopolistic elites, into a mystificatory discourse which serves to uncritically vindicate or justify the established political powers. In such instances, the symbols of a community become fixed and fetishized; they serve as lies. Over against this, there exists the *imaginaire* of rupture, a discourse of "utopia" which remains critical of the powers that be out of fidelity to an "elsewhere," to a society that is not-yet.[31]

For Ricoeur, the value of utopian discourse is its ability to envisage and summon us imaginatively to inhabit an "elsewhere" outside the given; for while this might encourage a turning away from "what is" in favor of what Keats calls the "pleasant smotherings" of imaginative escape,[32] it may also involve a keeping vigil for something missing or something more—something beyond the existing order. In which case, as an "exploration of the possible" that offers us "a new vantage on the given,"[33] it can serve a *revolutionary* purpose and would cease— in any simple or inevitable sense—to be a reactionary stance or a flight from sociopolitical concerns, as McGann uncritically assumes it is. Ricoeur explains the matter like this:

> This development of new, alternative perspectives defines utopia's most basic function. May we not say then that imagination itself—through its utopian function—has a constitutive role in helping us unthink the nature of our social life? Is not utopia—this leap outside—the way in which we radically rethink what is family, what is consumption, what is authority, what is religion, and so on? Does not the fantasy of an alternative society and its exteriorization 'nowhere' work as one of the most formidable contestations of what is?[34]

In short, for Ricoeur, since the possible precedes and clears the way for the actual, utopian discourse may serve a prophetic, emancipatory function by unfolding a world "in front of" the text that can change our ways of looking at things and open up new possibilities for being. In other words, its "fidelity to an 'elsewhere'" is less concerned with representation and more concerned with *transformation*—that is, initiating new vision or another way of being in

---

[31] Ricoeur, "The Creativity of Language," 29.
[32] Keats, "I Stood Tip-Toe upon a Little Hill," 132.
[33] *LIU*, 310 and 16.
[34] *LIU*, 310.

the world.[35] Ricoeur states, "The field of the possible is now opened beyond the actual, a field for alternative ways of living."[36] Thus, on this reading, contra McGann, utopian discourse turns out to be a form of ideology critique.

In summary, then, the key difference between the two thinkers is that whereas McGann evaluates the Romantics' transcendent imaginings in essentialist terms—which is to say, he sees them as *intrinsically* ideological—in Ricoeur's view, such literary visions are not *in themselves* either good or bad; their value is, rather, to be determined after the fact by the work's effects, "since only subsequent history will decide between sterile and creative discordances."[37] What's more, as Ricoeur points out in a Blochian vein, even this can only ever be a provisional assessment, for "what about aborted attempts? Might they not return one day, and might they not obtain the success that history refused them in the past?"[38] In alerting us to such possibilities, Ricoeur reminds us not only of the utopian potential that may be surreptitiously astir within ideology but also of the "anachronic" character of this potential, which can survive its pastness and remain open to the present. A brief illustration of these differences in practice may be helpful at this point.

As one of his examples of Romantic "false consciousness," McGann cites the climactic utopian vision conveyed by the Spirit of the Hour in Shelley's *Prometheus Unbound* (IV, 131–60). McGann's evaluation of this vision, which he suggests is a statement of Shelley's own liberal and reformist views, is curt and emphatic: it is "almost pure ideology."[39] How, by contrast, might we understand this passage in light of Ricoeur's more nuanced conception of ideology and utopia?

While Ricoeur would certainly recognize in Shelley's vision of the "yet to be" a "leap outside" the existing order to a "nowhere" place, he would, I think, not only dissent from McGann's one-sided negative reading of this mode of non-congruence, he would also encourage us to refrain from such essentialist evaluations altogether.[40] Instead, I suspect, conscious of the Janus face of utopian imaginings, Ricoeur would advocate a more pragmatic "post-hoc" appraisal, which takes cognizance of the vision's effects. Thus, although Shelley's millennial utopian vision might be a sophisticated literary form of wishful thinking, which unwittingly double-crosses itself in encouraging an attitude of quietist

---

[35] Ricoeur, *Freedom and Nature*, 54.
[36] "IUCI," 25.
[37] Ricoeur, "Science and Ideology," 245.
[38] Ricoeur, "Science and Ideology," 182.
[39] *TRI*, 120–1.
[40] Shelley, *Prometheus Unbound*, in *Shelley's Poetry and Prose*, III, iii, 56.

100   *Literature and Religious Experience*

complacency that furtively shores up the political order that the work was apparently supposed to subvert, it may also disclose new forms of society and bear witness to the alterability of things. As Ricoeur writes,

> The shadow of the forces capable of shattering a given order are already the shadow of an alternative order that could be opposed to the given order. It is the function of utopia to give the force of discourse to this possibility.[41]

In this way, by bringing into view "the shadow of another order" and offering us a variation on the real, Shelley's utopian vision of the world has a critical potential and can help to foster a counter-consciousness, which may in turn help to loosen the hold of the established order on the cultural imaginary. In Ricoeur's phrasing, utopian hope has "a *fissuring* power," in that it "effects a rupture in a closed order."[42] In which case, rather than being an evasion of reality, Shelley's envisioning of a counter-possibility would constitute a vital preliminary step toward sociopolitical change.

Some caveats are clearly in order at this point. First of all, it needs to be underlined that what we are concerned with here are shadows and possibilities—whose frail, modally qualified status is a kind of "as if," in contrast to the "is" of the actual; and as the scholastic adage reminds us, there is no necessary development from being possible to being actual. In the second place, it should be acknowledged that in venturing beyond the actual and turning us toward a world "elsewhere," utopian discourse draws us into a political space of risk and fragility, whose vision of another order can foster oppression as well as liberation. All of this is made clear by Ricoeur. What he also brings into view, however, with a gift for balancing suspicious and affirmative critical approaches, is the power of the possible—to contest, shatter, and reconfigure the actual. As Ricoeur succinctly expresses it, cultural revolution "proceeds from the possible to the real, from fantasy to reality."[43]

Ricoeur's less predetermining approach would seem to be especially appropriate in the case of *Prometheus Unbound*, since Shelley's utopian lyrical drama culminates with a magnificent paean to hope as a performative agency with the potential to bring about its own fulfilment:

> To defy Power which seems Omnipotent;
> To love, and bear; to hope till Hope creates

---

[41] "IUCI," 24.
[42] Ricoeur, "Freedom in the Light of Hope," in *The Conflict of Interpretations*, 412 and 411.
[43] "IUCI," 25.

Vision   101

> From its own wreck the thing it contemplates;
> Neither to change, nor flatter, nor repent;
> This, like thy glory, Titan, is to be
> Good, great and joyous, beautiful and free;
> This is alone Life, Joy, Empire, and Victory. (IV, 572–8)

As Terry Eagleton notes, "On this view, hope is not simply an anticipation of the future but an active force in its constitution."[44] This is a fine observation, which implies that Shelley's conception of hope isn't rooted in any present actualities, just as his vision of the future isn't simply an extension in time of the existing order. Rather, the utopian hope he envisages reaches beyond and seeks by dint of its own reaching to transform the current order of possibilities. Indeed, Shelley's performative conception of hope reverses the usual way of looking at things, since ordinarily our hopes are determined by the range what's possible; yet for Shelley what's possible may be determined and even *transformed* by hope.

3. Existential Hermeneutics

Let us turn now to the second point of divergence from McGann's account. The other key aim in *TRI*—aside from attempting to convince us that the Romantics' transcendent visions should be read as "dramas of displacement and idealization"—is "to persuade scholars that criticism ought to be trying not to reify, or recuperate, or repeat Romantic interests and experience."[45] In this way, in order to preserve a "critical vantage,"[46] McGann seeks to insulate the reader from identifying with the Romantics' enchanted imaginings. Ricoeur, by contrast, takes a much more positive view of readerly identification; for according to the latter's model of "existential" hermeneutics, whether the act of imaginatively entering into the proposed world of a text is pathological or productive, an instrument of quietism or emancipation depends on what it does to the reader or what the reader does with it.[47] (In espousing an approach that focuses on *praxis* and incites a move "from text to action," Ricoeur is in a sense closer than McGann to Marx, who famously proclaimed, "The philosophers

---

[44] Eagleton, *Hope without Optimism*, 84. Eagleton is discussing Ernst Bloch's performative conception of hope, which he illustrates with reference to *Prometheus Unbound*.
[45] McGann, *The Beauty of Inflections*, 334.
[46] *TRI*, 12.
[47] Ricoeur, *Interpretation Theory*, Conclusion.

have only *interpreted* the world, in various ways; the point is to *change* it.")[48] Moreover, in contrast to McGann, who sees the work of art as closed off in its pastness—or who imposes this condition of closedness upon it, blocking our ears like Odysseus to shield us from the work's enchanting effects—Ricoeur sees the artwork as a transtemporal resource and an archive of possibilities that remain open for appropriation by the reader across time.

This more pragmatic "Ricoeurian" approach, which recognizes the plural temporalities and productive capacities of imaginative works, is becoming increasingly prevalent in studies of art. For example, a number of art historians, such as James Elkins, Keith Moxey, Alexander Nagel, and Christopher Wood,[49] have started to call the segregating "authority of chronology" into question and—influenced by recent developments such as the turn to affect— are rethinking the nature of artistic time and exploring approaches that recognize the "autonomous achronological temporality" of artworks.[50] These "anachronic" critical approaches, which invert "the traditional preoccupation with the significance of the image at the moment of its production to that of its reception,"[51] emphasize the transhistorical presentness of the artwork and its ability to engender effects across time. As Keith Moxey puts it, artworks have a power that "exceed[s] the parameters of their chronological circumstances," which allows them to solicit "continuing responses … from those who encounter them through the ages."[52]

In the field of literary studies, too, an increasing number of scholars are becoming interested in the transmission of effects across time and are refusing to be "browbeaten by the sacrosanct status of period boundaries."[53] In the work of those associated with "post-critique," for example, we find a desire to explore alternatives to the dominant methodologies of "synchronic historicism," in which literary works are "stuck fast to neighboring phenomena in the same slice of time" and imprisoned in a "temporal container."[54] What they advocate in place of such approaches are "models of textual mobility and transhistorical attachment" that can help us to explore questions such as the following:

---

[48] Marx, "Theses on Feuerbach," 123. Ricoeur's version of this axiom is as follows: "By changing his imagination, man alters his existence." *History and Truth,* 127.
[49] See, e.g., Elkins, *The Object Stares Back* (1996); Moxey, *Visual Time: The Image in History* (2013); and Nagel and Wood, *Anachronic Renaissance* (2010).
[50] Karlholm and Moxey, *Time in the History of Art,* 2.
[51] Karlholm and Moxey, *Time in the History of Art,* 2.
[52] Karlholm and Moxey, *Time in the History of Art,* 27.
[53] Felski, *The Limits of Critique,* 154.
[54] Felski, *The Limits of Critique,* 154.

Why is it that we can feel solicited, buttonholed, stirred up, by words that were drafted eons ago? How can texts that are inert in one historical moment become newly revealing, eye-opening, even life-transforming, in another? And how do such flashes of transtemporal connection and unexpected illumination cut against the grain of progress narratives that drive the rhetoric of critique?[55]

The aim of such critics in exploring these "anachronic" alternatives is not to dispute the importance of historicist approaches but to consider what is lost when texts are treated as museum exhibits and insulated from more participatory forms of engagement. Rita Felski's comments on the subject are worth quoting at length:

> Historical criticism focuses on the meanings of texts *for others*: the work is anchored at its point of origin, defined in relation to a past interplay of interests and forces, discourses and audiences. ... One consequence of such historical embedding is that the critic is absolved of the need to think through her own relationship to the text she is reading. Why has this work been chosen for interpretation? How does it speak to me now? What is its value in the present? To focus only on a work's origins is to side-step the question of its appeal to the present-day reader. ... Yet the cumulative force of its past associations, connotations, and effects by no means exhausts a work's power of address. What of its ability to traverse temporal boundaries and to generate new and unanticipated resonances, including those that cannot be predicted by its original circumstances?[56]

In view of these losses, Felski and others are calling for approaches that seek to do justice to the "busy afterlife of the literary artefact" and "the transtemporal liveliness of texts,"[57] approaches, that is, that aren't condescending about the textual affordances that works of literature can elicit across time—such as

---

[55] Felski, *The Limits of Critique*, 154–5. This tendency is perhaps most prominent in Shakespeare Studies, where a widespread dissatisfaction with the prevailing methods of new historicism has encouraged the exploration of "presentist" approaches and the affective afterlife of literary works, which take cognizance of historical difference but focus attention on the meanings a text may generate for us in the present. In Romantic studies too, however, there are signs of what has been called a "post-historicist" turn; as Mark Canuel explains,

> For many years, "presentism" was taken to be a criticism applied to historicism that was guilty of not being historical enough. ... But some of the scholarship I describe as post-historicist moves beyond history in a way that shuns the kind of embarrassment over presentism that [scholars such as Alan Lui] may wish to encourage. The move we are seeing is often explicit and intentional, making Romantic literature into something that can speak directly to our own moment. (*British Romanticism: Criticism and Debates*, 11)

[56] Felski, *The Uses of Literature*, 10.
[57] Felski, *The Limits of Critique*, 154.

104 *Literature and Religious Experience*

escapism, enchantment, and identification—and are more inquisitive about the reader's experience of imaginary worlds and our productive affiliations with texts.

4. Conclusion

What I have attempted, rather hurriedly, to do in this chapter is to offer a more balanced and less prejudicial alternative to the one-sided critique of the visionary imagination that has long been dominant in Romantic studies. This alternative, as I have sought to show, is more hopeful but no less critical than McGann's approach, since it takes cognizance of the deceptive as well as the disclosive potential of idealized or imaginary worlds. Indeed, the proposed Ricoeurian alternative is arguably *more* critical, as it doesn't rule out certain options in advance and its interpretations are not foreordained by ideological precommitments.[58]

There are two dimensions to this alternative approach, which correspond to but contrast with the two prongs of McGann's critique. On the one hand, it evinces a hospitality to divergent possibilities, in that it is open to religious as well as secular constructions of the real.[59] On the other hand, it focuses attention on the experiences literature affords "in front of" the text, when the act of reading is allowed to become an existentially relevant exploration of the possible. This contrasts sharply with the paradigm of wittingly alienated reading that is commended to us in McGann's model of ideology critique, which favors a posture of disenthralled aloofness as it is assumed that the truth necessarily lies elsewhere than with the manifest content of the text.

In the hands of this sort of suspicious approach, literature loses some of its apostrophic or "transitive" character, as its calling out to us across time and space is muted when it becomes something simply to unmask or diagnose and the reader refuses the *invitations* of a text to enter imaginatively into its world.[60] In

---

[58] According to Christopher Castiglia, the "despondent nihilism" and "diffused suspicion" that characterizes McGann's brand of ideology critique is the outworking of a "disenchanted Cold-War disposition," which has been "maintained melancholically long past the Cold War's end." *The Practices of Hope*, 83 and 2.

[59] This critical openness to possibilities is underwritten by a sort of reflexive skepticism, which questions everything including its own questioning, and so paradoxically makes room for faith. As Byron puts it, "He who doubts all things, nothing can deny" (*Don Juan*, XV, 88). Ricoeur characterizes this posture of chastened openness as a "second naïveté," which encompasses both a "willingness to suspect" and a "willingness to listen." *Freud and Philosophy*, 27.

[60] In speaking of literature's "transitive" character, I am drawing on John Shearman's study of Renaissance art, in which he invokes the notion as a way of explaining how, rather than encouraging a posture of

Vision   105

this way, as Felski observes, "we are shielded from the risks, but also the rewards, of aesthetic experience."[61]

While Felski is apparently uninterested in the kinds of rewards with which this essay and volume are concerned, what I am arguing for might be described as a religious form of post-critique.[62] This might seem irrelevant when it comes to poems like "Ode to a Nightingale," which calls into question its own intimations of transcendence and keeps its distance from traditional religious frameworks of meaning in staging its vesperal moment of vision. What I want to suggest, however, is that even such "naturalized" moments of vision can "speak directly to our own moment" and open up possibilities for the present-day reader to appropriate and actualize "in front of" the text. Furthermore, even if such readerly experiences of transcendence are performative effects that are artfully induced by a literary construct, they can nonetheless offer us an analogue or foretaste of what, for a believer, is a reality to come.[63] In other words, I am proposing that literary moments of vision are an affordance structure or "laboratory of possible good,"[64] which can scaffold or, more tentatively, allow us to try out certain kinds of religious experience—for example, by enticing us into imagining a "beyond" or stepping into "a sort of oneness"—that is, catachrestic imaginings of a promised "not yet," which *pace* McGann "is not refuted by its non-being."[65]

Bibliography

Berger, Peter. *Redeeming Laughter: The Comic Experience of Human Existence.*
    New York: Walter de Gruyter, 1997.
Bloch, Ernst. *The Principle of Hope.* Vol. 3. Cambridge, MA: MIT Press, 1986.

---

    detached admiration, certain kinds of art seek to involve "the engaged spectator" in the world of the work, luring them into the events it stages and eliciting a sense of imaginative participation, as the viewer "becomes an accomplice in its aesthetic functioning." *Only Connect*, 57–8.

[61] Felski, *The Limits of Critique*, 188.
[62] For a discussion of the exclusive secularism of post-critique as practiced by Felski, see Branch and Knight, "Why the Postsecular Matters."
[63] Peter Berger speaks of transcendence "in a lower key," by which he means a momentary transcendence of "the reality of ordinary, everyday existence" that "does not in itself have any necessary religious implications." Even so, this transitory experience does involve "an intuition, a signal of true redemption, that is, of a world that has been made whole and in which the miseries of the human condition have been abolished." This is what he means by transcendence "in a higher key." Thus, for Berger, "lower" experiences of transcendence are distinct from but may open into a "higher" form of religious transcendence. *Redeeming Laughter* 205.
[64] Bloch, *Tübinger Einleitung in die Philosophie*, 222.
[65] Bloch, *The Principle of Hope*, 1202.

106 *Literature and Religious Experience*

Bloch, Ernst. *Tübinger Einleitung in die Philosophie*. Frankfurt am Main: Suhrkamp, 1970.

Branch, Lori, and Mark Knight. "Why the Postsecular Matters: Literary Studies and the Rise of the Novel." *Christianity & Literature* 67, no. 3 (2018).

Bush, Douglas, ed. *Keats: Selected Poems and Letters*. New York: Riverside Editions, 1959.

Canuel, Mark, ed. *British Romanticism: Criticism and Debates*. London: Routledge, 2015.

Castiglia, Christopher. *The Practices of Hope: Literary Criticism in Disenchanted Times*. New York: New York University Press, 2017.

Eagleton, Terry. *Hope without Optimism*. New Haven, CT: Yale University Press, 2015.

Felski, Rita. *The Limits of Critique*. Chicago: University of Chicago, 2015.

Felski, Rita. *The Uses of Literature*. Oxford: Blackwell, 2008.

Hopps, Gavin. *Romantic Enchantment: Fantasy, Theology and Affect*. Liverpool: Liverpool University Press, 2021.

Karlholm, Dan, and Keith Moxey, eds. *Time in the History of Art: Temporality, Chronology and Anachrony*. London: Routledge, 2018.

Keats, John. *The Letters of John Keats: 1814–1821*. Vol. 1, edited by Hyder Edward Rollins. Cambridge, MA: Harvard University Press, 1958.

Keen, Paul. *The Crisis of Literature in the 1790s: Print Culture & the Public Sphere*. Cambridge: Cambridge University Press, 2004.

Marx, Karl, and Friedrich Engels. *The German Ideology*. Vol. 5 of *Collected Works*. London: Lawrence and Wishart, 1976.

Marx, Karl. "Theses on Feuerbach." In *The German Ideology*, edited by C. J. Arthur. London: Lawrence & Wishart, 1970.

McGann, Jerome J. *The Beauty of Inflections: Literary Investigations in Historical Method and Theory*. Oxford: Clarendon Press, 1985.

McGann, Jerome J. *The Romantic Ideology: A Critical Investigation*. Chicago: University of Chicago Press, 1983.

O'Connor, Flannery. *Mystery and Manners*. New York: Farrar, Straus & Giroux, 1969.

Ricoeur, Paul. *The Conflict of Interpretations*. Edited by Don Ihde. Evanston, IL: Northwestern University Press, 1974.

Ricoeur, Paul. "The Creativity of Language." In *Dialogues with Contemporary Continental Thinkers: The Phenomenological Heritage*, edited by Richard Kearney. Manchester: Manchester University Press, 1984.

Ricoeur, Paul. *Freedom and Nature: The Voluntary and the Involuntary*. Evanston, IL: Northwestern University Press, 1966.

Ricoeur, Paul. *Freud and Philosophy: An Essay on Interpretation*. New Haven, CT: Yale University Press, 1970.

Ricoeur, Paul. *History and Truth*. Evanston, IL: Northwestern University Press, 1965.

Ricoeur, Paul. "Ideology and Utopia as Cultural Imagination." *Philosophic Exchange* 7 (1976): 17–28.

Ricoeur, Paul. *Interpretation Theory: Discourse and the Surplus of Meaning*. Texas: TCU Press, 1976.

Ricoeur, Paul. *Lectures on Ideology and Utopia*. New York: Columbia University Press, 1986.

Ricoeur, Paul. "Science and Ideology." In *From Text to Action: Essays in Hermeneutics, II*. London: Continuum, 2008.

Ruskin, John. *Modern Painters*. Vol. 2. London: George Allen, 1906.

Ruskin, John. *Modern Painters*. Vol. 3. London: George Allen, 1906.

Scarry, Elaine. *On Beauty and Being Just*. Princeton, NJ: Princeton University Press, 1999.

Shearman, John. *Only Connect ... Art and the Spectator in the Italian Renaissance*. Princeton, NJ: Princeton University Press, 1992.

Shelley, Percy Bysshe. *Shelley's Poetry and Prose*, ed. Donald Reiman and Neil Fraistat, 2nd ed. New York: Norton, 2002.

Sikka, Sonia. "On the Truth of Beauty: Nietzsche, Heidegger and Keats." *Heythrop Journal* 39 (1998): 243–63.

Stillinger, Jack, ed. "Imagination and Reality in the Odes of Keats." In *Twentieth Century Interpretations of Keats's Odes*, 1–16. Englewood Cliffs: Prentice-Hall, 1968.

Williams, Rowan. *Grace and Necessity: Reflections on Art and Love*. London: Continuum, 2005.

6

Metanoia: Tales of Transformation in Harriet Beecher Stowe and Wendell Berry

John Gatta

One line of fairly sharp contrast that has traditionally been drawn between novelistic writing and short fiction relates to characterization. Whereas the short story typically *reveals* something telling about its characters, a novel usually offers space enough to dramatize genuine *change* in one or more of its protagonists. Potentially, at least, the change in question may even reflect some ameliorative transformation of character—morally, psychologically, or spiritually.

So it strikes me as worth reflecting upon theological implications of this literary principle. What, in other words, can novelistic fiction tell us about prospects of achieving that self-transformation under grace, or transformation of a social order, that Judeo-Christian faith traditions have long associated with terms such as "conversion" and "*metanoia*"? Is it really possible for a human being to undergo a decisive shift in self-identity? If so, how might such a transformation take place? What might we take to be its existential character and consequences? What might it mean in practice for a person to experience *metanoia as an inward alteration—not simply of opinion or belief, but of disposition and consciousness*? And to what extent might a movement toward *metanoia* reflect a recovery, a process of recursive assimilation, rather than a drastic revision of one's primal identity?

I believe such questions could be profitably addressed by considering all sorts of novelistic fiction, penned by authors of many different faith persuasions or none. But my focus here is on just two relevant works, by authors who happen to share a fundamental grounding in Christian faith while differing considerably in their personality, literary approach, and historical context. One of these texts, Harriet Beecher Stowe's *Uncle Tom's Cabin*, is a well-known, enormously influential nineteenth-century novel—still controversial in our own day, as it had been from the first, but now more often invoked or disparaged than actually read on its own terms. The other work I want to consider is Wendell Berry's novella, *Remembering* (1988)—less familiar as a discrete title than Stowe's novel, though the work of a well-known contemporary author whose work encompasses several literary genres. Despite their evident differences, there is more common ground between these works than the Christian faith perspective that informs them. For the literary merit of both has been questioned—not always justly, in my view—insofar as the storytelling of each advances an extraliterary agenda as well: abolitionism, in the case of Stowe's fiction, and an anti-corporatized agrarianism, in the case of Berry's.

It helps to establish clearly from the outset that the linguistic root of our keyword, *metanoia*, signifies an inward *change*—by virtue of its "meta" Greek prefix—and, more pointedly still, a change of mind or heart.[1] As such, it is closely allied in biblical usage to "conversion" (i.e., "to turn," Greek *epistrepho*) though not synonymous with all constructions of that term. Critic Jay Parini argues, for example, that the common tendency to equate metanoia with remorse for wrongdoing and even with penitence amounts to a mistranslation, attributable to St. Jerome's rendering in the Latin Vulgate. Yet Parini acknowledges that *metanoia* calls indeed for a "letting go," a sacrificial "giving up an aspect of your former self" so as to turn "in a fresh direction."[2]

In any case, whether in scriptural usage or otherwise, repentance for sin cannot be viewed as the totality of *metanoia*'s import. Neither has *metanoia*'s sense of an inward turning and reflection always been construed, for ancient Greeks or for present-day humanitarians, in explicitly religious terms. Thus, the University of Connecticut, a public secular institution where I previously taught, has for years designated a campus-wide "Day of Metanoia" to encourage members of its learning community to reflect on topics such as race relations or earth-friendly ways of being.

Yet for souls attuned to transtemporal verities, including Stowe and Berry, the inward transformation realized in a person's *metanoia* or conversion experience may and often must be understood in broader faith perspective— as a metamorphosis involving not only a change of mind and heart but also a

---

[1] In New Testament usage, *metanoia* and its variant forms appears throughout the Synoptic Gospels, as well as in the Acts of the Apostles, but never as such in St. John's Gospel. It appears often but not always. in connection with "repentance," as involving an admission of prior wrongdoing. For entries describing how it figures in diverse biblical contexts, see *The Collegeville Pastoral Dictionary of Biblical Theology*, 830–5; *Harper's Bible Dictionary*, 861–3; and *The Oxford Companion to the Bible*, 646–7.

[2] Parini, *Living a Spiritual and Ethical Life*, 43–4.

renewed personal relation to the social order, the natural order, and the divine Source of it all. So contrary to popular usage, the change at issue here is more decisive than that commonly applied to a person's shift of allegiance from one denomination of Christian belief and practice to another. Stowe, for example, never regarded her own shift away from the Calvinist Congregationalism in which she was born and raised, toward her affiliation in later adulthood with the Episcopal Church, as a "conversion."[3]

The testimony that Stowe sets forth in *Uncle Tom's Cabin* is, nonetheless and unmistakably, all about "conversion." Written under the force of what Stowe took to be a kind of divine inspiration, this is a book that Frederick Douglass and other African Americans in conference agreed had been "plainly marked by the finger of God."[4] According to Stowe, she received this godly inspiration when she was seized by the inward vision of a beaten-down dying slave—the prototype of her Uncle Tom character—as she sat at the communion table of a parish church in Brunswick, Maine, where she was living at the time.

Literary criticism never quite knows what to make of a book that purports to embody prophetic utterance. But I think it's clear that *Uncle Tom's Cabin*, with all its narrative defects, digressions, and sentimental or authorial intrusions, simply cannot be judged by the formalistic standards of the well-wrought novel. I would therefore concur with critics such as Edmund Wilson, Ann Douglass, and Jane P. Tompkins, who concluded years ago that *Uncle Tom's Cabin* may not qualify as a great or even a good novel, judged by the usual belletristic criteria for fiction, but is nonetheless a great book.[5] It qualifies, in other words, as a masterwork of homiletic rhetoric by virtue of the artfulness with which Stowe aims to capture the hearts and minds of her readers.

It does this by combining the language of feeling, prevalent in the sentimental, domestic fiction of Stowe's day, with the apocalyptic urgency of evangelical preaching Stowe had absorbed from her father and brothers. The legacy of her father's evangelical passion animates much of this book. And among the whole brood of the Reverend Lyman Beecher's ministerial offspring, Harriet was arguably the most compelling preacher of them all.

---

[3] See my essay, "The Anglican Aspect of Harriet Beecher Stowe," 412–33. There I discuss the reasons for Stowe's shift in denominational allegiance, its implications, and evidence for her having officially joined the Episcopal Church.

[4] See Yarborough, "Strategies of Black Characterization," 68.

[5] See, e.g., Douglass, *The Feminization of American Culture*, 245. And in *Sentimental Designs*, Jane P. Tompkins argued cogently from a feminist standpoint that the communal, domestic rhetoric of nineteenth-century sentimental fiction by women authors such as Stowe warrants more admiration than traditionally accorded it, by virtue of its power to move reader and its appeal to higher calling.

112   *Literature and Religious Experience*

The argument that follows takes account of several forms and trajectories of *metanoia* that Stowe portrays, across diverse orders of her characterization in *Uncle Tom's Cabin*. Yet her ambition was larger still: not only to describe *metanoia* but also to stir readers toward experiencing and acting upon it for themselves. In that regard it is worth recalling that even in secular terms, many serious literary works addressed to audiences beyond the authorial self intend not only to entertain or to instruct but also to inspire some *change*—at least momentary and partial—in their readers. Edgar Allan Poe argued, for example, that short lyrical poems could conjure a strong impression, elevating souls briefly toward the contemplation of Beauty. Yet for a devoutly disposed writer like Stowe, literary imagination promised to stir yet more enduring, momentous changes in readers encountering her testimony. And the swiftly precipitated, unanticipated *metanoia* she had herself experienced first at age thirteen would help to inspire this ambition.

As is widely known, the stimulus for Stowe to begin composing this book in 1851 had a good deal to do with the feelings of moral indignation aroused in her by passage of the 1850 Fugitive Slave Law, which now forced northerners to confront the specter of slavery on their own ground. Evidently, too, the outrage Stowe felt over the forced division of families, including children and spouses, as slave members were legally sold away from one another, was fueled by her own trials as a grieving mother—that is, by the profound personal crisis she faced around the same time, when her beloved infant son Charlie died of cholera. No wonder Stowe says she wrote this book with her "heart's blood."[6] That searing experience of losing her child took place during a cholera epidemic in Cincinnati. And in this city, convulsed by race riots, just over the Ohio River from Kentucky, she had actually met fugitive slaves and ex-slaves. She had encountered fierce debates at her father's seminary in Cincinnati between gradualists like her father, who favored a policy movement toward eventual emancipation, and outright abolitionists, who argued what came to be her own view: that Christian belief demanded immediate and unconditional emancipation.

The case for immediate emancipation that Stowe presses in *Uncle Tom's Cabin* is addressed primarily, though by no means exclusively, to a readership of white, northern, middle-class or ruling-class mothers. Stowe believed that this audience, which included the prime movers and keepers of the nation's conscience, would

---

[6] Cited in Stowe, *Uncle Tom's Cabin*, 458. Excellent biographical treatment of matters germane to Stowe's composition of the book can be found in Hedrick, *A Life*; Koester, *A Spiritual Life*; and (with extensive textual commentary) Reynolds, *Mightier than the Sword*.

Metanoia 113

be particularly receptive to her argument that America's peculiar institution of bondage degraded both white and black, across both north and south.

The novel's often graphic pictures of flogging, murder, trauma-induced suicide, infanticide, and sexual assault of African Americans all contribute to this indictment. Stowe recognized that her readers might be most deeply moved by witnessing the system's destruction of families, or family coherence. In our own day, scenes exposed through mainstream or social media of forced, government-sanctioned family separations near America's southern border dramatize for us the potency of such images. Stowe saw the nation's union—if not its very soul—imperiled indeed by a practice that could legally put asunder wives from husbands and slave children from their mothers. An emotionally charged episode early in the story shows the slave character Eliza Harris, child in arms, desperately fleeing across ice floes in the Ohio River to save her son Harry from bondage and separation.

Drawing on her evangelical heritage, Stowe meant above all to convince readers that slavery was sin—and, thus, absolutely intolerable. Understood as sin rather than as social ill, crime, or political aggravation, slavery could never be reformed, as some were suggesting. It had to be expunged, totally and immediately. For Stowe, the original sin of American slavery not only divided slave families but also separated free citizens and slaveholders from their God, a God whose wrath and justice would soon bring cataclysm unless the nation repented speedily. Thus, Stowe's novel combines a heartfelt sermon to the congregation of all America with a stirring epic tale of flight toward freedom. Portraying such personal struggles to break free was, Stowe realized, a likely means of stirring sympathy—leading, in turn, toward *metanoia*—in her readers.

For this author, two different but affiliated orders of personal conversion were needed to avoid national peril: first, a massive moral-political conversion of citizens to the cause of emancipation; but also, coextensive with that imperative, the religious regeneration of hearts and souls in accord with the gospel teachings of Christianity. And Stowe promotes this two-pronged call for mass *metanoia* by incorporating three distinct classes of fictive characters into her narrative.

Representing a first class of souls in the novel's drama of salvation, figures such as the title character Tom and a character aptly named Evangeline (or Eva) qualify as model "saints" and catalysts for change. They are regenerate worthies in both senses—as antislavery exponents *and* as committed Christians—even though they would seem to be "once-born" types, in terms of William James's psychologized anatomy,[7] because they are never shown themselves to undergo

---

[7] James, *Varieties of Religion Experience*, 140.

an experience of drastic metamorphosis. Tom, Stowe's black hero who embodies a peculiarly feminized and maternal Christ, also fosters new birth in others, as does the white child saint Eva through an early death recounted with every adornment of nineteenth-century sentiment.

Modeled in part on an actual slave fugitive named Josiah Henson, Tom betrays only a few minor traits that accord with his disrepute in today's common parlance as an overcompliant African American. One must, of course, grant that Stowe writes from the perspective of a nineteenth-century white woman, viewing African Americans through the mostly favorable yet sometimes patronizing and stereotypical lens of what has been called "romantic racialism," as distinguishable from racism.[8] Nonetheless, her Uncle Tom is scarcely the Uncle Tom of today's popular disdain. Without elaborating on this much-discussed characterization for the purpose at hand, I would simply recall that Stowe's Tom, far from groveling to his masters, flatly refuses to cooperate at crisis moments, by virtue of his defiant and self-sacrificing love, when ordered under pain of death to do so. Readers or would-be readers of Stowe's book sometimes forget that Tom stands up to the slaveholding tyrant Simon Legree so firmly that he reduces Legree to blubbering desperation. Tom demonstrates that he *will die*—and does die, from a brutal beating—rather than betray two fugitive slaves named Cassy and Emmeline, and that defiance on his part is essential to their successful escape from Legree.

In stark contrast to saints such as Tom and Eva, the story's second but lowest class, that of confirmed reprobates, includes several slave traders together with the infamous Simon Legree. And it is pointedly ironic, with respect to Stowe's depiction of North/South tensions in this period, that Legree—by all odds the supreme villain of the tale, should actually be a Yankee, born and bred in New England, who had been transplanted to Louisiana.

Stowe's third class of characters, a group most germane to our consideration of *metanoia*, occupies a middle station between the other two classes and shows dynamic potential. These characters are neither saints nor hardened sinners. Stowe's white New Orleans planter, Augustine St. Clare; her black fugitive, George Harris; and her Kentucky state senator, John Bird, are all prime examples

---

[8] See George M. Frederickson, "Uncle Tom and the Anglo-Saxon Romantic Racialism in the North," rpt. in *Uncle Tom's Cabin*, 478–87. Admittedly, though, Stowe's racial attitudes are most open to critique with respect to her having supported, at least for a time and toward the close of *Uncle Tom's Cabin*, the highly controversial colonization movement that encouraged the emigration of freed blacks to Africa.

of what Pauline Calvinism would term "natural man." Stowe portrays them as sympathetic characters—not yet saints through much or most of the story but blessedly ripe for conversion.

From the start, George Harris plainly requires no radicalizing *metanoia* to recognize his need for liberation from bondage, or the rank injustice of slavery. Through much of the narrative, though, he remains skeptical about the justice, saving goodness—even the existence—of a God who has allowed brutal white masters to degrade his humanity, deny his talents, and separate him from his wife and child. "Is there a God to trust in?" he asks scornfully of an elderly white man who tries to console him. For "I've seen things all my life that have made me feel that there can't be a God. You Christians don't know how these things look to us. There's a God for you, but is there any for us?"[9]

Yet given the indignities Harris is forced to endure, Stowe attributes no blame to him for his religious skepticism, no sense that it requires moral repentance on his part. *Metanoia* in this case involves nothing of penitence. For only when Harris for the first time encounters communion with a Christian fellowship of acceptance, faith, and love, in the setting of Rachel Halliday's Society of Friends, can he finally experience the change of mind and heart recognizable as *metanoia* faith. Above all, Halliday's motherly solicitude for Harris, as she breaks bread over a shared meal with other loved ones, inspires this transformation. For Stowe, a leading manifestation and medium of God's salvation on earth was the redemptive, sacred force of maternal love. From the standpoint of her own gospel-grounded, domestic feminism, that theological principle suffuses *Uncle Tom's Cabin* as well as several of the novels she subsequently wrote. Increasingly she was drawn toward a Christianity displaying the motherly compassion of God in Jesus—and in Mary, the blessed Mother of God.[10]

Unlike Harris, Augustine St. Clare faces a tortuous, uncertain path toward that twofold *metanoia* of faith and moral principle he never quite attains within his lifetime, apart from a deathbed epiphany that comes too late to free those for whom he had vaguely meant to provide legal relief. St. Clare is a most reluctant Southern slaveholder, one who grants the cause of emancipation to be both just and inevitable. With his head, if not with heart and will, he qualifies as a convicted abolitionist. Thus tormented by internal tensions, self-loathing, and

---

[9] Stowe, *Uncle Tom's Cabin*, 114. Subsequent page citations are to this edition, indicated parenthetically in the text.
[10] I comment further on these themes in *American Madonna*, 53–71.

116   *Literature and Religious Experience*

near-despair, he denounces the "cursed" system of slavery as "the essence of all abuse," an original sin "from the devil" in which he knows he stands complicit (213–14).

Yet he lacks the will to change. Much as his famed ancient namesake, the bishop of Hippo, had once resolved in theory to turn away from habits of carnal self-indulgence so as to embrace Christian faith, but found himself delaying to do so in practice,[11] so also St. Clare had thought about preparing a proper will to protect his slaves "one of these days" (293). A fatal accident intervenes to thwart that intention.

Indeed, Stowe's naming of this character abounds in irony. Of course, St. Clare is no "saint." Moreover, he fails to embody that change of life that the historic St. Augustine had so memorably described in his *Confessions*. Neither, during most of his days, does St. Clare gain clear apprehension of what a change of heart requires of him, with regard either to advancing the cause of emancipation or professing faith in God's saving goodness. Stowe even suggests impishly that Tom the slave, rather than St. Clare the master, might better call to mind an ancient bishop of North Africa since Tom with "his grave, good-natured black face looked respectable enough to be a Bishop of Carthage, as men of his color were in other ages" (173).

Miss Ophelia, St. Clare's cousin from Vermont, marvels at these contradictions. She wonders how, after all, a person can know a given course of action to be sinful, acknowledge the need to repent of it, and yet fail to do so. St. Clare tells her he is "repenting" of his sin "all the time." But when she presses him, 'What do you keep on doing it for?" he queries her in turn: "Didn't you ever keep on doing wrong, after you'd repented, my good cousin?" (212).

Despite St. Clare's deficiencies, I believe his response on this particular point happens to ring true. From an Aristotelian standpoint, wherein someone's deep knowledge of the good establishes that person's likelihood to practice virtue, Ophelia's puzzlement makes sense. Yet from the contrary standpoint of St. Paul's existential realism, the human psyche apart from grace remains a tangle of self-contradictions, such that "the good that I would I do not; but the evil which I would not, that I do" (Rom. 7:19, KJV). Stowe shared St. Paul's recognition that conversion is never completed within this mortal life, such that even the new birth of *metanoia* never quite obliterates that lesser self of the old Adam.

---

[11] Augustine's oft-cited remark on the matter was "Give me chastity and continence, but not yet!" in *The Confessions of St. Augustine*, 194.

Conversion is apt to be elusive, psychically enigmatic, rather than always clearly situated in time.[12]

The novel's portrayal of St. Clare's death brings to light something else about Stowe's view of the *metanoia* experience in Christian context. When St. Clare at last glimpses a passage toward new birth on the occasion of his death, he experiences, paradoxically, not a thorough and novel makeover of his previous identity, so much as a return to communion with the best angels of his primal self, a recovery of his original standing as a child of God. True, the scene in question includes sentimental features—Tom's tearful leave-taking, or St. Clare's last calling out to "Mother"—at variance with contemporary literary tastes. The depiction of this character's *metanoia* moment nonetheless captures something genuine, resembling Buddhist enlightenment or *satori* more than penitential remorse, when he finally opens "his eyes with a sudden light, as of joy and recognition." Stowe allows a penetrating note of earnestness to color the way her unregenerate Augustine, having been sorely conflicted and self-estranged for years, ends up countering at the point of death a doctor's judgment that "His mind is wandering." "No!" he insists, "It is coming HOME, at last! (300–1). For once, albeit only for an instant, Clare knows who he is and where he belongs.

In several other episodes, too, Stowe illustrates how *metanoia* can effectively enlarge a person's imaginative, broadly integrative vision of reality. As a fiction writer, Stowe of course appreciated the moral reach of imagination, a human faculty divinely inspired—as per Samuel Taylor Coleridge's famed summation— to foster awareness of the vast web of interconnections encompassing all things, visible and invisible. The biblical sense of *metanoia* as conferring a heightened consciousness, a freshly expansive way of seeing reality, thus coincides with later accounts of a creative human faculty—namely, the Imagination—that far surpasses mere Fancy or make-believe.

Such linkage is dramatized, for example, by the scene early in Stowe's novel where Senator John Bird of Ohio is chastised by his wife Mary for having voted in his state legislature to prohibit the sheltering of runaway selves. Once the senator encounters flesh-and-blood fugitives at his door, however, in the person of Eliza Harris and her son, he realizes—with convicting encouragement from his wife— that his previous knowledge of such matters lacked imaginative engagement with reality. He had suffered from a fallacy of disembodied abstraction. "His idea of a

---

[12] Stowe's realization that conversion could be an obscure, enigmatically incremental process was subsequently deepened by the faith-crisis from which she emerged after Henry, her oldest son, drowned in 1857 without ever having testified publicly to an experience of personal conversion.

118   *Literature and Religious Experience*

fugitive," writes Stowe pungently, had only been "an idea of the letters that spell
the word,—or, at the most, the image of a little newspaper picture of a man with
a stick and bundle, with 'Ran away from the subscriber' under it'" (90).

What Senator Bird learns here is not that he should abandon all reason in
favor of free-floating emotion, for I think Stowe is too often misconstrued as a
naïve exponent of womanly sentimentality. The episode confirms instead John
Bird's need to combine reason and feeling, knowledge and compassion. His new
decision to speed the escape of Eliza and young Harry is scarcely irrational, then,
but founded on deeper thought. By applying a fairly rigorous logic of consistency
and biblical teaching, Mary Bird stirs her husband toward a change of mind
and heart that calls him back to his better self. Only in the light of discerning
imagination can the "letters that spell the word" point toward an authentically
signifying grammar, one that honors the humanity of actual living fugitives.

Just as Mary Bird had confronted her husband with a forceful imperative of
tough love, Stowe calls out her readers—yet still more severely—in her book's
closing bid for collective *metanoia*. In a chapter bearing the understated title
of "Concluding Remarks," she sets forth in her own hortatory voice a jeremiad
warning of wrath to come unless her readers seize the "day of grace" still open to
them, denounce the "accursed traffic" of slavery, and thereby hasten the millenni
alistic renewal of God's kingdom on earth. Only thus, she insists, is "this Union"
of states "to be saved."

That vision of salvation, a word of course laden with religious resonance as
the contrary of sin's dis-union, displaces for Stowe not only the future prospect
of Southern secession but also some Northern calls for separatist dis-union with
slaveholders voiced by radical abolitionists such as William Lloyd Garrison.
And in the light of the Civil War carnage that followed, the extremity of Stowe's
foreboding seems warranted. For by 1852, when the novel first appeared, she
deemed the nation headed swiftly toward cataclysm, a horrific consequence
of the original sin of slaveholding that rendered America vulnerable to divine
judgment. A destructive upheaval lay ahead—unless the citizenry Stowe
addressed moved with alacrity to welcome God's new birth in their souls. So in
her concluding, overtly homiletic chapter Stowe voiced a hope that such turn
and rescue might still take place. Ever the evangelist, Stowe ends up intoning,
before her congregation of all America, God's promise of salvation *if* those she
addresses awaken to their peril and respond now in faith:

A day of grace is yet held out to us. Both North and South have been guilty
before God; and the *Christian church* has a heavy account to answer. Not by

Metanoia 119

combining together, to protect injustice and cruelty, and making a common capital of sin, is this Union to be saved—but by repentance, justice and mercy; for, not surer is the eternal law by which the millstone sinks in the ocean, than that stronger law, by which injustice and cruelty shall bring on nations the wrath of Almighty God! (418)

Berry concludes his novella *Remembering* with a comparable surge of emotional appeal. Yet he otherwise portrays and evokes *metanoia* not through a profusion of characters spread across an episodic, sprawling narrative like that presented in *Uncle Tom's Cabin*, but as centered in the midlife struggle of its protagonist, Andy Catlett. Neither does Berry, in tracing Andy's progress from hellish despair and self-isolation toward saving communion with a larger yet localized community of life, invoke biblical language so overtly as Stowe had done.[13] Plainly, though, the conversion narrative set forth in *Remembering* retains an underlying Christian pattern and character, as evidenced above all through an all-suffusing tissue of allusions to Dante's *Divine Comedy* and Milton's *Paradise Lost*. Andy Catlett ends up traversing a long, convoluted passage toward conversion, a process that amounts to "a long choosing" in which he not only decides one thing or another repeatedly, but is also "chosen and chosen again."[14] In Dantesque terms, this journey takes him from an inferno of loss and desolation, through a sustained *purgatorio* of chastening search and discovery in diverse settings, to a paradisiacal self-restoration back on his home ground.

What I take to be *the* defining moment within this pilgrimage takes place after Andy reaches the Pacific Ocean, the continent's edge and the endpoint of his inchoate flight toward oblivion, at which point Berry's narrative voice reminds us how his geophysical pivot in California captures the figurative essence of conversion: "Though he has not moved, he has turned" (50). Having once *turned* in body and soul, in other words, he has already prepared to head east and *move* toward glimpsing a fuller vision of metanoia.

Andy Catlett is a Kentucky farmer and sometime agricultural journalist who has literally been dis-membered after losing his right arm to a corn thresher. The psychic and spiritual dislocation he suffers from this accident leaves him mired in self-pity, estranged from his wife and children, existentially lost. From the first, we learn that "he does not know where he is" (3). His unsettled state

---

[13] Though less conspicuously than Stowe, especially with respect to Andy Catlett's recorded perceptions, Berry does ground his overall narrative in biblical allusions and imagery, as Phillip J. Donnelly has ably recognized in "Biblical Convocation in Wendell Berry's *Remembering*," 275–96.

[14] Berry, *Remembering*, 50. Subsequent page citations are to this edition, indicated parenthetically in the text.

of mind and soul is underscored by Berry's narrative technique, which includes dream sequences, stream of consciousness recollections, multiple flashbacks, and nonlinear storytelling.

Andy's dislocated, dismembered state of mind is likewise mirrored in the geographic span of his wanderings. Before his final, restorative return to his farm home in Port William, Kentucky, he had been attending a dispiriting conference on food production systems and agricultural technology at a large university in the Midwest. From there he had found his way to San Francisco. And during the decade prior to his last, presumably permanent return to Kentucky, he had searched and traveled still more widely—living for three years in San Francisco, in addition to spending time in Ohio, Pennsylvania, and Chicago.

The inward course of Andy's *metanoia* thus follows roughly the trajectory of his outward, spatial wandering—which sees him repeatedly visiting or dwelling in distant sites but finally draws back to his home place in Kentucky. Like the Christian theological concept of a *felix culpa* or fortunate fall, however, this return involves not merely a resumption of the *status quo ante* but a more advanced stage of enlightenment. The novella's closing portrayal of Andy's *metanoia* vision thus reflects a paradoxical, recursive apprehension of deep knowing comparable to that which T. S. Eliot had voiced in the "Little Gidding" section of his *Four Quartets*: that "the end of all our exploring / Will be to arrive where we started / And know the place for the first time."[15]

But what finally enables Andy to turn and move beyond his hellish abyss of despair? Several influences apparently contribute to that progress—including some peculiar, unpredictable, and (as always) undeserved motions of grace that touch this character during his last stay in San Francisco. Despite Berry's usual identification with rural agrarianism, it is surprisingly in this urban setting, which likewise played a role in the author's own life story, that Andy eventually "reminds himself of himself," thus beginning to acknowledge his true identity within a "membership that chose him, yet left him free until he should choose it, which he did once, and now has done again" (38, 50).

Especially in the course of Andy's solitary musings in the city, memories well up in him that confirm his continued membership in Port William's extended community of life, a body encompassing both living and dead relations, as well as nonhumans within the larger community of creation. He calls to mind, for example, a luminous yet commonplace day of bathing in a local creek that Mat Feltner, his maternal grandfather, had once spent with one of Mat's relatives many

---

[15] Eliot, *Complete Poems and Plays*, 145.

years ago, before Andy was born. Andy could only "remember" this moment of idyllic respite from hard labor by drawing on the memory of his grandfather, who had told him about that which, in Wordsworthian language, amounts to a nodal "spot of time." Yet Andy comes to share the sentiment Mat had voiced about this moment, to the extent of subsequently remembering and making it his own: ' "I thought of all the times I'd worked in that field, hurrying to get through, to get to a better place, and it had been there all the time' " (48–9). Berry suggests that for Andy to remember such things amounts to more than indulging in idle nostalgia. Instead, it contributes substantially to a re-membering of his broken soul. Such memory corresponds, in fact, to that ritualized making-present-of-the-past known as *amannesis*, which Christians commonly associate with eucharistic celebrations and Jews with the Passover Seder.

Two other episodes recalled from Andy's stay in California's Bay Area can be identified as particularly relevant to catalyzing his spiritual turn of heart from despair toward personal salvation. One is his glimpse of a sea lion, as he gazes out into the waters of San Francisco Bay. He is strangely moved by the momentary sight of this animal who "looks around with the intelligent gaze of a man" and who, unlike him, is so evidently at home in that place of beauty it inhabits (42).

The other telling episode takes place at Washington Square in early morning, near the bench where a homeless person lies sleeping in this city of Saint Francis. Andy looks up at Saints Peter and Paul Church and reads there a famous line from Dante's *Paradiso* engraved on its face: "LA GLORIA DI COLUI CHE TUTTO MUOVE PER L'UNIVERSO PENETRA E RISPLENDE" (39). At this point, as he recalls an earlier visit to the Bay Area, that motto he had encountered by chance from Dante—another exile from home, from another time and place— begins to resonate more deeply with him. It stirs him to envision his home place not as a uniquely isolated enclave but as another face of that all-encompassing "glory" that is also discernible on the Pacific Coast: "But the whole bay is shining now, the islands, the city on its hills, the wooden houses and the towers, the green treetops, the flashing waves and wings, the glory that moves all things resplendent everywhere" (49).

The blessed release from anger and despair that Andy experiences as he finally reenters Port William at the novella's close derives from the expansive view of "membership" he has by that time acquired.[16] The spirit of Dante still

---

[16] A favorite term for Berry in both prose and poetic discourse, "membership" has rich spiritual, social, and ecological connotations throughout his corpus. These are linked in turn to St. Paul's vision of broad creaturely participation in the body of Christ. The theme is effectively elaborated in Bilbro, *Loving God's Wildness*, 146.

122 *Literature and Religious Experience*

accompanies him, too, in the form of a ghostly guide, "a man, dark as shadow" who walks ahead of him to lend instruction since, like himself, "the place, though it is familiar to him, is changed." Though Andy remains "dark to himself," still missing an arm, he finds himself made "whole" (100, 101). And the place he encounters now, through a kind of visionary dispensation, reveals itself to him as freshly permeable, through time as well as space. He sees its membership, like the "communion of saints" affirmed in the Apostles' Creed, fully embracing the dead along with the living:

> The dark man points ahead of them; Andy looks and sees the town and the fields around it, Port William and its countryside as he never saw or dreamed them, the signs everywhere upon them of the care of a longer love than any who have lived there have ever imagined …. Over town and fields the one great song sings, and is answered everywhere; every leaf and flower and grass blade sings. And in the fields and the town, walking, standing, or sitting under the trees, resting and talking together in the peace of a Sabbath profound and bright, are people of such beauty that he weeps to see them. He sees that these are the membership of one another and of the place and of the song or light in which they live and move.
>
> He sees that they are the dead, and they are alive. He sees that he lives in eternity as he lives in time, and nothing is lost. (102)

This rhapsodic, uplifting finale to Berry's fiction contrasts markedly with the grim warning of possible catastrophe with which Stowe had concluded *Uncle Tom's Cabin*. Overall, however, the two authors shared a good deal with respect to their fictive portrayal of *metanoia* experiences. Both were apt to conceive of such experiences as recursive, recurrent, multilayered, elusive, and psychically enigmatic rather than necessarily fixed in time. Thus, Berry endeavors in his novella to dramatize the recursive dimension of *metanoia* through his detailed enactment of memory processes, together with his limning of Andy's blessed return to Kentucky. Stowe's narrative becomes recursive insofar as her closing exhortation for readers to embrace a new birth of freedom, a collective turn toward *metanoia*, rests upon calling the nation back to honoring its original, putative faith in democratic ideals and Christian charity.[17]

The two fictions likewise converge, finally, insofar as they understand anyone's personal apprehension of *metanoia* to depend crucially upon the example and

---

[17] For a searching analysis of the ways in which Stowe's rhetoric throughout the novel invokes ideals from the Declaration of Independence and other foundational documents of the Republic, see Harold Bush, Jr., "The Declaration of Independence and *Uncle Tom's Cabin: A Rhetorical Approach*," 172–83.

intervention of others. Both acknowledge that *metanoia* changes necessarily take place within, and largely through, the agency of, God's "communion of saints." Whereas some versions of enlightenment might focus on an individual's solitary trial to complete a form of spirit-quest, neither *Uncle Tom's Cabin* nor *Remembering* embody such a story. Instead, a whole cloud of witnesses, living and dead, support Andy Catlett's eventual turn toward salvation, as Stowe likewise shows to be the case for George Harris, John Bird, and Augustine St. Clare.

Bibliography

Achtemeier, Paul J., ed. *Harper's Bible Dictionary*. San Francisco: Harper & Row, 1985.

Augustine. *The Confessions of St. Augustine*. Translated by John K. Ryan. New York: Doubleday-Image, 1960.

Berry, Wendell. *Remembering*. Berkeley, CA: Counterpoint, 2008.

Bilbro, Jeffrey. *Loving God's Wildness: The Christian Roots of Ecological Ethics in American Literature*. Tuscaloosa: University of Alabama Press, 2015.

Bush, Harold K., Jr. "The Declaration of Independence and *Uncle Tom's Cabin*: A Rhetorical Approach." In *Approaches to Teaching Stowe's Uncle Tom's Cabin*, edited by Elizabeth Ammons and Susan Belasco, 172–83. New York: Modern Language Association, 2000.

Donnelly, Phillip, J. "Biblical Convocation in Wendell Berry's *Remembering*." *Christianity and Literature* 56 (2007): 275–96.

Douglass, Ann. *The Feminization of American Culture*. London: Papaermac, 1996.

Eliot, T. S. *The Complete Poems and Plays*. New York: Harcourt, Brace & World, 1962.

Gatta, John. *American Madonna: Images of the Divine Woman in Literary Culture*. New York: Oxford University Press, 1997.

Gatta, John. "The Anglican Aspect of Harriet Beecher Stowe." *New England Quarterly* 73 (September 2000): 412–33.

Hedrick, Joan D. *Harriet Beecher Stowe: A Life*. New York: Oxford University Press, 1994.

James, William. *The Varieties of Religion Experience*. New York: New American Library, 1958.

Koester, Nancy. *Harriet Beecher Stowe: A Spiritual Life*. Grand Rapids, MI: William B. Eerdmans, 2014.

Metzger, Bruce M., and Michael D. Coogan, eds. *The Oxford Companion to the Bible*. New York: Oxford University Press, 1993.

Parini, Jay. *Living a Spiritual and Ethical Life*. Boston: Beacon Press, 2018.

Reynolds, David S. *Mightier than the Sword: Uncle Tom's Cabin and the Battle for America*. New York: Norton, 2011.

Stowe, Harriet Beecher. *Uncle Tom's Cabin: Authoritative Text, Backgrounds and Contexts, Criticism.* Edited by Elizabeth Ammons. New York: Norton, 2018.

Stuhlmueller, Carroll, ed. *The Collegeville Pastoral Dictionary of Biblical Theology.* Collegeville, MN: Order of St. Benedict, 1996.

Tompkins, Jane P. *Sentimental Designs: The Cultural Work of American Fiction, 1790–1850.* New York: Oxford University Press, 1985.

Yarborough, Richard. "Strategies of Black Characterization in *Uncle Tom's Cabin* and the Early Afro-American Novel." In *New Essays on Uncle Tom's Cabin*, edited by Eric J. Sundquist, 45–84. Cambridge: Cambridge University Press, 1986.

7

Belief: Marilynne Robinson's *Gilead* and James Wood's *The Book Against God*

Lori Branch

1.

On April 10, 2018, James Wood interviewed Marilynne Robinson at Harvard's Radcliffe Institute. The conversation was somewhat misleadingly titled "The Writer and the Critic," since Wood, Harvard's sole "professor of the practice of literary criticism," also has two novels to his credit.[1] More apt would have been "The Believer and the Skeptic," since Wood's questions orbit Robinson's faith, probing her belief in the resurrection, heaven, and an afterlife compensating for this one. He claims to be like Robinson "obsessed with resurrection," only "the problem is I *can't* believe it," and her novels, he suggests, are more on the side of doubt than are her essays. Robinson in turn subtly reframes each question. She believes in heaven, but Calvin taught her that the little revealed of it in Scripture indicates God would have us focus on life in this world; doubt is the friend, not the foe, of faith that, she says, is dialectical; resurrection isn't dogma for her so much as the only intuition that measures up to the unaccountable reality of life and consciousness. When a student asks whether religion is a necessary foundation for her social ethics, Robinson responds that an intuition of the sanctity of a human being "such that you want to give them dignity and the possibility of living out their lives by their lights" is a fundamentally religious impulse, however non-confessional, and Wood quickly interjects, "But there is no *reason* why it *needs* to be grounded *necessarily* in a notion of the divine"— to which Robinson retorts, "I think that you proceed from a different set of

---

[1] The interview was the Julia S. Phelps Annual Lecture in the Arts and Humanities and is accessible at https://www.radcliffe.harvard.edu/video/writer-and-critic-marilynne-robinson-and-james-wood-in-conversation.

126   *Literature and Religious Experience*

assumptions than I do. I think that if you see the sacred in anything, that *is* an intuition of the divine. It doesn't matter if it's quantum physics or your next-door neighbor."

Wood's questioning implies Robinson is naïve about her belief, unaware of deeper truths her fiction reveals, and that reason surely leads one to unbelief. In turn Robinson identifies, not without pique, the place their assumptions differ most markedly, around what constitutes reason, belief, and knowledge. In the charged coherence of these novelists' exchange we see the inextricability of modern belief and doubt: their pull, despite defensiveness and even hostility, toward relation with the other in the shared space of uncertainty, a deep literariness by which they seem inseparable from the narration of their repeated encounters. This, Wood's and Robinson's novels make even more plain.

2.

The child of evangelical Anglicans, Wood has been outspoken for three decades about his loss of faith. In his twenties, "Kierkegaard's masochism" finished off the apostacy begun in his teens and "finally rid me of belief." With or without God, life "seems a pointlessness posing as a purpose," and the advantage of living without God is that "the false purpose has at least been invented by man, and one can strip it away to reveal the *actual* pointlessness."[2] Wood's claim across *The Broken Estate* is that the great crisis of the nineteenth-century novel is this felt meaninglessness. "It was not just the ascent of science," explains Wood, but "the ascent of the novel that helped to kill off Jesus's divinity, when the novel gave us a new sense of the real, ... of how the real disposes itself in a narrative—and then in turn a new skepticism toward the real as we encounter it in narrative."[3] Good fiction "requests of us a doubleness," pulling us into believing that our own realities bear some relation with the "simultaneously not quite real and very real" ones in drama or fiction.[4] But this suspension of disbelief is only limited and metaphorical, rendering literature secular and secularizing:

> Fiction requests belief from us, but we can choose not to believe at any moment. This is surely the true secularism of fiction—why, despite being a magic, it is actually the enemy of superstition, the slayer of religions, the scrutineer of

[2] Wood, "The Broken Estate," 261.
[3] Wood, "Introduction," xxii.
[4] Wood, "Introduction," xviii.

falsity. Fiction moves in the shadow of doubt, knows itself to be a true lie, knows that at any moment it might fail to make its case. Belief in fiction is always belief "as if." Our belief is itself metaphorical—it only *resembles* actual belief, and is therefore never wholly belief.[5]

For Wood, the novel's "as-if" believing, never total and always in the shadow of doubt, cannot efface its truth, its fundamental access to reality. The novel is secularizing for Wood because it makes the reader judge of the text's truth, rather than acquiescent to its demands: "Fiction asks us to judge its reality; religion asserts its reality."[6]

Wood's version of religion, then, is the specifically modern kind that, particularly after the Reformation, reimagined itself in terms of modern epistemologies, a "faith" cashed out as certainty, demanding on reason's authority that we accept its truth. Certainly this is one version of belief, dominant by the nineteenth century and pervasive in fundamentalism. It is an error, though, to mistake this knowledge-like, assent-demanding version of belief for Christian faith throughout history. The ethos of *fides quaerens intellectum*—faith seeking understanding—reaches back a millennium to Anselm of Canterbury and, before him, to Augustine and the Cappadocian fathers, and as René Girard puts it, "the multiplicity of the Gospels" is itself "a call to interpretation."[7] Wood's faith-versus-fiction dilemma is a very nineteenth-century sort of crisis, one that lingers for anyone raised in that variety of "belief," to be sure. The *sine qua non* of Wood's unbelief is the sort of belief it is allergic to, which, Robinson insists, is not hers.

There are varieties of unbelief, too. Wood is no Colm Tóibín, who quipped in his review of *Lila* that "One of the purposes of literature … is to put religion in its place"—an easy task, since creating a religious protagonist in a novel "without making a dog's dinner out of the book" is, according to Tóibín, impossible: religious belief simply, astoundingly, defies meaningful realist representation.[8] Wood is no Philip Pullman either, no aspiring fifth horseman of the New Atheist apocalypse, and he has been quite critical of what he sees as its very old atheism that "helplessly replicates" an "over-simple discussion of God" and is thus "unable to offer a rich or meaningful account of the varieties of religious belief … [and] unbelief." For Wood, this is a loss. To rule out of bounds the category of the religious "robs all of us, whether believers or secularists,

---

[5] Wood, "Introduction," xx.
[6] Wood, "Introduction," xxi.
[7] Girard, "Anthropology of the Cross," 281.
[8] Tóibín, "Putting Religion in Its Place."

of some surplus of the inexpressible; it forbids the passing of the shadow of uncertainty over our lives." Novelists do what the New Atheists can't, Wood avers, which is to "struggle with unbelief and doubt," raising the question of "what it means to continue to need or make use of a religious language whose content is no longer believed in."[9]

Struggling with unbelief's uncertainties, Wood inhabits the "immanent frame" Charles Taylor describes in *A Secular Age*, a world in which multiple contingent aspects of modernity render naïve belief impossible and intentional belief one "embattled" option among many. Modernity has generated a "nova effect" of possible belief options, occupying a field that Taylor claims is bounded by the extremes of the "triple transcendence perspective" and its total denial. Thus unbelief, however insistent on its facticity and invested in "buffered" forms of selfhood, is also troubled, lacking accounts of purely immanent modes of human flourishing capable of confronting mortality, un-beset by what Wood more existentially calls "purposelessness."[10]

Unbelief's struggle with uncertainty is the anima and animus of Wood's debut novel, *The Book Against God*. To borrow his diagnosis of Robinson, this novel troubles unbelief more profoundly than his nonfiction does. Its charming, exasperating narrator, Thomas Bunting, is a card-carrying unbeliever: "The secularist, as I certainly consider myself, has a duty to be worldly, to take the pagan waters at spas of his own choosing."[11] His wife Jane, a concert pianist with long arms, a sleek ponytail, an attractively ample seat, and the desire to have a child, "has never been a secularist" (20), though she's not conventionally religious either. Jane once told Thomas that talking with someone who "really understands music" makes her feel as if she's met someone of the same religious faith. "She didn't mean me; I was a pagan, unable to pray with her. But it was lovely to touch the hem of that faith, to approach her single passion" (27).

In the novel's opening pages, we learn that Thomas's father, Peter, has died in the preceding year and that Thomas and Jane are no longer living together. The novel unfolds as Thomas cagily recounts how he both undermined their marriage and, he worries, killed his father—by his pathological lying: twice Thomas claimed his father had died to weasel extensions on overdue writing and taxes, and within the year Peter died in actual fact. Thomas also reveals that he hasn't finished his PhD thesis in philosophy in part because he's secretly

---

[9] Wood, "Notes on the New Atheism," 6, 7.
[10] Taylor, *A Secular Age*.
[11] Wood, *The Book Against God*, 10. Hereafter cited parenthetically.

writing the "Book Against God," or the BAG as he nicknames it, a covert operation against the faith of his Anglican-priest father, where he copies out "apposite religious and antireligious quotations" and develops theological and philosophical arguments (5).

Both the BAG and Thomas's chronic lying are driven by his war against uncertainty. Making small talk with Timothy Biffen, a theology colleague of his father's in Durham, Thomas finds himself trembling with anger because Timothy won't declare outright atheism, instead calling out Thomas's desire for an unattainable certainty: "I can't possibly say to you that because of this paucity of proof or suggestion that I don't think God exists, or that 'I don't believe'—whatever that word 'believe' means ... I can't commit myself to your kind of language of certainty. I can't even speak it, because if I do I am committing an intellectual lie" (169–70). "I can't help being certain!" Thomas retorts; neither can he believe in a God who created our world, "a place of horror and pain and bitter senseless longevity for millions and millions" (170). When Thomas adds that "even if He exists, I can't believe in Him and won't believe in him—He doesn't exist for me," Timothy parries wearily,

> Except that he palpably does exist for you, ... because you can't stop talking about "God." You can't say "He doesn't exist" ... and I can't say the opposite—I mean, I can't know that God does exist. Can you honestly say, hand on the heart, that you know the whole of religion is a colossal error? Can you look at our cathedral and just know that it simply represents an error, ancient ignorance, that it's just a big mistake? (172)

Thomas's hypersensitivity and zeal to convert Timothy to his cause indicate the fissures opening in his naïve secularism. Until this point he doesn't doubt it's possible to finish the BAG and be done with uncertainty once and for all, and this unrequitable desire for vindicated unbelief is the novel's engine, wrestling against its own inability—the BAG's, the novel's—not just to exorcise the question of God but to motivate a full-hearted way of living in the world. It's no coincidence that the thesis Thomas stalls out writing is on the Epicureans. Unable to make what Taylor calls a purely immanent account of human flourishing, Thomas finds it easier to attack the idea of God in the BAG and, in life, to lie, about anything whatsoever. Thomas's pestiferous prevarication, deliciously nettlesome to undergraduates, serves the dual purposes of insisting on a finally knowable truth and of avenging himself on others' trust, which can only appear to him as vulnerable gullibility.

130   *Literature and Religious Experience*

Thomas's resentment of others' truck with uncertainty manifests on a trip to his parents' when, alone in his room one night, Thomas pisses in a glass his mother Sarah will take from his bedroom the next morning, simply because he knows she'll pretend not to notice what it is. Wood's image captures Thomas brilliantly, full of scotch and piss and vitriol, at both the agnostic Timothy and his jovially believing parents. Thomas recalls how his father wrote reviews for a journal of theology, which sent him advance copies of books, and cheekily pasted a sticker from one of them on his favorite Bible: "This is an advance copy sent in lieu of a proof" (42). Peter tells Thomas, "Belief and unbelief are not absolutes, and not absolute opposites. What if they are rather close to each other, I mean belief shadowed by unbelief and vice versa … so that one is not exactly sure where one begins and another ends?" (49). Thomas seethes at this: "Peter, the supposed believer, the great parish priest, the former lecturer in theology, aerated his faith with so many little holes, so much flexibility and doubt and easygoing tolerance, that he simply disappeared down one of these holes" (49). Peter, like his canny wife Sarah, is no naïve believer, and this quite literally pisses Thomas off. He particularly resents his parents' "obvious fulfillment in marriage" (64), augmented by the endless repetition of daily rituals, a kind of devotion he cannot muster. "Oh, if I could only have learned from this," he muses; "I seem so incapable of repetition, so bad at sticking at anything, and I marvel now at this aspect of their lives, their emotional resourcefulness" (45–6).

This emotional resourcefulness extends to a blitheness about death Thomas found unnerving even as a child, when Peter performed his grandmother's graveside service and six-year-old Thomas ran away from the mourners, Peter pursuing him, calling, "Come back to the grave" (69). Retaining a certain childishness and lacking the resources to deal with either marital difficulties or death, Thomas faces both, and at the novel's climax his fabrications snowball until he tells a lie so "terrible" it "masters" him, faking an orgasm with Jane for fear of fathering the child she yearns for: "What right do I have to bring life into the world? To create a person who might, at some point in his life, wish that he were dead?" (201). Just as he can't finish his dissertation on the Epicureans, so in purely immanent terms Thomas cannot justify fathering a child.

Without knowing Thomas's predicament, Peter reveals that he too suffered such doubts and misgivings when Sarah was pregnant and "I was not sure that I had enough faith—faith in God, faith in the future—to be a father" (225). In the crucible of impending parenthood, Peter came to believe that "the creation of something out of nothing is an act of love" and "that we would rather be

Belief 131

alive than dead, even if life is painful, is proof that there is more love in the world than pain" (226). This unexpectedly intimate talk sadly turns out to be their last, and soon after, Peter dies of a heart attack. Thomas, raw with grief and defensive in the face of death, in the most painfully comic pages of the novel starts to quote from the BAG in his father's eulogy—the impropriety of which prompts Jane and the parish canon to remove him from the pulpit midstream.

At the end of the novel, Thomas is grieving, working odd jobs, living in a tiny bedsit, when Jane invites him to dinner. After the meal, she puts on a record, Svatislav Richter playing the slow movement of Beethoven's piano sonata number 30:

> The melody was, above all, very stable, neither joyful nor melancholy; instead, it seemed to be the essence of knowledge itself, the gold of truth, constant behind our stormy extremes as the sun is behind clouds. Yet there was another sound, not musical. Something like a man's sniffing. It was the pianist breathing!— heavy, almost impatient, as if he were wrestling with the music to secure its great medial serenity. The pianist was breathing quite hard through his nose as he wrestled with this sweet sound. It was the sound of hard work, but it was also the sound of existence itself—a man's ordinary breath, the give and take of the organism, our colourless wind of survival, the zephyr of it all.
>
> The evidence of human effort, of pain, was intensely moving. I hung my head as I listened. (255)

This epiphany of the pianist's laborious wrestling to create beauty recapitulates the novel's association of repetition and graceful effort, the defining elements of belief, ritual, and his parents' love, the majesty and poignance of which Thomas does not feel until this moment. Come morning, Thomas's thoughts return to his father's funeral, where his mother held his hand, and he suddenly remembers how, at his grandmother's graveside, his father also had held his hand.

> Is that right? Could that be? Why, then, did I only remember Father being cross with me and striding towards me in his black cassock. But the more I think about it, ... I am sure he held my hand. In my adult years I only held his hand to shake it, to say hello or goodbye. I would like to put my hand out now, and touch his. (257)

Jane's religious love of music together with the labored breathing of the pianist open up for Thomas a new feeling for his father's faith and love in their complexity, together with a longing to connect with his father, across the gap between their

132   *Literature and Religious Experience*

belief and unbelief, and despite uncertain memory. The novel's final paragraph then becomes a prayer to his father:

> Oh, Father, there were days so exciting when I was a little boy that each morning was a delicious surprise ... When anyone asks me, I say that my childhood was happy, and for once, for once, I am not lying. Wasn't it an orchard, my childhood? But why, then, the worm? Why the worm? Tell me. (257)

Thomas's prayer registers both a Miltonic fall and a conversion, not to his father's Christianity or to Jane's musical devotion, but from naïve to non-naïve, vulnerable postsecular unbelief. At the novel's end the fate of Thomas's marriage is uncertain, and his felt purposelessness remains. Thomas may be mocking our trust with his piss, but the hole his father has disappeared into is no evasive belief but the existential reality of death, and Thomas is able at least in longing to reach into that grave, into the field of uncertainty occupied by his father's faith and his inability to believe, to talk with a man he loves about both his love and his unbelief. Wood's nonfiction suggests considering what sort of belief and even religiousness animates this final paragraph, when his father's death and foundering marriage mitigate his railing about the suffering of abstract "millions." If, as Wood remarks, *To the Lighthouse* "turns on what it means to continue to need or make use of a religious language whose content is no longer believed in,"[12] at the end of *The Book Against God* this language indicates in part a desire for unbelievers and believers to converse and commune, to acknowledge how they inhabit a shared space of uncertainty, rendering any boundary between the religious and secular highly porous. The language of religion—prayer, fall, lamentation, longing, wrestling with faith and doubt—speaks to human experiences secularism does not exorcise. Wood may in fact mean his novel to be a book against God, but it stages a compelling postsecular peripeteia, revealing the way an isolated self bent on certainty and autonomy can come suddenly to sense the shocking fallibility of its own memory and reason, feeling its secular bufferedness as a lonely conundrum it would like to escape. Whether Thomas finds what he calls the "emotional resources" to break out of his habitual anger and condescension toward others' trust—the structures of feeling bound up in what Jacques Lacan calls the subjectivity of mastery—is the postsecular question with which the novel leaves us.

---

[12] Wood, "Notes on the New Atheism," 7.

Belief 133

3.

In contemporary fiction, we tend to find explorations of belief in novels that, for their realism, seem driven to sensational lengths to excuse what Tóibín fears will make a "dog's dinner" out of the book. The high-wire fabrications and funeral theatrics of *The Book Against God*; the gothic apocalypticism of Cormac McCarthy's *The Road*; the clairvoyant cult leader of James Howard Kuntzler's dystopian *World Made By Hand* series; the sharia France and Marian mysticism of Michel Houellebecq's *Submission*: each portrays mere consideration of belief as Kristevan abjection, a possibility "thrown under" anything resembling normal living as portrayed in realist fiction. Wood's second novel, *Upstate*, regrettably leaves Thomas's wrestling behind, tossing the possibility of genuine belief into the nonexistent laps of two overweight evangelicals who make an appearance only to prove that religion offers no existential insights worth taking seriously, reducing purposefulness and nihilism to matters of psychological disposition and the novel to a gloomy pulpit of determinism. It's all the more remarkable then, that Robinson's four *Gilead* novels are completely devoid of sensationalism, as opulent in quotidian Midwestern detail as in psychological realism. Thomas-caliber, self-avowed unbelief shares the stage with belief in each of them, their various incarnations of faith neither premodernly naïve nor modernly cashed out as provable propositions espoused as belief within the immanent frame.

Gilead telescopes Taylor's five-century religious transformation into the lives of three generations of ministers, all named John Ames, in the form of the youngest Ames's letter to his son, Robby. Where the first Ames—a fiery abolitionist minister who shed blood for his cause—stands in for the prophetic certainty and violence of the Wars of Religion, his son follows him in the ministry but like many Enlightenment Christians shuns enthusiasm and violence, which his father condescends to as his "domesticated" faith. The second Ames's eldest son and the narrator's brother, Edward, as if on Taylor's cue incarnates nineteenth-century crises of faith. Set to inherit his father's pulpit, his studies funded by their congregation, Edward instead returned from Göttingen "with a walking stick and huge mustache," having published a volume on Feuerbach and become an atheist. Edward warned his teenaged brother that leaving the "backwater" of Gilead was "like waking from a trance" and gave him *The Essence of Christianity* "thinking to shock me out of my uncritical piety."[13] Reflecting on Edward, Ames feels "in some ways as if I hardly knew him, and in others as if

---

[13] Robinson, *Gilead*, 27. Hereafter cited parenthetically.

134 *Literature and Religious Experience*

I have been talking to him my whole life," about Feuerbach and much else (24). In fact, the first thing we hear from Ames about Feuerbach is how wonderful he is on the joyful aspects of religion: "Of course he thinks religion could just stand out of the way and let joy exist pure and undisguised. That is his one error, and it is significant. But he is marvelous on the subject of joy, and also on its religious expressions" (24).

We find out late in the novel why the inner dialogue with Edward and Feuerbach has been so determinative for Ames—because Edward's loss of faith ultimately prompted their father to abandon belief and even to urge his younger son to leave it and Gilead with them:

> Well, all he accomplished was to make me homesick for a place I never left. I couldn't believe he would speak to me as if I were not competent to invest my loyalties as I saw fit. How could I accept the advice of someone who had such a low estimation of me? Those were my thoughts at the time. ... Then in a week or so I got that letter from him. I have mentioned loneliness to you, and darkness, and I thought then I already knew what they were, but that day it was as if a great cold wind swept over me the like of which I had never felt before, and that wind blew for years and years. My father threw me back on myself, and on the Lord. That's a fact, so I find little to regret. It cost me a good deal of sorrow, but I learned from it. (235–6)

Faced with the prospect of abandoning faith and home for father and brother, Ames remains in Gilead and keeps up his conversation with their unbelief for years, rereading Feuerbach alongside John Calvin and Karl Barth, through decades of lonely struggle.

These antagonistic forms of belief and unbelief—his grandfather's visionary fire and his brother's and father's rationalized faith that ultimately abandons religion as necessarily naïve—form the matrix of Ames's subsequent religious life. Ames's belief is thus inseparable from the modern experience of unbelief Wood shows us in Thomas, and like Thomas, Ames is drawn toward engagement across the secular/religious divide, in a way that is noncoercive and yet true to his faith experience. From this intergenerational crisis of faith, and having suffered the death of his wife and child, Ames serves in his father's pulpit for forty-five years, writing 2,500 sermons as his Book For God, wrestling with loneliness, anger, and covetousness, watching his best friend and local Presbyterian minister Robert Boughton raise a sprightly brood of eight. Ames's placid life is miraculously upended in his sixties by falling in love with Lila, a woman half his age, whom he marries and who bears their son. Ames assumes that his son will encounter

Belief 135

all the nineteenth-century arguments against God, and careful reasoning about God is as central to Ames's account of belief as to Thomas's unbelief, though their epistemologies differ. "Nothing true can be said of God from a posture of defense" (177), Ames writes, because proofs "are never sufficient to the question" of being itself and are impertinent, claiming for God "a place within our conceptual grasp" (178). Alienation from one's own thoughts and experiences, Ames comes to believe, is far more dangerous to belief than explicit attacks on it: "If the awkwardness and falseness and failure of religion are interpreted to mean there is no core of truth in it ... then people are disabled from trusting their thoughts, their expressions of belief, and their understanding, and even from believing in the essential dignity of their and their neighbors' endlessly flawed experience of belief" (146).

Ames's letter to Robby is in good measure an account of his own endlessly flawed experience of belief, its coming to dwell in Wood's "shadow of uncertainty" and for that becoming more true to itself. A "considerable disruption" spotlights this flawed experience a third of the way into the novel, the return to Gilead of the tortured black sheep of the Boughton family, Jack (122). Forty-three years earlier, Boughton announced at Jack's baptism that his son would be named after his friend, and Ames was so stunned that he felt unable to attend and bless the child properly (187–8). Jack's adolescent thievery and drunkenness furthered their alienation, and his adult unbelief frequently calls Edward to Ames's mind, prompting Ames to advise his son against the defensiveness he feels all too keenly:

> It precludes the best eventualities along with the worst. At the most basic level, it expresses a lack of faith. As I have said, the worst eventualities can have great value as experience. And often enough, when we think we are protecting ourselves, we are struggling against our rescuer. I know this, I have seen the truth of it with my own eyes, though I have not myself always managed to live by it, the Good Lord knows. (154)

Ames's weathered faith, like Peter's and Susan's, owns its vulnerabilities. The challenge Ames faces in Jack is like Jacob's in wrestling with the angel, grappling not so much with an adversary as with himself, to find the emotional resources to embrace the other as a source of blessing.[14] Ames here connects belief to encountering both God and others, recalling a piece of wisdom he relates earlier in the novel:

[14] Genesis 32.

136 *Literature and Religious Experience*

> This is an important thing, which I have told many people, and which my father told me, and which his father told him. When you encounter another person, when you have dealings with anyone at all, it is as if a question is being sent to you. So you must think, What is the Lord asking of me in this moment, in this situation? If you confront insult or antagonism, your first impulse will be to respond in kind. But if you think, as it were, This is an emissary sent from the Lord, and some benefit is intended for me, first of all the occasion to demonstrate my faithfulness, the chance to show that I do in some small degree participate in the grace that saved me, you are free to act otherwise than as circumstances would seem to dictate. You are free to act by your own lights. You are freed at the same time of the impulse to hate or resent that person. He would probably laugh at the thought that the Lord sent him to you for your benefit (and his), but that is the perfection of the disguise, his own ignorance of it. (124)

Extending the benefit of the doubt, even to one who insults us, is here likened to participating in the grace by which God saves us and thereby enjoying some partial freedom from impulse and spite such as plagues Thomas. Belief in Robinson's novel—always wrestling with unbelief yet not reducible to it—is more essentially a trust in God's provident care that frees Ames to engage life and others, including their unbelief, as unfolding within God's grace.

The rest of the novel explores what emotional resources Ames's endlessly flawed belief affords him for relating to Jack across the chasm of their religious difference. Their encounter resuscitates Ames's "sullen old reptilian self" (167) who, we learn, never overcame his revulsion at Jack's having abandoned a child he fathered out of wedlock, squandering the paternity Ames longed for (164). Ames realizes he has been "long in the habit of seeing meanness at the root" of everything Jack does (230), but trying to do better by him, he glimpses Jack's anger, sadness, and loneliness (184). In one wearying conversation about belief, Ames, suddenly moved to tears, abandons theological wrangling and tells Jack, "When this old sanctuary is full of silence and prayer, every book Karl Barth ever will write would not be a feather in the scales against it from the point of view of profundity" (173). Ames is embarrassed at crying, but exposure of his vulnerability draws Jack back to talk with his godfather about the all-consuming matter that has returned him to Gilead. Their subsequent conversation constitutes the great watershed of the novel, the blank page that sets off the main body of Ames's manuscript from the ending: Jack reveals that he has a common-law wife, Della, who is Black, and an eight-year-old son, and poses the pressing question of whether they might escape Missouri's miscegenation laws and live safely with him in Gilead (231). Jack's suffering love for his family radically alters

Ames's perception of him, and Ames records his story for his son, since Jack "is a man about whom you may never hear one good word, and I just don't know another way to let you see the beauty there is in him" (232).

Realizing how nearly impossible it would be for Jack to build a life with Della in all-white Gilead kindles in Ames a prophetic fire reminiscent of his grandfather: inasmuch as Gilead's citizens have turned a blind eye to racism in their midst and failed to live up to their abolitionist legacy, "this town might as well be standing on the absolute floor of hell for all the truth there is in it, and the fault is mine as much as anyone's" (233–4). His belief that encounter with the other is a question from the Lord thus allows Ames to be rescued by Jack both from their previous alienation and from blindness and complacency about racism; their encounter is the basis for Ames's deeper understanding of himself and the world—his repentance or *metanoia*, change of heart and mind. Where Jacob hopes in God's *hesed*, his steadfast love, wrestling with the angel and refusing to let go until he blesses him, Ames ultimately cannot let Jack go until Jack lets Ames bless him as he failed to do those forty-three years ago. Putting his hand on Jack's brow and pronouncing the benediction from Numbers, Ames no longer looks at Jack's unbelief as an affront but sees Jack's love, beauty, and suffering, alongside his own complicity in making Gilead a place where there is no balm for Jack. By the end of *Gilead*, the unbelieving other is neither dead like Peter at the end of *The Book Against God* nor an obese caricature like the evangelicals in *Upstate*, nor even simply a son ailing and blessed in hopes of healing, but Ames's sparring partner and rescuer. If the three generations of Ames's "begats" replay the transformation of belief across Taylor's secular age, the third Ames's inner revolution turns modernity's secular-religious opposition, the wrestling match between belief and unbelief, into a transforming embrace. How Robby and his children will wrestle with both religious and racial otherness is the question that remains.

4.

The epistemological wrestling match between belief and unbelief in *Gilead* and *The Book Against God* is a very masculine affair. For all Ames's beauty at the end of *Gilead*, it is the women of the three subsequent novels who attract Robinson's curiosity. Even in *Gilead*, it is Lila who blesses Jack before Ames does (200), who speaks with him in a way that takes the edge out of his voice (201), who chastises Ames for disregarding Jack's discomfort with himself (154), and

138 *Literature and Religious Experience*

who alone answers Jack's fear of reprobation with a hope that we learn in *Lila* is hard-won: "A person can change. Everything can change" (153). The focus of *Home* is Glory, Boughton's youngest child and an unheroic heroine worthy of Fyodor Dostoevsky's Alyosha, whose compassion elicits Jack's ridicule and offhand observation that she attracted a parasitic boyfriend by being a clearly "vulnerable" woman. When she repeats the word back to him hoping he catches its barb, he clarifies that by vulnerable he means religious: "Pious girls have tender hearts. They believe sad stories ... Little knowledge of the real world."[15] But Glory owns up to the vulnerability Jack, like Thomas, despises, and where Ames and Jack needle each other over predestination and Boughton cannot overcome his anger at Jack's unbelief, in the novel's central tableau Glory bakes bread, filling the house with its aroma and enabling a radiant, plain-cloth communion scene between her, Jack, and their father. Glory is able to commune with Jack, not to annoy him the way others do, because she refuses to try to "convert" him or to ensconce her faith in religious terminology, instead making the meaning of her belief in real relationship and dialogue with Jack.

Jack's wife Della resembles Glory, as Jack himself points out, not least in her vulnerable openness. In *Jack*, we learn that Della too is educated and believing, a high school English teacher raised by her African Methodist Episcopal bishop father in the separatist tradition of Marcus Garvey, who nonetheless falls in love with a white man. While Jack sees his preacherly good manners as the happenstance of upbringing, Della sees Jack's decency in spite of his unbelief and melancholy, thievery and alcoholism—what she calls his living "as if"—as poetry, a revelation of the miracle of his "holy human soul."[16] Metaphorical but not therefore dismissible, belief for Della is constituted by this ineradicable "as-if"-ness. Della is able to love Jack, allowing for his unbelief and even the possible truth of a nihilism that genuinely makes no sense to her (36). Unthreatened by his unbelief, she recognizes that they inhabit the same uncertainty, "just living on hints," and her love becomes the balm Jack could never find in the seeming certitudes of Gilead. In Della's love, we see something like Thomas's desire to reach out to his father across the gulf of unbelief and death that separate them; only Della finds in her belief and experience the emotional resources to reach across the divides of religious and racial difference, to take Jack's hand again and again, and to raise their child.

---

[15] Robinson, *Home*, 121.
[16] Robinson, *Jack*, 208. Hereafter cited parenthetically.

Belief 139

The closing of *Jack* uncannily echoes the end of *The Book Against God*, complete with Miltonic echoes. No place for them in Memphis, Jack and Della find themselves exiled, and "the world was all before them, such as it was":

> The knowledge of good. That half of the primal catastrophe received too little attention. Guilt and grace met together in the phrase despite all that. He could think of himself as a thief sneaking off with an inestimable wealth of meaning and trust, all of it offended and damaged beyond use, except to remind him of the nature of the crime. Or he could consider the sweet marriage that made her a conspirator with him in it, the loyalty that always restored them both, just like grace. (309)

The momentous "or" launching the novel's final sentence represents the possibility Jack rebuffs with the refrain he shares with Thomas and Wood, "I can't believe," the freedom he hardly knows he has, to tell a different story, to interpret and to imagine his life otherwise.

Jack's trenchant incredulity is scripted in part by the feminization of faith in the nineteenth century and its relegation to motherhood and the nursery. Edward, with his great mustache and the affectation of a walking stick, his need to portray himself as especially masculine and no longer a child, signals the crucial predecessor of that feminization of faith, the secularization of masculinity in Enlightenment and its attraction and antagonism toward the faith it feminizes. Reaching their summit in Della's love for Jack, the Gilead novels also dramatize another unplumbed truth, not simply secularism's masculinity, but its whiteness.

Bibliography

Girard, René. "The Anthropology of the Cross: A Conversation with René Girard." In *The Girard Reader*, edited by James G. William, 262–88. New York: Crossroad, 2015.

Robinson, Marilynne, and James Wood. "The Writer and the Critic: Marilynne Robinson and James Wood in Conversation." 2017–18 Julia S. Phelps Annual Lecture in the Arts and Humanities, April 24, 2018, at Radcliffe Institute for Advanced Study, Cambridge, MA. Recorded Lecture. https://www.radcliffe.harvard.edu/video/writer-and-critic-marilynne-robinson-and-james-wood-in-conversation.

Robinson, Marilynne. *Gilead: A Novel*. New York: FSG/Picador, 2004.

Robinson, Marilynne. *Home*. New York: FSG/Picador, 2008.

Robinson, Marilynne. *Jack*. New York: FSG/Picador, 2020.

Taylor, Charles. *A Secular Age*. Cambridge, MA: Belknap/Harvard University Press, 2007.

Tóibín, Colm. "Putting Religion in Its Place." Review of *Lila* by Marilynne Robinson, *The London Review of Books* 36, no. 20 (October 2014). Available online: https://www.lrb.co.uk/the-paper/v36/n20/colm-toibin/putting-religion-in-its-place (accessed September 2, 2020).

Wood, James. *The Book Against God: A Novel*. New York: Picador, 2003.

Wood, James. "The Broken Estate: The Legacy of Ernest Renan and Matthew Arnold." In *The Broken Estate: Essays on Literature and Belief*, 249–70. New York: Picador, 2010.

Wood, James. "Introduction: The Freedom of Not Quite." In *The Broken Estate*, xv–xxii.

Wood, James. "Notes on the New Atheism." *The Berlin Journal*, no. 19 (Fall 2010): 5–7.

8

Turning: Alabaster's Wager and the Experience of Conversion

James Kearney

In the summer of 1597 in the village of Cambridge, England, a young man by the name of William Alabaster made a wager with himself. The wager was a response—both calculated and impassioned—to an experience of religious conversion. As far as Alabaster was concerned, the stakes were nothing less than the fate of his immortal soul and the possibility in this world of laying claim to future forms of the self. The strange event of the wager not only reflects Alabaster's particular experience of conversion but also captures the ways in which he is attuned to what we might call a phenomenology of the self. Literary writing—here, devotional poetry and conversion narrative—was crucial both to Alabaster's conversion experience and to the wager he made in its wake.[1] In this brief essay, I dwell with Alabaster's depiction of his conversion, a life-altering event that leads to this strange and telling wager. Alabaster's account of his conversion serves also as a platform from which to address the ways such narratives both capture and create the forces—affective, formal, phenomenological—that surround and shape the obscure event of religious conversion. Alabaster's description of his experience of religious change draws in a range of phenomenological matters: the fraught temporality of experience, the doubt that necessarily attends what we might call a "truth-event," and the relation of ecstatic religious experience to a writing self and the writing of literature. In turning to Alabaster's turn, my hope is to attend both to religious experience as form and to the ways in which literary and narrative forms evoke and shape experience.

---

[1] For an account of the relation of Alabaster's literary production to his conversion, see Molly Murray's excellent *The Poetics of Conversion*, 36–68. In addition to Murray, I am indebted to Marotti, *Religious Ideology and Cultural Fantasy*, 98–109; G. M. Story's and Helen Gardner's edition of *The Sonnets of William Alabaster*; and especially Dana Sutton's *Unpublished Works of William Alabaster*.

1

In that fateful summer of 1597, Alabaster was a promising young Protestant divine with a secure living, a bride in waiting, and a bright future ahead of him.[2] A Fellow of and catechist for Trinity College, Cambridge, he had served as a chaplain on the Earl of Essex's Cadiz expedition, and on his return to England he continued to benefit from the Earl's favor. Alabaster had also begun to make a name for himself in the literary world of Renaissance England. In the early 1590s he wrote a Latin tragedy in a Senecan vein, *Roxana*, which was performed at Trinity College and evidently well received.[3] Alabaster was also working in the 1590s on an epic poem, *The Elisaeis*, early versions of which circulated among a select few. Referencing Alabaster's "heroick song" in progress, Edmund Spenser promoted the younger poet as someone destined for literary fame.[4] Written to celebrate Elizabeth's imminent defeat of Catholicism, the poem was, in fact, never completed.[5] And it was never completed because in 1597 this promising young man ran into Thomas Wright, a Roman Catholic priest, then under house arrest in London. As the story goes, the hope was that Alabaster, the brilliant young divine might convert the old priest. But it seems that things did not go as planned.

Conversion evokes transformation, some radical alteration or change.[6] The paradigmatic conversion-as-transformation in the Christian tradition is Saul's conversion to Paul on the road to Damascus recorded in Acts 9.[7] In a bravura reading, Alain Badiou seizes on Pauline conversion as radical event: "a thunderbolt, a caesura ... a conscription instituting a new subject."[8] In a more prosaic register, of course, conversion also simply means "to turn." And often the implication is of a rudimentary bodily turn. Why should the humble act

---

[2] See Sutton, *Unpublished Works*, xv–xxx; Murray, *Poetics of Conversion*, 36–68; Marotti, *Religious Ideology*, 98–109. Also see Coutts, "The Life and Works of William Alabaster."

[3] Performed at Trinity College, *Roxana* circulated in manuscript, several of which survive, and was printed in 1632. See Coldeway, "William Alabaster's *Roxana*: Some Textual Considerations."

[4] Spenser, *Come Home Againe*, lines 400–14.

[5] See O'Connell, "'The Elisaeis' of William Alabaster."

[6] Investigating the use of the term in the ancient world, Karl Morrison notes that in the context of philosophy and theology it was a metaphor borrowed from crafts like metallurgy to describe processes of material change. And religious conversion often carries this sense of an almost physical metamorphosis from one substance or thing to another. See Morrison, *Understanding Conversion*, 185, xiii.

[7] "And as he journeyed, he came near Damascus: and suddenly there shined round about him a light from heaven: And he fell to the earth, and heard a voice ..." Acts 9:3-4 (KJV).

[8] Addressing the prodigious strangeness of this thing that "*happened* ... purely and simply, in the anonymity of a road," Badiou suggests that this "encounter"—this foundational event—is sudden and singular, incalculable and unconditioned: "Nothing leads up to it." See Badiou, *Saint Paul*, 17–18 (emphasis added).

of turning carry such weight? Working within a phenomenological register of conversion might lead us to retain the positional or directional significance of turning toward or turning away, simple embodied movements tasked with extraordinary gravitas.[9] The commonplace turn in perspective or direction suggests a phenomenological reorientation that reshapes the self by reshaping one's relation to the world. One of the great poets of the turn is Badiou's erstwhile teacher Louis Althusser, whose account of ideology and subject-formation offers a version of the turn that is at once material and allegorical.[10] In a famously evocative passage, Althusser figures the workings of ideology as a hailing or address that solicits a turn.[11] Here, I am less concerned with the precision with which Althusser captures the workings of ideology than with the way he avails himself of the metaphoric and metaphysical richness of the turn.

For Althusser, this solicitation and turn is part of what Althusser calls his "little theoretical theatre" of address and recognition.[12] He imagines this simple dynamic in relation to what he calls "the most commonplace everyday" experience, for instance, a police officer hailing someone in the street.[13] In this "theoretical scene," the figure so hailed "will turn round" and "by this mere one-hundred-and-eighty-degree physical conversion" become "a *subject*. Why? Because he has recognized that the hail was 'really' addressed to him, and that 'it was *really him* who was hailed' (and not someone else)."[14] Spare and minimalist, the scene Althusser conjures is nonetheless striking in its evocation of embodied response: one *hears* a voice and turns to *see*, occasioning the body to reposition, reorient, and refocus. Looked at in a certain way, this "one-hundred-and-eighty-degree physical conversion" is reminiscent of the famous line from Revelation, with its entangling of senses, its strange synesthesia: "And I turned to see the voice."[15] The phenomenology of the scene, however, does not primarily reside in sensory perception or embodied motion but in intersubjective dynamics. One does not primarily turn to see or hear but

---

[9] In a brilliant analysis that attends to phenomenologies of "orientation," Sara Ahmed takes up the ways in which the relation of embodied self to world has implications for the way we think direction, rectitude, straightness in terms of the ethical and political. See Ahmed's *Queer Phenomenology*.

[10] Although "dramatist" might be more apt as Althusser was given to theatrical metaphors and to thinking in terms of the stage. On Althusser's relation to theater, see Balibar, "Althusser's Dramaturgy and the Critique of Ideology."

[11] On the figurative or allegorical aspects of Althusser's analysis, see Butler, *Psychic Life of Power*, 106–31.

[12] Althusser, "Ideological State Apparatuses," 174.

[13] Althusser, "Ideological State Apparatuses," 174.

[14] Althusser, "Ideological State Apparatuses," 174.

[15] Rev. 1:12 (KJV).

144 *Literature and Religious Experience*

to face. To face up to, perhaps, as Althusser suggests with his references to guilt and conscience, but also and more fundamentally to face in order to address and to be addressed.[16]

Althusser's analysis seemingly cannot escape the language and logic of religious experience, in the end turning to religion as his paradigmatic example. The episode he mobilizes from the Judeo-Christian tradition to disclose the logic of ideology is the scene in Exodus where Moses "turns" to "see" the bush that "is not burnt." When God in turn "saw" that Moses had "turned" to "see," "God called unto him," and Moses "said, Here am I."[17] For Althusser, religion specifically and ideology generally work as call and response, interpellation and turn, address and recognition. According to Althusser, the scene "obtains" from the hailed subject "the *recognition* that they really do occupy the place" designated "for them as theirs in the world, a fixed residence ... in this vale of tears."[18] Vale of tears alludes to Psalm 84, where once again we have the form of solicitation and turn, although the positions are reversed: "O LORD God of hosts, hear my prayer: give ear, O God of Jacob ... Behold, O God our shield, and look upon the face of thine anointed."[19] While the thought of figures like Althusser and Badiou suggests how consequential religious experience and the conversion event are for the ways that modern thought understands the relation of self to world, the point here is not to unearth the secret religious foundation of philosophical accounts of subject formation. Most immediately, the point is that Althusser's analysis offers insight into the figure of the turn and what it affords. And what Althusser recognizes is that the turn is often a form of address, that the turn is weighty because it implies an essential form—both familiar and momentous—of intersubjective experience.

Althusser's evocative scene has been queried for the ways in which it evokes an infinite regress; how does the addressee hear the call unless she already knows what or who she is in relation to the call, unless she already understands what it means to be addressed?[20] In some sense the subject must already be conditioned to turn. In a consequential strain of the Christian conversion narrative, this

---

[16] Althusser, "Ideological State Apparatuses," 172, 174, 181. On a phenomenology of facing in the early modern period, see the collection *Face-to-Face in Shakespearean Drama*, edited by Matthew Smith and Julia Reinhard Lupton.

[17] Exod. 3:3-4 (KJV). Althusser: "It is (really) I! I am Moses thy servant, speak and I shall listen!" ("Ideological State Apparatuses," 179).

[18] Althusser, "Ideological State Apparatuses," 178.

[19] Ps. 84:8-9 (KJV). Isabel Davis discusses Althusser's use of this psalm in a fascinating analysis of "calling" in late medieval literature ("Calling").

[20] See Butler's searching analysis in *Psychic Life of Power*.

circularity is paradoxical feature rather than bug.[21] If conversion as Pauline transformation—following a reading like Badiou's—is necessarily passive and unmediated, sudden and unconditioned, conversion as turn suggests that the addressed reorients because she *recognizes*, with the emphasis on knowledge repeating or rhyming. Always already solicited, the subject turns, the self or soul converts. Conversion as turn then exists somewhere between passive and active tenses; the figure of the turn—and this is crucial to Althusser's analysis—confounds our sense of agency.[22] In the Christian tradition, the model here is not Paul but Augustine, for whom the soul seems to collaborate in its own conversion, soliciting God's address.[23]

2

For his part, Alabaster attends to the riddles and paradoxes that propagate between Pauline and Augustinian models of conversion. When he arrives at the dramatic moment of his conversion experience, Alabaster explicitly articulates it as a Pauline event. "If I remember well," he writes, it was "as if those" scales ("squames") that

> fell from St. Paul's bodily eyes at his … [words missing in manuscript] … and understanding so was I lightened upon the sudden, feeling myself so wonderfully and sensibly changed both in judgment and affection as I remained astonished at my true state. I found my mind wholly and perfectly Catholic in an instant, and so to be persuaded of all and every point of Catholic religion together. … For I saw most evidently in my inward judgment that all were true …. And feeling this in my self upon the sudden with such inward light of evidence as I could not contradict, and with such force of affection as I could not resist, I leapt up from the place where I sat, and said to myself, "now I am a Catholic."[24]

---

[21] To be clear, in my view it is feature rather than bug in Althusser as well. On circularity as intrinsic to Althusser's model, see Butler, *Psychic Life of Power*, and Balibar, "Althusser's Dramaturgy and the Critique of Ideology."

[22] Butler captures this well:

> The "turning around" is a strange sort of middle ground (taking place, perhaps, in a strange sort of "middle voice"), which is determined both by the law and the addressee, but by neither unilaterally or exhaustively. Although there would be no turning around without first having been hailed, neither would there be a turning around without some readiness to turn. (Butler, *Psychic Life of Power*, 107)

[23] The dizzying paradoxes of such a turn are captured powerfully in the final lines of John Donne's "Goodfriday, 1613. Riding Westward."

[24] Alabaster, *Unpublished Works*, 118. I have modernized Alabaster's spelling throughout.

146 *Literature and Religious Experience*

In the first instance, Alabaster's "strange and powerful conversion" is framed in terms of knowledge and doctrine, belief and understanding: "all were true."[25] The knowledge that he arrives at is not new of course; he has a scholar's intimacy with the doctrines at stake. It is just that in this "instant" he feels the truth of this knowledge within himself, and he does so "with such inward light of evidence" that he "could not contradict" and "with such force of affection" that he "could not resist." Note that he figures the self as a resistant interlocutor or mulish impediment. Earlier, Alabaster had depicted this change as a divine decision to put an end to the "pride and presumption" of his "judgement" and "knowledge" of "truth and religion." He describes this as "almighty God" having decided or "determined to do me a greater turn."[26] The expression "doing a good turn"— an "act of good" will "that does good" to "another"[27]—is wonderfully evocative here. When calling on the homely idiom, Alabaster, a poet and scholar attuned to the resonances of languages, cannot have been unaware of the ways in which it echoes and shapes the "turn" at hand. Remarkably familiar in reference to "almighty God," the figure of "doing a good turn" suggests neighborly exchange and colloquial address.

The immediacy of the event ("upon the sudden," "in an instant") is obviously crucial, but Alabaster also carefully tracks his affective and intellectual reactions to this sudden change. He not only feels himself to be "wonderfully and sensibly changed" in "judgment and affection" but also feels this change to such an extent that he is "astonished" at his new, "true state." Alabaster's focus is neither his spiritual condition precisely nor some unfolding of truth but the strange *experience* of his altered relation—cognitive, somatic, affective—to knowledge. Yet Alabaster seems to have no direct knowledge of that transformation. Alabaster takes pains to emphasize the retrospective nature of the account ("if I remember well") and can only describe himself as "changed." We are already in the past tense. Moreover, the first we hear of the turn, of something having happened, is through the mediating reference to the scales that fell from Saint Paul's eyes. As Alabaster approaches the moment itself, the narrative seems to retreat, to withdraw from the immediacy that so characterizes it. Remarkably, there is even a gap in the manuscript at precisely the place where we might hope to find a relation of the ineffable event.

[25] Alabaster, *Unpublished Works*, 118.
[26] Alabaster, *Unpublished Works*, 113.
[27] *Oxford English Dictionary*, "turn (n.)."

Turning 147

I have argued elsewhere that conversion poses a problem for historical inquiry insofar as conversion narratives often register a "black box" effect in which the moment of transformation is elided.[28] In a sense this is what conversion narratives often *are*: stories organized around an explicitly unknowable moment or event. Alabaster is particularly reflective and expressive with regard to that unknowability. In a fascinating discussion of the phenomenology of the event, the philosopher Françoise Dastur observes that "we can speak about the event only in the third voice and in a past time, in the mode of 'it happened to me.'" Here, she reflects a surprising accord among figures as diverse as Giorgio Agamben, Badiou, and Jacques Derrida, philosophers of the event who seem to agree that the event is necessarily unpunctual, necessarily a retrospective (or prospective) phenomenon. For Dastur, this is not simply a function of the strange temporality that structures the event but is also internal to the "experience" of such an event, where we "experience our incapacity to experience."[29] In Alabaster's narrative the dramatic effect of the transformative moment arises, I suggest, from a vibrant and lyrical evocation of this strange experience of the "incapacity to experience."

3

By the end of the sixteenth century, the Christian conversion narrative was both an ancient, venerable genre *and* one that had become epidemic in the wake of the Protestant Reformation. Indeed, by the time of Alabaster's turn, the volume of such narratives would seem to suggest that the experience of conversion—that singular, existential event—was ubiquitous. The conversion narrative is not simply a record of a remarkable experience of course; it is necessarily a form that anticipates and shapes the event of the turn, a form that makes intelligible and authenticates experience. To be sure, the compelling qualities of Alabaster's conversion narrative are a function both of the particular and idiosyncratic features that shape it and of Alabaster's writerly inspiration and ingenuity. At the same time, Alabaster's story is terrifically familiar. If there is something that truly stands out about Alabaster's conversion amid the flood of such accounts in this historical moment—something beyond its lyrical artistry and narrative punch—it is its sophisticated relation to the conversion narrative as genre. Alabaster's story is not simply highly self-conscious regarding its own

[28] Kearney, "Tasting the Gospel."
[29] Dastur, "Waiting and Surprise," 185–6.

148   *Literature and Religious Experience*

generic commitments; it *performs* its relation to the conversion narrative. And its primary point of reference is Augustine.[30]

The conversion is framed in the first instance in relation to Alabaster's encounter with Thomas Wright, the recusant priest being held in "custody" in London.[31] The immediate cause of the conversion experience, however, is not Wright but a book lying on Wright's table:

> Wherefore it pleased Almighty God to take another more compendious way with Me ... That finding one day a certain English book lying upon the said Mr Wrights table (which I hope was put there by the providence of Almighty God for my conversion, as St *August.* recounteth the book of St *Antony* the monk his life was ... for the present conversion of two that lighted upon it) I asked Mr Wright what book it was, and he told me Mr William Rainolds ... in defense of the English translation of the new testament by the English Catholics in Rhemes. Whereupon I took the said book home with me, not suspecting what would follow.[32]

If Alabaster does not suspect "what would follow," readers familiar with the generic elements of the conversation narrative certainly will, grasping the "said book" as a version of Chekhov's gun.[33] The fateful book that Alabaster lights upon is, as he says, a text written by one William Rainolds. Before he turns to his encounter with this book, however, he first tells us more about this Mister Rainolds, a Catholic controversialist who, it turns out, is not only another convert but one also converted through a reading experience. Alabaster is here following his Augustinian model closely. When Augustine recounts his conversion in the *Confessions*, he famously surrounds his turn with the turns of others, making book eight of the Confessions a *matryoshka* doll of conversion stories. In his reference to "St *August,*" Alabaster cites an episode that Augustine records in the run up to his own conversion, a story in which two gentlemen are converted when they happen upon "the book of St *Antony,*" the desert monk. Following and replicating Augustine, Alabaster situates himself within a spiritual and hermeneutic community—ancient and extant, from Anthony to Rainolds—and authenticates his turn as an iteration within a living tradition.

---

[30] For a thorough account of Alabaster's relation to Augustine's conversion, see Murray, *Poetics of Conversion,* 36–68.

[31] Alabaster, *Unpublished Works,* 114.

[32] Alabaster, *Unpublished Works,* 114–15.

[33] As I have argued elsewhere, Augustine's influential account of his own conversion in the *Confessions* helped shaped what we might think of as the readerly or textual conversion, a form that became ubiquitous in the Reformation. In a post-Reformation world the scene of conversion is often a scene of reading. See Kearney, *Incarnate Text,* 140–77.

Turning 149

Beyond its evocation of the unknowable moment of change, Alabaster's narrative seems to be shaped by two prevailing concerns: this intimate and searching relation to other conversion narratives and the arbitrariness of the elements that shape the drama. With regard to the latter, Alabaster seems to be turning away from a Pauline model that emphasizes immediacy and toward an Augustinian model that emphasizes contingency and mediation. The famous "*tolle lege*" scene in the eighth book of the *Confessions* is, of course, anything but some unmediated experience of the divine. As the story goes, Augustine hears a voice, perhaps a child, perhaps chanting or playing a game. Rather than turn toward the voice to see, however, he listens to the injunction: "take up and read." Turning away from the voice, he turns toward the book and then turns to a random page and passage, lighting on the first thing he sees. When that passage speaks to him, he *knows*; at this moment, his turn is—*finally*, readers of the *Confessions* might think—sudden, instantaneous, complete. Augustine's turn is mediated in the first instance by a voice or voices, which do not explicitly speak to or address Augustine. It is crucial to the episode that we do not have anything like direct address; rather, we have an event that requires interpretation. The experience is subsequently mediated not only by the book to which he turns, but also by Augustine's seemingly strange act of bibliomancy, which seems to establish both the contingency of the elements that give shape to this event and the importance of that contingency.

Alabaster's account, likewise, reads as a series of random occurrences. He happens to take up a book, which he happens to take home with him.[34] Setting the scene, he writes that—having returned to his "lodging"—he took the "little book of Mr. William Rainolds" in hand as he sat down at his bedside after supper. Simply to pass the time, he tells us, he "began to read the preface thereof." He had not read "for the space of a quarter of an hour" when it was "as if those squames that fell from St. Paul's bodily eyes at his ... [words missing in manuscript]."[35] One of the things that makes the event come to life *as an event*—both for Alabaster and in the Augustinian tradition—is the ecstatic experience of a fundamentally interpretive or hermeneutic wonder. The affective joy of reading the signature of the divine in the world is a narrative element often deployed; and that joy is a function of discovering the divine not simply in the world but in the minute and seemingly random particulars of one's own life. A crucial aspect

[34] "finding one day a certain English book ... whereupon I took the said book home with me." Alabaster, *Unpublished Works*, 115.
[35] Alabaster, *Unpublished Works*, 118.

150   *Literature and Religious Experience*

of the phenomenology of the "turn" is *recognition*, particularly recognition of self in relation to world, law, god. As Althusser writes, "yes, it really is me."[36] In the Augustinian conversion narrative, there is no hailing, no direct address; one reads the signature of the divine precisely because the elements in question are both contingent and meaning-laden. And one *recognizes* this message or pattern in the contingent elements of one's own idiosyncratic narrative, and thus recognizes the message as addressed *to me*. A call and response in slow and protracted motion, Alabaster's conversion—like Augustine's—is then an intimate and forceful address, one that is received and authenticated in a certain sense via its very lack of immediacy.

In reading the signature of the divine in these contingent elements, of course, one necessarily reads providential design, divine agency. And happening upon the conversion experiences of others emerges as part of this is design; the new convert finds that he or she is part of an iterative pattern. And, on a certain level, this must be so; how else to solve the riddle of a singular event that is at the same time embedded in genre and tradition? If we are to believe the truth of the conversion experience, believe that these are more than writerly exercises in *imitatio*, then there must be some rationale for the ways in which these narratives seem to conform to the expectations of genre. And that rationale—divinity at work in and *through* the lives of men—is written into the genre from Augustine forward. Here we have generic design as the hand of god. Of course, if this formal consistency can be laid at the feet of providential design, it nonetheless points to a paradox at the heart of the Augustinian conversion narrative. If these formal and familiar elements help frame, shape, and mediate the unmediated experience at the heart of the narrative, then there must be some sense in which the unmediated experience is anticipated, expected. Moreover, if it is mediated in such a way that requires—and is authenticated by—an interpretive act, then one would need to know how to read this secret signature, how to hear this implicit and intimate address. And this means that one is in some sense equipped for this sudden and unfathomable turn.

In her attempt to grapple with the experience of the event, Dastur offers a complex account of the phenomenology of surprise. For Dastur, in the first instance, "we can only define" an event as

> what arrives unexpectedly and comes to us by surprise, what descends upon us … The event in the strong sense of the word is therefore always a surprise,

---

[36] Althusser, "Ideological State Apparatuses," 178.

something which takes possession of us in an unforeseen manner, without warning, and which brings us toward an unanticipated future.[37]

To a certain degree, this sounds not unlike other accounts of the event, including that of Badiou. Dastur's surprise, however, can never be absolute because on some level the event "requires the collaboration of the one who obeys" its call, its demand. Key to any phenomenology of the event is the "paradoxical capacity of expecting surprise."[38] Although she does not say this precisely, Dastur's thought here seems to suggest that the paradoxical capacity to expect the unexpected is a condition of possibility of surprise and therefore of the event. In any case, this paradox is crucial to the genre of conversion as it is intrinsic to the complex negotiation of agency and will characteristic of the experiential turn.

A fascinating component of Augustine's turn that distinguishes it from its Pauline antecedent is that Augustine *desires* such a spiritual transformation. One of the striking elements in Augustine's narrative is his repeated *failure* to will himself to turn away from his old life. And this speaks to the strange experience of agency at the heart of conversion as "turning." Looked at in a certain way, the *Confessions* is a trenchant psychological account of what we might think of, following Leslie Farber, as "willing what cannot be willed."[39] And this philosophical problem of the limits of the will bears on the strange phenomenology of the turn. If Augustine's narrative performs the "truth" that the turn cannot be willed, that such a transformation requires more than human agency or "more-than-human" agency, it also gestures to all the ways that the Augustine within the *Confessions* works to create the conditions of his own conversion. In other words, if the conversion itself manifests as a sudden revelation, the path will nonetheless have been laid for this revelation.

Looked at in a certain way, of course, religious practice is often the practice of creating the conditions of and for belief. Althusser's famous description of the workings of ideology—via the material practices of religion—works in precisely this way, of course: "Kneel down, move your lips in prayer, and you will believe." For Althusser, this is the everyday, material experience of ideology's interpellation or address.[40] Althusser is here paraphrasing the famous "wager" episode in the *Pensées* where Blaise Pascal invents modern decision theory to determine whether one should believe in god. The "scandalous" element that

---

[37] Dastur, "Waiting and Surprise," 182.
[38] Dastur, "Waiting and Surprise," 186.
[39] Farber, "Will and Anxiety," 152.
[40] Althusser, "Ideological State Apparatuses," 168.

152 *Literature and Religious Experience*

Althusser takes up is not the so-called wager itself but the ensuing suggestion that—having calculated that it is in one's best interests to believe—one should attempt to induce belief by acting the part, by engaging in the forms of belief.[41] The conditions of and for belief are not simply inscribed into material practices like kneeling, of course, but in all kinds of forms, including narrative and generic forms. The genre of the conversion narrative, for instance, works to create conditions of belief even as it frames and exalts an unconditioned moment outside human will or design. And this strange logic—the *form* of the unexpected—is not simply a philosophical riddle but manifests in and as experience. Often it manifests as the anxiety that Farber suggest attends "willing what cannot be willed." For Augustine, the problem of "willing what cannot be willed" and its attendant anxiety shape his experience before his conversion; for Alabaster, they shape his experience after the turn, when he attempts to establish and sustain what we might call, following Badiou, fidelity to the event.

4

Immediately after his turn, Alabaster begins conjuring possible futures, constructing narratives in which he plays a particular and familiar part:

> And eventimes I imagined my self to ... dispute for the Catholic faith; which I was resolved to defend, even unto death itself; and to suffer most gladly any kind of torture or persecution that man could lay upon me for the same.[42]

He envisions himself heroically defending his faith; as he writes, there was no "cogitation so pleasant and sweet unto me as to imagine myself" called before "the Council, or the Queen herself." And he dreams of suffering for that faith: "many a sweet hour" spent imagining himself "thrust into some dark dungeon with as many chains as I could bear." And when he sees himself in that "dark dungeon" awaiting his fate—suffering, torture, execution—he feeds himself "with the comforts which I conceived I should find there" including "what sonnets and love devices I would make to Christ, about my chains and irons."[43] Here, the generic expectations built into this narrative include the transformation of

---

[41] Pascal, *Pensées and Other Writings*, 152–8. Pascal is more equivocal about the notion that one can come to belief through habituation than Althusser's essay might lead one to believe.

[42] Alabaster, *Unpublished Works*, 120.

[43] Alabaster, *Unpublished Works*, 120.

Turning 153

suffering and fidelity into art, as Alabaster imagines this future self devising prison poetry, sonnets, and love devices addressed to Christ.

While the newly converted Alabaster is impatient for these tribulations to begin, he also longs for time to reflect on his experiential turn and to prepare himself for the public affirmation of his new faith. He prays for and believes he has been granted such an interim, a six-month "space of truce" to make ready.[44] As soon as he returns to Cambridge to enjoy this interim, Alabaster takes certain actions, including breaking off his wedding engagement, a painful ordeal

> for I had loved the party dearly and our friends had mutually agreed to the match, whereupon much discontentment was taken at me both of her friends and my own parents ... [some] affirming that the party was like to die for grief. But I being well assured in conscience that no obligation of necessity remained on my part I overcame at length by Gods assistance the assault.[45]

Having severed the relationship with this party he loved dearly—alienating family and friends in the process—Alabaster moves on to the next item on his itinerary, buying some books: "The next thing I attempted was to furnish myself with" necessary religious texts, "buying so many books" as "seemed sufficient" for the purpose "I had designed."[46] And Alabaster purchases these books because he will embark on a period of reading and reflection. With these meditations, he will prepare himself for the trials he foresees when he presents himself to the world. But he also extends and sustains that long moment of change and—in doing so—attempts to shore up, to bolster, his turn.

One could argue that—in this interim that he has claimed as his—Alabaster is engaged in practices that fortify what Badiou might call fidelity to the event.[47] For Badiou the truth of an event like Paul's conversion or the resurrection of Christ (or the French Revolution) does not have to do with knowledge but with praxis, forms of labor and endeavor that constitute an active commitment both to what has been disclosed in the event and to the consequences of that disclosure. In this six-month interim Alabaster is attempting to live the truth of what happened to him, the truth of his conversion event, even as he prepares himself to live that truth more fully and consequentially upon his declaration of faith and return to the world. He is not only engaged in a certain fidelity

---

[44] Alabaster, *Unpublished Works*, 121. "I made a particular prayer to almightie god, that hee would vouchsafe to spare me one halfe yeare of libertie before I were apprehended, to prepare myself to this combatt by study and reeding." Alabaster, *Unpublished Works*, 120.
[45] Alabaster, *Unpublished Works*, 121.
[46] Alabaster, *Unpublished Works*, 121.
[47] See Badiou, *Being and Event*, especially 232–7.

154 *Literature and Religious Experience*

to the event but also in a kind of training to remain faithful to the event. If Badiou's suggestive language helps us begin to think through the complexity of Alabaster's experience, it can only go so far as that experience does not quite map onto Badiou's conceptions of truth or event.[48] It might be more apposite to turn to another convert, the phenomenologically inclined philosopher Gabriel Marcel. Raised atheist or agnostic, Marcel converted to Catholicism in 1929. His remarkably searching philosophical reflections from that period are concerned with—among other things—commitment and fidelity in relation to time, with what it means to make pledges or promises on behalf of some future self.[49] These concerns would remain at the center of his philosophical project, and like Badiou, Marcel insists that fidelity is praxis.[50]

Alabaster describes this interim before his trials would begin as an idyllic time in which he could walk and think, communing with his god and with his soul:

> I was wont often to walk into the fields alone, and being then summer there I would set me down in certain corn fields, where I could not be seen nor heard of others and here pass the time in conferences between almighty God and my soul.[51]

This time is filled with earnest studies, interrupted periodically by the summer showers of affective irruptions:

> Thus then I passed on partly in studying, partly in praying, partly in solacing my self with cogitations of suffering for Christ stake, which was always the sweetest consolation of all the rest; And when the floods of tears came down upon me, I could do no less but open the gates to let them pass.[52]

Passing the time in these "conferences" between God and soul, Alabaster would "sometimes" do so "with internal meditation uniting my will to god," and "sometimes" do so by "forming and contriving the same meditations into verses of love and affection." He describes the creation of these verses as "hiding" the "fire under ashes."[53] The conceit here is that he is banking the embers of his devotional ardor, preserving it for future use.

---

[48] Apart from anything else, Badiou is concerned with events of a certain scope that have what we might call a world-historical significance.

[49] See Marcel, *Being and Having*, especially 9–153.

[50] For Marcel's phenomenology of fidelity, see *Creative Fidelity* and *Homo Viator*. Helen Tattam usefully situates Marcel's work in relation to philosophical thought on time. See *Time in the Philosophy*. Also see Cain, *Theory of Religious Experience*.

[51] Alabaster, *Unpublished Works*, 122.

[52] Alabaster, *Unpublished Works*, 122.

[53] Alabaster, *Unpublished Works*, 122–3.

Turning

155

This extraordinary image suggests the ways in which Alabaster's fidelity to the event of his conversion has become a project that he takes up. Alabaster does not simply believe that some future self will remain unchanged or insist that that future self remain bound to what he currently wills. Throughout this interim, Alabaster is engaged in what Marcel would call "creative fidelity." Acutely attentive to the flux of experience, Marcel addresses seriously the ways subsequent events can work to render promises and commitments fruitless. Fidelity, for Marcel, is both necessary and impossible. He follows Friedrich Nietzsche in thinking that the capacity to make promises, the ability to bind some future self, marks the human. But he also respects time's ability to render human intention absurd and remains wary of the hubris implicit in the presumption that one's current belief or commitment will carry the day. Thus, fidelity as praxis must be a form of ingenuity, creatively and fluidly responding to an ever-changing world, constantly revisiting and revising the relation between changing circumstances, changing selves, and living commitments. Commitment, for Marcel, "bids me to invent a certain *modus vivendi*."[54] Here, Marcel suggests that we must work to create and sustain ways or forms of life that shape the self in relation to promise and obligation. Of course, *modus vivendi* not only points to way of life generally but also refers idiomatically to a negotiated peace. The remarkable idea here is that one finds a way forward—a form of life—that is somehow a brokered or negotiated peace between urgent present and contingent future. And Alabaster seems to be thinking in precisely these terms, attempting to arrange some accommodation, some rapprochement between the certainties of present passions and an uncertain future that might well resist our claims on it.

Crucially, this is fidelity grounded in doubt. Marcel writes that fidelity "aspires to unconditionality," but it can of course only ever aspire.[55] The impossibility of some absolute, unconditional fidelity then shapes whatever fidelity we find. And it is this tragicomic gap between aspiration and reality that drives what Marcel would call "creative fidelity." When Alabaster writes of banking the embers of his poetic meditations, his hope is that "the reading" of these verses "might afterwards kindle" his "devotion at new time again."[56] Here, we have creative fidelity that does not seek to bind the will but to solicit an emotional response, to create perhaps a Proustian moment that will turn or return that future self to experiences past through an affective call or summons. In creating these verses,

[54] Marcel, *Creative Fidelity*, 162.
[55] Marcel, *Homo Viator*, 133.
[56] Alabaster, *Unpublished Works*, 123.

156   *Literature and Religious Experience*

Alabaster is, in some sense creating the conditions for future reading experiences. Embedded in this strange conceit is a theory of the aesthetic. Alabaster's belief is that the aesthetic form, the living design of his "verses of love and affection" can capture and preserve and transmit this *experience* in such a way that it will "kindle" devotional intensity. Belief, however, may be too strong a word here; it might be more accurate to say that Alabaster *wagers* that his art might bank this ardent experience for some later encounter, some future event.[57]

This is not, however, precisely the strange wager Alabaster makes with himself in relation to his turn. Immediately after addressing his "verses of love and affection" and his hopes for them, Alabaster writes that he "did set some times a certain strife and wager between" his "present affections and future." For its part, his "present" self bets that it can "devise sonnets now and so full of fiery love and flaming ardor towards Christ, that then it should serve for a pattern and sample for the time to come."[58] His future self is—or rather his "future devotions" are— also involved in this wager. And these future devotion "on the contrary part" wager that they can not only "maintain" but also

> increase the heat and vigor of love and affection in me, that when I should come afterwards to read over my former sonnets I might wonder rather at the coldness of them then gather heat by them.[59]

The "present" wagers that it can preserve ardor through art while the "future" scoffs at the presumption and proposes that the fire so preserved will seem cold when compared to the "heat and vigor" of its own "love and affection." The marginal note in the narrative reads "a wager betwixt present and future affections."[60] Alabaster proposes a wager concerning his fidelity to the event of the turn, and he offers these verses as the test. That *motion* is implicit in the experience of the turn is crucial here because, of course, one can always turn back, or turn again. In a way, we have returned to "willing what cannot be willed" but in a different register. This is not—as with Augustine—the inability to will the turn but the inability to will fidelity to the turn. Alabaster will be faithful to the event or not of course; what he gives voice to is intense desire, hope. Despite his bravura, this episode demonstrates how uncertain the future seems to him. And what he stages with both his poetry and his wager is an address; he will

---

[57] Strikingly, Marcel also uses the language of wagering to discuss fidelity; from a certain perspective, he suggests, "all fidelity seems incomprehensible, impracticable, a wager, and scandalous too." *Creative Fidelity*, 163.

[58] Alabaster, *Unpublished Works*, 123.

[59] Alabaster, *Unpublished Works*, 123.

[60] Alabaster, *Unpublished Works*, 123.

Turning 157

hail this future self in the hopes that these affective verses might speak to some Alabaster yet to come, call him in such a way that he will recognize both the call and the self that responds. Or, even better, that he will recognize these banked embers as a weaker or colder version of his current zeal.

In his conversion narrative, Alabaster indicates that these devotional forms have designs not merely on future Alabasters but on others: "And these verses and sonnets I made not only for my own solace, and comfort, but to stir up others also that should read them to some estimation of that which I felt in my self."[61] Ever the scholar-poet, Alabaster quotes pseudo-Dionysius in order to offer a sense of how this desire to "stir up others" engenders (once again) affective knowledge in himself: "for which cause my desire was so extreme ardent to impart this my happiness with others that I felt in me the true force of that St. *Dionysius Ariopagita* saith, *bonum est sui diffusivum*, the nature of goodness is to spread itself to many."[62] This desire to spread the word of his happiness is so strong that he comes to understand the truth of this aphorism via affective force ("felt in me the true force"). There is no way to know who may have been effected by Alabaster's verses during his lifetime or after, how these aesthetic embers might have enkindled others, or how faithful these others might have been to whatever turns the verses engendered. Regardless of what happened in any particular case, these aesthetic forms offer themselves as—among other things—voices that might summon, summons that might elicit recognition; they are addressed to those with ears to hear, and in their address might well create or help to create the conditions that afford hearing.

In the end, Alabaster seems to have lost this strange wager with himself. He would famously become a serial convert, would one way or another find himself turning and turning again. No writings exist—as far as we know at present—addressing these later turns explicitly, and so we cannot know how later versions of Alabaster looked back on this earliest conversion experience. And we cannot know how he felt about that remarkable interim when he endeavored to think his way through the paradoxical experience of the turn, singular and familiar, conventional and unfathomable; when he attempted to feel his way forward through intense certainty and inevitable doubt; when he sought a path that navigated the vagaries of affective ardor and the strange temporalities of the self; when he wagered on the continuity of emotional life and on what writing and literary form might promise or afford.

---

[61] Alabaster, *Unpublished Works*, 123.
[62] Alabaster, *Unpublished Works*, 123.

Bibliography

Ahmed, Sara. *Queer Phenomenology: Orientations, Objects, Others.* Durham, NC: Duke University Press, 2006.

Alabaster, William. *Unpublished Works of William Alabaster.* Edited by Dana Sutton. Salzburg: University of Salzburg, 1997.

Althusser, Louis. "Ideology and Ideological State Apparatuses." In *Lenin and Philosophy and Other Essays*, translated by Ben Brewster, 127–86. London: Monthly Review Press, [1971] 2001.

Augustine. *The Confessions.* Translated by Henry Chadwick. Oxford: Oxford University Press, 1991.

Badiou, Alain. *Being and Event.* Translated by Oliver Feltham. New York: Continuum, 2005.

Badiou, Alain. *Saint Paul: The Foundation of Universalism.* Translated by Ray Brassier. Stanford, CA: Stanford University Press, 2003.

Balibar, Étienne. "Althusser's Dramaturgy and the Critique of Ideology." *differences: A Journal of Feminist Cultural Studies* 26, no. 3 (2015): 1–22.

Butler, Judith. *The Psychic Life of Power: Theories in Subjection.* Stanford, CA: Stanford University Press, 1997.

Cain, Seymour. *Gabriel Marcel's Theory of Religious Experience.* New York: Peter Lang, 1995.

Coldeway, John. "William Alabaster's *Roxana*: Some Textual Considerations." In *Acta Conventus Neo-Latini Bononiensis*, edited by R. J. Schoeck, 413–19. Binghamton: State University of New York Press, 1985.

Coutts, Eleanor. "The Life and Works of William Alabaster, 1568–1640." Unpublished PhD dissertation, University of Wisconsin, 1956.

Dastur, Françoise. "Phenomenology of the Event: Waiting and Surprise." *Hypatia* 15, no. 4 (Autumn 2000): 178–89.

Davis, Isabel. "Calling: Langland, Gower, and Chaucer on Saint Paul." *Studies in the Age of Chaucer* 34 (2012): 53–97.

Farber, Leslie. "Will and Anxiety." *Salmagundi* 123 (Summer 1999): 141–60.

Kearney, James. *The Incarnate Text: Imagining the Book in Reformation England.* Philadelphia: University of Pennsylvania Press, 2009.

Kearney, James. "'Tasting the Gospel': Transformative Reading and Textual Intimacy among Early English Reformers." In *The Aura of the Word in the Age of Print*, edited by Jessica Buskirk and Samuel Mareel. New York: Routledge, 2016.

Marcel, Gabriel. *Being and Having.* Translated by Katharine Farrer. Westminster, UK: Dacre Press, 1949.

Marcel, Gabriel. *Creative Fidelity.* Translated by Robert Rosthal. New York: Farrar, Strauss and Company, 1964.

Marcel, Gabriel. *Homo Viator: Introduction to a Metaphysic of Hope.* Translated by Emma Crawford. New York: Harper, 1962.

Marotti, Arthur. *Religious Ideology and Cultural Fantasy*. Notre Dame, IN: University of Notre Dame Press, 2005.

Morrison, Karl F. *Understanding Conversion*. Charlottesville: University Press of Virginia, 1992.

Murray, Molly. *The Poetics of Conversion in Early Modern English Literature*. Cambridge: Cambridge University Press, 2009.

O'Connell, Michael. "'The Elisaeis' of William Alabaster." *Studies in Philology* 76, no. 5 (1979): 1–12.

Pascal, Blaise. *Pensées and Other Writings*. Translated by Honor Levi. Oxford: Oxford University Press, 1995.

Smith, Matthew, and Julia Reinhard Lupton, eds. *Face-to-Face in Shakespearean Drama: Ethics, Performance, Philosophy*. Edinburgh: Edinburgh University Press, 2019.

Spenser, Edmund. *Colin Clouts Come Home Againe*. In *The Shorter Poems*, edited by Richard McCabe, 518–62. London: Penguin Books, 1999.

Story, G. M., and Helen Gardner, eds. *The Sonnets of William Alabaster*. Oxford: Oxford University Press, 1959.

Tattam, Helen. *Time in the Philosophy of Gabriel Marcel*. London: Modern Humanities Research Association, 2013.

9

Guidance: Understanding Providence in George MacDonald's Fiction

Mark Knight

All men must make a kind of clothes
　　To shield their hearts from frost;
And circumstance is God's great web
　　To clothe the trembling host:
Shall we, because our thread is fast,
　　Think all our labour lost?[1]

References to a thread that guides or holds us can be found across a number of works by the Scottish writer George MacDonald (1824–1905). In the opening chapter of *Phantastes* (1858), his faerie romance for adults, the thread is just one of the tropes the protagonist, Anodos, reaches for to describe his anticipation of what awaits him in his late father's bureau: "Perhaps, like a geologist, I was about to turn up to the light some of the buried strata of the human world. ... Perhaps I was to learn how my father ... had woven his web of story. ... Perhaps I was to find only the records of lands and moneys."[2] MacDonald's characters and narrators experiment with multiple metaphors in other works, too, as they test the capacity of language to describe life experiences, but the thread seems to be of particular interest to MacDonald. It is woven into the plot of his novel for children, *The Princess and the Goblin* (1872), and here, in the epigraph I have selected for the start of this essay, it introduces various theological possibilities regarding the interaction of human and divine agency. If the thread signifies the means of finding our way safely through the complex maze of life, inspired by the help Ariadne gives Theseus in his encounter with the Minotaur, then its

---

[1] MacDonald, "An Old Sermon," 515.
[2] MacDonald, *Phantastes*, 43.

162   *Literature and Religious Experience*

function in the epigraph seems to be to emphasize divine direction (the web of circumstance) of our most basic labor. But this is not the only way of reading the epigraph. MacDonald's reference to the thread seems more concerned with weaving than Greek myth, in which case the trope encourages us to think of a guiding thread, the following of which enables human agency and our subsequent contribution to the warp and woof that clothe us. This second and more likely option makes MacDonald's final question rhetorical, with the fast(ened) thread being the very thing that makes our labor possible. But there are further complications before we settle on this reading. Is the thread secure or stuck? Should we view the web as a home or a trap? And is the trembling host the person who needs clothing or the consecrated bread of the Eucharist (and, by extension, Christ himself)? Not everyone who writes about MacDonald seems interested in such religious complexities, and there are certainly other productive ways of thinking about the threads that guide many of his protagonists on their journeys.[3] Yet the theological valences of the guiding thread are instructive, for our reading of MacDonald, and, more significantly for the purposes of this essay, the ways in which we think about our experience of providence.

Introducing the richness of his subject, David Fergusson explains in his book on providence that the term "refers literally to divine foresight and provision but its historic meanings are broader—these encompass purpose, direction, rule and vocation."[4] To talk about providence is to think about God's interaction with the world at all levels, corporate and personal, extraordinary and commonplace, macro and micro. The doctrine has consequences for how we think about prayer, suffering, agency, salvation, ecology, economics, and our narrative "sense of an ending," to name just a few affected areas.[5] Our view of providence might sustain the hope of ecological transformation and encourage us to find ways of participating in that work, or it might lead to resignation that our world is as it is meant to be; it might prompt those who pray to intercede in the hope of changing God's mind, or it might encourage a set of internal reflections that

---

[3] Other suggestive possibilities, and the lack of critical attention to anything explicitly theological, are evident in Albert D. Pionke's summary of three approaches to *Phantastes* in modern criticism: "First, MacDonald's overt investment in the sometimes-pathless, sometimes-upward-tending trajectory of his protagonist's manliness has invited numerous psychoanalytic readings of the novel" (22); "a second group of critics ... have sought to make sense of Anodos's twenty-one-day dream of development in Fairy Land by tracing MacDonald's ample borrowings from earlier writers" (22); and a third group have argued that the text "is constructed symmetrically around Anodos's visit to the library in the Fairy Queen's palace" (23). See "The Art of Manliness," 21–37.

[4] Fergusson, *The Providence of God*, 1.

[5] Kermode, *Sense of an Ending*. For more recent accounts of theology, literature and eschatology, see Fiddes, *The Promised End*; Kriner, *The Future of the Word*; and Tate, *Apocalyptic Fiction*.

Guidance   163

attempt to align one's mindset with the predetermined purposes of God. Given the sheer number of issues at stake, it is no surprise that theologies of providence vary enormously in the Christian tradition. Proceeding from different starting points and looking to various foci, these theologies end up in radically different places: accounts that insist on God's sovereignty, those more interested in trying to think about how providence accommodates the agency of others, those which see God himself as a participant in the temporality of existence, and so on. Aware of this range of possibilities, Fergusson insists early on in his study of providence that "despite some popular misconceptions, the doctrine of providence is not a Calvinist franchise."[6] It is an important observation, and one that should stop us from presuming that the Calvinist understanding of double predestination, in which some are elected for salvation and others for damnation, is a synonym for providence. Those who situate themselves within the Calvinist tradition reveal a great deal of variety in their writing on providence, and they are concerned with much more than one's destiny in the afterlife. Furthermore, these debates are only a small cross-section of a much larger set of conversations about providence, informed by numerous theologians with little or no connection to the thought of John Calvin.

MacDonald's understanding of providence was informed by Calvinism, both in his early exposure to Reformed theology and in the formal Congregationalist education he received as a student at Highbury Theological College after his undergraduate work at Aberdeen. Yet MacDonald's relationship with Calvinism was not straightforward. Although "the mature George MacDonald thought of himself as someone who had rejected Calvinism, ... [a point] often emphasized in secondary sources, ... it is important to grasp what precisely is and is not meant by this."[7] The aspects of Calvinism that MacDonald rejected included the idea that some individuals were destined to endure eternal punishment in hell and, more generally, the emphasis on a transactional judicial language that follows from thinking so heavily about God's sovereignty. MacDonald's theology underwent various shifts over the course of his life, as one would expect from any religious believer, but his reservations about aspects of Calvinism were more constant. MacDonald's questioning of elements in this tradition played a part in his short-lived tenure as a Congregationalist minister in Arundel; later, in his subsequent career as a writer, he protested repeatedly against unyielding instances of Calvinist doctrine and practice. That said, it would be misleading

---

[6] Fergusson, *The Providence of God*, 1.
[7] Larsen, *George MacDonald*, 101.

164   *Literature and Religious Experience*

to overstate MacDonald's break from Calvinism. Timothy Larsen has noted how the author continued to be invited to preach in a range of churches over the course of his life, some of them Calvinist, and Larsen also points out that "one of the most striking features of his [MacDonald's] theology is its robust, prominent, unflinching belief in divine providence."[8] There is, of course, a danger, here, of slipping back into the idea that providence belongs to Calvinism, but it does seem to be the case that MacDonald's particular theological upbringing shaped the role that providence went on to play in his thinking and imagination.

Writing in *The Miracles of Our Lord* (1870), MacDonald insists,

> But to the reader of my choice I do say that I see no middle course between believing that every alleviation of pain, every dawning of hope across the troubled atmosphere of the spirit, every case of growing well again, is the doing of God, or that there is no God at all—none at least in whom *I* could believe.[9]

Articulated in this short propositional form, the doctrine of providence seems stark and uncompromising, even if we add in the caveat that MacDonald thought his view was compatible with the agency of the created order.[10] The starkness only increases when we consider MacDonald's refusal to think of suffering as an exception to this rule. Although MacDonald considered suffering to be the consequence of a fallen world rather than God's initial goal for creation, he still thought the purposes of God could and should be discerned in such experiences.[11] Suffering, for MacDonald, offered an opportunity for spiritual development, and he thought that God's hand could be seen in it. It is a line of thought with a long history in the Christian tradition going back to the second-century Irenaeus, who sought to find a pedagogy of pain amid the early Christian experiences of persecution. The belief in suffering's developmental possibilities explains why MacDonald was so keen to plot instances of suffering eschatologically, not in the sense that our current struggles are offset by a later state of happiness in heaven

---

[8] Larsen, *George MacDonald*, 101. While I am not convinced by Larsen's account of how MacDonald sought to sabotage his career as a church minister, I do think the closer investigation of MacDonald's experiences at Arundel is helpful, and I am grateful to Larsen for documenting some of MacDonald's continuing connections with Calvinist communities. See Larsen, *George MacDonald*, 97.

[9] MacDonald, *Miracles of Our Lord*, 33.

[10] "He [God] begins with the building of the stage itself, and that stage is a world—a universe of worlds. He makes the actors, and they do not act—they *are* their part. He utters them into the visible to work out their life—his drama .... Instead of writing his lyrics, he sets his birds and his maidens a-singing." MacDonald, "The Imagination," 47.

[11] MacDonald's debt to Calvin is visible here: "In the very bitterness of tribulations we ought to recognise the kindness and mercy of our Father, since even then he ceases not to further our salvation. For he afflicts, not that he may ruin or destroy, but rather that he may deliver us from the condemnation of the world." Calvin, *Institutes of the Christian Religion*, book 3, chapter 8, section 6.

but in the sense that our momentary experiences take on a different hue when they are interpretable within a longer redemptive narrative. This eschatological thinking informs the advice given in *At the Back of the North Wind* (1871), when Diamond's struggle to come to terms with the cries of those who have drowned at sea is met with the following answer from the mysterious North Wind: "I will tell you how I am able to bear it, Diamond: I am always hearing, through every noise, through all the noise I am making myself even, the sound of a far-off song."[12] Although we may find the idea of melodious music accompanying and reworking the cries of the dying to be grating, North Wind's answer repeats a line of thought that MacDonald writes about on other occasions. At the end of *Phantastes*, for instance, Anodos insists that "I know that good is coming to me—that good is always coming, though few have at all times the simplicity and the courage to believe it. What we call evil, is the only and best shape, which, for the person and his condition at the time, could be assumed by the best good."[13]

Observing how this belief in the value of suffering was a recurring theme in MacDonald's work, Larsen sees a degree of amelioration in the fact that suffering was a fundamental part of MacDonald's own experience: "A man of sorrows and acquainted with grief, George MacDonald was forced to endure the deaths of four of his children, of his wife, and even of a granddaughter."[14] Sorrow and joy sound together throughout the personal correspondence of the MacDonald family, and it is more acceptable, perhaps, to hear someone talk positively about suffering when their words are not so much bitter medicine for others as the fruit of difficult personal experience. Even so, MacDonald's understanding of providence remains a stumbling block for many modern readers, including those, like me, who share many of his Christian commitments. Even if our own experience of suffering is limited, we can still be acutely aware of the severity of suffering experienced by others; and in our Western secular age, at least, we often no longer possess the conceptual framework required to imagine such events as anything other than the result of chance and/or human activity.[15] Yet there are still good reasons to consider what MacDonald has to say about providence, partly because this statement is not his final word on the matter, and partly because his more uncomfortable observations can be suggestive

---

[12] MacDonald, *At the Back*, 97.
[13] MacDonald, *Phantastes*, 273.
[14] Larsen, *George MacDonald*, 105.
[15] For Talal Asad, the consequence of this new secular framework for thinking about suffering is a desire to minimize pain: "A crucial point about pain, however, is that it enables the secular idea that 'history-making' and 'self-empowerment' can progressively replace pain by pleasure—or at any rate, by the search for what pleases one." Asad, *Formations of the Secular*, 68.

166   *Literature and Religious Experience*

for our thinking about theology—a prompt to reflect on areas that we might ignore otherwise. As MacDonald remarks elsewhere, "repose is not the end of education; its end is a noble unrest, an ever renewed awakening from the dead, a ceaseless questioning of the past for the interpretation of the future."[16] Put simply, MacDonald knows the grit involved in trusting providence, and his unfashionable belief in providence can still prove disconcertingly instructive, even if we do not wish to follow him in every path that it takes.

It is not surprising that MacDonald's reflections on suffering should experience difficulties. Problems arise for anyone who tries to offer an explanation for evil, hence the repeated failure of theodicies on both a theological and affective level.[17] We might say something similar about all talk of God, which is quickly stretched to breaking point when too much strain is placed on an isolated term or metaphor. This insight is at the heart of the historic balance between the cataphatic and apophatic in Christian thought, and MacDonald was similarly aware of the limits of theological language.[18] This goes some way to explaining why he tended to prefer literature, both poetry and prose, over doctrine as a means of thinking theologically. He read widely across the literary tradition, and his understanding of providence was informed by literary theologians such as Dante Alighieri, George Herbert, John Milton, John Bunyan, and Samuel Taylor Coleridge more than it was by systematicians.[19] According to Stephen Prickett, one of MacDonald's most influential modern interpreters, this literary theology is a legacy of Romanticism and its interest in the inner world of experience, the language used to describe this experience, and the resulting concern with ideas of creativity and development.[20] It is certainly true that MacDonald's reading was refracted through many of the Romantic influences that Prickett traces, but it is also worth remembering that an older tradition is at play when MacDonald looks to literary authors to help him think theologically: many of those MacDonald read predated Romanticism and had their own reasons for wanting to think about God through a profusion of literary forms.[21]

---

[16] MacDonald, "The Imagination," 1.
[17] For a useful introduction to the problems of theodicy, see Trakakis, "Anti-Theodicy," 124–44.
[18] A good collection of theological essays on the limits of language can be found in Davies and Turner, *Silence and the Word*.
[19] "The vastness of MacDonald's exposure to British literature is evident in his book *England's Antiphon* [1868], in which he takes the reader on a tour of six hundred years of poetry. He offers a theological context for this overview, with central focus on worship." Dearborn, *Baptized Imagination*, 26.
[20] See Prickett, Romanticism and Religion. He relays how "poetry is, for MacDonald, a *theological instrument*: a means of vision whereby opposites may be held simultaneously in focus" (86–7).
[21] A further reason for caution about the weight we give to Romanticism when understanding MacDonald's theology is to resist the idea that more literary approaches to theology are part of a modern secularizing arc. This is not Prickett's position, but it can be heard elsewhere, from the crucial role of Romanticism in Charles Taylor's narrative of our secular age to the still-influential argument of

Guidance

167

In some ways, there are a relatively stable set of theological concerns across the literary forms employed by MacDonald. Martin Dubois is right to insist that the sermons which are so "prominent in MacDonald's realistic fiction" are also a feature "in later fairy tales and fantasies … [suggesting] that these bear a closer relation to his preaching than has usually been thought."[22] And we might also consider how references to providence are evident in both MacDonald's realism and fantasy. At the same time, the explorations of providence are more limited in the realist novels, with MacDonald struggling to balance realism's requirement for explanatory details and internal cohesion with a depiction of providence that acknowledges the doctrine's mystery and complexity. Realism does not have to be straightforward or forthcoming. It is a form of writing that can hint, imply, and leave matters vague, as Daniel Wright has argued, and, as John Plotz reminds us, realism generated its own formal experiments as the nineteenth century went on.[23] But when plot lines emerge in the nineteenth century in a way that bears a recognizable relationship to the Christian narrative, they can sometimes seem trite, forced, and clumsily didactic. This is a danger to which MacDonald is prone: although his realist fiction differs from that of many of his religious contemporaries, one can still see why Ellen Wood complained that he had a "direct religious lesson to convey [in *Guild Court* (1867)] and works the thread of his caricature … directly in the web of his story."[24] By contrast, the genre of fantasy offered MacDonald greater theological freedom because it allowed what his much-loved Novalis called "a vision without coherence. An ensemble of wonderful things and events."[25] *Phantastes* contains a great deal of

---

M. H. Abrams that Romanticism naturalized a prior supernaturalism. In each case, there is a failure to see how elements of Romanticism, subjectivity and aesthetics particularly, can also be understood theologically, One consequence of the failure to see these theological possibilities is the repeated idea in some critical circles, inspired by the work of Robert Lee Wolff, that MacDonald is a doubting skeptic. Whatever weight we give to the influence of Romanticism on MacDonald, it is worth acknowledging the centrality of faith to his life and writing. The point was widely recognized by his contemporaries, from those, like John Ruskin, who sought his spiritual counsel, to the claim made by a Mr Hunter in the introduction to one of his public lectures, that MacDonald had "Christianized Christianity." George MacDonald, Letter to Louisa, September 17, 1890, in the Beinecke Manuscript Library, Yale, George MacDonald Collection, General MSS 103, Box 4, Folder 169.

[22] Dubois, "Sermon and Story," 577, 582.

[23] See Wright, *Bad Logic*, especially "Chapter 4. George Eliot's Vagueness"; and Plotz, *Semi-Detached*. For a contemporary example of an author successfully using a broadly realist frame to explore providence, see the novels of Marilynne Robinson.

[24] Wood, "Our Log-Book," 77. Given Wood's own propensity for didactic writing, there is a certain irony in her complaint.

[25] This quotation from Novalis is one of the epigraphs that MacDonald uses to orientate his readers in *Phantastes*. On a more general point, it would be wrong to make a hard division between MacDonald's realism and fantasy. Sections of the fantasy writing reads more like domestic realism, as in the latter stages of *At the Back of the North Wind*, and there are fairy tales in realist texts such as *Adela Cathcart* (1864). Commenting on the realist texts, G. K. Chesterton writes that "all of the inanimate objects that are the stage properties of the story retain the nameless glamour which they

168   *Literature and Religious Experience*

signifying detail, but the text is relieved of the pressure to offer a full explanation, in part, because of its resistance to a collapse into allegory: "It is no use trying to account for things in Fairy Land; and one who travels there soon learns to forget the very idea of doing so, and takes everything as it comes; like a child, who, being in a chronic condition of wonder, is surprised at nothing."[26]

Anodos's description of the attitude that fantasy cultivates and requires stands in contrast to the demystifying efforts of some of those who write about nineteenth-century fantasy and related areas. I am thinking specifically of the subfield of children's literature, where Jack Zipes and others have written extensively about the ideologies of fairy stories.[27] But we can see a related methodological emphasis in other criticism on the period, in books that focus on an area of fantasy, such as Molly Clark Hillard's *Spellbound: The Fairy Tale and the Victorians* (2014), and in works such as John Kucich's *Imperial Masochism: British Fiction, Fantasy and Social Class* (2006), which take up aspects of fantasy in the context of a wider critique. Although ideology is present in all types of literature, demystifying it seems to feel especially pressing for critics who write on fantasy, presumably because the strangeness of the genre compels us to try and make sense of what we read. To be clear, ideological criticism is valuable, and getting beneath or behind the appearances of fairyland can be important. I do not want to repeat the mistake of my namesake in *Phantastes*, the knight who blindly admires the worshippers clothed in white robes and is only saved when someone reveals what is really going on and realizes that the object of worship is a wolf that devours its worshippers. But suspicion can start to suffocate our reading practice when it becomes too pervasive, as Rita Felski and others have noted.[28] Anodos registers a similar concern in *Phantastes* when, overwhelmed by his shadow and succumbing to its influence, he starts to think that "in a land like this, with

---

    have in a literal fairy-tale. The staircase in *Robert Falconer* is as much of a magical ladder as the staircase in *The Princess and the Goblin*." G. K. Chesterton "Introduction," in MacDonald, *George MacDonald and His Wife*, 11.

[26] MacDonald, *Phantastes*, 67.

[27] Although Zipes sees MacDonald as a reformer, his reading of the Scottish author is still focused on ideology:

> No matter what form his writing took, MacDonald was bent on spreading his socio-religious convictions to large audiences. ... Like Dickens, he wanted to expose the deplorable material conditions and unjust social relations in England .... However, he never argued for a radical transformation of the hierarchical structure of society and government. Influenced by his agrarian upbringing, his politics were more inclined to take the form of safeguarding the natural rights and autonomy of individuals. (Zipes, *Fairy Tales and the Art of Subversion*, 103)

    Zipes's legacy can be seen in many of the works that appear in the Children's Literature and Culture book series published by Routledge.

[28] Felski, *The Limits of Critique*.

Guidance 169

so many illusions everywhere, I need his [the shadow's] aid to disenchant the things around me. He does away with all appearances, and shows me things in their true colour and form."[29] Left unchecked, the work of demystification can lead to the opposite of the illumination it promises, stopping Anodos (and his readers) from seeing and appreciating the world around them at all.

Contrary to what ideologically dominated criticism might lead us to believe, Anodos's wonder at the world around him does not stop him from questioning it, even more so after his visit to the library and his experience of becoming the things that he reads.[30] Yet the questioning is accompanied by an acute awareness of the limits of his knowledge. Anodos's reading of the library's fairy tales make a significant contribution here, as he realizes the extent to which his reproduction of them are representations that "must resemble translations from a rich and powerful language" into a "mean and half-articulate speech."[31] The lack of an omniscient narrator in *Phantastes* to offer additional explanation helps normalize the gaps in Anodos's understanding and models his intellectual humility as an appropriate response to the phenomena he experiences. And the use of stories within stories puts narrative at the center of our efforts to think about providence and grasp some of its threads.

Aware of the need to distinguish this humility from a blind acceptance of mystery that can become stifling and oppressive, MacDonald repeatedly invites readers to consider the source of the things they do not understand. The vague "Something" that "compels [Anodos] to go on" is never finally identified, and it is not the only thing that MacDonald leaves unexplained.[32] Yet there are hints that MacDonald is thinking about the Holy Spirit, arguably the most underdeveloped area of Christian theology in the whole of the nineteenth century and a doctrine with important implications for the way we understand providence. Some of the pneumatological references in *Phantastes* take the form of a Romantic and Platonic commitment to the primacy of Spirit, but others take on a more specifically Christian character. The woman who guides Anodos and fills him with an "unknown longing" recalls the feminized Wisdom described in Proverbs 9, an influential biblical passage that Christian readers have historically

---

[29] MacDonald, *Phantastes*, 117.
[30] The library scene can be found in ch. 11 of *Phantastes*. MacDonald's enthusiasm for questioning the world around him may provide a further explanation for his disagreement with Calvin's version of God's sovereignty. "Despite its pastoral benefits, Calvin's doctrine has its practical downside. In the face of life's fragility, it has the dubious effect of supressing complaint or questioning" (Fergusson, *The Providence of God*, 90).
[31] MacDonald, *Phantastes*, 148.
[32] MacDonald, *Phantastes*, 107.

170   *Literature and Religious Experience*

understood as referring to the Holy Spirit.[33] In the books of the New Testament, the Holy Spirit fulfills a similar role to the woman in MacDonald's tale, a figure who preserves, comforts, and guides individuals into all truth. The association appears to be present in Anodos's thinking as well, although it is not identified explicitly: "When the thought of the blessedness I experienced after my death in Fairy Land is too high for me to lay hold upon it and hope in it, I often think of the wise woman in the cottage, and of her solemn assurance that she knew something too good to be told."[34]

A further sign that the Holy Spirit is the one who animates the fantastic world of *Phantastes* can be found when the woman saves Anodos from the Ash tree. Her voice reminds him "of the sound of a gentle wind," a description that recalls the best-known symbol of the Holy Spirit in Christian theology.[35] It is an idea that MacDonald returns to elsewhere, again most notably in *At the Back of the North Wind*. There, the more sustained exploration of this biblical metaphor moves beyond gentleness to possibilities that are "quite impossible for me to describe," possibilities that are not reducible to some simple equation with the Holy Spirit, even though that link is striking.[36] North Wind's movements in this scene seem wild and untamed; they present to Diamond as bordering on the capricious, without finally undermining his confidence in her intrinsic kindness. Amid the storm, the form of North Wind is likened to a wave crashing into rocks—she "was much wilder, and twisted and shot and curled and dodged and clashed and raved ten times more madly than anything else in creation exception human passions." The choice of language here seems designed to recall the account of creation in Genesis, where the "Spirit of God moved upon the face of the waters."[37] It is an allusion that can help us understand how Diamond can register the chaos but still find comfort in the knowledge that he was "sheltered … by North Wind's arm and bosom."[38] And in selecting this maternal image, MacDonald gives us further reason to keep the biblical conception of the Holy Spirit in mind, without compelling us to make this association.

The ill-defined connection between North Wind and the Holy Spirit is theologically appropriate given the elusiveness of the person of the Holy Spirit in the Christian tradition. Whereas talk of the Father and of the Son offers a clearer language for imagining God, at least on the surface, the language theologians

---

[33] MacDonald, *Phantastes*, 45.
[34] MacDonald, *Phantastes*, 272.
[35] MacDonald, *Phantastes*, 72.
[36] MacDonald, *At the Back*, 95.
[37] Gen. 1:2.
[38] MacDonald, *At the Back*, 95.

Guidance 171

have at their disposal to describe the person and work of the Spirit is more limited. This is no accident, with the language of the Scriptures—"the wind bloweth where it listeth, and thou hearest the sound thereof, but canst not tell whence it cometh, and whither it goes"; "the Spirit itself maketh intercession for us with groanings which cannot be uttered"—setting the tone for subsequent theological reflection.[39] For Robert Jenson, this hiddenness has something to do with the way in which "God the Spirit is the perfecting Freedom that animates creation."[40] Jenson is alert to the risk of turning the Spirit into an operative principle rather than one of three triune persons, and keen, too, to remind us how, in Christian theology, the Father and the Son also participate in the work of creation. But he recognizes, as well, that in contrast to the Father and the Son, the references to the Spirit in the biblical tradition conceive of the Spirit almost exclusively in terms of God's ongoing activity, and it this movement and process that leads to some of the representational challenges.

Grappling with the question of how God's activity in the world through his Spirit might be represented, MacDonald makes repeated use of simile in his description of North Wind, as if to draw readers' attention to the insufficiency of the language being used:

> Her voice was like the bass of a deep organ, without the groan in it; like the most delicate of violin tones without the wail in it; like the most glorious of falling water without the clatter and clash in it: it was like all of them and none of them—all of them without their faults, each of them without its peculiarity: after all, it was more like his mother's voice than anything else in the world.[41]

The appeal here to music is noteworthy. Because music is the most nonrepresentational of all the art forms, it is better suited to exploring those aspects of God, and life more generally, that exceed physical description. Jeremy Begbie insists that "the world of music is capable of yielding highly effective ways of addressing and moving beyond some of the intractable theological aporias that modernity has bequeathed to us," and this capability extends to recording the providential activity of the Spirit.[42] Among the texts by MacDonald where this is most apparent is *Phantastes*. There is the moment when Anodos focuses on the effect of the woman's song rather than the song itself—"My whole frame quivered with joy, surprise, and the sensation of the unforeseen. Like a living

---

[39] Jn 3:8; Rom. 8:26.
[40] Jenson, *Systematic Theology*, 25.
[41] MacDonald, *At the Back*, 90.
[42] Begbie, *Music, Modernity, and God*, 1.

172   *Literature and Religious Experience*

soul, like an incarnation of Nature, the song entered my prison house."[43] And, later on, there is his more ambitious attempt to talk about the song itself, using anticipatory language that hints at the purpose of God's providential activity without finally putting that meaning into words: "As I lay, with my eyes closed, I began to listen to the sound of the leaves overhead. At first, they made sweet inarticulate music alone; but, by-and-by, the sound seemed to begin to take shape and to be gradually moulding itself into words."[44]

Music is not the only resource available to MacDonald as he explores an understanding of providence that is both tangible and beyond our reach. Once again, the form of fantasy proves useful, allowing MacDonald to take up more representational metaphors and adapt the properties of physical matter as required. In *The Princess and the Goblin*, this adaption results in a thread that is literalized at some points and left metaphorical at others:

> It was indeed very pretty stuff. There was a good bunch of it on the distaff attached to the spinning-wheel, and in the moonlight it shone like—what shall I say it was like? It was not white enough for silver—yes, it was like silver, but shone grey rather than white, and glittered only a little. And the thread the old lady drew out from it was so fine that Irene could hardly see it.[45]

I am struck here by the question of why MacDonald makes such efforts to describe something he considers unrepresentable. Might an answer lie in MacDonald's awareness that the thread, like providence more generally, requires moments of visibility if it is to serve any purpose in our thought? The workings of God may be unknowable, with the unpredictable appearances of the thread in *The Princess and the Goblin* serving to heighten the feeling of disorientation that accompanies our efforts to understand these workings, but if the concept of providence is to have any bearing on the theological choices we make, it needs some level of visibility, even if the threads of meaning are never properly in our grasp.

Like so much of MacDonald's other language for thinking about providence, the thread never loses its mystical qualities. In making this observation, I am aware how my own use of the metaphor meets another potential breaking point: I do not mean to suggest that a thread's constituent strands can be separated into the known and unknown, nor do I wish to imply that the moments where the thread becomes visible brings the full workings of providence into view. There is

---

[43] MacDonald, *Phantastes*, 242.
[44] MacDonald, *Phantastes*, 272.
[45] MacDonald, *The Princess*, 62.

good reason why MacDonald moves between metaphors when he explores the topic of providence. It is in keeping with the polyphonic approach to providence that Fergusson calls for in his study, an approach that can mobilize a multiplicity of metaphors, concepts and theological resources without asking too much of any of them.[46] As Fergusson explains, even those metaphors that initially seem amenable to constructive theological thought about providence run into difficulty. This is the case with music, for instance, which risks suggesting that "everything in creation contributes to an overall harmony. The danger here is of transposing moral and religious objections to suffering into artistic depictions of the shadow in the painting or the discordant note in the music which comprise a richer and more poignant performance."[47] And it can be a problem with the thread, when the fineness that was meant to suggest the limits of our knowledge is also read as a sign of the precarity of God's salvific work.[48]

In contrast to the problems I observed in MacDonald's propositional comments on providence, his literary explorations are better able to "concede the speculative limits of Christian theology, and to acknowledge its practical character."[49] While all literature is freed from the need to adhere to propositional formulations of theology that try and lay claim to orthodoxy, fantasy's open break from the constraints of reality gives it license to explore those theological truths that most obviously exceed our ability to understand them.[50] Providential language breaks down in books such as *Phantastes*, as it does in all theological writing, but the ensemble quality of MacDonald's faerie romance directs us to expect that this should be so. We are, after all, reading a "vision without coherence," so it is only to be expected that the text's theological insight should be partial and fragmentary. Crucially, though, the limitations of language

---

[46] Questions of language are just one part of Fergusson's study. For example, he emphasizes the need for theologies of providence to be less dependent on the model of a Father who asserts his will and more willing to think about the workings of providence via the Son and the Spirit.

> To put it another way, the work of providence tends historically to have been appropriate to the first person of the Trinity, with too little attention given to the enhancement of providence by the work of the Son and Spirit, whom Irenaeus described as the two hands of God in the economy of creation and salvation. Those two hands have not feature sufficiently in standard accounts with their exclusive focus on the sovereign will and rule of God as Father. (*The Providence of God*, 10)

[47] Fergusson, *The Providence of God*, 315.
[48] While that precarity is embraced by some theologians, it was firmly rejected by MacDonald.
[49] Fergusson, *The Providence of God*, 342.
[50] Debates about the limits and failures of theological language have been prominent since the second half of the twentieth century, beginning with Thomas Altizer's "death of God" theology in the 1960s, continuing with the linguistic turn in continental philosophy, and further developed in work by and conversations between thinkers such as John Caputo, Jacques Derrida, Kevin Hart, and Gianni Vattimo.

become an opportunity for further exploration rather than a barrier to action or an excuse for not thinking about providence at all. Anodos does not fully understand the worlds that he enters, but he is still required to note the qualities he finds there and act accordingly.[51] In making this distinction between narrative and proposition, I am cognizant of the larger and more involved debate in the late twentieth century between two different ways of doing theology.[52] Whatever we might think about that debate more generally, literary narrative offers a powerful account of providence, particularly when it is conveyed in a fantastical and eclectic form. That strange form is well suited to our experience of the world, which rarely proceeds in a linear and clear fashion, and the speculative nature of fantasy writing can risk insights and possibilities that otherwise seem prohibited. In Christian theology, providence is not a mechanical or generalizable account of the way the universe works, but the particular and strange story of God's action and our experiences of it. When that experience runs into difficulty or seems incomprehensible, as it inevitably does, the speculative mode integral to literary narrative can help stimulate the faith needed to carry on making "a kind of clothes" and not "think all our labour lost."

---

[51] Vernon White suggests, not uncritically, that a good deal of modern theology sees

> semiology as a replacement for all these hard questions about causality. Recognizing the reality of sign-making is, at root, the suggestion that events can always convey another transcendent meaning while retaining their empirical integrity. ... The underlying appeal here is to a radical category of transcendence in which divine action does not compete at all with empirical causation, and so there is no need to show how they relate. (*Purpose and Providence*, 110–11)

The focus on narrative that I am arguing for here makes that appeal to radical transcendence more difficult without preventing it altogether: we are encouraged to make sense of the story before us, even though we know that there may be other chapters as yet unread.

[52] For a more detailed consideration of narrative theology, see the work of Hans Frei, George Lindbeck, and Gerard Loughlin.

Bibliography

Asad, Talal. *Formations of the Secular: Christianity, Islam, Modernity*. Stanford, CA: Stanford University Press, 2003.

Begbie, Jeremy. *Music, Modernity, and God: Essays in Listening*. Oxford: Oxford University Press, 2013.

Calvin, John. *Institutes of the Christian Religion*. Edited by Henry Beveridge. Grand Rapids, MI: Eerdmans, 1989.

Davies, Oliver, and Denys Turner, eds. *Silence and the Word: Negative Theology and Incarnation*. Cambridge: Cambridge University Press, 2002.

Dearborn, Kerry. *Baptized Imagination: The Theology of George MacDonald*. Burlington, VA: Ashgate, 2006.

Dubois, Martin. "Sermon and Story in George MacDonald." *Victorian Literature and Culture* 43 (2015): 577–87.

Felski, Rita. *The Limits of Critique*. Chicago: University of Chicago Press, 2015.

Fergusson, David. *The Providence of God: A Polyphonic Approach*. Cambridge: Cambridge University Press, 2018.

Fiddes, Paul S. *The Promised End: Eschatology in Theology and Literature*. Chichester: Wiley, 2000.

Jenson, Robert W. *Systematic Theology Vol. 2: The Works of God*. New York: Oxford University Press, 1999.

Kermode, Frank. *The Sense of an Ending: Studies in the Theory of Fiction*. New York: Oxford University Press, 1967.

Kriner, Tiffany E. *The Future of the Word: An Eschatology of Reading*. Minneapolis, MN: Fortress Press, 2014.

Larsen, Timothy. *George MacDonald in the Age of Miracles*. Downers Grove, IL: InterVarsity Press, 2018.

MacDonald, George. "An Old Sermon with a New Text." *Good Words* 5 (1864): 515.

MacDonald, George. "The Imagination: Its Function and Its Culture." *The British Quarterly Review* (July 1867): 45–70.

MacDonald, George. *At the Back of the North Wind*. Edited by Roderick McGillis and John Pennington. Peterborough, ON: Broadview Press, 2011.

MacDonald, George. *Phantastes. Edited by Nick Page*. London: Paternoster, 2008.

MacDonald, George. *The Miracles of Our Lord*. London: Strahan and Co., 1870.

MacDonald, George. *The Princess and the Goblin*. Edited by Roderick McGillis. Oxford: Oxford University Press, 1990.

MacDonald, Greville. *George MacDonald and His Wife*. London: George Allen and Unwin, 1924.

Pionke, Albert D. "The Art of Manliness: Ekphrasis and/as Masculinity in George MacDonald's Phantastes." *Studies in the Novel* 43, no. 1 (2011): 21–37.

Plotz, John. *Semi-Detached: The Aesthetics of Virtual Experience Since Dickens*. Princeton, NJ: Princeton University Press, 2018.

Prickett, Stephen. *Romanticism and Religion: The Tradition of Coleridge and Wordsworth in the Victorian Church.* Cambridge: Cambridge University Press, 1976.

Tate, Andrew. Apocalyptic Fiction. London: Bloomsbury, 2017.

Trakakis, N. N. "Anti-Theodicy." In *The Cambridge Companion to the Problem of Evil,* edited by Chad Meister and Paul K. Moser, 124–44. Cambridge: Cambridge University Press, 2017.

White, Vernon. *Purpose and Providence: Taking Soundings in Western Thought, Literature and Theology.* London: Bloomsbury, 2015.

Wood, Ellen. "Our Log-Book." *The Argosy* (1867): 75–80.

Wright, Daniel. *Bad Logic: Reasoning about Desire in the Victorian Novel.* Baltimore, MD: Johns Hopkins University Press, 2018.

Zipes, Jack. *Fairy Tales and the Art of Subversion: The Classical Genre for Children and the Process of Civilization.* New York: Routledge, 1988.

10

Silence: Kidnapping, Abuse, and Murder in Early-Twenty-First-Century White Evangelical Fiction

Christopher Douglas

Why do you hide your face

Job 13:24

I called to my god, but he did not show his face,
I prayed to my goddess, but she did not raise her head

Ludlul bēl nēmeqi (Babylonian, 2nd millennium BCE, quoted in Korpel and de Moor, *The Silent God*, 263)

Theology has a hard problem and it has always been this: why are the gods silent and inactive in the face of human suffering and the existence of evil? What accounts for the unresponsiveness of the hidden god(s)?[1] The gods' silence becomes the hard problem particularly in moments of crisis, in the face of suffering and evil, when an individual or a community is in pain or historical trauma.[2] One answer to the hard problem is that some of the gods, or the God, are themselves responsible for the suffering endured, for reasons such as punishment or disciplining. But this explanation does not work in other situations, such as with undeserved suffering, or when humans seek to do good or seek the presence of the god(s).

The problems of divine hiddenness and suffering are distinct but related, the former sharpened by the latter.[3] Where are the gods? Why do they hide from us?

---

[1] Korpel and de Moor, *The Silent God*.
[2] Howard-Snyder and Moser, *Divine Hiddenness*, 5, 7.
[3] Schellenberg, "Divine Hiddenness," 513–14.

All theological traditions must attempt answers to these crucial questions. Those answers change across history and cultures, and some are better than others. The questions are articulated in our most ancient literary traditions: in Homer, by Babylonian theologians, in the Tanakh's book of Job and elsewhere, in the New Testament's Jesus, who quotes Psalm 22 in "My God, my God, why hast thou forsaken me?" These questions are found in the religious traditions across the Ancient Near East (ANE), including in what has been called the "Old Testament of the Old Testament," the clay tablets discovered at Ugarit in 1929 that reveal the "Canaanite" stories, practices and beliefs that were the religious-cultural matrix out of which ancient Israelite religion emerged.[4]

Biblical scholars no longer see the Bible and its divine beings as a unique work isolated from its ANE cultural context. In the Bible and the wider ANE, humans wondered about the silence and inactivity of the gods, and developed several methods for giving voice to the silence. The gods communicated through prophecy, dreams, divination such as throwing lots, interpreting thunder, the flight of birds, the entrails of animals, astrological observations, oil patterns on water, abnormal fetuses, curling patterns in smoke or water, or "through human representatives of the gods, such as priests, prophets, astrologers, diviners, magicians, spiritistic mediums, [and] scribes."[5] The ancients thought that the gods might be silent for reasons analogous to human silence: as punishment, because of human sin or noise or social injustice, or due to forbearance, incapacity, or divine sleep.[6] The ancient Israelites shared these methods of divination and explanations for the silence of the gods with their ANE neighbors. As Marjo Korpel and Johannes C. de Moor summarize, "just as in the world surrounding ancient Israel magical arts and divinatory techniques did exist in the pre-exilic period, but were gradually phased out when the biblical canon was formed and the holy Book became the only authoritative source of revelation."[7] Perhaps not coincidentally, the postexilic development of divine "speech" as revelation in a book as a primary authority coincided with the contraction of ancient Israelites' pantheon of gods into the singular God, reconfiguring the architecture of heaven if not its population.[8] This contraction sharpened the theodicy questions emerging from the hard problem of the hidden God's silence and inactivity in the face of Israel's woes.

---

[4] Korpel and Moor, *The Silent God*; Moberly, *The Old Testament of the Old Testament*, quoted in Smith, *Memoirs of God*, 95.

[5] Korpel and de Moor, *The Silent God*, 147, 308–11, 158.

[6] Korpel and de Moor, *The Silent God*, 239–40, 250–1, 259.

[7] Korpel and de Moor, *The Silent God*, 224.

[8] Fredriksen, "How Jewish Is God?," 200.

Silence 179

The hard problem that unsettled the ancients is no less with us today, magnified by our increased capacity for violence and our new understanding of violence and suffering in nature. Our questions about God's silence and inactivity in the face of human suffering are the subject of contemporary religiously interested literature, including both serious literary fiction and popular evangelical fiction. Adopting Wai-Chee Dimock's "deep time" approach to literary studies allows us to see that this contemporary literature is addressing the hard problem that the ancients would have recognized. Read alongside ANE traditions, including the Tanakh, we find that the silence of the gods in the face of human misery is a very old question, and that our millennia-old answers are problematically unfinished.

We begin to sense the shape of theology's hard problem by looking at *The Shack*, an evangelical novel that narrates a fantasy solution to it. *The Shack* is a twenty-first-century retelling of the Tanakh's Job. A family in the Pacific Northwest experiences the most terrible calamity when the youngest daughter is kidnapped, abused, and murdered. While her mother eventually finds strength and endurance in her Christian faith, the girl's father, Mack, loses his faith, unable to understand why God could have allowed this evil to happen to his daughter, or the suffering her loss causes him. It is the silence of God in the face of suffering, and the inactivity of God while evil destroys their daughter Missy, that is the hard problem the novel takes up. Its answer is a fantasy of divine presence and speech—showing its debt to Job—as Mack gets a chance to visit with God. Receiving an invitation to the site of the murder, Mack arrives and surprisingly finds the cabin in the woods magically transformed into a summer cabin by the lake, where he visits with the individual members of the Holy Trinity—God the Father, appearing as an African American woman, the Holy Spirit, appearing as an Asian American woman, and Jesus the Son, appearing as a Middle Eastern carpenter. This multicultural godhead spends the weekend with Mack, cooking, eating, hiking, and gardening. Through this fantasy of presence, God teaches Mack the things he cannot understand about the hard problem—and, in so doing, dissolves the hard problem of the silence and inactivity of God.

As I have argued elsewhere, *The Shack* is a reimagining of the biblical book of Job that strangely multiplies the number of divine beings responding to the problem of suffering. William Paul Young inadvertently rediscovered the ancient Israelite polytheism of three thousand years ago for the simple reason that justifying the gods' ways to humans is an easier task than justifying God's ways to humans.[9] Recent critical-historical Bible scholarship has uncovered

---

[9] See Douglas, "This Is *The Shack*."

180   *Literature and Religious Experience*

the pantheon of gods worshipped in ancient Israelite religion, gods whose genealogical traces lead us to *The Shack*'s divine characters. Rather than reprise this argument, I turn to how the novel undoes the problematic silence of God by narrating a powerful evangelical fantasy of divine speech and presence.

The popularity of this early twenty-first-century novel—over twenty million copies sold, made into a Hollywood film—is accountable to the fact that it recognizes that people experiencing terrible tragedy, grief, and depression deserve to have answers directly from God. God knows that Mack is lost since the tragedy that befell his family, and so God takes entirely appropriate action: seeking Mack and arranging a retreat with him—not a one-off, brief prayer session or vague feeling of presence that might or might not be Mack's imagination, but an actual weekend with God, a life-transforming encounter with the divine over days, giving him a chance to talk, listen, grieve, argue, reflect, rest, and then do it all again. This God seems to understand that a sacred text, ministering priest, or social church of Christ is not enough. That talking to an invisible, silent spirit and imagining a response is not enough. Mack's visit must be personal, extensive, tactile, and embodied; it must be like Jacob wrestling the divine being at the river, demanding a blessing. While *The Shack*'s hero experiences the silence of God in much the same way as Job, he is ultimately comforted by divine speech and presence in a way that Job is not. Mack is not encumbered, as Job is, by the conventional wisdom and platitudes offered by his friends about deserved human suffering and retributive divine agency. The seeming rules— of God's hiddenness, of our necessary ignorance, of the sufficiency of a book instead of the Holy One's direct presence, numinous and tactile—were broken for Mack, and this Christian fantasy of presence suggests a recognition that the rules deserve to be broken for everyone.[10] Its readers theologically intuit this, and God knows we need it.

In *The Shack*, God recognizes that we deserve a direct encounter with the divine, for only this will rescue us from the terrible tragedies of human suffering such as is experienced by Mack—or even from the emptiness and despair of everyday life. Maybe, as is hinted in Job, we won't be that impressed by the Lord's answers, or maybe, like Mack, the divine contact will seem to suffice. *The Shack*'s theological center, expressed in evangelical language, is the idea that humans are created to be in relationship with God and the novel shows us what that direct relationship should look like. While the popular novel expresses this idea in evangelical language, it is not different from the philosophy of religion's attempt

[10] Murray, "Deus Absconditus," 68.

Silence   181

to grapple with the hiddenness of God and its supposition that a perfectly loving God would make his existence known so that humans could have a relationship with him.[11] We should all get weekends with the Trinity at a beautiful summer cottage with a lake and garden; we love it when Mack gets what we all deserve.

But Mack's key question to God, as distilled in the film—"where were you when I needed you?"[12]—is only part of the problem, the smaller part. He should better have asked: "where were you when Missy needed you?" Just as the Job-like dialogue cycle in *The Shack* provides an explanation for God's silence even as it undoes God's silence, it likewise explains God's inactivity in preventing evil even as it partly undoes that inactivity, after the fact. *The Shack* argues that because of free will, God chooses not to exercise power to thwart human decisions. Thus, Missy's murderer's actions must be respected as a consequence of his exercise of free will, even at the cost of the pain, suffering, and death of other humans. Although *The Shack*'s theology on hiddenness and free will is phrased in popular, evangelical terms, it is not substantively different from arguments in philosophy of religion and academic theology.[13]

But it would have been easy for God to thwart the murder of Missy and none of us would have been the wiser. The specific sequence of events leading to Missy's murder shows us how. Missy is drawing at the picnic table when Mack is alerted to his two older children, out on a canoe on the lake. Mack waves at them, and one of them lifts her paddle to wave in return. "It is remarkable how a seemingly insignificant action or event can change entire lives," the narrator remarks.[14] Somehow, one person waving her paddle in the air causes a canoe with two sitting people to capsize. Though they are wearing lifejackets, that of Mack's other child becomes tangled and he is trapped beneath the capsized canoe. Fortunately, "all the instincts [Mack] had honed as a teenage lifeguard came roaring back" as he flings himself into the water to save his son from drowning.[15] Meanwhile, the killer, who happens to be lurking nearby at that exact moment, takes advantage of the distraction to abduct Missy.

It is a baroque set of improbable events. Of course, sequences as intricate as this must have happened repeatedly in human history—billions of chance

---

[11] Schellenberg, "Divine Hiddenness," 510.

[12] *The Shack*, 2017, movie trailer, 1:39, https://www.imdb.com/video/vi113292825? playlistId= tt2872518.

[13] For example, Howard-Snyder and Moser summarize: "God hides and thus permits inculpable nonbelief (at least in principle) in order to enable people *freely* to love, trust, and obey Him; otherwise, we would be coerced in a manner incompatible with love" (9).

[14] Young, *The Shack*, 42.

[15] Young, *The Shack*, 43.

182 *Literature and Religious Experience*

incidents, the butterfly in the Amazon, chaotic amplifications, that have led in unlikely ways to human misery, suffering, and death. God could certainly have intervened at any moment in this chain of cause and effect, breaking any one of these links. Maybe override Mack's decision to wave. Or Kate's decision to wave back, or wave back with her paddle. Maybe not allow the rules of physics to be so oversensitive that one raised paddle tips a canoe with two seated adolescents. No one would notice if God intervened to disentangle Josh's lifejacket. No one would be the wiser to the overruling of free will if Missy decided to run down to the lake as Mack leapt in. Or if the killer decided to lurk elsewhere. Imagine how sacred to God human free will has to be to not gently, silently, invisibly intervene to slightly alter the chain of events to save this young girl's life. A slight wrinkling of the anthropomorphic eyebrow, an almost unnoticeable raising of the pinky, and all would be well.

But we learn, in fact, that God's respect for free will and his policy of nonintervention are selective. Arranging a weekend with Mack is one important miracle that alters his life—and those of others. In one sequence near the end of Mack's visit, God the Father—now instantiated as a Native American man— shows Mack the killer's trail and leads him to Missy's body. This helps Mack properly mourn—they have a funeral for Missy, who is buried in a beautiful handmade wooden casket crafted by Jesus the carpenter—but which also allows Mack, now knowing the trail and the hiding spot, to later lead police to Missy's body, which allows them to also capture the killer, who is brought to trial. God directly intervenes, creating a process that leads to the killer's capture and likely execution: in 2007, when Young published *The Shack*, Oregon had the death penalty. But this God who now helps catch and perhaps execute the killer demurred to alter sequence step leading to Missy's murder—the lifted paddle, the tipped canoe, the stuck lifejacket, Missy drawing, and all of the particular events that led the killer to that exact place and time. The ways of God are mysterious indeed. I would like to suggest that this novelistic fantasy of divine speech and action unconsciously grasps the insufficiency of traditional answers to the hard problem, and so provides a picture of a more active, just, present God.

The Shack is an evangelical Christian fantasy of presence, of the silent, hidden God who reveals himself to commune with humans in pain and who undoes prior inactivity to intervene, offering healing and justice. It is the kind of answer an anguished parent of a murdered child might call out for, as Job did. But almost none of us have a divine encounter like Mack and Job do, breaking all the normal rules of traditional Christian theology which tells us that God must remain hidden and silent because "were God to reveal himself to everyone,

Silence 183

then fear of divine punishment, desire for our future wellbeing and desire to please God would overwhelm all incentive to choose evil, rendering morally significant choices impossible."[16] This theology holds that if the omnipotent, omniscient, omnipresent, and benevolent God were to be present and speak clearly to humans—appear everywhere, to everyone, all at once, speaking in all our languages—then this would violate human free will because we would be forced to acknowledge his divinity and speech. So, our free will as to whether to believe in God or to understand what his views are, depends on ignorance— uncertainty about his existence and, for Christians or in societies with a Christian heritage, uncertainty about whether and how the Bible speaks truly about him.[17] Traditional Christian theology ingeniously tries to transform the hard problem into a necessity: we *must* not know in order for free will to work. God must remain hidden and silent and we must not be sure if he exists, or if and what he communicates to us, so that we can make our choice to believe freely. In traditional Christian theology, this free will rule even appears to supersede God's power, as though it were a law preceding him, something he didn't choose. God is presumed to have imposed a rule about free will that requires his hiddenness and silence—but sometimes we tell stories about breaking this rule, as for Mack and Job.

This theology doesn't make much sense. As with evolution, God is surely responsible for the consequences of the system he creates and for the suffering and evil the systems entail.[18] In undoing God's silence and inactivity, *The Shack* is a fantasy of a more just God working under more humane rules. Another early twenty-first-century white evangelical novel addressing God's silence and inactivity, and the seeming necessity that humans be unsure about God's views, is Lynn Austin's historical Christian romance, *Candle in the Darkness* (2002). In some ways, Austin's novel takes *The Shack*'s tale of kidnapping, abuse, and murder, and magnifies it on a national scale, where the experience of human suffering and evil is multiplied millions of times—"Sixty Million and more," as Toni Morrison enumerates.[19]

Austin's novel is set during the Civil War, where a young white Virginia woman grows up questioning the ethics of slavery around her and decides to support the Union cause, seeking the abolition of slavery on Christian grounds. If *The Shack*

[16] Dougherty and Parker, "Hiddenness of God," §5.
[17] See Murray, "Deus Absconditus."
[18] Theodicies that really grapple with evolution and the silence of God end up abandoning some of the qualities of classical Christian theology, such as omnipotence. See Haught, *God After Darwin*, 41; Korpel and de Moor, *The Silent God*, 299–300; Dougherty and Parker, "Hiddenness of God," §2.
[19] Morrison, *Beloved*, xi.

184   *Literature and Religious Experience*

is an evangelical fantasy in which God's inscrutable silence and inactivity are spectacularly broken, *Candle in the Darkness* is an evangelical fantasy of moral clarity, portraying a coming of age story in which a morally sentient human discerns the injustice around her and learns the courage to do good, seek justice, and defend the oppressed (as Isaiah might put it; 1:17). Caroline Fletcher is the only child of a wealthy slave-owning family in Richmond, and the novel follows romance conventions as she comes of age in Southern aristocratic society. The novel traces Caroline's emerging discernment as she begins to question the peculiar institution her family and society are built around. After her mother dies, she briefly lives with her aunt in Philadelphia and engages with Christian abolitionist society and theology. But the novel is at pains to show that this young Southern white woman is already a Christian abolitionist before being infected by Northern ideas. Feeling naturally close to the captive people who take care of her growing up (in a way her cold mother does not) and watching their suffering—as when her nanny's son is sold off because, Caroline later pieces together, the son is her half brother, the result of her own father's repeated raping of her nanny—gives Caroline human empathy for other people in distress.

This empathy and love is doubled by Christian discernment as she matures. Like *Uncle Tom's Cabin* and unlike some other contemporary Christian fiction—Marilynne Robinson's *Gilead* being the most glaring example[20]—*Candle in the Darkness* faces fairly squarely the fact that both proslavery and antislavery positions in the antebellum period were supported by Christian theology. Caroline grows increasingly aware that her Christian views differ from the Christian ethos of her family, cousin, fiancé and his family, and Southern society at large. In one episode, a young Caroline attends an outdoor church service on her cousin's plantation, where her uncle reads scripture to the stolen people whom he keeps in legal bondage: "Servants, obey in all things your masters according to the flesh; not with eyeservice, as menpleasers; but in singleness of heart, fearing God."[21] The uncle later preaches, "It's His will that some of you are slaves. Your earthly masters are God's overseers. Blessed are the faithful, those who are submissive, obedient. They will inherit the kingdom of heaven."[22]

Candle in the Darkness deserves credit for recognizing the real religiosity of what Frederick Douglass termed "Christian slavery." Austin's solution to the problem of Christian slavery is also like Douglass's—she portrays it as

---

[20] See Douglas, *If God Meant to Interfere*, 84–116.
[21] Austin, *Candle in the Darkness*, 60. See Col. 3:22.
[22] Austin, *Candle in the Darkness*, 60.

Silence 185

inauthentic and, in a further move, contrasts it with purportedly more real religiosity of the kidnapped African Americans. It is her family's enslaved Eli who teaches young Caroline about "Massa Jesus" in a way that affects her more deeply than official white Christianity: "I was pretty sure that Eli's Jesus was the same person who the minister preached about every Sunday in church, but the stories sounded better when Eli told them. They sounded as though they might have really happened."[23] Later, she sneaks out with her young cousin and spies on a nighttime Christian enslaved community where Eli preaches and which seems more authentic, with "sheer joy."[24] Whereas her cousin Jonathan thinks slavery is "part of God's plan. It's in the Bible," Eli preaches about God saving the Israelites from Egyptian captivity in due time.[25] Young Caroline recognizes the theological difficulty: "Jonathan and Eli couldn't both be right."[26]

The novel fantasizes moral clarity insofar as it portrays a young white evangelical Southerner growing up in a slaveholding family and culture who nonetheless comes to see the better ethics of African American Christianity and Northern abolitionist Christianity. In a Philadelphia church one day, she reflects, "All my life I had heard Scripture used to defend slavery, but at the lecture that day, for the first time, I heard the Bible quoted to oppose slavery."[27] But admiring abolitionist passion doesn't stop her from rebuking the preacher, whose views are morally correct but without proper Christian empathy: "The Negroes are not a *cause*. They are *people!*"[28] With Eli as her spiritual mentor, Caroline's faith grows more certain about the wrongness of her society, even as the Civil War commences. As her Southern cousin and fiancé go off to fight for the cause, in fact, Caroline courageously risks herself to help her Philadelphia cousin, now a Union soldier imprisoned in Richmond, organize a prison break of Union soldiers, and then conceals her escaped cousin in her home. She later acts as a spy, gathering information about Confederate military positions and passing the information through a spy network to the Union army.

Called by God, and typologically linked to the story of Rahab who conceals Israelite spies, Caroline commits treason against the Confederacy. She is discovered in the closing months of the war, placed under house arrest, abandoned by her fiancé, and faces possible hanging before Union forces enter Richmond and defeat the Confederate States. In the meantime, she teaches her

---

[23] Austin, *Candle in the Darkness*, 34.
[24] Austin, *Candle in the Darkness*, 67.
[25] Austin, *Candle in the Darkness*, 70, 68.
[26] Austin, *Candle in the Darkness*, 71.
[27] Austin, *Candle in the Darkness*, 111.
[28] Austin, *Candle in the Darkness*, 113.

nanny to read, and she eats meals with her "servants" around the kitchen table. They eat together and pray together, with Caroline eventually imagining that "they had adopted her into their family," and while most other abducted people take the opportunity to escape to approaching Union forces—one dimension of enslaved people's agency that en masse turned the war against secession into a war against slavery[29]—Caroline's do not.[30] While from one perspective there is a little bit of Uncle Tom-ism in their reluctance to escape when they have a chance, from a better perspective they are committed to a political project: circumstances have thrown them into a situation where an extremely rare white ally is willing to risk her life to commit espionage against the Confederacy, possibly helping and hastening the defeat of evil and arrival of freedom for millions of their fellow captives across the South.[31] They partner with and enable Caroline's treason, choosing the Christian struggle of human flourishing and justice.

All of which is great. Hopefully readers cheer for Caroline as they cheer for Mack. But insofar as these evangelical novels are fantasies, they are fantasies because they portray not what was or is but what should have been and should be. Caroline's story of a morally autonomous white Southern Christian coming to recognize the evil of slavery and betray her society to bring the system down almost never happened. Why was Caroline's moral clarity vanishingly rare? The answer, I contend, was God's studied policy of silence and inactivity. In *Candle in the Darkness*, Caroline knows that the Union is also "asking for God's blessing on their cause" and wonders, "Which side was right? God couldn't be on both sides, yet both sides prayed to Him, believed in Him."[32] Though both Caroline and Austin believe God prefers freedom to slavery, and Eli believes God uses the war to draw individuals into closer evangelical relationship with him, the novel's recognition that both the North and the South believed in the theological premise of their struggles unintentionally suggests that God's policy of silence and absence were critical to Christianity's moral ambivalence about the evil institution.

As evangelical scholar Mark Noll argues, the Civil War was a "theological crisis" because when it came to one of the great evils in the modern and early modern period, Christians could not clearly discern if or what God thought about the kidnapping, torture, rape, and suffering of tens of millions of people. God kept silent. What we had instead was a book, but "during the antebellum era

---

[29] Hahn, *The Political Worlds*, 55–114.
[30] Austin, *Candle in the Darkness*, 303, 413, 249.
[31] Austin, *Candle in the Darkness*, 326.
[32] Austin, *Candle in the Darkness*, 188–9.

Silence 187

confusion beset whites who turned to Scripture for guidance on slavery"[33]—"The country had a problem because its most trusted religious authority, the Bible, was sounding an uncertain note."[34] In what was largely an intra-evangelical struggle where both sides approached the Bible with the expectation it was "a plain book whose authoritative deliverances could be apprehended by anyone who simply opened the covers and read," the Bible was catastrophically polyvocal.[35] Proslavery Christians wove a web of specific references from the Tanakh and New Testament—Gen. 9:25-27, 17:12; Deut. 20:10-11; Jesus's silence about slavery; 1 Cor. 7:21; Rom. 13:1, 7; Col. 3: 22, 4:1; 1 Tim. 6:1-2; Philemon[36]—into a biblical defense of the evil institution of American slavery, even as antislavery Christians had to rely on a more ethereal set of broad "general principles" that seemed to weaken the authority of the biblical text.[37] As with other historical moments, the ambivalence of the sacred anthology we have instead of God's direct voice and actual presence has been the occasion for catastrophic evil. While believers like Austin might imply through the contrast of authentic slave religion with joyless slaveholding religion that the former had the presence of the Holy Spirit in a way the latter did not, this distinction is not noticeable to neutral historical observation. The still small voice tended to confirm everyone's priors.

"Truly, you are a God who hides himself, O God of Israel, the Savior," the Isaiah poet mused (45:15). My argument here is not that *Deus absconditus* caused this occasion of vast suffering but that his policy of silence and ambivalent revelation made the problem much worse. Douglass recalls one master who attended a Methodist tent revival meeting where he "experienced religion." Contrary to the hopes of some of his abductees, Auld did not become more "kind and humane" after being born again. On the contrary, describes Douglass, "prior to his conversion, he relied upon his own depravity to shield and sustain him in his savage barbarity; but after his conversion, he found religious sanction and support for his slaveholding cruelty."[38] After conversion, Auld would quote scripture sanctioning the torture he inflicted, whipping an enslaved person while citing Jesus's line, "He that knoweth his master's will, and doeth it not, shall be beaten with many stripes."[39] How many millions of times such biblically sanctioned torture occurred is unknown. God's policy of silence, and the poor

[33] Noll, *The Civil War*, 63.
[34] Noll, *The Civil War*, 50.
[35] Noll, *The Civil War*, 21, 20.
[36] Noll, *The Civil War*, 34–5.
[37] Noll, *The Civil War*, 41, 45.
[38] Douglass, *Autobiographies*, 52.
[39] Douglass, *Autobiographies*, 53; See Lk. 12:47.

188   *Literature and Religious Experience*

compensation of an ambivalent, polyvocal sacred anthology, has, in increasing the self-righteousness of proslavery Christians, been itself the occasion for increased human suffering and evil.

In their closing theological rumination in *The Silent God*, Korpel and de Moor write, "If God is silent, man must speak. Divine silence is an invitation to speak in his name."[40] But, citing the words of a Christian Nazi, they partly acknowledge the difficulty that comes with speaking for the silent God. Like Austin and Douglass, they determine that other people's religious convictions with which they disagree must be inauthentic, "a thin varnish."[41] "This example," they argue, "shows that the decision to speak words of God is a *moral* one. Believers have to ask themselves honestly, 'Is it a word of God I am going to speak? Or will I speak what I myself or what others want to hear?' "[42] We should all practice such worthy moral self-examination. But as Austin and Noll reveal, theological traditions justifying evil are communal, durable, and highly resistant to moral critique. *A Candle in the Darkness* is a fantasy about the Christian moral clarity that should have been but was not.

Despite the horrors of hundreds of thousands of dead, characters including Caroline pray to God because they continue to believe that he makes micro-level decisions, day-to-day, of who lives and who dies due to combat, wounds, or disease. Another ancient story about God's silence—the book of Job—suggests a different view. "Why do you hide your face, and count me as your enemy?" Job asks God, and after several rounds asking to plead his case before God, God responds from his whirlwind.[43] While Job is an everyman, speaking for us all, his plea is theologically grounded in his personal experience: his ten children killed, body diseased, property destroyed, social status mocked by his friends' conventional wisdom that his woes must be the fruit of unacknowledged sin. But the God who breaks silence is God as Systems-Designer. He draws Job's attention away from his personal circumstances of suffering to consider cosmological creation and its chaotic workings, meteorological energies, animal ecosystems. God directs Job's consideration to the animal world, asking him rhetorically if he can "hunt the prey for the lion" or who "provides for the raven its prey," and later

---

[40] Korpel and de Moor, *The Silent God*, 287.

[41] Korpel and de Moor, *The Silent God*, 295. Julie Ingersoll writes of this rhetorical move: "An impediment to the analysis of the place of violent religion in the United States has been the hegemonic character of Christianity and the authenticating discourses of Christians themselves, as they work to legitimate their own versions of their tradition while denying 'authenticity' to the various other expressions of it, most especially violent expressions." Ingersoll, "Classification Matters," 227.

[42] Korpel and de Moor, *The Silent God*, 295.

[43] Job 13:24.

Silence 189

ruminates about the hawk that "it spies the prey," after which "its young ones suck up blood."[44] Consider the System, the Systems-Designer tells Job. In this species-level view, individual lives do not matter. Violent suffering, including these predator-prey relations, are part of nature. The System is working as it should.

This answer should strike us as not good enough. It is not good enough for Mack or Caroline. It is not good enough for the "Sixty Million and more" people who experienced slavery as God hid, mute. It may not even have been good enough for the Job poet, who questions whether we live in a moral universe. Indeed, the ambiguity of the book may suggest that when it comes to justice, Job—and maybe other humans—might be more righteous than God. Thus, of God's rhetorical question to Job, "Will you even put me in the wrong? / Will you condemn me that you may be justified?"[45] James Harding writes, "The form of the rhetorical question, which entices the reader into not questioning the assumptions upon which it rests, hides the disturbing truth that Job was right. The rhetorical question dissuades Job, and the reader, from responding by asserting that Job has made YHWH out to be wicked, and he was right."[46] This piece of ANE wisdom literature "allows the reader to confront the possibility that a human may be more righteous than the deity."[47]

To pose this possibility, as Job does ambiguously, is to begin to seriously grapple with the ethics of the hard problem of God's silence and inactivity in the face of evil and human (and nonhuman animal) suffering. *The Shack* and *Candle in the Darkness* are not equipped for this task. Like other evangelical fiction, these novels work to silence doubt and ambiguity, to dispel rather than investigate difficult theological problems.[48] Serious literary fiction addressing such questions, in contrast, has tended to abandon conceptual elements of the moral universe that so entranced the Job poet 2,500 years ago. In Cormac McCarthy's *Blood Meridian*—a novel also seemingly concerned with the predator–prey relations characteristic of the System—the terrifying character of the judge asks his murderous crew, "If God meant to interfere in the degeneracy of mankind would he not have done so by now?"[49] Barbara Kingsolver's *The Poisonwood Bible*, meanwhile, has a narrator muse about natural suffering, "Back then I was still a bit appalled that God would set down his barefoot boy and

---

[44] Job 38:39-41, 39:28-30.
[45] Job 40:8.
[46] Harding, "A Spirit of Deception," 164.
[47] Harding, "A Spirit of Deception," 164-5.
[48] See Douglas, "This Is *The Shack.*"
[49] McCarthy, *Blood Meridian*, 153. See Douglas, *If God Meant to Interfere*, 221-44.

girl dollies [i.e., children] into an Eden where, presumably, He had just turned loose elephantiasis and microbes that eat the human cornea. Now I understand, God is not just rooting for the dollies."[50] The System is working as it should. A somewhat parallel set of questions about the silent, hidden God emerges at the end of E. L. Doctorow's *City of God*, where a new Jewish convert reflects on the lessons of the Shoah. He reviews the catastrophic flipside of Korpel and de Moor's theological rumination "Divine silence is an invitation to speak in his name."[51] Doctorow's convert instead prays to the hidden, silent God:

> Even among those of us clinging to a love of You and an irrepressible longing for Your love ... there is a risen suspicion, that You are part of the problem. Men use You at will for their most hideous purposes. You do not seem to resist—anyone who wants You, and for whatever foul, murderous reason, can have You.[52]

These examples of serious literary fiction deem traditional answers to the hard problem of God's silence and inactivity in the face of evil and suffering unworkable.

Karl Barth recognized the difficult work of bearing witness to the silent God of history who wants us to be a "responsible partner."[53] I would like to suggest that this responsibility now surely requires us to help God understand that the current arrangement is not working—that it is, in fact, making things worse. Perhaps what we need now, accordingly, is a commensurate ethically engaged literature and religion criticism that can begin to take these challenges seriously and, with the literature itself, help our partner understand that his policy of silence is not working.[54] An ethical criticism might seek answers from God directly, as Job did, and not be content to rehearse the conventional theological platitudes, as Job's friends were.

The hard problem has become even worse in the last few decades because we don't even know about whom we're talking. Recent biblical scholarship, joined with archeological and inscriptional evidence, strongly indicates that the God at the center of the Abrahamic faiths is a historically fashioned amalgamation

---

[50] Kingsolver, *The Poisonwood Bible*, 529. See Douglas, *If God Meant to Interfere*, 60–83.

[51] Korpel and de Moor, *The Silent God*, 287.

[52] Doctorow, *City of God*, 266.

[53] Karl Barth, *The Church Dogmatics*, vol. 3/4 (Edinburgh: T&T Clark, 1961), 75, quoted in Korpel and de Moor, *The Silent God*, 291.

[54] Thus, rather than conclude that divine hiddenness is evidence for atheism and naturalism (Schellenberg, "Divine Hiddenness," 509), I am arguing that we might assume divine existence but for reasons of limited knowledge, goodness, or power, that he / they do not sufficiently comprehend the extent to which their silent hiddenness is an ethical problem, and that it is our job to convince him / them and call for a change of rules.

of several other pagan deities, drawing on their different names and characteristics: El, the high god of the Ugaritic / Canaanite pantheon; Yahweh, the storm god probably introduced into the pantheon through trade from the South; Baal, Ugarit's patron god of war and fertility; Anat, his sister, the warrior goddess who slays death; Asherah, consort of El who may have prefigured the Bible's female personified Wisdom.[55] Who is the God we fashioned from these other gods? It is not clear about or to whom we are talking and praying anymore, and it does not appear that he or they care about human (and nonhuman animal) suffering. That must change. It is clearer than ever, as we move into a season of violence and the death throes of the white Christian supremacy in the United States that has been its governing mode for four centuries, that we desperately need better communication from the divine. The world has had enough. It is well past time for a different kind of communal petition: that the god(s) break their silence and emerge from hiding.

Bibliography

Austin, Lynn. *Candle in the Darkness*. Bloomington, IN: Bethany House, 2002.

Dimock, Wai-chee. *Through Other Continents: American Literature across Deep Time*. Princeton, NJ: Princeton University Press, 2008.

Doctorow, E. L. *City of God*. New York: Random House, 2000.

Dougherty, Trent, and Ross Parker. "Hiddenness of God." In *Routledge Encyclopedia of Philosophy*, Taylor and Francis, 2016. Available online: https://doi.org/10.4324/97804 15249126-K3574-1.

Douglas, Christopher. *If God Meant to Interfere: American Literature and the Rise of the Christian Right*. Ithaca, NY: Cornell University Press, 2016.

Douglas, Christopher. "This Is *The Shack* That Job Built: Theodicy and Polytheism in William Paul Young's Evangelical Bestseller." *Journal of the American Academy of Religion* 88, no. 2 (June 2020): 505–42.

Douglass, Frederick. *Autobiographies*. New York: Library of America, 1994.

Fredriksen, Paula. "How Jewish Is God?: Divine Ethnicity in Paul's Theology." *Journal of Biblical Literature* 137, no. 1 (2018): 193–212.

Hahn, Steven. *The Political Worlds of Slavery and Freedom*. Cambridge, MA: Harvard University Press, 2009.

Harding, James E. "A Spirit of Deception In Job 4:15? Interpretive Indeterminacy and Eliphaz's Vision." *Biblical Interpretation* 13, no. 2 (2005): 137–66.

---

[55] An excellent layperson's introduction to this scholarship is Smith, *Memoirs of God*; see also Douglas, "This Is *The Shack*."

Haught, John F. *God After Darwin: A Theology of Evolution*. 2nd ed. New York: Westview Press, 2008.

Ingersoll, Julie. "Classification Matters: Hiding Violence in Christianity in the United States." *Journal of Religion and Violence* 7, no. 3 (2019): 227–30.

Kingsolver, Barbara. *The Poisonwood Bible*. New York: HarperPerennial, 1998.

Korpel, Marjo C. A., and Johannes C. de Moor. *The Silent God*. Leiden: Brill, 2011. ProQuest Ebook Central.

McCarthy, Cormac. *Blood Meridian*. New York: Vintage, 1992.

Moberly, R. W. L. *The Old Testament of the Old Testament: Patriarchal Narratives and Mosaic Yahwism*. Minneapolis, MN: Fortress Press, 1992.

Morrison, Toni. *Beloved*. New York: Vintage, 2004.

Murray, Michael J. "Deus Absconditus." In *Divine Hiddenness: New Essays*, edited by Daniel Howard-Snyder and Paul Moser, 62–82. Cambridge: Cambridge University Press, 2001.

Noll, Mark A. *The Civil War as a Theological Crisis*. Chapel Hill: University of North Carolina Press, 2006.

Schellenberg, J. L. "Divine Hiddenness." In *A Companion to Philosophy of Religion*, 2nd ed., edited by Charles Taliaferro, Paul Draper, and Philip L. Quinn, 509–18. Oxford: Wiley-Blackwell, 2010.

Smith, Mark. *Memoirs of God: History, Memory, and the Experience of the Divine in Ancient Israel*. Minneapolis, MN: Fortress, 2004.

Young, William Paul. 2007. *The Shack: Where Tragedy Confronts Eternity*. Newbury Park, CA: Windblown Media.

11

One: Poetic Love in Ibn ʿArabī

Jeff Sacks

The world in its entirely is the lover and the beloved.

Ibn ʿArabī, *al-Futuḥāt al-makiyya*

1.

"At the campsite, now abandoned, stay and call her / name as your heart is softly torn away," Muḥī al-Dīn Ibn al-ʿArabī (1165–1240) wrote in a volume of poetry entitled *Tarjumān al-ashwāq* (Translator of Desires).[1] The verse addresses another, to whom it responds, and as it does so it tells its addressee to "stay" and "call her name": *qif bi-al-diyār wa-nājihā.* The use of the verb "qif," to "halt" or "stop," in the imperative, indexes the Arabic poetic tradition, and, in particular, the tradition of the *nasīb*, the opening of the pre-Islamic, *jāhilī* ode, as it is exemplified in the ode of Imruʾ al-Qays, which begins, famously, with the same verb in the same mode: "qifā," "halt."[2] If Imruʾ al-Qays opens this ode in the dual, Ibn ʿArabī opens the line I'm reading here in the singular, "qif," and so we may wonder about the mode of address in this passage in Ibn ʿArabī, and about the way in which it reiterates the poetic tradition to which it relates itself and through which its form is given to us. In the *nasīb*, language opens in relation to loss, because one speaks, already, addressing another, a beloved, in a linguistic context where something or someone has departed and is no longer. And yet this departure is never final—the marks of the *aṭlāl*, the remains of the campsite, will

---

[1] Ibn ʿArabī, *Bewildered*, 23/Ibn ʿArabī, *Tarjumān al-ashwāq*, 101.
[2] On the *nasīb*, see Stetkevych, *Zephyrs of Najd.*

194   *Literature and Religious Experience*

never, finally, have disappeared—and it therefore convolutes a desire to locate a point of origin in poetic speech. It is not that the poem promises a unification of the lover and the beloved, because in the terms of the poetic to which Ibn 'Arabī relates himself and which he repeats, language already takes place on the far side of a departure and a disappearance. In the context of the *nasīb*, not only is unmediated interlocution not promised, but the poem's indifference to it—its indifference to a giving of sense—is what allows for the taking place of this or that poetic utterance at all. The absence of the beloved, the mere fact that the beloved will already have departed and disappeared, is what gives poetic speech, and it is this gift that Ibn 'Arabī turns to, and which he forwards, when he says the word "qif," as he gives this word away yet again.

In what follows I'll privilege this forwarding of the poetic, as we are given to read it in *Tarjumān al-ashwāq*, in its relation to the sense in which Ibn 'Arabī speaks of God and world, of "al-ḥaqq" and "al-khalq," in his *Fuṣūṣ al-ḥikam* (Bezels of Wisdom).[3] We are asked to read this relation, in Ibn 'Arabī, in the intersection of the poetic with love, and in Ibn 'Arabī's explication of the relation between the lover and the beloved and the indeterminacy this relation implies and reiterates, which it sends out to us—and which the poem expounds as it gives to us a particular sense of the world and language. It is a sense that, if it affirms a distinction between God and world, between "al-ḥaqq" and "al-khalq," it occasions a fundamental disorder in the drawing of that distinction, which Ibn 'Arabī convolutes and to which his language, at the same time, cannot cease returning. In this chapter I consider Ibn 'Arabī's writing in this sense, where language speaks to us of God and world, and the distinction between then, and where it must reiterate and ruin the distinction upon which it nevertheless relies in order to speak and to offer a word—to offer any language at all.

To approach this sense of language, God, and world I wish to underline that if the poet, in *Tarjumān al-ashwāq*, asks us to halt and call out, the addressee of this call remains indeterminate. The pronoun "hā," in the words "wa-nājihā," "and called her name," may refer to "her," but it may also refer to "them," in the plural—for example, the remains of the abandoned camp and its "abodes," "diyār"—or to "it."[4] And so "hā" may refer to a particular individual, a young woman, Niẓām, the daughter of Abū Shujā' Zāhir ibn Rustum ibn Abī al-Rajā

---

[3] Ibn 'Arabī, *Bezels of Wisdom*/Ibn 'Arabī, *Fuṣūṣ al-ḥikam*. In what follows I capitalize following standard, English-language practices; I occasionally modify the translation to provide a more literal rendering, or offer an alternate translation between brackets.

[4] Nicholson, in *Tarjumān*, 96, renders the passage as follows: "Halt by the dwelling-places and call to them, wondering at their loneliness, with exquisite lamentation."

One   195

al-Iṣfahānī, with whom Ibn ʿArabī studied the ḥadīth collection of al-Tirmidhī—
"As for the Shaykh, I studied with him [*samaʿnā ʿalayhi*] Abū ʿĪsā al-Tirmidhī's
book of ḥadīth"—and whom Ibn ʿArabī met in Mecca, in 1202 AD.[5] Ibn ʿArabī
writes, in his introduction to *Tarjumān al-ashwāq*, that Niẓām was "a slender
young woman who drew the attention of those near her, whose beauty graced
us, whether one spoke or listened, who dazzled our gatherings, who was named
Niẓām, and who was nicknamed 'The Eye of the Sun and Radiance'" (8), and
of whom the poems contained in *Tarjumān al-ashwāq* are an "imitation": "I
imitated her [*fa-qalladnāhā*] in my composition of this book [*min naẓminā fī
hādhā al-kitāb*], which consists in the most beautiful poems, which I wrote in a
pure, eloquent language [*bi-lisān al-nasīb al-rāʾiq*] and well-suited expressions
of love" (9). The poems, he tells us, did not reach the object they sought to
imitate—"I didn't reach in their composition even some of what my soul
found and what our intimacy provoked, in her generous affection, her refined
knowledge, her delicate language, and her pure beauty" (9)—even as the poems
point, everywhere, to her: "For every name I mention in this part [in the
poems—JS] alludes to her, and with each abode I lament I mean hers [*wa-kull
dār andabuhā fa-dāruhā aʿnī*]" (9).

It is as if the name of the beloved, Niẓām, is in excess of itself and its
reference; the pronoun "hā" points at once to Niẓām and to the beloved in the
tradition of the *nasīb*, to which Ibn ʿArabī explicitly alludes in the sentences
I'm translating here. The "pure, eloquent language" of Ibn ʿArabī's poems,
which mirror, in their form, Niẓām—and I might underline that the word
"niẓām" means "order" or "arrangement"; it is a word, in Arabic, for "verse"
and even for "poetry"—is, in the Arabic I've translated here, "bi-lisān al-nasīb
al-rāʾiq"; the "abodes" that Ibn ʿArabī tells us he laments, "kull dār andabuhu,"
is reiterated, in the plural form, "diyār," in the line of the poem we've begun
to read: *qif bi-al-diyār wa-nājihā*. The poem speaks to us of a single beloved,
which is, everywhere, multiplied, in excess of itself. And the poem, therefore,
reiterates a relation to a tradition that it does not merely repeat, because the
tradition itself, the tradition of the *nasīb*, may be what is alluded to in the word
"hā"; the tradition of the *nasīb* may be the beloved to which Ibn ʿArabī calls
out and about which we may not say that it is merely exterior to the poem,
because it is only through its reiteration that the poem becomes what it is. It is
this sense of the poetic that is mirrored, in Ibn ʿArabī, in the reflection on God

---

[5] Ibn ʿArabī, *Tarjumān al-ashwāq*, 7.

196   *Literature and Religious Experience*

and world, "al-ḥaqq," and "al-khalq," and which Ibn ʿArabī asks us to read in the commentary he provides on *Tarjumān al-ashwāq*.

2.

To speak of the beloved, in these pages in Ibn ʿArabī, is to speak in the language of the *nasīb*, "bi-lisān al-nasīb al-rāʾiq," and it is at the same time to speak of "the divine," "al-ilāh," of "the reality," "al-ḥaqq," and of "the essence," "al-dhāt," a feminine singular noun that is a name for the transcendent essence of God. Ibn ʿArabī underlines, in relation to the poems contained in *Tarjumān al-ashwāq*, that "I persist, in what I've composed, in gesturing to divine manifestations, spiritual revelations, and heavenly correspondences" (9), and it is in this sense that he explains, in his commentary on the poetic volume, in relation to the line that immediately precedes the one I've cited here, that the "ruins," "ṭulūl," of the abandoned camp—"Stay now at the ruins in Laʿlaʿi, fading/ and in that wasteland grieve for those we loved"—are "the traces of the abodes of the divine names in the hearts of the gnostics [*athar manāzil al-asmāʾ al-ilāhiyya bi-qulūb al-ʿārifīn*]."[6]

And so to read these passages in *Tarjumān al-ashwāq* is to read them in relation to the divine names, and to write of the divine names, in Ibn ʿArabī, is to write of God in relation to a distinction Ibn ʿArabī draws, in *Fuṣūṣ al-ḥikam*, between the "single" and the "multiple": "Man [*al-insān*, "the human being"—JS] is multiple [*kathīr*] and not single of essence [*aḥadī al-ʿayn*], while God [*al-ḥaqq*, "the reality"—JS] is single of essence, but multiple with respect to the divine names [*aḥadī al-ʿayn kathīr bi-al-asmāʾ al-ilāhiyya*]."[7]

I want to linger with this moment in Ibn ʿArabī, where the explication of the names of God intersects with the poetic, and to do so I want to underline the mode of explication, the language practice, of Ibn ʿArabī. We may consider this mode in that, in the English-language rendering of the passage in *Fuṣūṣ al-ḥikam* I've transcribed here, the word "but" is supplied—"God is single of essence, *but* [my emphasis—JS] multiple with respect to the divine names"—even as it does not appear in the Arabic text. The editor of the Arabic edition, Abū al-ʿAlāʾ ʿAfīfī, whose 1946 Beirut edition has become the standard, does not provide editorial supplement; the Arabic text places the two sentences, each next to the other,

---

[6] Ibn ʿArabī, *Bewildered*, 23/Ibn ʿArabī, *Tarjumān al-ashwāq*, 101; Ibn ʿArabī, *Dhakāʾir al-aʿlāq*, 86.
[7] Ibn ʿArabī, *Bezels of Wisdom*, 210/Ibn ʿArabī, *Fuṣūṣ al-ḥikam*, 169.

One   197

and because it does this, the disjunction implied in their joining, Ibn 'Arabī's parataxis of argument, suggests itself as a protocol for reading Ibn 'Arabī. The writing of the paradox in *Fuṣūṣ al-ḥikam*—single of essence, multiple with respect to the divine names—does not require the precaution of a "but," or even of a comma, which I've supplied in this gloss, but is merely stated. It is a statement that implies a "general ontological thesis,"[8] which refers to a field of distinctions, between the single and the multiple, the temporal and the eternal, and the "originated"—"It is established that the originated [*al-muḥdath*] is dependent on that which brings it about, for its possibility. Its existence is derived from something other than itself [*fa-wujūduhu min ghayrihi*], the connection in this case being one of dependence [*fa-huwwa murtabaṭ bihi irtibāṭ iftiqār*]"—and, following the philosopher Ibn Sīnā, in the *Ilāhiyyāt* (Metaphysics) of his *Shifā'* (The Healing), what must have the quality of "necessary existence":

> It is therefore necessary that that which is the support should be essentially and necessarily itself [wājib al-wujūd li-dhātihi, "necessarily existent in itself"—JS], self-sufficient and independent of any other. This it is that bestows existence [al-wujūd, "being"—JS] from its own essential being [bi-dhātihi, "from its essence"—JS] on dependent existence [li-hādhā al-ḥādith, "on this originated being"—JS], in this way becoming related to it [fa-intasaba ilayhi].[9]

This being, which is "necessarily existent in itself," is related to the "originated" being, not only because it gives being to it, but also because it cannot separate itself from its distinction from it. The terms, as Ibn 'Arabī writes them, and as he gives them to us, are at once articulated and disarticulated, and because of this the distinctions he elaborates are rendered indistinct. It is an indistinction that is drawn through a paratactic writing practice that mirrors the ontological form it traces; the language of Ibn 'Arabī does not tell us that what is is this "but" that, but only that it is "this that," and it therefore speaks to us of a sense of being that, irresolvable to the distinctions he affirms and collapses, fails to be itself and can do nothing but call out to another: *qif bi-al-diyār wa-nājihā*.

If "the reality," "al-ḥaqq," is a name through which distinctions are drawn, Ibn 'Arabī presses upon the names "the essence," "al-dhāt," and "the lord," "al-rabb," to speak of the relation between God and beings: "Know that that which is termed 'God' [*Allah*] is one through the essence [*aḥadiyyun bi-al-dhāt*] and all through the names [*kullun bi-al-asmā'*]. Each created being [*kull mawjūd*, "each

---

[8] Izutsu, *Sufism and Taoism*, 82.
[9] Ibn 'Arabī, *Bezels of Wisdom*, 54/Ibn 'Arabī, *Fuṣūṣ al-ḥikam*, 53. On "wājib al-wujūd," see Sīnā, *The Metaphysics of the Healing* (*Al-Shifā': al-Ilāhiyyāt*.

198 *Literature and Religious Experience*

being"—JS] is related to God [*Allah*] only as being its particular lord [*rabbihi*], since its relationship to God as the all is impossible."[10] It is through the divine names that God becomes manifest in the world—"Do you not understand that the reality is manifest through the attributes of relative beings [*al-muḥdathāt*, "originated beings"—JS]" (92/80)—and this manifestation is also called, in Ibn 'Arabī, "khalq," "creation." The created world is at once distinguished from and indistinct from "the reality," or from God. Ibn 'Arabī explains of "khalq" that "there is, in it, a distinction [*ikhtilāf*], because when you look at it from one standpoint, you say, 'It is the reality [*ḥaqq*],' and when you look at it from another standpoint you say 'It is creation [*khalq*],' and it is, in itself, not 'the reality' and not not 'the reality' [*wa huwwa fī nafsihi lā ḥaqq wa lā ghayr ḥaqq*]," and we might, therefore, underline that "al-ḥaqq" may be nothing more or less than a locus for the articulation and collapse of a field of distinctions—a word through which "the essence," "al-dhāt," and "the lord," "al-rabb," and also "the reality," "al-ḥaqq," and "the creation," "al-khalq," are drawn apart and related.[11]

"The essence" is what does not have a relation to created beings; "the lord," "al-rabb"—or, differently, "the divinity," "al-ilāh"—is a name that indexes such relations, and it is for this reason that God is "multiple with respect to the divine names." "Al-rabb" is a name for God where a sense of relation is implied, but "the essence," "al-dhāt," "as being beyond all of these relationships, is not a divinity."[12] Yet the word "as," in the English-language rendering I've transcribed, translates a conditional clause: "It is then the case," this passage might also be translated, if somewhat literally, "that the essence, were it to be denuded of these relations [*thumma inna al-dhāt law taʿarrat ʿan hādhihi al-nisab*], would not be a divinity [*lam takun ilāhan*]." The word "law," "were it to be," introduces a conditional clause that dramatizes the aporetic quality of Ibn 'Arabī's sentences; the sentence says: were "the essence" to be denuded of relationality, of a relation to relations, it would not be "the divinity," but it is not denuded of relations in this way, and so it *is* the divinity, but only insofar as as it is "the divinity" by not participating in relations with "created" or "contingent" beings—which is to say, by being "al-dhāt." The sentence defines the categories it distinguishes—"al-dhāt," "al-ilāh"—by disorganizing the difference between them. "All goes back to him and his names," but there is, in Ibn 'Arabī, a "radical ambiguity," a fundamental indetermination, to which we must return in reading Ibn 'Arabī.[13]

---

[10] Ibn 'Arabī, *Bezels of Wisdom*, 106/Ibn 'Arabī, *Fuṣūṣ al-ḥikam*, 90.
[11] Ibn 'Arabī, *al-Futuḥāt al-makiyya*, 7.410.
[12] Ibn 'Arabī, *Bezels of Wisdom*, 92/Ibn 'Arabī, *Fuṣūṣ al-ḥikam*, 81.
[13] Chittick, *The Sufi Path*, 213, 211.

There is in indistinction between "al-khalq" and "al-ḥaqq," between the world and God, and yet God, as "the essence," "al-dhāt," is, merely, itself, "self-subsisting":

> Glory be to him who alone is evidence of himself alone, and who is self-subsisting. There is nothing in being [al-kawn] but what is implicit in the divine unity [al-aḥadiyya], and there is nothing in the imagination but what is implicit in multiplicity [al-kathra]. Whoever holds to multiplicity is with the cosmos [al-ʿālam, also, "the world"—JS], the divine names, and the cosmic names. Whoever holds to the unity is with the reality [al-ḥaqq] in his essence [min haythu dhātihi] as self-sufficient beyond all worlds. His essence being self-sufficient beyond all worlds, he ["the reality," "al-ḥaqq"—JS] is independent of and beyond all nominal relationships, since the names, while implying him [kama tadullu ʿalayhā, as they point to "it," "the essence"—JS] also imply the relations named [musammayyāt], whose effects they manifest. (125–6/104–5)

The "names," Ibn ʿArabī writes, "point to the essence," which is "self-sufficient beyond all worlds," just as, kamā, they imply "the relations named"; the names of God mediate the relation between "the essence," "al-dhāt," and "the world," "al-ʿālam," even as this is a relation that is not a relation, and that is, merely, an "implication," a "pointing." Insofar as God is "the reality," "al-haqq," and insofar, therefore, as it is "the essence," "al-dhāt," what we are given to read is an aporetic sense of the being of God, where God is "al-ḥaqq" in its indistinction from "al-khalq," "al-dhāt" in its indistinction from "al-ʿālam."

And yet God, Ibn ʿArabī reminds us, is "one"; he cites the chapter of the Qurʾān entitled "al-Ikhlāṣ," "Sincerity," as follows:

> "Say: he, God, is one [qul huwwa Allah aḥad]," in his essence; "God, the eternal refuge [Allah al-ṣamad]," in respect to our dependence on him [min ḥaythu istninādinā ilayhi]; "He begets not," in his identity or in relation to us [min ḥaythu huwiyyatuhu wa-naḥnu]; "Nor is he begotten," as in the preceding verse; "He has no equal," as in the preceding verse. (126/105)

Ibn ʿArabī continues,

> Thus does he describe himself and isolate his essence in the words "God is one," although the multiplicity manifest through his attributes is well known among us. We, for our part, beget and are begotten, we depend on him and we compete one with another. However the unique one transcends all these attributes, having no need of them or of us. (126/105)

200   *Literature and Religious Experience*

A tension is reiterated: if "we" are dependent upon God and rely upon it, if we are grounded through it and lean upon it, *nastanid ilayhi*, and if, with this leaning, God transcends relation and time, this is only insofar as the explication of this "dependence" reiterates a field of categories that intersect.

"One may not abstract God [*Allah*] from the world, which is his manifestation,"[14] and we may think this incapacity for abstraction in relation to the categories *Fuṣūṣ al-ḥikam* intersects, which it articulates and collapses, at the moment at which Ibn ʿArabī offers a reflection on "the essence," "al-dhāt," in relation to "God's unity," "aḥadiyyat Allah": "God's unity, in respect of the divine names that require our existence, is a unity of many [*aḥadiyat al-kathra*], while in respect of his complete independence of the names and us [*al-ghaniyy ʿannā wa-ʿan al-asmāʾ*], it is a unity of essence [*aḥadiyat al-ʿayn*], for both of which the name the one [*al-aḥad*] is used, so take note."[15] If "the One is regarded as the all-embracing Being—the ultimate ground of all existence,"[16] if the one, as "the essence," is "absolutely unconditioned,"[17] and if, further, "Being is one and changeless, while the existent things never remain still for an instant,"[18] the unity of God, if also "the essential unity of being,"[19] "the Oneness of Being,"[20] divides. There is a unity of multiplicity, "al-kathra," and a unity of essence, "al-ʿayn," and yet this division, if it mirrors the distinction, in terms of modes of being, between "al-khalq" and "al-ḥaqq," it does not secure the being of either of these but gives to us their indistinction. Each sense of unity spoken of in the language of Ibn ʿArabī cannot be separated from a prior division between multiplicity and unicity—between an understanding of "the divinity," "al-ilāh," with respect to the divine names, on the one hand, and with respect to God's transcendence, in relation to "the essence," "al-dhāt," on the other—which the name "the one," "al-wāḥid," recalls and withholds. The "one," then, in Ibn ʿArabī, ceases to be itself, it ceases to be "one," as it gives to us, merely, an experience of reading where language disidentifies the terms it cannot cease defining—where, in a reiteration of categories, language dissolves the distinctions it sets in play and sends, aporetically, at us. It is an experience that, without a desire to resolve language into its sense, an atemporal meaning, merely gives to us a temporal practice that, without end, is what "language," in Ibn ʿArabī, is.

---

[14] Ghandour, *Die Theologische Erkenntnislehre Ibn al-ʿArabīʾs*, 264.
[15] Ibn ʿArabī, *Bezels of Wisdom*, 126/Ibn ʿArabī, *Fuṣūṣ al-ḥikam*, 105.
[16] Al-ʿAfīfī, *Mystical Philosophy*, 170.
[17] Chodkiewicz, *Seal of the Saint*, 125n31.
[18] Chittick, *The Sufi Path*, 125.
[19] Al-ʿAfīfī, *Mystical Philosophy*, 146.
[20] Chodkiewicz, *Seal of the Saints*, 163.

One   201

3.

In Ibn 'Arabī we are given a sense of oneness, where what is said to be "one" is not itself; where "one," including the absolute oneness which is the "unity," "aḥadiyya," of "the essence," "al-dhāt," ceases to be what it is. We may consider this sense of oneness in relation to Ibn 'Arabī's discussion of the unlimited distinction of God, understood as "the absolute being," from limits: "One who is distinguished from what is limited," he writes, "is himself limited because he is not that thing; to deny all limitation is itself a limitation, the absolute being limited by his own absoluteness [*wa-al-muṭlaq muqayyad bi-al-iṭlaq*]."[21] The qualities of the transcendent and the absolute may "only be assented to in relation to the divine essence [*al-dhāt al-ilāhiyya*]," where the world "is nothing but an image of the reality disclosing itself [*al-ḥaqq al-mutajallī*] in its names and attributes," but this "essence," itself, is convoluted in the distinction that is to be drawn between it and, at once, "the divinity" and "the lord."[22] There is an infinity of names—"The names of God are infinite because they are known by all that derives from them, which is infinite, even though they derive from a number of sources, which are the matrices or abodes of the names"—and yet this infinitude is returned to a single being, which, being solely itself, shelters its unity.[23]

It is this unity that gives a sense of being and its meaning: "He permeates through [*fa-huwwa al-sārī fī*] all beings called created and originated, and were it not the case, existence [*al-wujūd*, "being"—JS] would have no meaning [*mā ṣaḥḥ al-wujūd*]" (135/111), and this "permeation," Ibn 'Arabī underlined in a passage I've cited above, is a "gift," "i'ṭā'." Because of the particular sense in which being is given, and because of the "permeation" it implies, and which encompasses God— "For divinity [*al-uluhiyya*] implies and requires that which depends on it, just as lordship [*al-rubūbiyya*] requires servanthood" (148/119)—Ibn 'Arabī is able to write of God that "He is being itself [*fa-huwwa 'ayn al-wujūd*]" (135/111). "The reality, in its essence, is beyond all need of the cosmos" (148/119), but "Lordship, on the other hand, does not enjoy such a position" (148/119); and yet "lordship," as soon as it is distinguished from "the essence," is immediately brought back to its relation to it: "Indeed, the lord is, in its reality and qualification, none other than this essence ['*ayn hādhā al-dhāt*]" (148/119). "The real exists in itself,"[24] but there is, already, differentiation: "When, however, differentiation and opposition

---

[21] Ibn 'Arabī, *Bezels of Wisdom*, 135/Ibn 'Arabī, *Fuṣūṣ al-ḥikam*, 111.
[22] Al-'Afīfī, *al-Ta'liqāt*, 2.127.
[23] Ibn 'Arabī, *Bezels of Wisdom*, 68/Ibn 'Arabī, *Fuṣūṣ al-ḥikam*, 65.
[24] Sells, *Mystical Languages*, 84.

202   *Literature and Religious Experience*

arise by virtue of the various relationships, the reality begins to describe itself as the bestower of compassion on his servants."[25] The time of this differentiation "forms an aporia,"[26] because, in order to speak of "the essence," "al-dhāt," in its distinction from "the lord," "al-rabb," differentiation must already be in play. Because of this, just as there is, already, differentiation, there is, already, a giving of names—there is, already, we might also say, language—with the "compassion," "al-shafaqa," of God, and it is this compassion, a "divine mercy," which gives to us the gift of being, and if also of language—and the foundational indistinction between them—in Ibn ʿArabī.[27]

In his commentary on *Fuṣūṣ al-ḥikam*, ʿAbd al-Razzāq al-Qāshānī (d. 1330) elaborates the relation between the divine names, on the one hand, and the distinction between "the absolute being," "al-muṭlaq," and "the contingent being," "al-mumkin" on the other, and I turn to his commentary here to clarify the sense of the distinctions Ibn ʿArabī draws. "Lordship," al-Qāshānī writes, "is not beyond all need of the cosmos, for the one who is beyond all need of the totality is none other than the essence itself."[28] The distinction between "lordship" and "the essence" intersects with the distinction between what is "necessary" in its being and what is, merely, "contingent," because the latter is given place to only through its disclosure in the divine names. "The contingent being," al-Qāshānī explains, "does not have being in itself [*laysā lahu bi-dhātihi wujūd*], for it has no being except in relation to it [*fa-lā wujūd lahu illā bihi*, where "it" refers to "the reality," *al-ḥaqq*—JS]" (200). "There is no thing," he further emphasizes, "other than what is through him" (200); because all beings other than "the reality" are contingent, they all depend upon it for their being: "The contingent being [*al-mumkin*] is not able to exist in itself [*li-dhātihi*], because if it did, it wouldn't be contingent and it would exist necessarily [*fa-yakūn fī al-wujūd wājiban*]" (200–1). "He is being in its totality / and he is the one through whose / being my being is established," Ibn ʿArabī writes,[29] and this "establishment" of the being of contingent beings, understood, as it is in these passages in al-Qāshānī, in its relation to the necessary being, is routed, in Ibn ʿArabī, through a reflection on the divine names. "The essence is one and the determinations various [*wa-al-ʿayn wāḥid wa-ikhtalafat al-aḥkām*]" (86/77), Ibn ʿArabī emphasizes, and these

---

[25] Ibn ʿArabī, *Bezels of Wisdom*, 148/Ibn ʿArabī, *Fuṣūṣ al-ḥikam*, 119.

[26] Sells, *Mystical Languages*, 66.

[27] Ibn ʿArabī, *Bezels of Wisdom*, 147/Ibn ʿArabī, *Fuṣūṣ al-ḥikam*, 119; and "All creatures [*al-mawjūdāt*, "all beings"—JS] are indeed words of God [*kalimāt Allah*], stemming as they do from 'Be,' which is the word of God" (178/142).

[28] ʿAbd al-Razzāq al-Qāshānī, *Sharḥ ʿalā Fuṣūṣ al-ḥikam*, 218–19.

[29] Ibn ʿArabī, *Bezels of Wisdom*, 135/Ibn ʿArabī, *Fuṣūṣ al-ḥikam*, 111.

determinations are the manifestations of the divine names. "Unity has three levels," al-Qāshānī wrote:

> The unity of the essence [al-dhāt], without consideration of multiplicity, and this is the essential, absolute unity [al-aḥadiyya al-dhātiyya al-muṭlaqa]; and the unity of the names [aḥadiyat al-asmāʾ], with the multiplicity of attributes, and this is the divine unity [al-aḥadiyya al-uluhiyya], and God, considered in this way, is one [wāḥid], and considered in the first way, absolutely one [aḥad]; and the third is the unity of lordship [aḥadiyat al-rububiyya].

This, he continues, "is the unity of the multiplicity of acts and effects, which are ascribed, finally, to the essential identity [al-huwiyya al-dhātiyya] itself."[30] And yet this routing—and this is the aporetic, and, I'll also want to argue, the poetic dimension of Ibn ʿArabī's language, where his text reiterates the paratactical form and mode its argument can take on—destabilizes the terms of the philosophical tradition with which Ibn ʿArabī is engaged (in the reflection on "necessary being" in Ibn Sīnā, and which al-Qāshānī elaborates in the passages of his commentary I've translated here) just as it gives to us the sense of the "whole" and the "one" in Fuṣūṣ al-ḥikam.

We may consider this sense in Ibn ʿArabī's discussion of "elevation," in its relation to the number "one"; "elevation is," Ibn ʿArabī explains, "one of God's most beautiful names":[31]

> The elevated is one of God's most beautiful names [wa-min al-asmāʾ al-husnā al-ʿalī]; but above whom or what, since only he exists, and he is elevated in his essence [fa-huwaa al-ʿalī li-dhātihi]? More elevated than whom or what, since only he is and he is elevated in himself [li-nafsihi]? In relation to existence [al-wujūd] he is the very essence of existing beings [ʿayn al-mawjūdāt]. Those beings named relative beings [fa-al-musammā muḥdathāt] are elevated in themselves [li-dhātihā], since they are none other than he [wa laysat illa huwwa]. (85/76)

The discussion of "elevation" points to a contamination between the form of "the essence," "al-dhāt," and "the divinity," "al-ilāh," a term through which God is considered from the point of view of the divine names:

> There is nothing in being other than the essence [wa-laysa illā al-ʿayn alladhī huwaa al-dhāt], which is elevated in itself, its elevation being unrelated to any

---

[30] ʿAbd al-Razzāq al-Qāshānī, Sharḥ ʿalā Fuṣūṣ al-ḥikam, 187.
[31] Ibn ʿArabī, Bezels of Wisdom, 85/Ibn ʿArabī, Fuṣūṣ al-ḥikam, 76.

204 *Literature and Religious Experience*

other. Thus, from this standpoint, there is no relative elevation, although in respect of the aspects of existence there is differentiation. Relative elevation exists in the unique essence [al-ʿayn al-wāḥida] only insofar as it is many aspects [min haythu al-wujūh al-kathīra].

"Thus, in a certain sense," Ibn ʿArabī continues, "it may be said that he is not he and you are not you [*lidhālika naqūl fīhi huwwa lā huwwā; anta lā anta*]" (85/76). The semicolon provided by the editor of the modern Arabic edition does not exist in premodern Arabic textuality, and it works, in this Arabic edition, to manage the indistinction brought about in Ibn ʿArabī's writing; the English-language translator provides the word "and"—"Thus, in a certain sense, it may be said that he is not he *and* [my emphasis—JS] you are not you"—to provide reassurance, a shock absorber for reading, in affirming the distinction between "he" and "you," and in affirming the distinction between the sense in which "he is not he" is distinct from "you is not you." The "relative elevation" that "exists in the unique essence" creates the indistinction between "the unique essence," which is "elevated in itself," because its elevation is "unrelated to any other," and that sort of being for which elevation is "relative"; and yet this sort of being, insofar as its being manifests the divine names, and because "he [*al-ḥaqq*—JS] is the very essence of existing things," is "elevated in itself" because it is "none other than he and his elevation is absolute not relative." The "contingent" being manifests an elevation that is at once relative and absolute, just as the being of "the essence" becomes convoluted in its relation to the quality of being elevated, if only in a relative sense, which characterizes the contingent being.

It is this contamination that opens the threat of multiplicity—"Multiplicity exists only in the divine names" (85/76) and, therefore, not in "the essence," "al-dhāt"—and it is, therefore, at this point, that Ibn ʿArabī turns to the number "one": "The numbers derive from the one [*al-wāḥid*] according to the well-known groupings," Ibn ʿArabī opens; he continues, "Thus the one makes number possible, and number deploys the one" (86/77). "One" is exterior to number but makes number possible; it is contained within number because number is derived from it, and it is therefore outside of enumeration: "Each unity is a reality in itself, like nine or ten down to the lowest and upward *ad infinitum*, although none of them are comprehensive, each of them being a collection of ones [*al-āḥād*]" (86/77), and, as Ibn ʿArabī writes of the number "one," "the plural number is derived from it, so we speak of the plural in relation to it and understand the plural through it [*fa-al-jamʿ yaʾkhudhuhā fa-naqūl bi-hā minhā, wa-naḥkum bi-hā ʿalayhā*]" (86/78). "One" is distinct from number but intersects with it as its ground; it is that in relation to which we are able to make a determination, a judgment, in relation to number, and, therefore, to recognize the difference between the single and the multiple, between what is on the side of "aḥadiyya" and what is on the side of "kathra." The intersection of "one" with "number" mirrors the intersection of "relative" with "absolute" elevation, and the creator with created beings: "Whoever has understood what I have said about numbers, namely, that to deny them is to affirm them, will know that the transcendent reality is the relative creature [al-ḥaqq al-munazzih huwwa al-khalq al-mushabbih], even though the creature be distinct from the creator" (86–7/78). "One," then, is and is not what it is; it is outside of number and relation (it is, following al-Qāshānī, "the absolutely one," "al-aḥad," rather than merely "the one," "al-wāḥid"), just as it manifests and is convoluted through them.

4.

One is "one" and "not one," or, paratactically, it is "one not one," at once what it is and what is in excess of itself. We may understand this excess in relation to love, and it is in this sense that the reading of the divine names in *Fuṣūṣ al-ḥikam* compels attention to *Tarjumān al-ashwāq*, just as the reading of *Tarjumān al-ashwāq* compels attention to the divine names. "Love [al-ḥubb] arises," Ibn ʿArabī writes in *Fuṣūṣ al-ḥikam*, "only for that from which one has one's being, so that man loves that from which he has his being, which is the reality [al-ḥaqq]" (274/217). But if the distinction drawn between "that from which one has one's being," which, Ibn ʿArabī tells us, is "the reality," "al-ḥaqq," and the one whose being "the reality" gives—which Ibn ʿArabī has called, in the several languages of his text, "the contingent being," "al-mumkin," and "the originated being," "al-muḥdath"—then the distinction between the lover and the beloved becomes indistinct. Ibn ʿArabī writes of this in a poem included in the final chapter of *Fuṣūṣ al-ḥikam*, where the speaker, in the first person, is "the reality": "The beloved longs to see me, and I long even more to see him [yuḥinnu al-ḥabīb ilā ruʾyatī, wa-innī ilayhi ashaddu ḥanīnan]/ The hearts beats fast, but destiny bars the way, I groan in complaint and so does he" (273/216). The indistinction of the one from the other—of "the beloved," "al-ḥabīb," from the lover, "I," "anā"—is intensified absolutely, to encompass the distinction between "al-ḥaqq" from "al-khalq," and "the necessary being," that being which is "wājib al-wujūd," from "the contingent being," "al-mumkin."

206 *Literature and Religious Experience*

We might say that this intensification is what poetic love, in Ibn ʿArabī, is; poetic love is what takes place where this or that thing, whichever thing—for example, what is said to be "one," merely what it is—is at once more and less than itself, reaching out to another, leaning toward and upon it, and, one might say, loving it, intensively, where "I" longs to see the beloved "even more," as Ibn ʿArabī wrote, than he wishes to see "me." It is as if there is, in "love," "al-ḥubb" already "ʿal-ʿishq,ʾ" "an excess in love [*ifrāṭ al-maḥabba*]," a term that intersects, itself, Ibn ʿArabī writes, with "al-gharām": "And among the qualities of lovers is, also, *gharām*, which is the lover's being exhausted in the beloved [*al-istihlāk fī al-maḥbūb*] in the persistence of grief [*al-kamd*]," which is "the most intense sadness of the heart [*ashadd ḥuzn al-qalb*]."[32] In Ibn ʿArabī, and with this excess, "the beloved is always already lost,"[33] and it is for this reason that what we are given to read is not "a contraction tending toward perfect synchrony," where relation, as a relation of "proportion,"[34] would privilege a stabilizing unity but merely an incapacity to distinguish the poles of the lover and the beloved, and the creature and God, which is "absolutely transcendent with respect to the Universe,"[35] as it is "the original ground of all being" and its sense.[36]

"The gnostic allots to everything its proper due,"[37] and what is due in the reading of Ibn ʿArabī is to relieve his language of our desire to impose upon it the sense we wish to have accorded it, a determinate meaning exterior to and above language and its temporal practice. And to read Ibn ʿArabī is, therefore, to do so as we ask for forgiveness for our desire to allocate to it a coherency to which it may not, finally, be recalled: "I forgave her as I heard her speak," Ibn ʿArabī wrote in *Tarjumān al-ashwāq*, "grieving as I grieved, with a wounded heart [*fa-ʿadhartuhā lammā samaʿtu kalāmahā/ tashkū kamā ashkū bi-qalbin mūjaʿ*]."[38] The indistinction of the being of the lover from the beloved, and of the world from God, is mirrored in the question of reading, to which we are put in Ibn ʿArabī. Because Ibn ʿArabī's language gives to us this indistinction, without wishing anything in return, it makes manifest in language a fundamental discombobulation of being, where the being of the "absolute God," "al-ilāh al-muṭlaq," as Ibn ʿArabī writes, neither encompasses nor does not encompass itself, where it remains incommensurate in relation to itself and what it is, and

---

[32] Ibn ʿArabī, *al-Futuḥāt al-makiyya*, 3.504, 508, 510.
[33] Sells, *Mystical Languages*, 112.
[34] Corbin, *Alone with the Alone*, 66, 129.
[35] Nasr, *Three Muslim Sages*, 106.
[36] Izutsu, *Sufism and Taoism*, 203.
[37] Ibn ʿArabī, *Bezels of Wisdom*, 276/Ibn ʿArabī, *Fuṣūṣ al-ḥikam*, 219.
[38] Ibn ʿArabī, *Bewildered*, 24/Ibn ʿArabī, *Tarjumān al-ashwāq*, 103.

One 207

where all that we can do is yield, again and again, to an incapacity to read and, finally, to decide:

For the absolute God [al-ilāh al-muṭlaq] cannot be contained by anything [lā yas'uhu shay'], being the very essence of everything and of itself [li-annhu 'ayn al-ashyā' wa 'ayn nafsihi]. Indeed, one cannot say either that it encompasses itself or that it does not do so [lā yuqāl fīhi yas'u nafsahu wa-lā lā yas'uhā]. So understand! God speaks the truth and he is the guide along the way [wa-Allah yaqūl al-ḥaqq wa-huwwa yuhdī al-sabīl].[39]

Bibliography

Al- 'Afīfī, Abū al-'Alā'. *Al-Ta'liqāt*. In Ibn 'Arabī, *Fuṣūṣ al-ḥikam*, edited by Abu al-'Alā' al-'Afīfī. Beirut: Dar al-Katib al-'Arabi, [1946] 2002.

Al- 'Afīfī, Abū al-'Alā'. *The Mystical Philosophy of Muhyid Din Abnul Arabi*. Lahore: Ashraf Press, 1979 [Cambridge University Press, 1939].

Al-Qāshānī, 'Abd al-Razzāq. *Sharḥ al-ustādh al-fāḍil wa-al-'ālim al-kāmil al-Shaykh 'Abd al-Razzāq al-Qāshānī 'alā Fuṣūṣ al-ḥikam*. Beirut: Manushurāt al-Jamal, 2017.

Chittick, William C. *The Sufi Path of Knowledge: Ibn 'Arabī's Metaphysics of Imagination*. New York: State University of New York Press, 1989.

Chodkiewicz, Michel. *Seal of the Saints: Prophethood and Sainthood in the Doctrine of Ibn 'Arabī*. Translated by Liadain Sherrard. Cambridge: Islamic Texts Society, 1993.

Corbin, Henri. *Alone with the Alone: Creative Imagination in the Sufism of Ibn 'Arabi*. Translated by Ralph Manheim. Princeton, NJ: Princeton University Press, [1969] 1998.

Ghandour, Ali. *Die Theologische Erkenntnislehre Ibn al-'Arabī's*. Hamburg: Gryphus, 2018.

Ibn 'Arabī, Muḥī al-Dīn. *Al-Futuḥāt al-makiyya*. Edited by Ahmad Shams al-Din. Beirut: Dar al-Kutub al-'Ilmiyya, 2011.

Ibn 'Arabī, Muḥī al-Dīn. *Bewildered*. Translated by Michael A. Sells. Sausalito, CA: The Post-Apollo Press, 2018.

Ibn 'Arabī, Muḥī al-Dīn. *Bezels of Wisdom*. Translated by R. W. J. Austin. Mahwah, NJ: Paulist Press, 1980.

Ibn 'Arabī, Muḥī al-Dīn. *Dhakā'ir al-a'lāq*. Edited by 'Abd al-Ghānī Muhammad 'Ali al-Fāsī. Beirut: Dar al-Kutub al-'Ilmiyya, 2006.

Ibn 'Arabī, Muḥī al-Dīn. *Fuṣūṣ al-ḥikam*. Edited with commentary by Abū al-'Alā' 'Afīfī. Beirut: Dar al-Katib al-'Arabi, [1946] 2002.

Ibn 'Arabī, Muḥī al-Dīn. *Tarjumān aal-ashwāq*. Beirut: Dar al-Sadir, [1955] 2003.

---

[39] Ibn 'Arabī, *Bezels of Wisdom*, 284/Ibn 'Arabī, *Fuṣūṣ al-ḥikam*, 226.

Izutsu, Toshihiko. *Sufism and Taoism: A Comparative Study of Key Philosophical Concepts*. Berkeley: University of California Press, 1984 [1966–1967].

Nasr, Seyyed Hossein. *Three Muslim Sages: Avicenna—Suhrawardī—Ibn ʿArabī*. Delmar, NY: Caravan Books, 1976 [Harvard University Press, 1964].

Nicholson, Reynold A. *The Tarjumān al-Ashwāq: A Collection of Mystical Odes*. London: Royal Asiatic Society, 1911.

Sells, Michael. *Mystical Languages of Unsaying*. Chicago: University of Chicago Press, 1994.

Sīnā, Ibn. *The Metaphysics of the Healing (Al-Shifāʾ: al-Ilāhiyyāt)*. Translated by Michael Marmura. Provo, UT: Brigham Young University Press, 2006.

Stetkevych, Jaroslav. *Zephyrs of Najd: The Poetics of Nostalgia in the Classical Arabic Nasīb*. Chicago: University of Chicago Press, 1993.

12

Humankindness: *King Lear* and the Suffering, Wisdom, and Compassion within Buddhist Interbeing

Unhae Park Langis

Ulysses in William Shakespeare's *Troilus and Cressida* avows, "One touch of nature makes the whole world kin" (3.3.169).[1] In the context of his argument, he means that we are all alike through a particular kind of human nature—that we love novelty as distraction. In a different but related context, he could well have been talking about the interdependence and interpenetration of everything in the world. In fact, it is in this latter Gaian sense of the world as a living organism that ecologists and environmental advocates have co-opted and deployed the aphorism toward the protection of natural resources and sustainable practices. The double sense of *nature* as the elemental environment and the essence of humankind implies the interdependence between the two within a micro-macrocosmic ecosystem. At the cusp of modernity, Shakespeare and his contemporaries were among the last heirs and subscribers in the West of a monistic cosmic order, or Oneness, a belief in the spiritual interconnectedness and inherent unity of all phenomena, and that happiness is linked to living according to this wisdom.[2] This Oneness often begins with a cosmogonic understanding that all things derive from the same source (the broadest, etymological sense of religion as "linking back") or are manifestations of the same principle—energy, consciousness, life force, be it Greek *pneuma*, Hindu *prana*, Chinese *qi*, or Native American Great Spirit.[3] Whereas secularists may affirm the interconnectedness of physical phenomena without a spiritual complement, ancient wisdom traditions involving oneness entail naturalistic

---

[1] Greenblatt et al., *Norton Shakespeare*. Citations to *King Lear* are from the conflated text, pp. 2479–553.
[2] Garfield et al., "The Oneness Beliefs Scale," 357; Garfield, "Buddhism-based Spirituality," 2.
[3] McEvilley, "The Spinal Serpent," 69.

210   *Literature and Religious Experience*

philosophies and mythologies of physical interdependence. Remarkably similar ethical ideals of lovingkindness arose around the world, grounded in the belief of spiritual oneness.[4] Despite expected cultural variances, its numerous iterations—Buddhist lovingkindness, Stoic *philanthropia*, Greco-Christian *agape*, Confucian *yen*, or Native American caring for all living and nonliving things[5]—converge on an ethic of unlimited, altruistic divine love toward fellow humans and other entities, a devotion to God as synonymous with a devotion to the Good.

The theme of oneness and compassion is prevalent in literature of all genres. In verse, the Native American poet Manitongquat's "A Prayer to Humankind: A Poem of the Heart" is but one expression of the wisdom of indigenous cultures in the New World:

> Life is the Sacred Mystery singing to itself,
> dancing to its drum, telling tales, ...
> and we are all that Spirit,
> our stories all but one cosmic story
> that we are love indeed,
> that perfect love in me seeks the love in you ....[6]

The idea of oneness in this brief excerpt accords not only with "How is your heart?," the common greeting among Mayans in their numerous languages but also on the Mayan notion of unity: *In lak'ech. Hala ken* (I am another you. You are another me).[7] In the Old World, thirteenth-century pantheistic Persian poet Sa'di Shirazi articulates this unity through the notion of a single cosmic being:

> All human beings are members of one frame,
> Since all, at first, from the same essence came.
> When time afflicts a limb with pain
> The other limbs at rest cannot remain.
> If thou feel not for other's misery
> A human being is no name for thee.[8]

This four-thousand-year-old "discourse of macranthropy—of the universe as a single huge anthropomorphic being"[9]—was widely disseminated from Mesopotamia to Egypt and Greece for centuries, judging by its familiarity among Hellenic and Hellenistic philosophers:

---

[4] McEvilley, *The Shape of Ancient Thought*, ch. 2; Nerburn, *Wisdom of the Native Americans*, 15.
[5] Pigliucci, "Stoicism"; Templeton, *Agape Love*, 83; Nerburn, *Wisdom of the Native Americans*, 15.
[6] Manitongquat, "A Prayer to Humankind."
[7] Valdez and Paredes, "In lak'ech: You Are My Other Me"; Tecpaocelotl, "In lak'ech Is New Age."
[8] Shiraz, *Gulistan*.
[9] McEvilley, *The Shape of Ancient Thought*, ch. 2.

Chrysippus:	"If a person is cut in his finger, the whole body suffers."[10]
Sextus Empiricus:	"In the case of unified bodies there exists a certain 'sympathy' …, since when the finger is cut, the whole body shares in its condition."[11]
Seneca:	"*membra sumus corporis magni*, we are all the limbs of a large body."[12]
Plotinus:	"When one member is cut, it is the mass of the body which is cut; the soul feels pain not merely as a mass, but as a living mass."[13]
Alexander of Aphrodisias:	"Nothing comes to be in the universe in such a way that there is not something else which follows it with no alternative and is attached to it as to a cause."[14]

These statements together remarkably resemble an often misquoted environmental slogan attributed to John Muir: "When we try to pick out anything by itself, we find it hitched to everything else in the Universe."[15]

Environmentalists and activists invariably attribute the key concept of interdependence not to Hellenic/Hellenistic sources but rather to more culturally resonant Eastern sources of Taoist and Buddhist mindfulness. This is not the occasion to discuss the complex reasons for this phenomenon. Suffice it to say that "whereas in the East the concept of a living Earth has been a staple of Eastern philosophical and religious thought, in the West it has been dominated since the seventeenth century by a mechanist paradigm leading eventually to the Industrial Revolution." More importantly, as Bruce Scofield notes, "its eclipse for the last three centuries is a deviation from two millennia of Western natural philosophy,"[16] yet the notion that "we are all kin" was second nature to Shakespeare and his contemporaries, the heirs of ancient Greek philosophy, who lived before this eclipsing of Oneness in the West. One German study confirms why sustaining humankindness is species-wise—embracing Oneness boosts satisfaction in all facets of life[17]—and such a worldview will be critical in our resilience to combat pandemics, politico-economic

---

[10] Rosenmeyer, *Senecan Drama*, 111–12; von Arnim, *Stoicorum veterum fragmenta*, 2.1013.
[11] Sextus Empiricus, *Against the Mathematicians*, 9.80.
[12] Seneca, Epistle 95, line 52, glossed in Rosenmeyer, *Senecan Drama*, 111; Gummere, *Epistles*.
[13] Guthrie, *Plotinos*, 467.
[14] Sharples, *Alexander of Aphrodisias*, 192.3–14.
[15] John Muir misquoted: http://vault.sierraclub.org/john_muir_exhibit/writings/ misquotes.aspx.
[16] Scofield, "Gaia: The Living Earth," 157.
[17] Edinger-Schons, "Oneness Beliefs," 1–12.

212 *Literature and Religious Experience*

inequalities, and climate change simultaneously. Nurturing lovingkindness on firm moral and religious grounding may be our only salvation.

Besides poetry, the literature of compassion in the genre of novels is also abundant. Sara Letourneau's claim that novels can lift her "spirits because their characters took the time to show kindness, tolerance, or sympathy toward others"[18] resonates with Ruth Ozeki's Buddhist-inflected *A Tale for the Time Being* and Anthony Doerr's Pullitzer Prize-winning Second World War novel, *All the Light We Cannot See*. The classical canon featuring compassion expansively includes works from Leo Tolstoy and Charles Dickens to Victor Hugo and Thomas Hardy. Hugo's *Les Miserables* notably depicts a memorable scene of mercy: when the police escort ex-convict Jean Valjean to return silverware he had stolen at the occasion of Bishop Bienvenu Myriel's hospitality, the latter merely chides abject Valjean for forgetting the silver candlesticks and making him vow to "use this money in becoming an honest man."[19] Through such a demonstration of enlightened charity, Monseigneur Bienvenu Myriel, as his name suggests, practices the universal ethic of Oneness: unlike those "who toil at extracting gold, he toiled at the extraction of pity. Universal misery was his mine. The sadness which reigned everywhere was but an excuse for unfailing kindness."[20] This is that "special concern on the part of world religions for the weak and defenseless, the vulnerable and voiceless"—in Arthur Templeton's words, "a call to follow in the footsteps of the Muhammad, Confucius, the Old Testament prophets, and many more by seeking to become agents of healing for the suffering of the world."[21]

Of all the literary works that explore the "milk of human kindness" (*Macbeth*, 1.5.15) or its lack, *King Lear* bears special interest as Shakespeare's iconic tragedy about suffering, wisdom, and compassion. Shakespeare adds to his familiarity of the Hellenic and Hellenistic philosophies of Oneness an aesthetic power of irony when the ethic of humankindness is violated *a fortiori* as octogenarian Lear is cast out into a raging storm by his own kin in this powerful meditation on ingratitude. As meteorology mirrors the terror of the human experience, *King Lear* examines nature in multivalent and embedded senses as the elemental environment, the essence of humankind, and the interaction between the two— embodied in the concepts of "nothing" and "kindness." These two notions intently lie also at the heart of Buddhism, the quintessential religion that posits

[18] LeTourneau, "Compassion in Literature."
[19] Hugo, *Les Misérables*, 97.
[20] Hugo, *Les Misérables*, 53; Brombert, "Salvation from Below," 221–3.
[21] Templeton, *Agape Love*, 99–100.

Humankindness 213

human suffering and offers a path into wisdom and compassion, and through this cluster of affinity offers a fitting framework by which to explore *King Lear*.

Consistent with premodern traditions of holistic mind–body wellness in the East and West, the Buddha acted as a spiritual physician, who, having cured himself of suffering, spread his teachings to help others.[22] According to tradition, his first discourse after enlightenment spells out his course of treatment against suffering in the Four Noble Truths, together affirming an end to suffering through a life of compassion and wisdom in following the Eightfold Path.[23] The Buddha's teaching, as Walpola Rahula discerns, centers on the deleterious idea of self "as an imaginary, false belief" with no corresponding reality,

> produc[ing] harmful thoughts of "me" and "mine," selfish desire, craving, attachment, hatred, ill-will, conceit, pride, egoism, and other defilements, impurities, and problems. It is the source of all the troubles in the world from personal conflicts to wars between nations. In short, to this false view can be traced all the evil in the world.[24]

Such is the image of *King Lear*, peopled with characters burdened by "self-aggrandizement, the pursuit of selfish desires, and the attachment to the things of the world."[25] These symptoms of ignorance are the very focus of Buddhist spiritual practice.

The cure for suffering, rooted in ignorance, is wisdom understood as the awareness that all phenomena lack intrinsic existence and that the self, "without an inner core," is rather a constantly changing matrix of five psychophysical aggregates (body, sensation, perception, intellect, and consciousness), mapped as "sensory and mental events" in "temporal and causal" interdependence.[26] Though we may perceive our selves as tangible entities with dense mass, the world at the atomic or subatomic level is seamlessly interconnected and completely empty of self. This Buddhist concept of no-self is best articulated in Thich Nhat Hanh's concept of interbeing:[27] instead of nihilism, nothing suffused through everything entails living free from self-attached craving and drawing

---

[22] Emmanuel, *Companion to Buddhist Philosophy*, 29. McEvilley, *The Shape of Ancient Thought*, ch. 13, notes that Democritus offers a similar account of desire, impermanence, and suffering in Fragment 235.

[23] Santideva, *The Bodhicaryavatara*, 153. The Eightfold Path consists of the following practices: right view, right intention, right speech, right action, right livelihood, right effort, right mindfulness, and right meditation (concentration).

[24] Rahula, *What the Buddha Taught*, 51.

[25] Templeton, *Agape Love*, 65.

[26] Westerhoff, "Nāgārjuna," 3.3.

[27] Hanh, *Peace Is Every Step*, 95–6.

214   *Literature and Religious Experience*

purpose and energy from the organic web of connectedness rather than a mental construct of separate selves with no corresponding reality.

Emotionally, such kinship in Buddhism centers on lovingkindness. Like its Greco-Christian version *agape*, selfless love, lovingkindness, as the Pali word *metta* and its roots indicate, is to treat another gently as a friend. In meditation, it is a wish for all beings to be free from suffering; more importantly in conduct, it means directing one's attention to the happiness or suffering of others. Lovingkindness, antidotal to selfishness, anger, and fear, awakens us to the truth of being, "a sense of unity beyond suffering," beyond fragmentation and alienation.[28] Insight into "the whole world kin" kindles a newfound way of life guided by kindness and wisdom. Though not manifesting no-self in its radical form, Shakespeare's tragedy, nonetheless, reveals transformation when Lear, unencumbered by attachment and self-interest, offers compassion to unfortunate others and envisions a Nirvana-like happiness of "singing like birds i' the cage," transcending the endless flow of contentious life into the very "mystery of things" (5.3.9, 16). Ultimately, when the audience must deal with Cordelia's senseless death, we too might be bolstered by the Buddhist karmic worldview of interbeing.

To be sure, drama and *dharma* (here meaning Buddha's teachings that "hold" us from falling into states of suffering) appear as odd bedfellows: what does theatrical "sound and fury / Signifying nothing" have to do with monks meditating in lotus position?[29] Let me note in this short essay what distinguishes modern scholars and practitioners from ancient Buddhist tradition: the Buddha's eminently practical stance to spiritual practice. The imperative of living ultimately calls one back to reconcile oneself with *dharmas*, here meaning the "constituent elements" or phenomena in life that "hold their own nature" yet are ultimately insubstantial.[30] The Buddha, regarding metaphysical and other irresolvable questions as obstacles to spiritual progress, met them, indeed, with Noble Silence.[31] The Pyrrhonian Skeptics' similar adherence to ontological indeterminacy is a key point of convergence in the shared tradition of *ascesis* (spiritual practice) from India to Greece, regardless of the path chosen— Buddhist mindful and moral living toward enlightenment; Aristotelian practical wisdom, or Stoic suspension of judgment and *ataraxia* (equanimity).[32] In

---

[28] Salzberg, *Lovingkindness*, 19.

[29] Shakespeare, *Macbeth*, Act 5, sc. 5, lines 26–7.

[30] Buswell and Lopez, "Many Meanings of Dharma." This is in a nutshell the aim of everyday Zen.

[31] *Malunkyaputta Sutta* 63, clarified in McEvilley, *The Shape of Ancient Thought*, ch. 13.

[32] According to Gombrich, *How Buddhism Began*, 106, and Vetter, *The Ideas and Meditative Practices of Early Buddhism*, xxii, the Buddha underscored "different ways of obtaining salvation for different types of individuals," much like Aristotle who made allowances for individual ethical development

Humankindness 215

examining a spiritual journey, I argue that Lear, within the triangulation of suffering, wisdom, and kindness, experiences watershed moments of awakening during which he taps into something like Buddhist interbeing. Such a claim is plausible because much like global Shakespeare, "the essence of Buddhism isn't 'Buddhist,' " as French biologist-turned-monk Matthieu Ricard notes, "it's universal" and particular: on the one hand, Buddhism "touches the basic mechanisms of the human mind" and, on the other, it "considers that each person has to start where they are and use the methods that match their nature and their personal capacities."[33]

1.

In divesting power to his daughters, King Lear discovers just how "slenderly [he] know[s] himself" (1.1.291–2)—his own nature, as well as the nature of kindness and love, and how they are mutually constitutive of greater Nature. Although intending to "unburthened crawl toward death" (1.1.39), Lear, during and after the division of his estate, proves his attachment to ego—embedded in the commiserable anxiety that old age brings—by conditioning his gift to praise and by clinging to "the name and all the additions to a king" (1.1.136). According to eighth-century Indian Buddhist master Santideva, seeking "praise" to feel "delight" is "absurdity, ... simply the behaviour of a child."[34] Lacking the skill of spiritual adepts, who choose ethically appropriate actions based on "understanding as well as good intention," Lear mistakes desire, the "near enemy" of lovingkindness, for what he really seeks—the raw but true kindness that Cordelia tenders him when with her response of "Nothing" (1.1.88), she refuses to situate her love in "an economy, exchangeable for wealth and power."[35] Indeed, according to Sean Lawrence, Lear claims to offer "absolute gifts" to his daughters when he is actually demanding "absolute obligation," the retention of a centurial retinue.[36] The impossible situation forces her to dial it back down to zero, which simultaneously intimates the infinite: in the paradoxical language of the Zen koan, nothing is everything; everything, nothing.[37] Downsizing Lear

---

based on varying psychohumoral makeup. For a review of scholarship on Greco-Buddhism, see Mills, "Skepticism and Religious Practice in Sextus and Nāgārjuna," 92.

[33] Revel and Ricard, *The Monk and the Philosopher*, 138.
[34] Santideva, *The Bodhicaryavatara*, VI.97.
[35] Santideva, *The Bodhicaryavatara*, 145; Lawrence, *Forgiving the Gift*, 94.
[36] Lawrence, *Forgiving the Gift*, 92.
[37] See Soeng, *The Heart of the Universe*, 7: "form is emptiness, ... emptiness is form."

should recognize the wisdom of "less is more" in Cordelia's one-word reply, "Nothing," but ego prevents him from recognizing that *his* conditioning of gift has more to do with transaction than Cordelia's apparently stinting love. Instead, inflated by the two elder daughters' fustian, Lear takes Cordelia's sudden deflation of pomp to plain speaking as an ungracious public affront to his royal person.

To probe the analogy suggested earlier, Cordelia's shocking answer, "Nothing," plays out like a koan, a Zen story or situation involving a dialogue or event between master and student. By skillfully wielding language, the koan aims to "shock" in order to create "an opening wedge" for an epiphany.[38] This sudden dousing of water does not work with Lear, too self-immersed to realize that he himself has driven Cordelia to a crash landing in this high-stakes competition. Exhibiting moral blindness, Lear's famous reply to Cordelia, "Nothing will come of nothing" (1.1.89), reminds us of a Chan koan:

> Emperor Wu of Liang asked the great master Bodhidharma, "What is the highest meaning of the holy truths?" Bodhidharma said, "Empty, without holiness." The Emperor said, "Who is facing me?" Bodhidharma replied, "I don't know." The Emperor did not understand ....

> When Bodhidharma first met Emperor Wu, the Emperor asked, "I have built temples and ordained monks; what merit is there in this?" Bodhidharma said, "There is no merit." He immediately doused the Emperor with dirty water.[39]

Lear resembles Emperor Wu in that, though intending to do the right thing, they both reveal their attachments and delusions in seeking "praise" to feel "delight," their inability to reside in no-self with the insight that nothing is everything. At the level of ordinary language, what Emperor Wu hears is nonsense, but in the embodied experience of emptiness and no-self, Bodhidharma's negative statements assert that the potent moral-metaphysical implications of emptiness apply in "an 'uroboric' or self-destroying path" even to bodhisattvas aspiring to buddhahood and "holy truths" like the emptiness doctrine itself.[40] By clinging to social status and merit like Emperor Wu, Lear misprises the generosity that undergirds Cordelia's "nothing." His ego-logic is unable to process Buddhist non-dualist logic, by which nothing is everything and vice versa.[41] Beyond the fustian of the elder sisters, Lear is left with nothing as we see later, whereas

[38] Yu, "Ta-hui Tsung-kao," 224.
[39] Wu, *Blue Cliff Record*, 1, 3.
[40] McEvilley, *The Shape of Ancient Thought*, ch. 17.
[41] Nagatomo, "Japanese Zen Buddhist Philosophy."

Cordelia's plain-speaking "nothing" expands to the plenitude of her filial bond. Her "nothing" is a lesson in thusness, everything that her filial piety should be, everything that we cannot discern when we do not attend to the present with full mind and heart.

Dumbstruck in the absence of delightful praise, Lear behaves, as Santideva would say, "like a child that howls a wail of distress when his sandcastle is broken."[42] In violently yanking Cordelia from his heart and purse, Lear instantiates the tragic irony embedded in the sheer self-destructiveness of humans, as described in Santideva's teaching: "Hoping to escape suffering, it is to suffering that they run. In the desire for happiness, out of delusion, they destroy their own happiness, like an enemy."[43] For his error, Lear, like Emperor Wu, will karmically be doused with torrential water. In so doing, Lear sets off a chain of actions within a matrix of nothing, suffering, and kindness—key elements interacting within the Buddhist ontology of connectedness, converging in a spiritual practice of mindfulness and compassion.

Goneril's sharp "censure" and order "to disquantity" his "insolent retinue" (1.4.176, 184, 224) stun Lear into the truth of her unkind nature and further into a query into the very nature of things. Doubting that she is properly his daughter, he turns inward, questioning his own self, his body, his speech, his senses:

Doth any here know me? This is not Lear.
Doth Lear walk thus? Speak thus? Where are his eyes?
Either his notion weakens, his discernings
Are lethargied—Ha! waking? 'Tis not so.
Who is it that can tell me who I am? (1.4.201–4)

This questioning remarkably resembles the Buddhist chanting of the Heart Sutra, intended to instill no-self: "No eyes, no ears, no nose, no tongue, no body, no mind."[44] Since the antagonism between Goneril and him is so far from his conception of the parent–offspring relationship, Lear would rather think it is a bad dream. He is coming to learn, however, as the Fool suggests, that he is "Lear's shadow," for "the marks of sovereignty, knowledge, and reason" (206–9) falsely convey that he has daughters—affectively and morally as opposed to biologically. Even though Lear impugns his identity, knowledge, and sovereign reason rhetorically, extending this skepticism substantively in the Buddhist sense of no-self might bring novel insight into the play. In the *Vinaya*, which sets rules

---

[42] Santideva, *The Bodhicaryavatara*, VI.93.
[43] Santideva, *The Bodhicaryavatara*, I.28.
[44] Soeng, *Heart of the Universe*, 67.

218   *Literature and Religious Experience*

for the Buddhist monastic community, we find a method other than meditation for gaining release from craving, namely, through discriminating insight, which Tilmann Vetter explains as "knowing that things we normally consider to be the self or belonging to the self cannot be or belong to the self if this self is conceived of as not suffering."[45] For the purposes of this "disidentification," the self is divided into its aggregates—form (body), feeling, apperception, dispositions, perception. In this discourse called the *Anattapariyaya*, the Buddha, typically addressing monks, examines each aggregrate as to whether or not it can be the self:

> What do you think, monks, is visible form permanent or impermanent?— Impermanent, Sir.—Now what is impermanent, is this unpleasant or pleasant?— Unpleasant, Sir.—Now, what is impermanent, unpleasant [and] bound to change, is it proper to regard it in such a way: this is mine, this I am, this is my self?—Surely not, Sir.[46]

After repeating the same line of syllogistic reasoning with the other aggregates, the Buddha concludes with each of the aggregrates:

> Therefore, monks, whatever visible form there is, past, future [or] present, inward or outward, gross or subtle, inferior or excellent, at a distance or nearby, all visible form should be looked upon with right discriminating insight in this way: this is not mine, this I am not, this is not my self .... When a noble disciple, who is learned, looks upon visible form, [etc.] in such a way, he has enough of visible form, [etc.] .... Having enough, he frees himself from desire; by being freed from desire he is released.

Through a similar disidentifying process, by which he distances himself from "the marks of sovereignty, knowledge, and reason" (1.4.207), Lear gains embodied knowledge of the Buddhist three marks of existence in active interplay: impermanence (loss of sovereignty and its trappings), suffering, and no-self. Earlier dismissing his Fool's ramblings as "nothing" (1.4.111), Lear is now pitifully "disquantitied" to "an O without a figure" from a worldly perspective, but being a "shadow" (176, 168, 206) of himself, from a Buddhist perspective of nothing is everything, may well be a mark of awakening to interbeing.

The sense of self, Ajahn Sucitto explains, arises out of empirical experience and ensuing social conditioning through language,[47] according to the link known as

---

[45] Vetter, *Ideas and Meditative Practices*, 35.
[46] *Vinaya* I and *Majjhima Nikaya* 22 I, quoted in Vetter, *Ideas and Meditative Practices*, 37.
[47] Sucitto, *Turning the Wheel of Truth*, 69.

name-and-form in the Buddhist chain of dependent origination, which explains how the phenomenal world came to be.

As Thomas McEvilley further notes, "The processes of sense-perception and linguistic reification constitute name-and-form, or *maya*, as they do the world of *doxa* for Parmenides."[48] When the impermanence of life reduces Lear from the apex of society to "houseless poverty" (3.4.28), he is abruptly awakened to the social constructedness of "name and form" in human world-making—if not quite the metaphysical insubstantiality of Buddhist emptiness. The loss of his retinue, previously so important as visible markers of his royal identity, instantly becomes immaterial, and the dispute of "additions" vs. the "disquantity[ing of his] train" (1.4.224) is suddenly put to rest.

This essay aims to explore Lear's spiritual journey within the Buddhist strand of the wisdom tradition of Oneness. A larger treatment would cover not only a complementary analysis of ingratitude on the part of Lear's daughters consumed by self-attached craving but also an exploration of karma, the physical manifestation of mental and moral phenomena. Through a statement like "One *touch* of nature makes the whole world kin" (*Troilus and Cressida*, 3.3.169, my emphasis), Shakespeare, like his peers much influenced by Senecan drama, shows his understanding of *sympatheia*, the Stoic counterpart to Buddhist concepts of interdependence and karma. As Cicero's translation of "touch" as *contagio* suggests,[49] the subtle, intricate, and sometimes self-implicating operation of pneumatic karma in *King Lear* highlights viral infection, the pervasion of psychophysical dis-ease—so resonant in the collective grappling and grieving during the Covid-19 pandemic as well as the simultaneous outrage unleashed by the unceasing police murders of African Americans.[50] As a longer study would show, Lear's own karmic implication in his adversity makes him forbear ("I will endure") and "shun" (3.4.19, 22) mental afflictions that manifest in unwholesome actions, but what is more important here about his eschewing anguish is that it opens up space for wholesome interaction.

When Kent tells him to seek shelter in the hovel, Lear's attention widens beyond himself to his fool: "Come on, my boy. How dost, my boy? my fellow? / ... Poor fool and knave, I have one part in my heart / That's sorry yet for thee" (3.2.66–71). The wholesome side of suffering opens Lear into mindful compassion as he implicitly acknowledges the Fool's caring for him. Helping

[48] McEvilley, *The Shape of Ancient Thought*, chs. 2 and 13, on deconstructing norms and Herodotus awareness of "the distinction between *physis*, or nature, and *nomos*, or culture."
[49] Cicero, quoted in Rosenmeyer, *Senecan Drama*, 111.
[50] Mulligan, "Pandemic, Recession, Unrest."

220   *Literature and Religious Experience*

the Fool, he helps himself: compassion, like mercy, is "twice blest," blessing "him that gives and him that takes" (*Merchant of Venice*, 4.1.181–2). Awakening to another's distress, Lear finds temporary relief from his own suffering: "This tempest will not give me leave to ponder / On things would hurt me more" (3.4.25–6). Instead of cursing or wallowing in sorrow, Lear channels his energy into an appeal, one of the most famous meditations on kindness in Western literature:

> Poor naked wretches, wheresoe'er you are,
> That bide the pelting of this pitiless storm,
> How shall your houseless heads and unfed sides,
> Your looped and windowed raggedness, defend you
> From seasons such as these? O, I have ta'en
> Too little care of this! Take physic, pomp;
> Expose thyself to feel what wretches feel,
> That thou mayst shake the superflux to them,
> And show the heavens more just. (3.4.29–37)

Here, Lear not only takes the Fool's kernel of Stoic wisdom to fit his "content with his fortunes" (3.2.74) but also extends beyond that to evoke compassion and justice among his aristocratic peers, who have neglected the concerns of the destitute and deprived. To this end, the Fool is instrumental to Lear's return to nature, his love of humanity, and connectedness to the world.

The injunction, "Take physic," is the most compressed expression of the idea familiar in both Eastern (Ayurvedic and Buddhist) and Western (Aristotelian-Galenic) mindbody traditions of seeking wholeness in nature (*physis*). Nature, in Stoic cosmology, is "the universe itself seen as an ordered whole (*kosmos*) determined by a principle of structure (*logos*) and law (*nomos*)."[51] *Physis*, simultaneously, refers to "the little world of man" in the premodern concept of micro-macrocosmic correspondences effected by pneumatic *sympatheia*. Accordingly, the imperative "Take physic," means to "heed nature" mindfully, to heal thyself by knowing and acting in kinship with other beings and justly interacting with the natural world. Cosmic wisdom, indeed: in a pandemic world where twenty-three million renters could be facing eviction and homelessness by October 2020,[52] we, too, could certainly "take physic," singly and collectively, and especially the corporate "persons" and flawed institutions inordinately accountable in these times of pandemic, climate change, and persisting economic

---

[51] Stephens, "Stoic Naturalism," 276.
[52] McKay, Gilman, and Neumann, "20 Million Renters Are at Risk of Eviction."

and social inequalities. The particularly harsh manifestations of Nature—the raging storm—make it admittedly challenging for Lear to feel kinship there. Nonetheless, he undergoes a fully embodied experience that poignantly reveals to him that lovingkindness is more substantial than anything else in the phenomenal world.

Lear no longer craves "additio[n]" (1.1.141); his actions show a realization of "having enough." As his later comment to Gloucester indicates, he profoundly understands the nature of human suffering: "We came crying hither; … / the first time that we smell the air / We wail and cry …. / When we are born, we cry that we are come / To this great stage of fools" (4.6.172–7). Buddhist texts also state that "on account of birth there is decay and death." Lear has awakened to the insight that Buddhists designate as "the spotless Dharma-eye," which allows one to the "apprehend the impermanence of seemingly stable things, when one knows they have ever begun to exist."[53] The first noble truth of suffering in the embodied human experience refers to not only birth, physical pain, and aging but also the illusory sense of self as constructed by the aggregrates.[54] Acutely if not durably, Lear has learned that the only cure for "addition," or craving and grasping in Buddhist terms, is reduction prompted by the insight of nothing.

The fruit of this moral awakening to kinship is generative lovingkindness. Albeit with increasing mental instability, Lear connects with Edgar, disguised as a madman, whom he assumes is another "discarded fathe[r]" like himself. In the complex workings of karma in the premodern psychopneumatic understanding of the world—fumes of ingratitude and other poisons diffusing against portentous meteoric skies—it is eminently conceivable that Lear, a victim of filial ingratitude, "more sinned against than sinning" (3.2.58), encounter and ally himself with Edgar, a twice-removed victim of the sexual indiscretion of his father and the karmic machinations of a spiteful, ungrateful "bastard" son against his stepbrother and father. After solicitous concern, Lear holds Edgar up as "the thing itself; unaccommodated man [as] no more but a poor, bare, forked animal as thou art" (3.4.98–100): in Buddhist terms, nothing and everything. To Lear, "unaccommodated" is "sophisticated," especially since he later addresses Edgar as a "learned Theban" "philosopher" (142, 145)—which, I suspect, is a reference to the Indian "naked philosophers" and their Jain and Buddhist *ascesis* (hence, *gymnosophists*), probably encountered by both Skeptic Pyrrho, traveling

---

[53] *Nikaya* 74, quoted. in Vetter, *Ideas and Meditative Practices*, 38; *Samyutta Nikaya* II.25, quoted in McEvilley, *The Shape of Ancient Thought*, ch. 13, and other similar passages of Epictetus and the Buddha in ch. 25.

[54] Vetter, *Ideas and Meditative Practices*, 73.

with Alexander the Great's entourage, and Neoplatonist Plotinus, studying in Alexandria, near Thebes.[55] Emulating their ascetics and enacting generosity toward Edgar, Lear tears off his clothes—"Off, off, you lendings!" (100). Knowing that material possessions are but borrowings during our short lease on earth, he "consider[s] … well" "the thing itself," and perhaps that nothing is everything. In *All's Well*, Parolles, a "braggart" who was disgracefully "found an ass," sustains himself with *thusness*, the wonder of merely being: "simply the thing I am / Shall make me live" (4.3.310–13). Perhaps it is not a stretch to say in Sharon Salzberg's words that "both the clear, open space of 'nothing' and the interconnectedness of 'everything' awaken" Lear to his "true nature": "We see that nothing is stagnant and nothing is fully separate, that who we are, what we are,"—"poor, bare, forked animal[s]" (3.4.99–100)—"is intimately woven into the nature of life itself. Out of this sense of connection, love and compassion arise."[56] From complaining about not having a hundred followers in 1.4 and 2.4 to stripping off his clothes in 3.4, Lear exhibits an extraordinary transformation from a conditioned state of acquisitiveness and status-mongering to one of inner abundance, which impels him to share his garments with another less protected against the pelting rain. Unlike the conditioned apportioning of his estate to his daughters in 1.1, this sharing is without expectation of reward or recognition. Through heartfelt giving to persons socially and economically more deprived than himself, Lear becomes awakened to the universal condition of suffering, its inherent causes, and the way to relieve pain through compassion and concern for others. Though his hard-earned peace and insight inexorably yield to the weight of his "abusèd nature" (4.7.15), madly rambling Lear still retains the wisdom gained that he is not "ague-proof" but a mortal who will "wear out to nought" and that true insight is not what is perceived by the senses in the conditioned world: "A man may see how this world goes with no eyes" (4.6.103, 133, 146).

Lear's unexpected reunion with Cordelia in 4.7 and 5.3 briefly sparks hope of redemption. As expected, Lear returns to himself from a disidentified state resembling Buddhist no-self, in which he did not feel his hands as properly his and felt kinship with others "mightily abusèd" (4.7.53). As much as he seeks a rational understanding of self, "Would I were assured / Of my condition" (4.7.56–7), the Buddhist hope remains that such recovery of reason will not vitiate newly

---

[55] McEvilley, *The Shape of Ancient Thought*, chs. 9, 13, and 22 on Diogenes, Pyrrho, and Plotinus, respectively. For other historical references and another plausible reading around Persian hospitality, see, respectively, Langis, "Virtues in Buddhism: Equanimity, Mindfulness, and Compassion in *Hamlet*," and Kaufman, "Ancient Persian Virtues in the Age of Shakespeare."

[56] Salzberg, *Lovingkindness*, 19, 113.

Humankindness 223

gained insights into interbeing. We see, indeed, that Lear retains his "Reason in madness" (4.6.169), wisdom dearly gained from suffering when refusing to confront his daughters for "censure" (5.3.3), he prefers, instead, a renunciatory life, the Nirvana-like happiness of "singing like birds i' the cage," transcending the endless flow of contentious life into the very "mystery of things" (5.3.9, 16). At the same time, Lear, clear-eyed about having to face punishment, vows that "the good-years shall devour [Goneril and Regan], flesh and fell, / Ere they shall make us weep! We'll see 'em starve first" (24–5). In so doing, he has recovered fortitude in the stance of Buddhist-Stoic forbearance and patience. Lear was indeed progressing on the three practices of the patience *paramita* (perfection)— from enduring those who wish us harm, to enduring difficulties in our body and in the environment, to enduring the emptiness" of phenomena[57]—only to be obstructed by Cordelia's sudden death. In dramatizing innocent Cordelia's death as an image of doomsday horror, Shakespeare pushes the envelope of life's insubstantiality—in the Western tradition of shadow existence from Plato to Roman role-playing—toward Buddhist nothing/everything.

Death relieves Lear, but the spectators, alongside Edgar and Albany, remain behind to be unsettled by Cordelia's death. Shakespeare, as artist, could easily have let Cordelia live—let us feel good that the good guy wins and the bad guy dies. Instead, he lets her die senselessly, thereby highlighting permanent mysteries of human life that we encounter daily—just turn on the news to the deaths of George Floyd and other black and brown martyrs of police violence. Ultimately, the audience's grappling with Cordelia's senseless death, through the dramatic experience of co-suffering, may be the "seed" of insight into "the life of things," which, unlike the "germens" (3.2.9) of ingratitude, may open up otherwise foreclosed possibilities of growth for us.[58] A Buddhist response to Cordelia's death schooling us for equanimity and compassion entails a shifting of perspective in two important ways. First, we can accept her death because Cordelia, herself, acting with full conviction and no regret, is the type of selfless martyr who would say "Why *not* me?" instead of "Why me?" Second, as radical as it sounds, Buddhist interbeing reveals a compassionate stance toward our perceived enemies and persecutors. Take the example of the Tibetan Buddhist monks who underwent ordeals of torture. Surprisingly, these monks were *not* experiencing feelings of fear, rage, dehumanization, and isolation commonly associated with post-traumatic stress disorder.[59] They had the breadth of vision

---

[57] Yen, *The Six Paramitas*, 24.
[58] Khapa, *Ocean of Eloquence*, 92; Makeham, *The Buddhist Roots*, 22.
[59] Salzberg, *Lovingkindness*, 232–4.

to shun dualistic thinking and to see that antagonists in any conflict are two sides of the same problem: as emotional beings, we're "all entangled in the same web of violence," though we may play different parts in "the unjust institutions, social systems, and ideas that perpetuate suffering."[60]

Even as we enjoy his art, Shakespeare's insistence that we face hard truths of reality encourages in us a stance of humility and humankindness enhanced through a Buddhist lens. We'll need to bank on these qualities with the various challenges ahead—pandemic, climate change, and persisting inequalities. Counteracting activist burnout, mindfulness allows the mental reserves to respond with alacrity and forcefulness in situations of injustice demanding action like #BlackLivesMatter's insistence upon a full-out transformation of policing. As the examples of Gandhi and Martin Luther King eminently reveal, proper actions of humankindness and justice flow more effectively from lives grounded in equanimity, from people who are at peace with themselves and a universe that may appear adverse. If we are to survive as a species, we must collectively become *Homo sapiens* in truth.

Bibliography

Brombert, Victor. "*Les Misérables*: Salvation from Below." In *Modern Critical Views: Victor Hugo*, edited by Harold Bloom, 196–215. New York: Chelsea House, 1988.

Buswell, Robert, and Donald Lopez. "The Many Meanings of Dharma: Deciphering Buddhism's Most Common Word." Available online: https://tricycle.org/magazine/many-meanings-dharma/.

Chernus, Ira. *American Non-Violence: The History of an Idea*. Maryknoll, NY: Orbis, 2004. Available online: https://spot.colorado.edu/~chernus/NonviolenceBook/ThichNhatHanh.htm.

Edinger-Schons, L. M. "Oneness Beliefs and Their Effect on Life Satisfaction." *Psychology of Religion and Spirituality* (2019): 1–12.

Emmanuel, Steven. *A Companion to Buddhist Philosophy*. London: Wiley, 2015.

Empiricus, Sextus. *Against the Mathematicians*. Available online: https://www.stoictherapy.com.

Garfield, Andrew M. "The Oneness Beliefs Scale: Buddhism-based Spirituality and Concern for Others and the Environment." University of Wisconsin-Madison, 2013.

Garfield, Andrew M., Brian Drwecki, Colleen F. Moore, Katherine V. Kortenkamp, and Matthew D. Gracz. "The Oneness Beliefs Scale: Connecting Spirituality

---

[60] Chernus, *American Non-Violence*, ch. 13.

with Pro-Environmental Behavior." *Journal for the Scientific Study of Religion* 53 (2014): 356–72.

Gombrich, Richard. *How Buddhism Began: The Conditioned Genesis of the Early Teachings*. London: Athlone Press, 2006.

Gummere, Richard, trans. *Epistles*. Cambridge: Loeb Classical Library, [1917] 2015. Available online: https://www.loebclassics.com/view/seneca_younger-epistles/1917/pb_LCL077.65.xml.

Guthrie, Kenneth, trans. *Plotinos: Amelio-Porphyrian Books, 22–33*, vol. 2. In *Plotinos: The Complete Works*. London: G. Bell, 1918.

Hugo, Victor. *Les Misérables*. Translated by Louise Hapgood. Minneapolis, MN: First Avenue Editions, 2015.

Kaufman, Sheiba K. "Ancient Persian Virtues in the Age of Shakespeare." In *Shakespeare and Virtue: A Handbook*, edited by Julia Reinhardt Lupton and Donovan Sherman. Cambridge: Cambridge University Press, 2022.

Khapa, Tsong. *Ocean of Eloquence: Tsong Khapa's Commentary on the Yogacara Doctrine of Mind*. Translated by Gareth Sparham. Albany, NY: SUNY Press, 1993.

Langis, Unhae P. "Virtues in Buddhism: Equanimity, Mindfulness, and Compassion in *Hamlet*." In *Shakespeare and Virtue: A Handbook*, edited by Julia Reinhardt Lupton and Donovan Sherman. Cambridge: Cambridge University Press, 2022.

Lawrence, Sean. *Forgiving the Gift*. Pittsburgh: Duquesne University Press.

LeTourneau, Sara. "The Power and Importance of Compassion in Literature." Available online: https://saraletourneauwriter.com/2016/11/08/importance-compassion-literature/.

Makeham, John, ed. *The Buddhist Roots of Zhu Xi's Philosophical Thought*. Oxford: Oxford University Press, 2018.

Manitongquat. "A Prayer to Humankind: A Poem of the Heart." Context Institute. Available online: https://www.context.org/iclib/ic01/manitong/.

McEvilley, Thomas. "The Spinal Serpent." *RES: Anthropology and Aesthetics* 24, no. 1 (1993): 67–77.

McEvilley, Thomas. *The Shape of Ancient Thought: Comparative Studies in Greek and Indian Philosophies*. New York: Allworth Press, 2002. Epub.

McKay, Katherine, Sam Gilman, and Zach Neumann. "20 Million Renters Are at Risk of Eviction; Policymakers Must Act Now to Mitigate Widespread Hardship." Aspen Institute, June 19, 2020. Available online: https://www.aspeninstitute.org/blog-posts/20-million-renters-are-at-risk-of-eviction/.

Mills, Ethan. "Skepticism and Religious Practice in Sextus and Nāgārjuna." In *Ethics without Self, Dharma without Atman*, edited by Gordon Davis, 91–106. New York: Springer, 2018.

Mulligan, Susan. "Pandemic, Recession, Unrest." *U.S. News*. June 2, 2020.

Nagatomo, Shigenori. "Japanese Zen Buddhist Philosophy." *Stanford Encyclopedia of Philosophy*. Available online: https://plato.stanford.edu/archives/spr2020/entries/japanese-zen/.

Nerburn, Ken, ed. *Wisdom of the Native Americans*. New York: MJF, 2010.

Nhất Hanh, Thích. *Peace Is Every Step*. New York: Random House, 2010.

Pigliucci, Massimo. "Stoicism." Internet Encyclopedia of Philosophy. https://www.iep.utm.edu/stoicism/.

Rahula, Walpola. *What the Buddha Taught*. New York: Grove Press, [1959] 1974.

Revel, Jean-François, and Mattieu Ricard. *The Monk and the Philosopher*. New York: Schocken Books, 2011.

Rosenmeyer, Thomas. *Senecan Drama and Stoic Cosmology*. Berkeley: University of California Press, 1989.

Salzberg, Sharon. *Lovingkindness: The Revolutionary Art of Happiness*. Boston: Shambala, 2008.

Santideva, *Śāntideva: The Bodhicaryavatara*. Translated by Kate Crosby and Andrew Skilton. Oxford: Oxford University Press, 1995.

Scofield, Bruce. "Gaia: The Living Earth. 2500 Years of Precedents in Natural Science and Philosophy." *Scientists Debate Gaia* (2004): 151–60.

Shakespeare, William. *The Norton Shakespeare*. Edited by Stephen Greenblatt, Walter Cohen, Jean Howard, and Katharine Eisaman Maus. New York: Norton, 1997.

Sharples, R. W., trans. *Alexander of Aphrodisias: On Fate*. London: Duckworth, 1983.

Shirazi, Sa'di. *Gulistan*. Translated by Edward Eastwick. London: Taylor & Francis, 2014, 1880. Epub.

Soeng, Mu. *The Heart of the Universe: Exploring the Heart Sutra*. New York: Simon and Schuster, 2010.

Stephens, William. "Stoic Naturalism, Rationalism, and Ecology." *Environmental Ethics* 16, no. 3 (1994): 275–86.

Sucitto, Ajahn. *Turning the Wheel of Truth: Commentary on the Buddha's First Teaching*. Boston: Shambhala, 2010.

Tecpaocelotl. "In lak'ech Is New Age." Available online: https://tecpaocelotl.livejournal.com/37886.html.

Templeton, John. *Agape Love*. Conshohocken, PA: Templeton, 1999.

Valdez, Luís, and Domingo Martinez Paredes. "In lak'ech: You Are My Other Me." Available online: http://vue.annenberginstitute.org/perspectives/lak%E2%80%99ech-you-are-my-other.

Vetter, Tilmann. *The Ideas and Meditative Practices of Early Buddhism*. Leiden: Brill, 1988.

von Arnim, Hans. *Stoicorum veterum fragmenta*. Leipzig: Teubner, 1903–24.

Westerhoff, Jan Christoph. "Nāgārjuna." *Stanford Encyclopedia of Philosophy*. Available online: https://plato.stanford.edu/archives/spr2019/entries/nagarjuna/.

Wu, Yüan. *Blue Cliff Record*. Translated by Thomas Cleary and J. C. Cleary. Boston: Shambala, [1977] 2005.

Yen, Sheng. *The Six Paramitas*. Elmhurst, NY: Dharma Drum, 2001.

Yu, Chun-Fang. "Ta-hui Tsung-kao and Kung-an Ch'an." *Journal of Chinese Philosophy* (1979): 211–35.

13

Gift: The (Im)possible Conditions of Grace in Herman Melville

Tae Sung

Out of natural courtesy he received, but did not appropriate. It was like a gift placed in the palm of an outreached hand upon which the fingers do not close.

Herman Melville, *Billy Budd*

1. A Pragmatist Mediation

A pragmatist approach to the religious experience of gifts begins not by determining their metaphysical sources but by tracking their phenomenological conditions and effects. For pragmatists like William James, it can never fully be determined whether religious experiences such as conversion or divine inspiration come from a theological or physiological source. Yet we can still track their effects on moral action because they produce dynamic sources of agency, or what I will call *dynamic gifts,* that open up new spheres of power to do things otherwise difficult or impossible.[1] These dynamic gifts include what Charles Taylor has called moral sources like divine grace that enable people to reach for their highest ideals, such as universal justice and benevolence.[2] By

---

[1] James calls these dynamic sources "dynamogenics," which are experiences that energize individuals. In his time, dynamogeny referred to experiments that measured physiological responses to stimulation. For James, such stimulation included religious experiences like the reception of theological grace and spiritual gifts. The term, "dynamic gift," is intended to be both a reference to James's use of dynamogenics and the biblical notion of power (*dunamis*) that comes from spiritual gifts (*charismata*). For a fuller discussion of James's psychology of dynamic gifts and the relationship between religious experience and language, see Sung, "'A New Sphere of Power,'" 52–79.

[2] Taylor is not often associated with pragmatism. But in a very interesting article, "What Is a Pragmatist?" published in *Pragmatism, Critique, Judgment: Essays for Richard J. Bernstein,* Taylor makes a distinction between two kinds of pragmatism—broad and radical—and finds himself

228 *Literature and Religious Experience*

engaging in various rituals like prayer or liturgy, individuals can experience shifts in consciousness that release abrupt and spontaneous bursts of energy that are then called redemption or salvation. But for Taylor, as it is for James, not everyone who participates in a religious ritual or ceremony experiences an abrupt and spontaneous burst of energy from a dynamic gift. For example, one may participate in the ritual of communion without ever receiving a dynamic gift of faith. This gap between two kinds of religious experiences, between participation and reception, like the difference between what Taylor calls buffered and porous selves, reveals how religious experiences of the gift are conditioned by social imaginaries or interpretive frameworks in different ways.[3]

Without examining these interpretive frameworks, a religious experience of the gift can turn into their etymological other as poison, a point emphasized by Jacques Derrida, whose argument remains often misunderstood. Derrida writes about the impossibility of a free and unmeasured gift that cannot appear without disappearing into an economy of exchange.[4] For as soon as it appears, its freedom, its purity is annulled by some form of obligation and reciprocity in such a way that the gift may turn out to be another means of domination, interest, and resentment.[5] Thus, for Derrida, thinking about the impossibility of the gift "activates our critical or ethical vigilance."[6] But contrary to reductive readings of Derrida, this vigilance is not simply negative but more precisely apophatic.[7] The impossibility, in negating the phenomenological appearance of the gift, opens up the very condition of hope, a kind of vigil for an *aneconomic* gift that remains unappropriated by an economy of exchange and yet produces a dynamic source of empowerment. In other words, there is a difference between a material or symbolic gift that circulates in an economy of exchange and a dynamic gift that

---

sympathetic to the former, especially as it is practiced by someone like Richard Bernstein. This article is also very interesting because it offers a bridge between his more robust engagement with William James in *Varieties of Religion Today* and *A Secular Age*.

[3] Secularity as an interpretive framework can change the conditions of possibility for the reception of dynamic gifts so that what was once an experience of the grace of God might now be interpreted as mere coincidence or another form of repayment, investment, or scam.

[4] Derrida, *Given Time*.

[5] Consider, for example, the political rhetoric of gifts as a substitute for bribery and blackmail, as when then-presidential candidate Mitt Romney blamed the gifts of big government for his loss in the 2008 elections or when the Saudi King gave $35 billion in gifts to his people during the height of the Arab Spring protests.

[6] Derrida, *Given Time*, 15.

[7] Critics of Derrida's writing on the gift often reduce it to the idea that there is no gift as such because they are bound by economies of exchange. I will argue that this is only a partial reading. For example, Alan Jacobs makes a compelling argument for a hermeneutics based on charity and gift-exchange to which I am very sympathetic. But he offers a puzzling claim that Derrida's argument amounts to a kind of Platonic self-sufficiency and Cartesian hermeneutics, despite both being key targets of deconstruction. See *A Theology of Reading: The Hermeneutics of Love* (New York: Westview Press, 2001), 80.

opens up the experience of moral agency. For Derrida, this latter experience comes from the very absence and deferral of an impossible gift that releases dynamic sources of agency to sustain both the vigilance necessary to keep track of the aporias of gift-exchange, as well as the ability to keep giving and receiving from one another even if we must do so differently.[8]

Despite their likelihood of being framed as oppositional figures, my aim will be to take another approach, pragmatist in method, by mediating without collapsing Derrida's and Taylor's discourse about gifts.[9] Though they approach this discourse from two different directions, one important point on which they can both agree is that there is no unmediated experience of dynamic gifts, which are anticipated, undermined, and directed by interpretive frameworks.[10] While these frameworks do not generate an experience of dynamic gifts, they do condition its possibility. What Taylor and Derrida help us to see are the dual risks to this hermeneutic insight. While Taylor worries about what he calls the dilemma of mutilation in a secular age without dynamic gifts and Derrida worries about how gift-economies can be used to dominate others, both are concerned with locating somewhere in the experience of gifts sources of agency to resist and overcome such risks. If there is to be a dynamic gift, what we gain

---

[8] See, for example, Derrida's writing on hospitality, which explores the double-bind of this gift and its risks. Derrida, *Of Hospitality*.

[9] Judged by his own remarks about Neo-Nietzscheans, Taylor may be the first to distance himself from Derrida's writings on the gift, much the way that John Milbank has argued strongly against Derrida. Despite the important overlap between Taylor and Milbank, my reading situates Taylor's writing about grace and gifts somewhere between Derrida's impossible gift and Milbank's ontological gift. One example is Taylor's description of the way communal gifts create "a bond where each is a gift to the other; where each gives and receives, and where the line between giving and receiving is blurred" (*A Secular Age*, 702). While Milbank holds onto the possibility of such communal exchanges purified of their agonistic tendencies, Derrida, as I will argue in the final section, blurs the line the way Taylor does here. For Milbank on the gift, see "Can a Gift Be Given?," 119–61; *Being Reconciled*.

For an exemplary model of this kind of pragmatist mediation, see Richard Bernstein's *Beyond Objectivism and Relativism*, which mediates between Hans-Georg Gadamer and Derrida in a way that is similar to what I am trying to do here. The pragmatist reading of Gadamer's *Truth and Method* is especially important for this chapter because it helps to establish the inextricable link between hermeneutics and experience.

[10] This attempt to locate a dynamic gift that exceeds gift-exchange goes beyond more prevalent debates about whether gifts operate unilaterally or reciprocally. See Peter Leithart's *Gratitude*, which argues that the history of gift theories has shifted back and forth between reciprocal and unilateral models. My objective here is to get at a more fundamental question about the conditions that make the experience of gifts possible beyond the subjectivity or objectivity of gift-exchange. This is what Derrida attempts to do when he brings Heidegger's ontology of Being into his discussion of gifts:

That is why, if there is gift, it cannot take place between two subjects exchanging objects, things, or symbols. The question of the gift should therefore seek its place before any relation to the subject, before any conscious or unconscious relation to self of the subject—and that is indeed what happens with Heidegger when he goes back before the determinations of Being as substantial being, subject, or object. (*Given Time*, 24)

230 *Literature and Religious Experience*

from insisting that Taylor and Derrida be read together is that in every religious experience of the gift, we must remain vigilant while also keeping vigil.

Perhaps better than any other literary figure, Herman Melville anticipated these discourses about the experience of gifts. On the one hand, he is relentless in his critique of gift-exchange. Especially in "Bartleby, the Scrivener" and *The Confidence Man*, related experiences with charity and grace are almost impossible to distinguish from investment and indebtedness. As a result, some critics conclude that gifts like grace cannot exist in Melville's fiction. On the other hand, however, his critique of gift-exchange can lead us to another question about what happens when our interpretive frameworks cannot account for experiences that exceed economic categories. This chapter will examine how Melville not only remains vigilant against an economy of gifts, but also keeps vigil for dynamic gifts.

2. The Dilemma of Melville's Vigilance

Critics like Hildegard Hoeller and Rachel Cole have written powerfully on the impossibility of the gift in Melville's writings. Their readings highlight Melville's vigilance in keeping track of the way gifts are, as Melville puts it, "quicken[ed] with the Wall street spirit."[11] This kind of vigilance, however, goes only halfway and does not reach what Derrida called "the immeasuring extent" of experiencing "a gift that cannot make itself [a] present."[12] The result is a Melville who anticipates all the contradictions of gift-exchange but fails to generate any hope. If, as Derrida, Taylor, and other theorists have argued, the gift is fundamentally about an openness to experiencing dynamic sources of agency and the possibility of generating new movements, then Melville's vigilance would leave us adrift like the castaway Pip or the missing whaleboat the Rachel seeks.[13] Before responding to Hoeller and Cole, this section will first summarize their arguments and then rely on Taylor to examine what is at stake with just a negative interpretation of the gift in Melville.

Hoeller offers the only book-length study of the gift in American literature, which includes strong and insightful readings of how the gift and "its collision with the market" fundamentally structures the plots and themes of several

---

[11] Melville, *Confidence-Man*, 49.
[12] Derrida, *Given Time*, 29.
[13] See also Agamben, *The Time That Remains*; Badiou, *Saint Paul*; and Kim, *Melancholic Freedom*.

nineteenth-century texts, including Melville's last published novel.[14] According to Hoeller, *The Confidence Man* "seeks out the (im)possible gift ... in the face of a capitalist world of strangers driven by self-interest."[15] The story takes place on the Mississippi river aboard a steamship called the Fidele. It's April Fool's Day. The narrative is structured episodically in different parts of the ship as a confidence man appears in a dizzying array of guises to test what Hoeller calls "the possibility of charity amongst strangers."[16]

In one instance, he is a mute and deaf beggar with fair cheek and flaxen hair holding a sign that says, "Charity thinketh no evil." He reappears next described as "a grotesque negro crippled" called the Black Guinea, whose "game of charity" is questioned by one "limping, gimlet-eyed, source-faced person."[17] Black Guinea defends himself by listing people on the boat who can vouch for him, including a man with a long weed in his hat and another with a gray coat and white tie. Not seeing them in the crowd, a merchant decides to demonstrate his confidence by donating a half dollar coin only to drop his business card unknowingly. Later, he is approached by a John Ringman wearing a hat with a long weed in it. Ringman recognizes an old acquaintance in the merchant who is embarrassed by his inability to recall the gentleman but nevertheless takes out his wallet to give him one banknote, which is soon exchanged for a larger one, as Ringman's story of personal calamity unfolds. And that's only three disguises in the first thirty pages of the novel.

Even more interesting than the number of his masks are the responses to the confidence man's request for donations. Some are suspicious. Others willingly give only to reveal how self-interested their donations are. Those who were suspicious are eventually made to give through sympathy, guilt, gratitude, and so forth. The very clergyman, who vigorously defended the crippled beggar against the limping man earlier but "mutely eyed the suppliant" in doubt when it was time for his own donation, is forced to make another decision a few chapters later whether to give, this time, to the representative of the Seminole Widow and Orphan Asylum, who wears a gray coat and white tie. The clergyman recognizes his dress and asks if he knows Guinea. The representative vouches for him and then admonishes the clergyman to be more charitable "by strangling the least symptom of distrust."[18] So, the clergyman not only entrusts a coin for the

---

[14] See Hoeller, *From Gift to Commodity*.
[15] Hoeller, *From Gift to Commodity*, 160.
[16] Hoeller, *From Gift to Commodity*, 160.
[17] Melville, *Confidence-Man*, 19.
[18] Melville, *Confidence-Man*, 42.

232 *Literature and Religious Experience*

representative to give to Guinea next time but also gives to the newly formed asylum charity, which, as it turns out, records and publishes donors' names. How convenient.

From the very beginning, then, is a conflict between a dynamic gift (charity) and its circulation in a gift-economy (game of charity). Such scenes represent well Derrida's argument that what we experience when we give or receive a gift can be bound up in aporias of gift-exchange. Givers calculate the costs of their donations and receivers wither from their indebtedness. According to Hoeller,

> Melville depicts the impossibility of the gift, the way in which the clergyman tries to reason himself into giving and out of giving. He is searching for a way to decide, but the moment of decision is outside of logos. The minute the gift has been given, the clergyman needs to turn it into a debt or a gain for him, annul it as a gift, and make it a record or a way of making amends. Melville, over and over, captures this moment.[19]

This moment is the experience of when gifts between strangers become a return on investments and when gifts, even between friends, as in the story of China Aster, turn into loans that result in resentment and ruin.

This "methodization of the world's benevolence," as Melville called an economy of charity, raises profound ethical questions that Cole examines in her reading of "Bartleby, the Scrivener," whose subtitle is, of course, "A Story of Wall Street," about a lawyer" who employs and then abandons the scrivener whose preference interrupts the logic of Wall Street.[20] For Cole, the story is a conflict between our responsibility to others and our responsibility to ourselves. In her interpretation, self-interest wins out. It becomes the "only way [for the lawyer] to be in good standing with his colleagues [by preferring] no one beside himself. To put this in practical terms, if he wants their recognition as a legitimate member of the social world, he will have to thrust Bartleby out."[21] The conclusion Cole draws from "this acutely critical vision of the lawyer's social world—which [she takes] to be synonymous, given its location, with American capitalism—[is that] to give unto others, even when there is plenty to go around, is social suicide."[22] In other words, in an economy of exchange, there is no room to experience a dynamic gift from what Derrida calls the wholly other. Ethical responsibility is,

---

[19] Hoeller, *From Gift to Commodity*, 164.
[20] See Cole, "The Lawyer's Tale."
[21] Cole, "The Lawyer's Tale," 124.
[22] Cole, "The Lawyer's Tale," 124.

in the end, measured in an algebra of rational calculation, which must remove Bartleby because he is unaccountable.

In each of these narratives, Hoeller and Cole see the impossibility of a gift that cannot appear without disappearing into an economy of exchange. The economic circulation of religious gifts like charity results in indebtedness, return on investments, social capital, or suicide. If that is all there is to the religious experience of gifts, then we do well to remain vigilant. But in Taylor's mind, we are faced with a dilemma when we do not make a hermeneutic distinction, which is necessarily an experiential distinction between economic gifts and dynamic gifts. Without such a distinction, our vigilance extends beyond the experience of indebtedness that results from gift-exchange to the experience of dynamic gifts that include the gifts of nature and genius in Romantic terms, the epiphanic in modernist literature, the phenomenological givenness of experience, all of which Taylor argues are modern substitutes for divine grace. For Taylor, what we experience in the reception of such gifts are dynamic sources of empowerment that enable us to reach for our highest ideals, such as universal justice and benevolence, which require moral sources to sustain our efforts. Without receiving a dynamic gift that opens up the experience of what James calls abrupt and spontaneous bursts of energy to empower us in the pursuit of justice, Taylor argues that we risk a dilemma of mutilation that may be "our greatest spiritual challenge."[23]

The challenge of this dilemma is that without experiencing such dynamic sources of empowerment, we will be saddled with moral demands that not only remain unfulfilled but also result in forms of violence. According to Taylor, it was Dostoyevsky who saw how "an ideology of universal love and freedom can mask a burning hatred, directed outward onto an unregenerate world and generating destruction and despotism."[24] And Nietzsche understood, "if morality can only be powered negatively, where there can be no such thing as beneficence powered by an affirmation of the recipient as a being of value, then pity is destructive to the giver and degrading to the receiver, and the ethic of benevolence may indeed be indefensible."[25] Nietzsche's unsettling conclusion is to do away with benevolence and to replace it with a very different kind of moral imperative to affirm the will to power even at the expense of others. Nietzsche is wrong, Taylor says, only if dynamic gifts like grace exist.

---

[23] Taylor, *Sources of the Self*, 521.
[24] Taylor, *Sources of the Self*, 517.
[25] Taylor, *Sources of the Self*, 516.

234   *Literature and Religious Experience*

Taylor goes on to argue that this dilemma, which is the same dilemma that I think Melville is wrestling with, is particularly acute in a secular age because conditions of belief can close or disclose the religious experience of dynamic gifts. Whether individuals are buffered or porous to such experiences is significant because we live in an age that "makes higher demands of solidarity and benevolence on people today than ever before. Never before have people been asked to stretch out so far, and so consistently, so systematically, so as a matter of course, to the stranger outside the gates."[26] Taylor goes to great lengths to study how conditions of belief have changed over time so that buffered selves are no longer able to experience dynamic gifts.[27]

The key condition to the experience of dynamic gifts is the role of interpretive frameworks that mediate what we experience in a collective social imaginary. Interpretive frameworks, which are like maps that provide spatial and temporal orientation, include the stories we tell to help make sense of our place within a larger social imaginary, which Taylor defines as "the way that we collectively imagine, even pretheoretically, our social life in the contemporary Western world."[28] While we can never fully articulate our collective social imaginaries, narratives serve a hermeneutic function that helps us to interpret whether the glass is half empty or full, whether an experience is mere coincidence or divine intervention. Interpretive frameworks provide a phenomenological openness to the possibility of experiencing a gift that might be given and thereby received. Otherwise, dynamic gifts might come and go unnoticed, resulting in the loss of their moral source.[29]

How gifts are defined and imagined have a profound impact on whether we experience them as sources of indebtedness or empowerment. Without the interpretive frameworks that place us in a phenomenological openness to the possibility of dynamic moral sources, the experience of dynamic gifts may

---

[26] Taylor, *A Secular Age*, 695.
[27] It is not insignificant that Taylor returns to the last chapter of *Sources of the Self*, which was about the role of dynamic moral sources in modernity, in the final section of *A Secular Age*, which examines the cross-pressures and dilemmas that result in an immanent frame. Taylor's most explicit writing about dynamic gifts appear precisely when he evaluates different sources to sustain moral ideals:

> Now one might conclude that this kind of response to the image of God in others is not really a possibility for us humans, and one might not be able to make sense of this notion of our being given to each other. I think this can be real for us, but only to the extent that we open ourselves to God, which means in fact, overstepping the limits set in theory by exclusive humanisms. If one does believe that, then one has something very important to say to modern times, something that addresses the fragility of what all of us, believer and unbeliever alike, most value in these times. (*A Secular Age*, 703)

[28] Taylor, *A Secular Age*, 703. For his work on interpretive frameworks, see Taylor, *Sources of the Self*, chs. 1 and 2.
[29] See also my reading of Taylor and Marilynne Robinson: "'In the Way of the Gift.'"

no longer be a possibility for us. Then, our moral sources are constricted, and the burden of our ideals becomes greater. Because these frameworks mediate and condition our experiences, certain modes of language, that is, certain vocabularies, definitions, and narratives of dynamic gifts, can close or disclose their possibility. If this is indeed a postsecular moment as some critics suggest, then reading Melville's fiction through a postsecular framework can help to reexamine the hermeneutical conditions that make impossible certain religious experiences and to allow us to ask again, after the demise of the secularization thesis, what conditions are necessary to experience a dynamic gift.[30]

3. An Unappropriated Gift

I agree with Hoeller and Cole that Melville offers a powerful critique of gift-exchange. But I see these narratives not so much as a critique of gifts as such but as a critique of the conditions that reduce gifts to their exchange value alone. There is, then, another question in Melville besides whether gifts exist or not. There is also the question of what happens when we no longer have the interpretive frameworks to experience gifts in noneconomic terms and how such aneconomic gifts might condition our modes of exchange in more dynamic ways. And this question of interpretive framework resides not just with the characters' experiences in the novels but in the readers' experience also. Is it possible to read and interpret the gift other than through economic categories? The significance of this question is that without an alternative framework, the experience of what I'm calling dynamic gifts may no longer be a possibility for us. After our critical vigilance, what remains of our vigil for dynamic gifts?

What I would like to propose here is that we can discern another side to Melville's vigilance by examining what Derrida called the gift's immeasuring extent. For Derrida, there cannot be a phenomenology of the gift because it cannot appear without disappearing into the circle of economic exchange. Nevertheless, its relation to the circle can still be thought, which is to say that the gift must be experienced apophatically rather than phenomenologically: "If the figure of the circle is essential to economics, the gift must remain *aneconomic*.

---

[30] By the postsecular I do not mean a particular recontextualization of religious faith such as John McClure's partial faith or Amy Hungerford's postmodern belief, which Tracy Fessenden has persuasively critiqued as still being beholden to the secularization thesis. Instead, as I use the term, postsecularism refers more broadly to the possibilities of rethinking all forms of religious belief after the demise of the secularization thesis. See McClure, *Partial Faiths*; Hungerford, *Postmodern Belief*; and Fessenden, "The Problem of the Postsecular," 154–67.

236   *Literature and Religious Experience*

Not that it remains foreign to the circle, but it must *keep* a relation of foreignness to the circle, a relation without relation of familiar foreignness."[31] This is Derrida's vigilance—not that there is no experience of the gift, but that if there is, the experience must be deconstructed in order to get at a noneconomic gift: "So the gift does not exist and appear as such; it is impossible for the gift to exist and appear as such. But I never concluded that there is no gift. I went on to say that if there is a gift, through this impossibility, it must be the experience of this impossibility."[32] To experience the impossibility of the gift is different from its appearance, which must always be tracked, vigilantly, lest it result in the kind of indebtedness that Melville depicts so powerfully. But when Derrida writes, "The gift is the impossible," he immediately clarifies, "Not impossible but *the* impossible. The very figure of the impossible. It announces itself, gives itself to be thought as the impossible."[33] Thinking through this experience of impossibility, that is, keeping an unappropriated relation of foreignness to the circle, requires what he calls a "measureless measure," which is a noneconomic framework for thinking the gift in a way that reconditions the circle of giving differently.

But what is the purpose of thinking, of measuring this immeasurable gap between gift and economy? It is not a matter of deciding between a pure gift and mere exchange. It is about having an interpretive framework that allows the impossibility of the gift to loosen the circle, to keep it from drawing ever tighter around what John Caputo calls an uninterrupted narcissism.[34] We cannot fully escape the circle, but thinking the gift can loosen it just enough to make room for an immeasurable gap from which an experience of a dynamic

---

[31] Derrida, *Given Time*, 7. Italics in original.
[32] From a conversation with Derrida, Jean-Luc Marion, and Richard Kearney published as "On the Gift: A Discussion between Jacques Derrida and Jean-Luc Marion," in John Caputo and Michael J. Scanlon's *God, the Gift, and Postmodernism* 59.
[33] Derrida, *Given Time*, 7.
[34] Caputo, *The Prayers and Tears of Jacques Derrida*, 172:

> But it is no less true that the aneconomic gift keeps the circle turning, so that the circle depends upon the very thing it excludes, the gift. The circle needs the gift no less than the gift cannot avoid the circle. For Derrida's point is not to find a spot of simple exteriority to the circle, but to loosen the circle and to create an opening for the tout autre. The point is not to escape the circle nor even to enter it in the right way but to know how to breach it in the right way. That is why Derrida says that there are many narcissisms, various degrees of narcissism, the best of which are hospitable and welcome to the other. There is always a movement of narcissism in any gift and indeed without a movement of narcissistic reappropriation, the relation to the other would be absolutely destroyed. Even above, the affirmation of the other, would be impossible without the trace of narcissism. When I love that good of the other, that is the good I love. And the most hospitable, open-ended narcissism, the good I seek for myself is the good of the other.

> See also Caputo and Scanlon's *God, the Gift, and Postmodernism* for important essays and interviews with Derrida and Jean-Luc Marion about the gift in relation to theology.

Gift 237

power can enable us to be more hospitable toward the wholly other that must not be reduced simply to another subjectivity. This is why Derrida writes, "If there is gift, it cannot take place between two subjects exchanging objects, things, or symbols ... But the subject and the object are arrested effects of the gift, arrests of the gift."[35] By negating the economy of a gift-exchange between subjects and objects, Derrida opens us to experience a more dynamic gift that constitutes every economic exchange. Having an interpretive framework for this aneconomic gift can condition our giving and receiving in a way that discloses an immeasurable gap from which the gift can empower us, from which we can experience dynamic sources of agency both to make room for the wholly other and to sustain our vigilance against the aporias of the gift.

In contrast to Hoeller and Cole, Branka Arsic's work demonstrates this more nuanced reading of Derrida and Melville. Though she does not explicitly write about the gift, her reading of what she calls the impersonal in "Bartleby" offers, I think, one opening into the kind of immeasurable gap that Derrida and Taylor seek.[36] For Arsic, Bartleby is a figure of depersonalized passivity. This kind of passivity is what Melville called in *The Confidence Man* an original, which Arsic describes as the experience of impersonal forces that pass through characters and generate their own forms and worlds. Like Derrida's aneconmoic gift, Bartleby's passivity is "a present without presence to itself" and makes possible the experience of a dynamic force that escapes existing categories and forms.[37] In other words, it does not already belong to the circle of economic exchange. This impersonal force is similar to what I am calling a dynamic gift. Arsic only hints at the possibility of this connection when she cites Derrida's *The Gift of Death*, but in the crucial scene in the story, a dynamic gift is what passes through Bartleby to the attorney.

Most readers will remember it. The passage comes near the end of the story after Bartleby has been removed from the office and now resides in the Tombs. The lawyer visits him one last time only to find Bartleby "profoundly sleeping" with dim eyes still open, ready to give the gift of death, a gift without the possibility of reciprocity. And here is the measureless gap that Melville provides. The lawyer writes, "Something prompted me to touch him. I felt his hand, when a tingling shiver ran up my arm and down my spine to my feet."[38] That tingling shiver. It's a small detail, one that is also open to the risk of reading too much

[35] Derrida, *Given Time*, 24.
[36] See Branka Arsic, "Bartleby or the Impersonal," in *Passive Constitutions or 7 ½ Times Bartelby*.
[37] Derrida, *Given Time*, 99.
[38] Melville, *Melville's Short Novels*, 33.

238   *Literature and Religious Experience*

into it. But dismissing it, as the lawyer seems to do, has its own risks too. It is precisely because such an experience has no economic value in the lawyer's mind that the shiver runs up and down without consequence.

Without an interpretive framework that anticipates the possibility of a dynamic gift from a tingling shiver, the lawyer is unable to experience anything more than a dead body. But Arsic provides an alternative framework for how the reader might experience what the lawyer does not:

> Instead of touching a dead body he actually feels Bartleby's hand, feeling the transmission of a shiver all over his body, a shiver meaning a trepidation or an excitement, in a word, life. Life trembles when the infinite overwhelms the finite, when all the categories and words break down. That is why the narrative ends with this trembling and as this trembling, with a life that comes from "death" and so negates it; the narrative ends with a touch that touches the infinite.[39]

The shiver can, of course, be interpreted in purely naturalistic terms of biological affect. But there is another hermeneutic tradition rooted in a more, rooted in a more mystical, mystical or pneumatological framework that could see through such an experience the effects of dynamic gifts. In Melville's time, such a framework could be traced both back through Emerson to at least Jonathan Edwards's discourse on religious affections and forward to its development in the religious pragmatism of William James.[40]

Melville's place in this tradition remains highly contested. But as Giles Gunn has argued, too rarely has Melville's work been interpreted as a prefiguration of especially the religious dimensions of Jamesian pragmatism.[41] Seeing this connection allows us to examine Melville's vigilance more precisely as a way to question what happens when we run up against the limits of economy, when our interpretive frameworks reduce gifts to mere objects of economic exchange. So, when the lawyer assumes his all-too-brief role as the dispenser of the gifts of charity, he calculates it as "mere self-interest" and "a great safeguard to its possessor."[42] In this framework, there is no room to consider that he may experience a dynamic gift from an immeasurable gap, and so the shiver makes no difference.

---

[39] Arsic, "Bartleby or the Impersonal," 107.
[40] Robert Richardson writes that dynamogenics "is the long-standing American interest in awakening to new life and new power, the great theme of Thoreau and Emerson and Whitman, the great theme too of Jonathan Edwards, now carried to the new American century by William James" (*In the Maelstrom of American Modernism*, 489).
[41] See Gunn, *The Pragmatist Turn*.
[42] Melville, *Short Novels*, 25.

The same might be said of the last chapter of *The Confidence Man*, where evidence of the gifts of faith and charity is sought after in the Bible. The confidence man, who perhaps believes in the gift more faithfully than any other, says, "There is a chapter, ... which, as not amiss, I must read you. But this lamp, solar-lamp as it is, begins to burn dimly."[43] If we think about this figure of solar lamps as interpretive frameworks that illuminate our reading of texts, here in one of the most relentless critiques of charity and gift-exchange I can think of, it could be said that Melville at least leaves open the possibility of renewal. If so, perhaps it will be like the moment when Billy Budd just before his hanging blesses Captain Vere, a benediction which produces a dynamic experience that the surgeon cannot rationally account for. As Melville describes slightly earlier in a different passage about how Taihitians received the Gospel, "it was like a gift placed in the palm of an outstretched hand upon which the fingers do not close."[44] What might it mean for a gift to be received but unappropriated? It would be to remain vigilant about the aporias of the gift while keeping vigil for its dynamic sources of agency.

Bibliography

Agamben, Giorgio. *The Time That Remains: A Commentary on the Letter to the Romans.* Translated by Patricia Dailey. Palo Alto, CA: Stanford University Press, 2005.

Arsic, Branka. *Passive Constitutions or 7 ½ Times Bartelby.* Palo Alto, CA: Stanford University Press, 2007.

Badiou, Alain. *Saint Paul: The Foundation of Universalism.* Translated by Ray Brassier. Palo Alto, CA: Stanford University Press, 2003.

Bernstein, Richard. *Beyond Objectivism and Relativism: Science, Hermeneutics, and Praxis.* Philadelphia: University of Pennsylvania Press, 1983.

Caputo, John. D. *The Prayers and Tears of Jacques Derrida: Religion without Religion.* Bloomington: Indiana University Press, 1997.

Caputo, John D., and Michael J. Scanlon. *God, the Gift, and Postmodernism.* Bloomington: Indiana University Press, 1999.

Cole, Rachel. "The Lawyer's Tale: Preference, Responsibility, and Personhood in Melville's 'Story of Wall-Street.'" In *Melville's Philosophies*, edited by Branka Arsic and K. L. Evans. New York: Bloomsbury, 2017.

Derrida, Jacques. *Given Time: I. Counterfeit Money.* Chicago: University of Chicago Press, 1992.

---

[43] Melville, *Confidence-Man*, 250.
[44] Melville, *Billy Budd*, 121.

240   *Literature and Religious Experience*

Derrida, Jacques. *Of Hospitality: Anne Dufourmantelle Invites Jacques Derrida to Respond*. Translated by Rachel Bowlby. Palo Alto, CA: Stanford University Press, 2000.

Fessenden, Tracy. "The Problem of the Postsecular." *American Literary History* 26, no. 1 (2014): 154–67.

Gadamer, Hans-Georg. *Truth and Method*. New York: Bloomsbury, 2004.

Gunn, Giles. *The Pragmatist Turn: Religion, the Enlightenment, and the Formation of American Literature*. Charlottesville: University of Virginia Press, 2017.

Hoeller, Hildegard. *From Gift to Commodity: Capitalism and Sacrifice in Nineteenth-Century American Fiction*. Lebanon: University of New Hampshire Press, 2012.

Hungerford, Amy. *Postmodern Belief: American Literature and Religion since 1960*. Princeton, NJ: Princeton University Press, 2010.

Kim, David Kyuman. *Melancholic Freedom*. New York: Oxford University Press, 2007.

Leithart, Peter. *Gratitude: An Intellectual History*. Waco, TX: Baylor University Press, 2014.

McClure, John. *Partial Faiths: Postsecular Fiction in the Age of Pynchon and Morrison*. Athens: University of Georgia Press, 2007.

Melville, Herman. "Bartleby, the Scrivener." In *Melville's Short Novels*, edited by Dan McCall. New York: Norton, 2002.

Melville, Herman. *Billy Budd, Sailor*. Edited by Harrison Hayford and Merton M. Sealts Jr. Chicago: University of Chicago Press, 1962.

Melville, Herman. *The Confidence-Man: His Masquerade*. Edited by Hershel Parker and Mark Niemeyer. New York: Norton, 2006.

Milbank, John. "Can a Gift Be Given? Prolegomena to a Future Trinitarian Metaphysic." *Modern Theology* 11, no. 1 (1995): 119–61.

Milbank, John. *Being Reconciled: Ontology and Pardon*. New York: Routledge, 2003.

Richardson, Robert D. *William James: In the Maelstrom of American Modernism*. New York: Mariner Books, 2007.

Sung, Tae. "'A New Sphere of Power': Religious Experience and the Language of Dynamic Gifts in William James." *William James Studies* 12, no. 2 (2016): 52–79.

Sung, Tae. "'In the Way of the Gift': The Postsecular Conditions of Grace in Marilynne Robinson's *Gilead*." *Humanities* 9, no. 32 (2020).

Taylor, Charles. *Sources of the Self: The Making of the Modern Self*. Cambridge, MA: Harvard University Press, 1989.

Taylor, Charles. *Varieties of Religion Today: William James Revisited*. Cambridge, MA: Harvard University Press, 2002.

Taylor, Charles. "What Is a Pragmatist?" In *Pragmatism, Critique, Judgment: Essays for Richard J. Bernstein*, edited by Seyla Benhabib and Nancy Fraser. Cambridge, MA: MIT Press, 2004.

Taylor, Charles. *A Secular Age*. Cambridge, MA: Harvard University Press, 2007.

14

Fantasy: Magical Experiences and Postsecular Fiction

Zhange Ni

Fantasy, currently a new dominant cultural form on the global scale, is a postsecular genre because it encapsulates and participates in the survival and flourishing of magic in the modern world. It is scholarly consensus that, as a self-conscious literary mode, fantasy emerged in the post-Enlightenment West, in the wake of the establishment of scientific rationality that delineated the boundaries of the real or the possible. This explains why fantasy is defined by its preoccupation with fabricating the impossible.[1] Fantasy also aims at triggering desires and emotions peripheral, if not antithetical, to the making of the interiorized modern subjectivity.[2] Around the same time that fantasy became a distinctive mode/genre of literature and other arts, the modern concepts of magic and superstition were formulated. Both terms denote experiences, practices, and traditions in opposition to scientific rationality, a dominant discourse of the secular age, and incompatible with the liberal—or, more bluntly put, Protestant—model of religion in the form of interiorized, privatized, and depoliticized.[3] Playing with "false" science and "improper" religion to enact the impossible and undesirable, fantasy has postsecular potential because it produces in its writer and reader cognitive as well as affective responses that exceed the purview of secular modernity and subvert the dominant value systems by experimenting with alternative modes of subject-formation and world-building.

---

[1] James and Mendlesohn, *Fantasy Literature*.

[2] Studying entertainment magic, Simon During demonstrates that it effects responses and competencies prior to the interiorized subjectivity of the modern individual and exemplifies desires linked to alternative modes of subjectivities. He applies this observation to fantasy literature, too (2002).

[3] Styers, *Making Magic*.

Existing theories of fantasy tend to emphasize the epistemological hesitation experienced by the reader while reading a fantastic text. By contrast, critics of fantasy blame it for offering mindless escape from social reality and providing facile wish fulfillment. Rather ironically, it is those same critics who duly acknowledge the affective aspect of fantasy that induces feelings, emotions, and embodied performances. For them, the "sin" of fantasy is not just its disregard of the boundaries set up by human rationality but also its prioritization of the "unruly" affects, by way of which the prevailing order could be challenged. Not unlike fantasy, the modern category of religion used to be studied within a largely rational framework. This explains why Donovan Schaefer calls for a centralization of affects and experiences, arguing that religion does not always operate on the cognitive plane and needs to be approached as embodied, lived experiences prior to, underneath, or outside of the regime of linguistic construction.[4] Although a verbal art, fantasy literature is an adventure beyond the symbolic regime of language and demands the attention of scholars of religion interested in the interpolation of affect into rational description on the supernatural.

I claim at the outset that fantasy is not just a literary genre but also describes the experience of writing or reading fantastic texts, where a whole variety of "impossible" phenomena are encapsulated. Some of these experiences of the writer, of the reader, and within the text may be deemed religious. We could try to identify the religious import of the author's creative act, debate whether the fans' enthusiastic embrace of a cultural product is indicative of the rise of a new religiosity, or pay attention to the imagined experiences within the fantastic text. In the last regard, the experiences enacted in and by fantasy, which is defined by these experiences in turn, have often been deemed as magical rather than religious. Resonating with Schaefer, Ann Taves focuses on experiences in her study of religion and understands them as not intrinsically religious but becoming religious after people deem them so.[5] Religious meaning is attributed to experience after its occurrence. On this basis, I emphasize that the experiences labeled religious are further divided into the proper and the improper, the latter being magical. Religious and magical experiences overlap considerably on the phenomenal level. The distinction between them is made by the power of secularism in the modern world.

---

[4] Schaefer, *Religious Affects*.
[5] Taves, *Religious Experience Reconsidered*.

Recently, scholars have made efforts to question the epistemic, affective, and moral-political supremacy of the secular and to consider the discursive (trans) formation of religion—both proper and improper—in diverse contexts. These attempts constitute the postsecular turn. Studying the formation of the secular, Talal Asad discusses the role played by imaginative literature in the training of secular subjects and sensibilities. According to him, imaginative literature, not unlike liberal religion, is pushed away from the realm of scientific inquiries and endowed with the task of cultivating the moral, spiritual character of the modern individual.[6] Fantasy, a peculiar type of imaginative literature overlooked by Asad, does not honor the limits of empirical reality or human rationality. Nor is it primarily concerned with the individual's quest for existential truth. As a result, the reality-escaping and wish-fulfilling fantasy suffers marginalization, stigmatization, and even suppression. However, its escape from consensus reality and fulfillment of deviant wishes constitute a conduit for the haunting of the precluded and disavowed magic. This haunting has been undermining the secular order, which involves an entire set of presumptions, attitudes, dispositions, and discourses that shape the experiences of writers, readers, and fictional characters.

In what follows, I outline the genealogies of magic and its close synonym, superstition, in Section 1, highlighting their role in demonizing the other for the sake of maintaining a particular form of the self in relation to the world and validating some religious experiences at the expense of others. Section 2 is devoted to an examination of the definitions and defenses of fantasy offered by Rosemary Jackson, Brian Attebery, and J. R. R. Tolkien. I argue that scholars of fantasy need to abandon their secularist assumptions and pay due attention to magic as it phenomenally overlaps with religion and is conceptually kept apart from it. In this regard, Tolkien, whose *The Lord of the Rings* series paved the way for the fantasy boom in the 1960s, viewed the fantastic art as a practice and product of magic. Since his notion of magic does not do full justice to the history surveyed in section one, I expand and revise his theory of fantasy in the third and final section. To explore the postsecular work of fantasy that retrieves and resignifies magical experiences, I read two fantasy novels, Neil Gaiman's *American Gods* and Mengru Shenji's *Foben shidao* (*The Buddha Belongs to the Dao*, hereafter *The Dao*) to conclude this essay.

---

[6] Asad, *Formations of the Secular*.

244   *Literature and Religious Experience*

1. Genealogies of Magic and Superstition

Magic and superstition are terms with long and complex histories, aimed at a variety of targets at different times and places by different people. They are labeling expressions with negative connotations, intrinsically biased, politically charged, vague, and flexible but not completely empty as signifiers. Ideas, practices, and the embodied experiences that undergird them are not intrinsically magical or superstitious but labeled so when they disrupt a particular arrangement of the cosmic order. The cosmic order is a shifting configuration, serving the interests of the ruling elites of the Greek polis, Roman Empire, medieval Christendom, and the modern system of the nation-state and the capitalist market.

In the Greco-Roman world, despite their respective origins, magic and superstition became synonyms, covering a whole gamut of nontraditional and unsanctioned phenomena outside the boundaries of the civic religion of the day and used as polemical tools against personal enemies, those of inferior social or gender status, or the cult practices of foreigners and outsiders. Magic and superstition continued to be synonyms for early Christian writers, who turned the pagan religion of the Greco-Roman world into a superstition, an inappropriate way of worshiping false gods. They also believed that all practices of magic invoked demons and were indistinguishable from superstition.[7]

From the thirteenth century on, thanks to the translation of Greek natural philosophy back into Europe from the Islamic world, attempts were made to investigate the hidden powers within nature and to separate magic from superstition. Against this background, natural magic emerged as an alternative to demonic magic.[8] However, fears of the devil did not abate but escalated in late medieval Europe. Demonic magic—superstition, sorcery, and witchcraft— was targeted for eradication in order to uphold the Christian order as well as to expedite the rise of a new hegemony: modern science that aimed to explore and exploit a disenchanted world and its mechanical, impersonal forces.[9]

In the modern period, magic and superstition were again used interchangeably. Researching magic as an analytical category in social sciences, Randall Styers emphasizes the role played by this category in the making of the modern subject in relation to the material world and social order.[10] Debates over magic helped to channel human needs into a rationalized scientific realm and a spiritualized

---

[7] Graf, *Magic in the Ancient World*; Martin, *Inventing Superstition*.
[8] Kieckhefer, *Magic in the Middle Ages*.
[9] Cameron, *Enchanted Europe*.
[10] Styers, *Making Magic*.

religious realm. Deviant impulses, experiences, and behavior consequently were relegated to the trashcan of magic. Not just an intellectual error but "a symptom of psychological impairment and marker of racial or cultural inferiority," magic was to be removed to facilitate the process of modernization, or, more specifically, the rise of nation-states, colonial empires, and global capitalism.[11]

A close synonym of magic, superstition is understood as magical—that is, irrational and impious—thought and practice rooted in long-standing folk traditions both within and beyond Europe. Studying superstition as a label deployed by the modern state, Jason Josephson-Storm points out that the nation-state promotes a set of scientific truths, protects religion as long as it conforms to the liberal model, and "invest[s] significant energy in purging the superstitious as the true enemy of modernity or secular governance."[12] It turns out that the entangled binary of religion and the secular is actually a trinary formation of religion, the secular, and magic/superstition.

The underlying agenda for the discussion and regulation of magic and superstition is to mold the modern subject, or, more precisely, what Sylvia Wynter calls the ratio-centric Man: the political subject of the state and the bio-economic subject of the market.[13] This ratio-centric figure is also the ethnoclass Man and excludes women, the working class, and the non-European "primitives" as not being fully human. Although Wynter contends that the ratio-centric Man was the modern transfiguration of the theocentric Christian, who disappeared in the secularization process, Wouter Hanegraaff stresses that the post-Enlightenment condemnation of magic/superstition in the name of science did not abandon but reinscribed the Christian superiority over the pagan others.[14]

Both scientific and Christian authorities were concerned with policing magic to help "produce a population of predictable, rational workers and citizens who conform to the needs of the capitalist marketplace and the modern bureaucratic state."[15] Along this line of inquiry, Silvia Federici reexamines the history of witch-hunting, demonstrating that the colonized Native Americans, the enslaved Africans, and women in Europe are versions of Caliban and the witch, whose productive and reproductive labor, through a brutal and sustained extermination of the demonic magic they practiced, was "placed under the control of the state and transformed into economic resources."[16]

---

[11] Styers, *Making Magic*, 27.
[12] Josephson-Storm, "Re-Theorizing Secularism," 4.
[13] Wynter, "Unsettling the Coloniality."
[14] Hanegraaff, *Esotericism and the Academy*.
[15] Bever and Styers, *Magic in the Modern World*, 12–13.
[16] Federici, *Caliban and the Witch*, 170.

246   *Literature and Religious Experience*

Beyond the Euro-American West, the building of the modern state and the capitalist market was also an urgent need in places such as twentieth-century China. In their struggle to enlighten the nation, strengthen the state, and boost economic growth, Chinese intellectuals eagerly embraced the triad of science, religion, and superstition (translated as *mixin*, meaning deluded belief). To pursue modernization, the Chinese state—that is, the Qing, Republican, and Communist states—promoted science, reformed Chinese religions, and launched a series of anti-superstition campaigns to purge magical elements in native traditions. Fantasy stories from the West were carefully kept outside of China, where realist novels and science fiction were passionately translated and popularized. Worse still, the secular state in the late 1920s even banned, or at least discouraged, the publication of fantasy novels that reinvented the magical practices of Chinese religions as well as the adaptation of these texts into fantasy films, blaming these works for having corrupted the mind of the masses by reviving "feudalistic superstition."[17]

2. Fantasy: Literature of Magic/Superstition

While the secular state and its elites worried about the subversion of superstition as carried forward by fantasy, little attention has been paid to it by scholars of religion and the secular. Similarly, scholars of fantasy have yet to study the genre with reference to the modernist triad of science, religion, and magic. Discussing disenchantment as a salient feature of modernity, Asad describes it as "a direct access to reality, a stripping away of myth, magic, and the sacred," and attributes the production of this feature to "the growing habit of reading imaginative literature."[18] He mentions also the split between history and myth, the former scientific, secular, dependent on "an attitude of skeptical inquiry in pursuit of authenticity" and the latter closely associated with so-called imaginative literature, or religion and the arts generally speaking, and regarded as "the original way of apprehending spiritual truth."[19] However, he neglects to mention fantasy, literature of magic, the third pole standing apart from and mediating between (secular) history and (religious) myth.

---

[17] Ni, "Xiuzhen (Immortality Cultivation) Fantasy."
[18] Asad, *Formations of the Secular*, 13, 14.
[19] Asad, *Formations of the Secular*, 43, 52.

The myth that keeps distance from history and the myth that gets stripped away are not the same. The former refers to a literary technique for imposing aesthetic unity on the fragmented individual experience and providing a fictional foundation for the groundless secular values. It is a secular technique, a mode of reading that quests in invented realities for existential messages rather than empirical truth. Myth in the second sense belongs to "the world we have lost" as described by Charles Taylor, "one in which spiritual forces impinged on porous agents, in which the social was grounded in the sacred and secular time in higher times, a society moreover in which the play of structure and anti-structure was held in equilibrium; and this human drama unfolded within a cosmos."[20] I suggest we replace myth in this sense with magic to avoid confusion.

Notably, when Asad discusses imaginative literature, he reads poets such as Samuel Taylor Coleridge, T. S. Eliot, and Adonis. The promotion of poetry as a surrogate religion envisioned by Matthew Arnold seems to have left its impact on Asad's work on the secular. If we shift our attention to the realist novel, I argue that it not only practices the mythical technique but also stays within the limits of empirical history. Although the realist novel is distinct from historical records in that its characters and events are not real, its imagination does not move beyond the human subject's sensorial experience within positivist history.[21] Like Immanuel Kant's "religion within the limits of reason," the realist novel is the play of human imagination within the same limits, that is, imagination constrained by the rules of representation. It tells stories of the embodied self's realization to train the moral character of the reader. Depending on the technique of myth as a reading strategy, the realist novel shares with the liberal model of religion the same task of guiding the modern subject in self-cultivation toward self-fulfillment.

What interests me, however, is what was subsumed against and underneath the realist novel, namely, the non-realist fantasy. Unfortunately, the confines of history and the mythical technique still serve as the major points of reference in the study of fantasy. For instance, Jackson, one of the early scholars of fantasy, celebrates the fantastic mode for unleashing repressed desires to dismantle the bourgeois category of the "real," "the concept of 'character' and its ideological assumptions," but excludes popular fantasy that invokes magic and invents otherworlds from the fantastic mode.[22] She believes that magic has been

---

[20] Taylor, *A Secular Age*, 61.
[21] Jameson, *The Antinomies of Realism*.
[22] Jackson, *Fantasy, the Literature of Subversion*, 175–6.

248   *Literature and Religious Experience*

surpassed by religion and science and the return of the "outdated" magic signals an escape from human history and the stabilization of the status quo.

Unlike Jackson, Attebery focuses his research on genre fantasy. He defines myth as "any collective story that encapsulates a worldview and authorizes belief."[23] Myth comes from the premodern and non-Western worlds, while fantasy is a modern attempt to reframe and recontextualize myth. For Attebery, the realist novel, myth, and fantasy are all symbolic structures not expected to be concerned with the question of propositional validity. More specifically, realist fiction invites metonymical reading because the invented characters and stories are still connected to reality. In comparison, both myth and fantasy, more fictional than the realist fiction, are to be read metaphorically (or, according to Asad, mythically). Myth and fantasy differ in that the former designates sacred narratives offering moral teachings while the latter is to extend entertainment to children, women, and the lower classes. Although without the cultural authority of the former, fantasy, fundamentally playful, provides a space for cultural negotiation.

I acknowledge the value of Attebery's metaphorical reading but find it inadequate. The traditional myths, Western or non-Western, contain stuff most likely untamable by this secular practice. Their radically heterogeneous views of the self, human history, and extrahuman nature are often incommensurable with what is allowed by scientific rationality and spiritualized religion. Fantasy reinvents magic, the unacknowledged third capable of destabilizing the established triad; fantasy is comprised of more than didactic or amusing stories already domesticated by a metaphorical reading.

The primary goal of fantasy is neither the representation of the real, which it troubles, nor the cultivation of the modern subject, a task it avoids. Fantasy ventures beyond the confines of history and rejects the mythical technique, on the one hand, and reintroduces magical elements such as gods, demons, and human interactions with supernatural powers and allows writers and readers to indulge in the thrill of magic, on the other. Fantasy is "a work mediated through—and in a telling sense defined by—those elements," after they have been allegedly singled out and exiled from the disenchanted universe of the modern era.[24] Starting from the Romantic era, fantastic elements in fiction "were widely regarded as superstitious, to be tolerated only if supported by evidence of actual belief or if supported by didactive or moral purpose."[25] That is to say, even though fantasy

---

[23] Attebery, *Stories about Stories*, 2.
[24] Clute and Grant, *The Encyclopedia of Fantasy*, 921.
[25] Wolfe, "Fantasy from Dryden to Dunsany," 10.

Fantasy   249

provides a shelter for magic, the magical was forced to hide behind the historical and the mythical for survival. It is Tolkien who foregrounded the magical as the defining feature of fantasy in his classic essay "On Fairy-Stories." According to him, fantasy comprises more than stories featuring magic. It involves magic as its practice and product. Presenting an apologetic of fantasy against its cultured despisers, Tolkien developed his own theorization of magic.[26]

I characterize Tolkien's strategy as retrieving the tradition of natural magic while circumventing the irredeemably derogatory term "superstition" and the demonic side of magic associated with it. In his preparatory notes for the 1947 published version of the essay, magic is defined as "the special use (real, imagined, or pretended) of powers that, though they must derive ultimately from God, are inherent in the created world, exterior to God."[27] Breaking away from post-Enlightenment scientific rationality but conforming to the teachings of Christian theology, he posited the existence of Faërie, a mysterious realm behind the sensible world, a reservoir from which magical practices endeavor to draw. Faërie also refers to the power running that realm, which is still part and parcel of the created nature. The third meaning of the term, then, is a peculiar mode of magic that channels that occult power toward the pursuit of aesthetic beauty, such as the beauty of a literary work. Although natural magic is regarded as a precursor to modern science, Tolkien pushed his natural magic onto an artistic track.

Tolkien divided magic into the technical and artistic types and identified Faërie with the latter. He strongly opposed the former, which resorts to "the vulgar devices of the laborious, scientific magician."[28] For him, technical magic "produces, or pretends to produce, an alteration in the Primary World ... [and desires] *power* in this world, domination of things and wills."[29] Artistic magic, or simply human art, is a practice that produces secondary belief—willing belief in nonexistent things and events. The epitome of artistic magic is the sub-creative art of fantasy literature. What fantasy is capable of achieving is sub-creation, the human creation of make-believe otherworlds, which are internally consistent and unconstrained by the given facts of the primary world.

Tolkien claimed that fairy stories, under the influence of their predecessors, mythical stories, practice sub-creation rather than representing consensus reality or carrying metaphorical or mythical messages. Fantasy literature is not

[26] Tolkien, Flieger, and Anderson, *Tolkien on Fairy-Stories.*
[27] Tolkien, Flieger, and Anderson, *Tolkien on Fairy-Stories*, 253.
[28] Tolkien, Flieger, and Anderson, *Tolkien on Fairy-Stories*, 33.
[29] Tolkien, Flieger, and Anderson, *Tolkien on Fairy-Stories*, 64.

250 *Literature and Religious Experience*

a lower form of art bearing the stigma of superstition but the true essence of art, an aesthetic mode of magic that taps the underlying powers of nature to alter existing forms and create new ones. Sub-creation is a human magic aimed at re-creating, although only partially, the realm of Faërie in this world and imitating and partaking in the creative capability of God, which is primary. For Tolkien, the experience of writing fantasy (sub-creation) and that of reading it (secondary belief) are both religious.

Tolkien should be positioned within the camp of scholars, artists, and practitioners who strove to revive and revamp magic in modernity. Tolkien positively resignified the wish-fulfilling and reality-escaping functions of fantasy, turning both into fantasy's strengths. His sub-creative art satisfies some primordial desires, such as the desire "to survey the depths of space and time" and the desire "to hold communion with other living things."[30] These desires break the mechanical rules of the material world and subvert an anthropocentric configuration of the social order. By satisfying these desires, Tolkien's sub-creative art promises recovery, freedom of things from human possessiveness; escape, freedom of humans from the iron cage of modern life; and the consolation of happy endings, freedom to hope for utopia amidst dystopian reality.

Positively resignified, magic is able to provide an invaluable repository of resources for challenging the asserted norms and hidden presumptions of modernity and to assume the role of social critique and subversion.[31] In our endeavor to foreground experience, a category distinct from though overlapping with belief, ritual, and institution, we are to be reminded that the processes in which certain experiences become religious are processes of legitimation and repression. The allegedly improper magical experiences are worthy of our particular attention because they constitute a site where the entanglement of the phenomenal and the political is readily discernible.

Having acknowledged the contributions made by Tolkien, I disagree with his assertion that only technical magic seeks changes in the primary world. Artistic magic, especially the subcreative art of fantasy, can be used to confront worldly powers and call for radical changes. I also notice that what is conspicuously missing in Tolkien's defense of fantasy is the othering function of magic. Tolkien was familiar with the medieval debates over natural and demonic magic. Demonic magic is not completely absent in his conceptualization. His Faërie is a realm of *both* occult powers *and* magical beings called fairies or spirits. He even

---

[30] Tolkien, Flieger, and Anderson, *Tolkien on Fairy-Stories*, 35.
[31] Styers *Making Magic*; Josephson-Storm, *The Myth of Disenchantment*.

Fantasy 251

acknowledged the moral ambiguity of fairies. However, he did not worry about the angelic or diabolical nature of fairies because he believed that the modern person was less frightened thanks to the protection of religion (Christianity) and the fact that science and modern life in general had become the new demons.

After all, Tolkien is a theocentric Christian rebelling against the ratio-centric Man but still tethered to the ethnoclass Man. Although he expected fairy stories to challenge the hegemony of science and technology, he adopted the perspective of Christian theology and adhered to church teachings. He challenged one channel (science) while leaving the other (religion) largely untouched. To reiterate a point I made earlier, magic and superstition have always been negative labels used by those in power to demonize the other. Avoiding the term "superstition" and dismissing the topic of demonic magic, Tolkien did not bother to resignify the negative image of the subhuman others, the superstitious subjects condemned by secular and religious authorities. The evasion of the role of magic and superstition as othering mechanisms is both symptomatic of and responsible for his inattentiveness toward the demonized others and subsequently the racism, sexism, and class discrimination in fantasy literature.[32]

I emphasize that a positive resignification of magic entails both Tolkien's retrieval of "good" magic—his effort to fit some experiences into the proper (Christian) model of religion—and an examination and debunking of the logical structure of the demonizing paradigm that makes "bad" magic (that is, superstition) by denouncing other experiences. I propose to revise Tolkien's key concepts of subcreation and Faërie. What Tolkien developed is a theological explanation of how fantasy subcreates, how fantasy draws on the power of Faërie to recreate, to a limited extent, that alternate realm in this world. Apparently non-Christian worldviews and human-divine relationships in particular are beyond his scope. And, calling the fantastic art of the writer sub-creation while the reader's reception of the otherworld secondary belief, he suggested that there is a creator–believer hierarchy between the writer and the reader.

What I propose is a magical technique of reading that goes beyond secondary belief to explore what the fantastic art has subcreated—various recreated Faërie-lands that are phantasmatic manifestations of what has been precluded from or concealed within the reality of a particular moral-political-cosmic order. This magical reading looks for the falsity that must be denied to make the empirical

---

[32] For a critique of how race has been represented in fantasy literature, see Young, *Race and Popular Fantasy Literature*.

252 *Literature and Religious Experience*

truth of science and the existential truth of religion possible. Practicing the magical method of reading, the reader, not just a secondary believer, participates in the ongoing process of subcreation of the fantastic art beyond the boundaries of Christian theology. Likewise, the writer has an entire range of religious, or, magical, traditions to draw on in his/her subcreation.

3. Practicing Magical Reading, Resignifying the Demonic

The demonic aspect of magic cannot be ignored. The demonic magic of the marginalized people needs to be picked up as a tool to confront the injustice and inequalities in the primary world and bring about real changes. To the same end, the demonic magic of the dominant power that maintains a particular configuration of the real is to be uncovered and dismantled, such as the demonic science Tolkien attacked and the magical tricks of commodity capitalism. Acknowledging the two faces of demonic magic, I suggest we reconceptualize Faërie as either the life-worlds of the non-modern, non-Western peoples or the hidden, mystical dimension of the established world order. The occult power of Faërie comes from the alternative cosmologies, epistemologies, and embodied experiences of the subhuman others; or, it is the very logic of global capitalism that commercializes everything, including desires, emotions, and experiences. Rooted in and aspiring toward Faërie, sub-creative art sheds light on the constructedness of history and the ideological function of myth. Correspondingly, magical reading looks beyond the historical and the mythical to read fantasy as an experiment with channeling human experiences toward the possibilities of subject formation and world-building exceeding the realms of secular science and liberal religion, both in service to the capitalist order.

To substantiate my claims above, I read *American Gods* and *The Dao*, two fantasy novels reinventing demonic magic. Both novels are published in the early twenty-first century. They are set in contemporary America and China, respectively. *American Gods* follows the adventure of its protagonist, an ex-convict named Shadow Moon, who journeys across America to run errands for Mr. Wednesday, a mysterious old man who turns out to be the American version of Odin, the main deity in the Nordic pantheon. There is an impending war between the old gods brought over to America by immigrants from around the world and a group of new gods, representing modern technologies, who are eager to take over. Working for Mr. Wednesday, Shadow helps him to rally the old gods against the new but discovers that the war has been plotted by Odin to

Fantasy 253

acquire the power of the fallen gods on both sides. Eventually, Shadow stops the war just in time and leaves America in an act of self-exile.

The Dao, the Chinese counterpart of *American Gods*, tells the story of Zhou Qing, an ordinary college graduate at the beginning of the novel, who practices Daoist alchemy to pursue immortality. Resorting to murder and plunder instead of traditional cultivation techniques such as meditation, visualization, and breathing exercises, Zhou succeeds in transcending the human world, that is, transporting himself to the realm of the immortals, who are household figures in Chinese mythology and folklore. These "Chinese gods" either choose to side with Zhou the new power or to fight against him to guard the old order. After a brutal battle that wipes out numerous gods on both sides, the protagonist establishes a new cosmic order, accomplishing what Odin fails to do in *American Gods*.

The two novels break the secular rules of artistic representation by refusing to "observe unities of time, space and character, doing away with chronology, three-dimensionality and with rigid distinctions between animate and objects, self and other, life and death."[33] Gaiman's America is an impossible world in which animals talk, the dead return, and gods live among humans. The human world in the Chinese novel is merely a lower state coexisting with the impossible realm of the immortals. The superstition *American Gods* features is the interdependent relationship between humans and spirits. The superstition at the center of *The Dao* is the quest for immortality, a perennial theme of Chinese religion and culture later viewed as an obstacle in the modernization process. Reinventing their respective demonic magics, *American Gods* sub-creates the Faërie-land as the non-modern, non-Western worlds of the marginalized, while *The Dao* sub-creates the demonic order of global capitalism.

The morally ambiguous spirits are characters in both novels, living among the immigrants or in some parallel universe, all enwrapped in struggles for survival or domination. Gaiman did extensive research on world mythology, reading myths from Africa, Asia, the Americas, and pagan Europe. Likewise, *The Dao* is a no less ambitious project built on modern Chinese scholarship collecting and compiling native mythology from various historical periods and geographical areas. Both novels attest to Attebery's point that fantasy is a modern attempt to rewrite myth. However, they also frustrate Attebery's metaphorical reading and call for a magical reading that traces and taps the hidden powers the fantastic art of these texts has invoked.

---

[33] Jackson, *Fantasy, the Literature of Subversion*, 12.

Gaiman's novel consists of two plotlines. On the one hand, there is Shadow's journey across America as narrated from a third-person limited perspective. On the other hand, there is the second narrator, a character in the novel and one of the old gods, Mr. Ibis, the American incarnation of Thoth, the Egyptian god of wisdom and writing. He tells four stories, all entitled "Coming to America," about a group of Viking pirates, an indentured servant girl from Ireland, twins captured from Africa and sold into slavery in the Caribbean, and a Siberian priestess traveling with her tribe into America. These immigrants bring with them the pagan gods in Nordic, Irish, African, and Siberian myths. The first and last stories form a colonizer-colonized pair. The Viking pirates, together with their god Odin, landed in today's America in 813 CE to conquer the indigenous tribes there, the first of which arrived around 10,000 BCE and had forgotten their original gods before the colonizers, first the Vikings and then the Puritans, wiped their history. The two episodes in the middle occurred in the first and second half of the eighteenth century, respectively, with Essie Tregowan (the Irish girl) and Agasu and Ututu (the African twins) arriving in America in 1721 and 1778, respectively.

The two plotlines invite two possible readings of the novel, one mythical, the other magical. We could read Shadow's fantastic journey in present-day America as an allegory of the modern individual's quest for self-identity by navigating himself between cultural heritages (old gods) and modern institutions (new gods). Or, we may want to read the "Coming to America" series as the primary storyline, as the title of the novel is "American Gods," not "Shadow's Journey." In this magical reading, stories of the immigrants and their gods work as a portal that connects us to the history of global capitalism, a history in which the subjugation of women, indentured labor, and slave trade founded the rise of capitalism on a global scale. These stories bring back what had to be obliterated to make that history real and possible—that is, the lived experiences of the racial, class, and gendered others clinging onto their superstition and excluded from the figure of the ethnoclass, ratio-centric Man. These experiences contending with and suppressed by the institutionalization of the new gods of global capitalism have resurfaced thanks to fantasy's preservation of superstition.

Compared with *American Gods*, *The Dao* thwarts the mythical technique more radically. This novel has triggered heated discussion among its readers over the question of the demonic cultivator. First of all, the cultivator is a figure from premodern China, who seeks to transcend various human limitations, to ascend to higher realms of existence, and to integrate himself/herself into the primordial Dao. The Chinese cultivator is indeed an exotic magician at odds with the modern individual seeking self-realization. What's more, the cultivator in *The Dao* does not simply replicate the image of the traditional cultivator, although both stand aloof from history and myth in the modern Western sense. While the traditional cultivator does follow moral rules, his/her modern transfiguration is portrayed as demonic. The novel makes no attempt at whitewashing the protagonist's inglorious path toward immorality, along which he ruthlessly murders his competitors and plunders their magical tools. The other cultivators are no exceptions, driven only by the accumulation of power. They are the evil magicians against whom Tolkien positioned his artistic magic.

The fantastic art of *The Dao* subcreates anti-heroes and nightmarish otherworlds. Genre fantasy has been critiqued for painting an overly simplistic picture in which good always triumphs over evil, but *The Dao* is a counterexample. The realm of the immortals, or, the Chinese inflection of Faërie, is an exacerbated version of the human world in terms of fierce competition and violent conflict, with both governed by the same cosmic Dao, which is amoral and inhuman. *The Dao* does not conceal but reveals the foundational violence that has been rendered unseen, unheard, and unsaid by the social, economic, and political order that such violence undergirds.

I read the demonic Dao as capital, while the cultivator the so-called human capital, a ratio-centric Man practicing endless self-training and self-enterprising to merge himself into the ever-expanding capital. While *American Gods* revisits the colonial history of global capitalism from the perspective of the subhuman others, *The Dao* engages with a new phase of capitalism, neoliberalism marked by the penetration of the principle of competition from the marketplace into all social spheres. What the novel subcreates is the making of the neoliberal subject and the gradual unlocking of the strictly hierarchical neoliberal world to him. The novel does not pretend to represent reality. Nor does it offer moral edification or escapist entertainment. Subject to magical reading, it pushes us to face up to the invisible heart of darkness that is throbbing within reality as it is, most intriguingly by reinventing the impossible magical/superstitious experience of immortality cultivation.

To sum up, magic inside fantasy novels is twofold: the everyday experiences of the subhuman others and the magic of commodity, competition, and capitalist expansion that capitalizes on human experiences to generate non-experience. Writing and reading these novels, writers and readers strive to retrieve the former and resist the latter. While Tolkien presented the endeavor of the writer as subcreative magic that brings otherworlds into being, I suggest that the reader may practice magical reading to examine the perilous realms and their hidden powers that serve as a repository for subcreation. Whereas the genre of fantasy provides a platform for magic and superstition to persist in the modern secular world, fantasy, the experiences of writers, readers, and characters inside the texts, has been performing the postsecular work, questioning the hegemony of science, the ideal model of religion, and the domination of the capitalist modern West as the only possible version of reality and then looking for the alternatives of being human and existing in the world. Aesthetic magic as conceived by Tolkien is not without its political agenda in the primary world.

Bibliography

Asad, Talal. *Formations of the Secular: Christianity, Islam, Modernity.* Stanford, CA: Stanford University Press, 2003.

Attebery, Brian. *Stories about Stories: Fantasy and the Remaking of Myth.* New York: Oxford University Press, 2014.

Bever, E., and R. Styers. *Magic in the Modern World: Strategies of Repression and Legitimization.* University Park: Pennsylvania State University Press, 2017.

Cameron, Euan. *Enchanted Europe: Superstition, Reason, and Religion 1250–1750.* Oxford: Oxford University Press, 2010.

Clute, John, and John Grant, eds. *The Encyclopedia of Fantasy.* New York: Macmillan, 1997.

During, Simon. *Modern Enchantments: The Cultural Power of Secular Magic.* Cambridge, MA: Harvard University Press, 2002.

Federici, Silvia. *Caliban and the Witch.* New York: Autonomedia, 2004.

Feher, Michel. 'Self-Appreciation; or, the Aspirations of Human Capital.' *Public Culture* 21, no. 1 (2009): 21–41.

Gaiman, Neil. *American Gods* (Tenth anniversary edition). New York: William Morrow, 2011.

Graf, Fritz. *Magic in the Ancient World.* Cambridge, MA: Harvard University Press, 1997.

Hanegraaff, Wouter J. *Esotericism and the Academy: Rejected Knowledge in Western Culture.* Cambridge: Cambridge University Press, 2012.

Jackson, Rosemary. *Fantasy, the Literature of Subversion.* London: Routledge, 2008.

James, Edward, and Farah Mendlesohn. *The Cambridge Companion to Fantasy Literature.* New York: Cambridge University Press, 2012.

Jameson, Fredric. *The Antinomies of Realism.* London: Verso, 2013.

Josephson, Jason A. *The Myth of Disenchantment: Magic, Modernity, and the Birth of the Human Sciences.* Chicago: University of Chicago Press, 2017.

Josephson, Jason A. "The Superstition, Secularism, and Religion Trinary: Or Re-Theorizing Secularism." *Method & Theory in the Study of Religion* 30, no. 1 (2018): 120.

Kieckhefer, Richard. *Magic in the Middle Ages*. New York: Cambridge University Press, 1989.

Martin, Dale B. *Inventing Superstition: From the Hippocratics to the Christians*. Cambridge, MA: Harvard University Press, 2004.

Mengru Shenji. *Fobenshidao* [The Buddha Belongs to the Dao]. Shijiazhuang: Huashan wenyi, 2008.

Ni, Zhange. "Xiuzhen (Immortality Cultivation) Fantasy: Science, Religion, and the Novels of Magic/Superstition in Contemporary China." *Religions* 11, no. 1 (2020): 25.

Schaefer, Donovan O. *Religious Affects: Animality, Evolution, and Power*. Durham and London: Duke University Press, 2015.

Styers, Randall. *Making Magic: Religion, Magic, and Science in the Modern World*. New York: Oxford University Press, 2004.

Taves, Ann. *Religious Experience Reconsidered: A Building-Block Approach to the Study of Religion and Other Special Things*. Princeton, NJ: Princeton University Press, 2009.

Taylor, Charles. *A Secular Age*. Cambridge, MA: Harvard University Press, 2009.

Tolkien, J. R. R., Verlyn Flieger, and Douglas A. Anderson. *Tolkien on Fairy-Stories* (expanded edition with commentary and notes). London: HarperCollins, 2008.

Wolfe, Gary. "Fantasy from Dryden to Dunsany." In *The Cambridge Companion to Fantasy Literature*, edited by Edward James and Farah Mendlesohn, 5–20. Cambridge: Cambridge University Press, 2012.

Wynter, Sylvia. "Unsettling the Coloniality of Being/Power/Truth/Freedom: Towards the Human, After Man, Its Overrepresentation—An Argument." *CR: The New Centennial Review* 3 no. 3 (2003): 257–337.

Young, Helen Victoria. *Race and Popular Fantasy Literature: Habits of Whiteness*. New York: Routledge, 2015.

15

Idolatry: Meaning, Power, and "Ideas" of Idolatry in *Heart of Darkness* and *Demian*

Larry D. Bouchard

A confession: for years I began a course in Religion and Modern Fiction with Joseph Conrad's novella, *Heart of Darkness* (*HOD*, 1899–1902) and recently changed to Hermann Hesse's *Demian* (1917–19) for reasons I am now reconsidering—reasons concerning *idolatry*.[1]

My course asks, *what is religion?* At any time, this question intersects with ideology, violence, and suffering. The Abrahamic faiths interpret such intersections in terms of idolatry, perhaps *the* basic form of sin.[2] Idolatry treats contingent matters—signs, fabricated images, nations, selves—as if of divine meaning and power. Since human expressions of religion are finite and limited—yet powerful and meaning-rich—idolatry can seem inevitable. John Calvin called the mind a "factory" of idols; Karl Barth deemed religion itself idolatry (except when sanctified by grace). No idolatry, no religion.

Critiques of idolatry, ancient to postmodern, turn on links between *power* and *meaning*. Because power and meaning are intimate yet incommensurate, they are hard to theorize. I believe when thought reaches an impasse, we should search for stories or images that narrate or visualize the impasse. So, I propose a meander. Start with Conrad and Hesse; detour among appreciative and critical studies of religion, meaning, and power; then return to "ideas" and "idols" pictured in the fiction.

---

[1] See my "Openings and Closures in Religion and Literature," 46–57; some material here follows that essay.

[2] Farley, *Good and Evil*, 119–138; Marion, *God without Being*, 25–52.

1.

HOD had advantages. It is short; its three parts lend themselves to three introductory discussions, raising issues of morality and doubt that haunt modern imaginations. It anticipates other stories of race, memory, and religion in the course, including Shūsaku Endō's *Silence*, Marilynne Robinson's *Gilead*, and Toni Morrison's *Beloved. HOD* also explores the narrative representation of subjectivity. On a long, airless evening a sailing yawl, the *Nellie*, is stalled on the Thames between the outflowing current and inflowing tide; there Marlow tells four affluent passengers of another river journey. Among them, a frame narrator subtly reacts as Marlow, sitting in in the lotus position and resembling an "idol," recounts the story of Kurtz, an ivory agent of "unsound method" in a place left unnamed, the Congo Free State.[3]

That Marlow sits like an idol will be repeated, referring to his posture, not his attitude. Yet idolatry is everywhere. Implicitly equating Roman colonizers of Britain with rapacious Europeans in Africa, Marlow ironically contrasts them with the *Nellie*'s businessmen and their "devotion to efficiency"—ironic, for no actual contrast is intended.

> The conquest of the earth, which mostly means the taking it away from those who have a different complexion or slightly flatter noses than ourselves, is not a pretty thing when you look into it too much. What redeems it is the idea only. An idea at the back of it; not a sentimental pretence but an idea; and an unselfish belief in the idea—something you can set up, and bow down before, and offer a sacrifice to. (7)

The "idea" involved ivory, and the Europeans in Africa "were praying to it" (27). Marlow learns that Kurtz, reputedly a musician, artist, and "universal genius," was "hollow at the core" and "an—extremist." A journalist reports Kurtz "had the faith ... he could get himself to believe anything" (72, 90). In Europe his rhetoric inflamed his colonialist admirers with rationales of moral virtue, and in Africa he made his abject laborers worship him.

However, my first teaching aim was to show the effects of Kurtz's demonic rule and portentous death on Marlow's subjectivity *as he narrates* the journey. It is a story of storytelling, story receiving, and retelling. Another point was that while *religion* does not occur in the text, *faith, belief, symbol, preaching, meditating, sin,* and *sacred* do. Conrad alludes to scripture, Virgil, and Dante, and the climax is a

---

[3] Conrad, *Heart of Darkness*, 4.

Idolatry 261

revelation: Marlow sees a change passing over Kurtz's face, "as though a veil had been rent." His dying words—"The horror! The horror!"—were "the appalling face of a glimpsed truth" (86, 88). The novella, a critique of empire and racism that nonetheless inflect its own language and despair, also discloses a religious dimension.

By *dimension*, or *vision*, I mean (1) a *thematic world* (themes of idolatry, atrocity, restraint, "infinite pity") encompassing (2) *circumstances, activities, and persons* (Conrad, Marlow, Kurtz, certain Europeans and Africans) with (3) *histories, cultures, practices* (Christian, Buddhist—but African?), which (4) get *focused and refracted* through formal and stylistic structures (plot, imagery, irony, movement), prompting us to interrogate this world.[4] Whether religious or not, such dimensions entail shareable meanings and feelings inviting exploration. We enter a world that "faces" us and impels us to respond.[5] When I taught *HOD* as the first text, I offered two avenues toward its religious dimensionality. The first concerned Marlow's meditation on exploitive idolatry. His narrative is analogous to a religious teaching, wherein we face our own dark capacities. Lest that seem too allegorical, there is another adjective overhanging the tale, "inconclusive." The passengers knew they were in for "one of Marlow's inconclusive experiences" (8).

My other approach shifted from meditation to confession. Marlow returns to Europe and visits Kurtz's fiancée. Though he "hate[s], detest[s], and can't bear a lie," neither can he tell the truth when she requests Kurtz's final words. Out of a "feeling of infinite pity," he says they were "your name." He expects judgment on this lie but no, "The heavens do not fall for such a trifle" (95–6). Yet his lie obsesses him, and the narrative is a confession of how near he came to the abyss that claimed Kurtz. He wants to tell the truth of Kurtz's horror and of how he has kept loyal to "the nightmare of my choice" (80). He affirms Kurtz as one who "judged" the horror, although what judgment remains unclear. On Kurtz himself, on Europe, the Congo, or whatever underlies it all? At the end of his tedious report on the "Suppression of Native Customs" Kurtz scrawled, "Exterminate all the brutes!" (62). If Marlow now confesses *his* proximity to Kurtz, what does that make *us*? Marlow's priest? Are we to absolve him, or prescribe his penance? If he wins our understanding, does he make us complicit? Must his confession become our own?

---

[4] On reference in fiction, see Gerhart, "Generic Studies," 309–25. On reference and "possible world[s]," see Ricoeur, *Interpretation Theory*, 87.
[5] On encountering narratives as persons, see Newton, *Narrative Ethics*.

262   *Literature and Religious Experience*

However provocative its pedagogical advantages, *HOD* was a hard sell. Its range of experience is narrow. Its few women are badly stereotyped. The Africans—Kurtz's "woman," Marlow's crewmembers, dying "shapes" and "shadows," "savages"—are accorded none of their arts or traditions. Marlow discovers bonds of "kinship" with them (44, 62) belatedly and ambiguously. While virulent imperialism is damned, *HOD*'s racial and political fatalism can imagine no alternatives. Chinua Achebe finds its projections so offensive as to leave misbegotten its ironic purpose of critique: to expose faith, moral education, sincerity, and spiritual and material progress as values deployed to justify exploitive abjection.[6] Marlow, oddly protective of Kurtz's memory, is appalled by his "exalted and incredible degradation ... He had kicked himself loose of the earth" (82).

So I chose another short novel, composed in Switzerland in 1917. *Demian* is a Bildungsroman appealing to serious late adolescents—"the story of Emil Sinclair's youth." It has desirable features for introducing religion and modernist fiction: intriguing myths and beliefs (a gnostic deity, Abraxas), intellectual friendship (Emil with his guide, Demian), sexuality and androgyny (images of Beatrice, Demian, and his mother Lady Eve), and speculations on good and evil, nature and spirit. *Demian* refracts religious, philosophical, and literary sources: the Bible, Augustine's *Confessions*, Hinduism, Gnosticism, Hegel's dialectic of spirit, themes from Nietzsche and Jung. The prologue interweaves enigmas and aphorisms echoing Romanticism: an individual is a "priceless, unique experiment of nature." "Every person's story is, important, eternal, divine." "In each of us spirit has become form, in each of us the created being suffers, in each of us a redeemer is crucified." "Many a one never becomes a human being, but remains a frog, lizard, or ant." "We can understand one another, but each of us can only interpret himself."[7] Are we to take these statements at face value?

In a way yes, for such propositions are "materials"' for art and may be granted their own terms. But also no, for it is as *patterns of difference* that they contribute to form and vision. Hesse, for instance, apparently locates God not in *transcendence* but *immanence* (in nature and in mind or spirit, *Geist*). *Apparently*, for this distinction may be questioned. Jung's collective unconscious is immanent in mentality yet transcends cultures and species. And while Max Demian has been deemed a "fictional transfiguration of Jesus," Christian form

---

[6] Achebe, "An Image of Africa," 1–20.
[7] Hesse, *Demian*, 1–2.

Idolatry 263

emptied of Christian content, we should ask, what is *content*?[8] To reimagine paradigms from the Bible or other sources may not completely erase meanings that were always multivalent.

I do want to show where *Demian* values plurality in religious discourse and practice. When Emil rejects one of his guides—a church organist who reads Gnosticism via analytical psychology—he judges Pistorius doctrinaire and "antiquarian." It is not the content Emil rejects but the stasis. Pistorius "led me along a path that had to go beyond even him, and leave him behind."[9] It is this content-rich yet self-surpassing path that makes *Demian* good for introducing issues of generality and particularity in religious experience. Yet the longer I consider it in light of meaning and power, the more I question its being more embracing of plurality and accepting of uncertainty than *HOD*. *Demian* may be *less* critical of idolatries in hermeneutical experience (experiences of understanding and interpretation that define human existence). As my meander continues, I detour—visiting certain impasses to interpreting religion, meaning, and power.

2.

I confess to being a junky for definitions-of-things-like-religion. In college I came across Paul Tillich on faith as "the state of being ultimately concerned" and learned his definition had grandparents: Calvin on piety as gratitude, Friedrich Schleiermacher's "feeling of absolute dependence," William James's "total reaction upon life," Rudolf Otto's sense of fearful yet fascinating mystery, Martin Buber's "eternal Thou." And children: Langdon Gilkey's "traces of ultimacy," David Tracy's "limit-to" and "limit-of" experiences, John Caputo's love of "the impossible"—postmodern lingo for God as love-commanding-love.[10] Caputo takes it from Augustine's "What do I love when I love my God," from "God is love" (1 Jn 4:8), and from the extended *shema*: "Hear, O Israel! The LORD is our God, the LORD alone. You shall love the LORD your God with all your heart and with all your soul and with all your strength" (Deut. 6:4-5). These definitions trace to Abraham and Moses, but I also like Daisetz Suzuki

---

[8] Ziolkowski, *Fictional Transfiguration*, 151–63, especially 158.
[9] Hesse, *Demian*, 82.
[10] Tillich, *Dynamics of Faith*, 1; Gerrish, *Grace and Gratitude*, 20; Schleiermacher, *Christian Faith*, 24; James, *Varieties of Religious Experience*, 35; Otto, *Idea of the Holy*, 7, 12–34; Buber, *I and Thou*; Gilkey, *Naming the Whirlwind*, 308; Tracy, *Blessed Rage for Order*, 92–3; Caputo, *On Religion*, 1.

264 *Literature and Religious Experience*

on religion as enlightenment.[11] He probably appeals to those discovering the Buddha via Immanuel Kant, although Buddhist and modern enlightenments are different. These approaches to religion are cautious about infinitizing the finite; yet each discerns matters infinite, adjacent to limits in experience.

Tracy does not define religion but notices that with religion we do find limit experiences and questions. Easiest to diagram are limit questions, which touch the boundaries of their domains. Imagine, say, *ethics* as a circle. In it ask, *why ought we to be ethical?* Then imagine this question as an arrow starting within ethics yet wanting to arc beyond its circle. It "still has the form of a moral question ('ought') but ... does not actually function ethically. In fact ... we cannot really produce a *moral* argument for being moral."[12] The question not only "transcends" moral discourse but may produce a shock—an experience of transcendence. Tracy distinguishes two sorts of limit. *Limit-to* questions arise within a domain and come *to* its limit. The arrow, "Why ought we to keep promises?" reaches the ethical world's edge. But *limit-of* questions arc over the edge, intimating an "other side" *of* the limit.

Limit-of inferences resist ordinary conceptualization; they require metaphors, narratives, lyrics, mystic tones, and images—associated with revelations and practices that "answer" limit-to questions—like symbols of covenantal grace (Judaism, Christianity), moksha (Hinduism), or enlightenment (Buddhism). The logic of limit implies such answers come in extraordinary forms that generate multiple interpretations over time. Which is wondrous! Except when clear, distinct ideas are what we crave. Perhaps idolatries of "the idea," which anxiously crave to control matters transcending definitional control, begin here.

For all that, limit experience is but one telltale of religion. Tracy quotes anthropologist Clifford Geertz's definition of religion as a "cultural system" of symbols that act upon people affectively and cognitively, instilling "conceptions of a general order of existence." Moreover, religious symbol systems clothe "these conceptions with such an aura of factuality" as to make the conceptions feel "uniquely realistic."[13] Yet Tracy omits the "paradigm" by which Geertz introduces the definition: "Sacred symbols function to *synthesize* a people's ethos—the tone, character, and quality of their life, its moral and aesthetic style and mood—and their world view—the picture they have of the things in sheer actuality are, their most comprehensive ideas of order."[14] When symbols and rituals function *as*

[11] Suzuki, "Enlightenment," 33–44.
[12] Tracy. *Blessed Rage for Order*, 102; my italics.
[13] Tracy. *Blessed Rage for Order*, 92; Geertz, *Interpretation of Cultures*, 90.
[14] Geertz, *Interpretation of Cultures*, 88–9; my italics.

religion, ethos and worldview (ought and is) fuse and people internalize the fusion. Implicitly, secular cultures lack such syntheses; for Matthew Arnold, Christian moral ethos and scientific worldview no longer fuse.[15]

Just as the *shema* exemplifies religion for Caputo, it could also work for Geertz. *God's oneness* is worldview synthesized by the *shema* (symbol and ritual) with ethos stretched to include *loving God with one's whole being and neighbor as oneself*. In the Qur'an, God's unity defines worldview; ethos is *taking eternal refuge* in divine unity (Suras 112, 114). Ethos and worldview can gloss Buddhist recitals of the Three Refuges and Christianity's Lord's Prayer. If all cultures have codes reflective of worldview (imagining how the world goes around) and ethos (how life should be lived) not all cultures fuse "is" with "ought." But such synthesizing is what Geertz thinks religious traditions *do*: they produce, within their "aura of factuality," a sense of order that resists chaos or "bafflement" but which outsiders may find baffling.[16] Learning a religion is analogous to learning a language, where total immersion excels grammar books. Geertz's approach has proven persuasive even to cognoscenti in different traditions.

Yet strengths may hide weaknesses, as in critiques of culture theory by Catherine Bell and Kathryn Tanner. Let me first say that philosophical and cultural *Kritik*—aiming to diagnose and repair structures of thought and practice—participates in traditions of emancipation.[17] The Hebrew prophets exposed oppressive idolatry; when secular critics trace distortions of ideology and bias, they too expose idols. The beauty of critique is liberation; its hammer is iconoclasm, where claims, seemingly comprehensive, are shattered by reasoned doubt. Here, the doubts concern culture theory's expectations of wholeness, its overvaluing of order, and its blindness to insinuated power.

Tanner would be the more peaceable prophet, hoping to revamp theologies of culture. Though she indexes Geertz but twice, the anthropologies she repairs must answer to "post-Geertzian" criticisms: for being inattentive to historical processes, privileging internal consensus and stability, downplaying social conflict, and construing cultures as "sharply bounded" and "self-contained." Tanner less refutes modern theories than softens their edges while retaining their better insights. Cultural meanings somewhat transcend history but are fully historical; cultures are holistic and bounded, yet their boundaries are porous; they not only entail internal conflict but also facilitate reform. "The

---

[15] See Scott, *The Poetics of Belief*, 39–61.
[16] Geertz, *Interpretation of Cultures*, 100.
[17] Ricoeur, "Hermeneutics," 9.

266 *Literature and Religious Experience*

differentiating function of the modern notion of culture is also retained ... but the account of cultural difference is modified substantially." Cultural identity is "a hybrid, relational affair, something that lives between as much as with cultures."[18] Cultures, hence religions, have internal diversity and external relations through which political and social change occur and communal self-idolatry resisted.

Whereas Tanner reforms academic claims about culture's function to secure wholeness, Bell identifies mystifications of power behind such claims. While "ritualization" may seem to fuse ethos and worldview or mediate the sacred, what ritual really does is manage power needed to make such distinctions. Hers is a critique both of theorists and practitioners, with more sympathy for the latter. Here I should state the obvious: everything requires *power*. To diminish power diminishes the forms it empowers. Critiques of oppressive or illusory power must assume that power itself is neutral or "good." To liberate is to redirect power; paradoxes like "the power of powerlessness" know this. So asking of meaning and power is a fundamental not just a political-cultural question—something to remember whenever "power" demands critique.

Bell begins with droll deconstructions of thinkers from Durkheim to Geertz, whose loops of reasoning invent the binary tensions—for example, ethos and worldview, action versus thought, sacred and profane—that ritual supposedly resolves, when, actually, rituals are strategies "for ascribing such distinctions to realities *thought* to transcend the powers of human actors."[19] Now, when old-fashioned hermeneuts learn that matters of meaning are really about power, we worry the claim is reductive: meaning reduced to structures of domination, everyone positioned in zero-sum games, power eclipsing predications and expressions. Matthew Arnold's "Dover Beach" would be not about the absence of God or pathos of faith but the poet's anxiety projected against chaos and others—and similarly "God's Grandeur" by Gerard Manley Hopkins and, say, Humpty Dumpty and Cinderella. I parody, but that seems the impasse when critique dwells on some extrinsic singular, like power, anxiety, or desire. However, power for Bell and Michel Foucault is more interesting than coercive control.

Yes, it positions and strategizes. Yet power is often indirect, insinuating from within and without, bottom up and top down, more in local webs than hierarchies, shifting, changing, entailing dominance certainly but also resistance and the implied consent of those whom power plays. Power must *effect* the freedom it affects; when strategy denies agency, rather than working through

---

[18] Tanner, *Theories of Culture*, 40–55, 57, 58.
[19] Bell, *Ritual Theory, Ritual Practice*, 74 (my italics); see also 206.

Idolatry 267

plural agents, it is not social power but brute force. Social power is relational. It is what we *are* together, more or less and from time to time, not some metaphysical substance we *have*. Foucault can define power so inter-relationally as to approach synonymy with *reality as meaningful*. Bell agrees and comes close to a hermeneutical dialectic of meaning and power: "Only by staying free of the substantive approach ... can one truly analyze power in terms of human relations."[20] But how close does she come?

For Bell, ritual entails "misrecognition." Rituals project sacred-profane distinctions onto realities "thought to transcend" human experience (Tracy's limit-of). She thinks what we should be asking is who gets to make these mystifying distinctions. It is the "ritualizers" who employ ritual to *establish or sustain the social power needed to make them*. Bell agrees with masters of suspicion like Ludwig Feuerbach or Karl Marx that people are averse to think themselves manipulating or manipulated by ritual schemes.

> The production and objectification of structured and structuring schemes ... involve a misrecognition of the source and arbitrariness of these schemes. These schemes tend to be experienced as deriving from powers or realities beyond the community and its activities, such as god or tradition, thereby depicting and testifying to the ultimate organization of the cosmos.[21]

Could people in actual traditions agree with this, without irony? Well, religious folk do enjoy their ironies. I once explained Bell to a group of "pastor-theologians" and some agreed that securing power was indeed what they did on any given Sunday. The notion that gaps between ritual story and ritual reality must remain obfuscated does not always hold. Ritualizers and ritualized may acknowledge the contingencies of their sacraments without emptying them of transcendence or depth. Moreover, there is another way to read *misrecognition* besides structural self-deception, moving us toward a less iconoclastic critique of idolatry.

There is an implication in a hermeneutical line from Schleiermacher to Hans-Georg Gadamer that understanding is grounded in *misunderstanding*. It's first a matter of finitude. To understand a complex thought or event is asymptotic— you never quite get there, a gap remains. The more you grasp a text's aspects the

---

[20] Bell, *Ritual Theory, Ritual Practice*, 199. See Foucault, A History of Sexuality, 1: 93: "Power's condition of possibility ... is the moving substrate of force relations which, by virtue of their inequality, constantly engender states of power, but the latter are always local and unstable ... Power is everywhere; not because it embraces everything, but because it comes from everywhere."
[21] Bell, *Ritual Theory, Ritual Practice*, 206–7.

268   *Literature and Religious Experience*

more aspects appear, still to be understood. This is so even before Schleiermacher considers hasty judgment, bias, and malice. "Misunderstanding occurs," he says, "as a matter of course."[22] With Martin Heidegger and Gadamer, the limits of understanding appear in interplays of projection and resistance. When we encounter anything, we project—from life experience and historical traditions—*fore-understandings*. Gadamer provocatively calls them *prejudices*. Our initial prejudices may illuminate the encounter ("this figure must be a tree") or may not ("no, it's a flowchart"). Mere "fancies," says Heidegger,[23] will be resisted—what Gadamer calls "being pulled up short by the text."[24] Without projecting from experience and tradition, understanding can never begin. Yet if my projections are *not* resisted to some extent by what I would understand, then for all I know I am peering into a mirror.

Understanding is sustained by projection and resistance via dialogue—unless dialogue's critical powers are subverted. Consider the "performative" distortions possible in discourse that *effects* social situations. Normally, saying *I promise* creates new spaces of obligation and expectation. Even simple assertions may count as performative speech, anticipating agreement or disagreement.[25] However, meaning's proximity to power especially appears in deceptive utterances, overt or unwitting. What Jürgen Habermas calls "systematically distorted communication" is the *lie* made structural—ideologized, operating behind the back of dialogue, hence unrecognized by all parties.[26] Ritual, for Bell, would normalize performative distortion. However, if misrecognition is but one path of *misunderstanding*, then a critical framework for ritual-religious meaning becomes more capacious.

Rituals misunderstand not necessarily from covert coercion—though they may—but from limits of knowing and action. Disjunctions between ritual expectations and realizations are occasioned by plural meanings within traditions as well as by strategic advantages. *As to plural contingencies*: Victor Turner thought the abundance of role paradigms in a society's "forest of symbols" implies that the outcome of a ritual process, while probable, will be uncertain. Which paradigms grab and transform my liminal, pliable self may

---

[22] Schleiermacher, *Hermeneutics*, 110.

[23] Heidegger, *Being and Time*, 195.

[24] Gadamer, *Truth and Method*, 268.

[25] Austin, *How to Do Things with Words*. On deceptive speech acts, see Habermas, *The Theory of Communicative Action*, 1: 294.

[26] Habermas, "Hermeneutics' Claim to Universality," 294–319, arguing that Gadamer's view of dialogue cannot repair discourse distorted systematically.

Idolatry 269

be anticipated but not necessitated.[27] Bell herself notices how the flexibility with which lay believers treat official teachings is important to their efficacy.[28] *As to culpability*: Tillich thought the only *adequate* religious symbols are those showing their own contingency in pointing toward the infinite.[29] Our tendency to control sacred symbols by equating them with their ultimate referent is how Tillich conceives the thrall of idolatry.

3.

Suppose meaning and power are on intimate yet incommensurate terms—like *map* and *territory*—hard to theorize. Their ad-hoc relations might yet be narrated, imaged. As it happens, Conrad and Hesse narrate pictures of signing, *semiosis*. Marlow recounts,

> Now when I was a little chap I had a passion for maps. I would look for hours at South America, or Africa, or Australia, and lose myself in all the glories of exploration. At that time there were many blank spaces on the earth, and when I saw one that looked particularly inviting on a map (but they all look that) I would put my finger on it and say, "When I grow up I will go there." (8)

This picture of "passion," musing on empty spaces and fingering maps, catches something of how signs play between the virtual and actual. The continents where young Marlow forgot himself are mere names, virtual realities, triggering associations but referring to little in particular.[30] It requires a finger and nerve to animate a map. When dynamically related to Marlow, the map's meaning and power and his become momentarily entangled.

In the semiotics of Charles Peirce, Marlow's map is first an *icon*, a sign based on resemblance. Should I unfold an outline map within its territory, say the Congo, there will be a point on the map the same as the point where I stand. Momentarily map, earth, and I merge. A curiosity, but it inspired desires, "glories of exploration"—"I will go there." The map pushes Marlow, points him, now becoming the sign Peirce terms *index* or *indicator*. "When I grow up" also

---

[27] Turner, "Betwixt and Between," 93–111; on Thomas Becket, see Turner, *Dramas, Fields, and Metaphors*, 60–97.

[28] Bell, *Ritual Theory, Ritual Practice*, 184–93. On gauging multivalent discourses, see Ochs et al., "Value Predicate Analysis," 93–113.

[29] Tillich, *Dynamics of Faith*, pt. 3, "Symbols of Faith." See Marion, *God without Being*, 22–4, on iconic concepts.

[30] On Ferdinand de Saussure's dyadic sign as merely "virtual," see Ricoeur, *Interpretation Theory*, 7.

270   *Literature and Religious Experience*

suggests how the map interprets Marlow to himself, becoming the third basic sign, the *symbol*.[31] His map shows how signs are nexuses of feeling, meaning, and power and are contingent, vulnerable—as if a map could suffer.

> True, by this time it was not a blank space any more. It had got filled since my boyhood with rivers and lakes and names. It had ceased to be a blank space of delightful mystery—a white patch for a boy to dream gloriously over. It had become a place of darkness. (9)

The map iterated a *surfeit* of meanings, as more Europeans fingered and darkened Africa.[32] Romantic musings became namings, with hints of violent inscription. We are accustomed to condemning dreams of "delightful mystery" screening violence; however, a surplus of meaning (Paul Ricoeur) may differ from a surfeit. One is an overflow that *opens itself to witnesses*, the other a distortion *obscured under a glut of names and notions*.[33] Conrad intuits the difference in another picture of semiosis.

> The yarns of seamen have a direct simplicity, the whole meaning of which lies within the shell of a cracked nut. But Marlow was not typical … to him the meaning of an episode was not inside like a kernel but outside, enveloping the tale which brought it out only as a glow brings out a haze, in the likeness of one of these misty halos that sometimes are made visible by the spectral illumination of moonshine. (6)

Marlow's "haze" of meaning spreads from the tale's "glow" to encompass hearers or readers in its "misty halo," further illuminated by other sources, "moonshine"—while "the yarns of seamen" promise dubious clarity. The contrast is illuminated by Peirce's triadic sign. To the sign-sense dyad he adds a third, the *interpretant*: *sign* and *object* are for *another in some context*. The interpretant, still part of an abstract model, concretizes semiosis. Signs become realities that affect and effect relations (hazes of meanings). Like Marlow's finger, the interpretant connects signs in space and time. A sign's interpretant can become a new sign, with another interpretant, becoming another sign, *ad infinitum*. The most exemplary signs are symbols—"words, sentences, books, and conventional signs."[34] Peirce's triad, sign–object–interpretant, approximates the predicative structure of sentences.

---

[31] Peirce, *The Essential Peirce*, 161–3, on icon, index, symbol, also maps.
[32] Conrad inscribing the very dichotomies he destabilizes. On blank/white (*blanc*), see Derrida, "White Mythology," 5–74.
[33] See Marion on witnessing the "saturated phenomenon," in *Being Given*, 211, 216–19.
[34] Peirce, *The Essential Peirce*, 274.

Idolatry 271

Although Ricoeur defines sign and symbol somewhat more narrowly than Peirce, both theorists consider sentences exemplary. Sentences imply power, not only when promising or commanding but also in predication itself. For Ricoeur, predicating utterances are the units of actual discourse. We *make* sentences. We bring nouns and verbs together to reflect and project "worlds." *Bringing together* implies and requires power. Meaning and power are still not convertible—their terms remain incommensurate. But as they are not alien to dialogical reflection, such reflection is not irreparably blind to power's distortions. Distancing critique happens, though fallibly, *within* understanding and reflection.[35] Discourse practices—including explanatory procedures, multivalent dialogues, hypothesizing narratives—can identify damages done by and suffered by signs, such as Marlow's map.

It might seem the "blank spaces" that so attracted Marlow would be liabilities compared to "rivers and lakes and names." But vagueness maintains possibilities that singular naming can foreclose. Peirce suggests the most indubitable beliefs are semantically "vague" and so retain flexible applicability[36]—whereas overdeterminations may contribute to idolatries of the idea. I shall return to Conrad, but now some "pictures" of semiosis in Hesse.

Emil leaves the ambiguous safety of home for school, where he falls into debauchery. From his dark wood he sees the girl he calls Beatrice, after Rossetti's painting of Dante's guide. In sublimated fervor, he attempts to paint her portrait from memory. His efforts are resisted—then a new face surfaces from his unconscious.

> It was something different, something unreal, but no less valuable. It looked more like a young man's face than a girl's ... a sort of divine image or sacred mask, half-male, half-female, ageless, equally strong-willed and secretly alive. That face had something to say to me, it belonged to me, it made demands on me. And it resembled somebody, I didn't know whom. (53)

The "dreamy" icon obsesses him. First it resembles Demian, later Emil himself. "It depicted that which constituted my life, it was my inner self, my fate, or my *daemon*" (54). He captions it from Novalis, "A man's fate and his character are two names for the same concept."

The picture and those that follow exemplify Gadamer's hermeneutics, even though Hesse follows a psychoanalytic concept of individuation. Emil encounters

---

[35] On Gadamer and Habermas, see Ricoeur, "Hermeneutics and the Critique of Ideology."
[36] Ochs, *Peirce, Pragmatism and Logic*, 9, 180–1.

something. From experience and tradition he projects a fore-understanding, Beatrice. Dante is in mind, mediated by Dante Gabriel Rossetti's painting. But this projection is resisted, so Emil revises—now the face resembles Demian—then revises again—now it seems himself. At this point resistance and revision might continue, but stops; the portrait becomes a mirror, the face freezes into a concept from Novalis and Heraclitus. Emil paints a sparrow hawk breaking from a shell, which he sends to Demian—who replies, "The egg is the world. Whoever wishes to be born must destroy a world. The bird is flying to God. The god is named Abraxas" (59). Another picture provokes Emil's resistance: "I questioned it, I made accusations against it, I caressed it, I prayed to it; I called it mother ... beloved ... whore ... Abraxas," until he discerns Jacob wrestling God for a blessing. "I wanted to kneel before it, but it was so firmly inside me that I could no longer separate it from myself" (77). The image blends into Beatrice, Demian, Lady Eve, and again himself. Marlow's tales were inconclusive; Emil's images tend to settle into singular meanings.

Demian implies a critique of idolatry—Europe "had gained the whole world, while losing its soul" (96)—but less self-critically than *HOD*. As Emil describes Demian and Lady Eve's salon with its outer and inner circles of elites ("astrologers and kabbalists, even a follower of Count Tolstoy ... practitioners of Hindu yoga, vegetarians, and others" [95]), the inner circle distances itself from all such creeds; they were "stillborn and useless," only "symbols."

> There was only one thing we conceived as our duty and destiny: for each of us to become so completely himself, so completely in harmony with the creative germ of Nature within himself, living in accordance with its commands, that the uncertain future would find us ready for any eventuality, whatever it might bring. (96)

The eventuality is the Great War. Demian's and Emil Sinclair's critiques of it are puzzling, given Hesse's near pacifism: the war is a creative process of individuation through which persons and civilizations must pass to become truly themselves. Demian predicts people will greet the fighting with blind excitement. "But you'll see, Sinclair, that this is just the beginning ... New times are dawning, and for those who cling to the old, the new will be horrible. What are you going to do?" (104–5). Demian's ambivalent enthusiasm is imaginable in August 1914, but what of Emil's? His is a retrospective, psychodynamic theodicy.[37] "Deep down, something was evolving. Something like a new humanity." The war's passions

---

[37] See Emmanuel Levinas's critique of theodicy in "Useless Suffering," 91–101.

Idolatry 273

weren't directed against the enemy; their bloody results were merely the outward materialization of people's inner life, the split within their souls, which desired to rage and kill, destroy and die, so that they could be reborn. A gigantic bird was fighting its way out of the egg, and the egg was the world, and the world had to fall to pieces. (107)

And it is here I sense that Conrad's inconclusive narrative—leaving Marlow "apart, indistinct and silent, in the pose of a meditating Buddha" (123)—breaks a link of religion with violence Hesse nearly forges. The link is the idol, not the image or pose but the idol of the Idea. While Plato's *eidos* is eternal, our *conceptions* of the eternal are contingent. Yes, *Demian* criticizes doctrines frozen in overdeterminations, a critique Emil turns upon Pistorius. And whether one thinks Hesse's pastiche of Gnosticism, Nietzsche, Jesus, and Jung is tenable for understanding religion, it does address religion and modernity creatively. (The flipped interpretations of Cain and Abel and the Prodigal Son are midrash-like as well as avant-garde.) However, the way Emil justifies the war as evolutionary generativity betrays an obsession to explain; a concept of self-world integration becomes a world-destructive theodicy.

If Hesse *momentarily invents an idol*, Conrad *momentarily undoes one*. True, as Marlow learns of Kurtz he grows obsessed with his "extremity" and "voice"— speaking from a limit "beyond the threshold of an eternal darkness" (94). He differentiates himself from Kurtz's revelation almost regrettably: "He had made that last stride, he had stepped over the edge, while I had been permitted to draw back my hesitating foot" (88).[38] He fears his lying did Kurtz injustice; nonetheless, he has done justice for his auditors, teaching us to attend without consoling explanations. "Nobody moved for a time. 'We have lost the first of the ebb,' said the Director" (96), who was listening with the others. Unmentioned is what touches every sign in *HOD*, suffering. We cannot "account for" the sufferings we witness except through attention and "restraint," a virtue Marlow praises (51) and which applies to interpretation. Hermeneutical restraint demurs from immediately explaining the suffering it attends. Marlow remembers with jarring regret the death of his African helmsman. I like to think the *Nellie*'s skipper is attending to Marlow's narrative of suffering when he misses the ebbing tide.[39]

Demian also ends with suffering. Emil goes to war, envisions Lady Eve in an apocalyptic shell burst, and awakens wounded near someone recognized as Demian. Emil has experienced Demian as a kind of Jesus, figured within his self's

---

[38] See Krieger, *The Tragic Vision*, 154–94.
[39] On Levinas and "ethics of attention," see Geddes, *Kafka's Ethics of Interpretation*, 127–8.

274   *Literature and Religious Experience*

"black mirror." As "friend and guide," Demian promises to be with him always, as an image and as Emil's "own image."[40] Even so, this epiphany is prefaced by Emil's suffering:

> In the morning I was awakened; I was to be bandaged. When I was properly awake, I turned over quickly toward the neighboring mattress. A stranger was lying on it, someone I'd never seen.
>
> The bandaging hurt. Everything that has been done to me since then has hurt. (109)

In that hurting, another narrative waits. Like Marlow's tale, Emil's does not end in certainties, which is good. Yes, it might have been better to engage the unknown neighbor beside him, but of that we are not told—only of Demian, ever the idea in Emil's mind.

***

Meanings have powers—performative, interrogative, indicative—that open spaces to persuade—by logic, emotion, or trust. Powers prompt troubled questions. Who gets to predicate, who gets to persuade? How are such determinations disclosed or concealed?

Questions like these return to pluralities and ambiguities in religious experience and tradition. Scholars and disciplined followers of religions discover flexibilities and surprises, rooted in the polysemy of scriptures, images, liturgies, and historical contingencies. Religious traditions have multi-aspect ratios, empowering them to understand their own limits and transformations through history. Extreme absolutism is rarer than hostile critics of religion surmise, but real. Productive vagueness gets refused, over-definitions sharpened, while insecure (or falsely secure) prophets and critics "gun up" their signs and territories.

Fictional works idolize too—but can become critiques of idolatry as they interrogate worlds and readers. Conrad's novella, marred by the ideologies it exposes, is more wary of its abyss than Hesse's, which concludes with a psycho-theodicy of war. *Demian* remains worth teaching, for Emil's idols neighbor our own, we critical apologists for religious studies and literature. Yet Marlow is the more chastened prophet of suffering.

---

[40] See Ziolkowski, *Fictional Transfiguration.* The novel's last line makes Demian quasi-religious: "*him, him,* [*Ihm,* unusually capitalized] my friend [*Freund*] and guide [*Führer,* also 'master,' 'leader']"—this in 1919.

Bibliography

Achebe, Chinua. "An Image of Africa: Racism in Conrad's *Heart of Darkness*." In *Hopes and Impediments: Selected Essays*, 1–20. New York: Doubleday, 1989.

Austin, J. L. *How to Do Things with Words*. Cambridge, MA: Harvard University Press, 1962.

Bell, Catherine. *Ritual Theory, Ritual Practice*. New York: Oxford University Press, 1992.

Bouchard, Larry D. "Openings and Closures in Religion and Literature: *Heart of Darkness* or *Demian, Life of Pi* or Something New." In *Teaching Religion and Literature*, edited by Daniel Boscaljion and Alan Levinovitz, 46–57. New York: Routledge, 2019.

Buber, Martin. *I and Thou*. Translated by Ronald Gregor Smith. Edinburgh: T&T Clark, 1937.

Caputo, John. *On Religion*. London: Routledge, 2001.

Conrad, Joseph. *Heart of Darkness*. Edited by Owen Knowles. London: Penguin, 2007.

Derrida, Jacques. "White Mythology: Metaphor in the Text of Philosophy," translated by F. C. T. Moore. *New Literary History* 6 (1974): 5–74.

Farley, Edward. *Good and Evil: Interpreting the Human Condition*. Minneapolis, MN: Fortress, 1990.

Foucault, Michel. *A History of Sexuality*, vol. 1. Translated by Robert Hurley. New York: Vintage, 1990.

Gadamer, Hans-Georg. *Truth and Method*, 2nd rev. ed. Edited and translated by Joel Weinsheimer and Donald Marshall. New York: Continuum, 1989.

Geddes, Jennifer L. *Kafka's Ethics of Interpretation: Between Tyranny and Despair*. Evanston, IL: Northwestern University Press, 2016.

Geertz, Clifford. *The Interpretation of Cultures*. New York: Basic Books, 1973.

Gerhart, Mary. "Generic Studies: Their Renewed Importance for Religious and Literary Studies." *JAAR* 45 (1977): 309–25.

Gerrish, Brian A. *Grace and Gratitude: The Eucharistic Theology of John Calvin*. Minneapolis, MN: Augsburg Fortress, 1993.

Gilkey, Langdon B. *Naming the Whirlwind: The Renewal of God-Language*. Indianapolis: Bobbs-Merrill, 1969.

Habermas, Jürgen. "On Hermeneutics' Claim to Universality." Translated by Jerry Dibble. In *The Hermeneutics Reader*, edited by Kurt Mueller-Vollmer, 294–319. New York: Continuum, 1988.

Habermas, Jürgen. *The Theory of Communicative Action*, vol. 1. Translated by Thomas McCarthy. Boston: Beacon, 1981.

Heidegger, Martin. *Being and Time*. Translated by John Macquarrie and Edward Robinson. New York: Harper and Row, 1962.

Hesse, Hermann. *Demian*. Translated by Stanley Appelbaum. Mineola: Dover, 2000.

James, William. *The Varieties of Religious Experience*. New York: Modern Library, 1902.

Krieger, Murray. *The Tragic Vision: The Confrontation of Extremity*. Baltimore, MD: Johns Hopkins University Press, 1973.

Levinas, Emmanuel. "Useless Suffering." In *Entre Nous: On Thinking-of-the-Other*, translated by Michael B. Smith and Barbara Harshaw, 91–101. New York: Columbia University Press, 1998.

Marion, Jean-Luc. *Being Given: Toward a Phenomenology of Givenness*. Translated by Jeffrey L. Kosky. Stanford, CA: Stanford University Press, 2002.

Marion, Jean-Luc. *God without Being: Hors-Texte*. Translated by Thomas A. Carlson. Chicago: University of Chicago Press, 1991.

Newton, Adam Z. *Narrative Ethics*. Cambridge, MA: Harvard University Press, 1995.

Ochs, Peter. *Peirce, Pragmatism and the Logic of Scripture*. Cambridge: Cambridge University Press, 1998.

Ochs, Peter, Nauman Faizi, Jonathan Teubner, and Zain Moulvi. "Value Predicate Analysis: A Language-Based Tool for Diagnosing Behavioral Tendencies of Religious or Value-Based Groups in Regions of Conflict." *JSSR* 58, no. 1 (March 2019): 93–113.

Otto, Rudolf. *The Idea of the Holy*. Translated by John W. Harvey. Oxford: Oxford University Press, 1917.

Peirce, Charles. *The Essential Peirce*, vol. 2. Bloomington: Indiana University Press, 1998.

Ricoeur, Paul. "Hermeneutics and the Critique of Ideology." In *Hermeneutics and the Social Sciences*, translated by John B. Thompson, 63–100. Cambridge: Cambridge University Press, 1981.

Ricoeur, Paul. *Interpretation Theory: Discourse and the Surplus of Meaning*. Fort Worth: Texas Christian University Press, 1973.

Schleiermacher, Friedrich. *Christian Faith*, vol. 1. Translated by Terrence Tice, Catherine L. Kelsey, and Edwina Lawler. Louisville: John Knox, 2016.

Schleiermacher, Friedrich. *Hermeneutics: The Handwritten Manuscripts*. Edited by Heinz Kimmerle. Translated by James Duke and Jack Forstman. Missoula, MT: Scholars Press, 1977.

Scott, Nathan A. *The Poetics of Belief: Studies in Coleridge, Arnold, Pater, Santayana, Stevens, and Heidegger*. Chapel Hill: University of North Carolina Press, 1985.

Suzuki, Daisetz T. "Enlightenment." In *Ways of Understanding Religion*, edited by Walter H. Capps, 33–44. New York: Macmillan, 1972.

Tanner, Kathryn. *Theories of Culture: A New Agenda for Theology*. Minneapolis, MN: Fortress, 1997.

Tillich, Paul. *Dynamics of Faith*. New York: Harper, 1957.

Tracy, David. *Blessed Rage for Order: The New Pluralism in Theology*. New York: Seabury, 1978.

Turner, Victor. "Betwixt and Between: The Liminal Period in *Rites de Passage*." In *The Forest of Symbols*, 93–111. Ithaca: Cornell University Press, 1967.

Turner, Victor. *Dramas, Fields, and Metaphors: Symbolic Action in Human Society.* Ithaca, NY: Cornell University Press, 1974.

Ziolkowski, Theodore. *Fictional Transfigurations of Jesus.* Princeton, NJ: Princeton University Press, 1972.

Afterword

Terry Eagleton

The idea of experience crops up in many forms in these essays, two of which (Unhae Langis's piece on *King Lear*, and Christopher Douglas's meditation on the silence of God) reflect, among other things, on the idea of suffering. It is an aspect of human life that might well lay to rest the dreary old cliché that all experience is good for you. Tasting a range of malt whiskies can be good for you, but being roasted over a fire is not. Emerson thought that all experience was worth having, an opinion not shared by the inhabitants of San Quentin. Oscar Wilde was equally skeptical about the value of experience, calling it the name we give to our mistakes. To put something down to experience means to regret that one was ever foolish enough to do it. As for suffering, the evangelists are careful to insert the Gethsemane scene into their narrative in order to show that Jesus, to put it mildly, has no desire for the experience of crucifixion. On the contrary, he is clearly panicking. If he did desire it, he would be a suicide rather than a martyr. Martyrs do not want to die because they place a supreme value on their life. This is why they give it up.

That a study of religious experience should look to literature is scarcely surprising. For literature is one of the subtlest forms of phenomenology we have, and as such, it lends itself to such notions as grace, evil, and redemption rather more readily than logical positivism or thermodynamics. It is in conveying a sense of how it feels to live through a situation that the creative writer has the edge over the historian, though the hierarchy is reversed when it comes to explaining the structural determinants of such states of affairs. According to Mark Knight, it is by turning to fiction that the Scottish writer George MacDonald comes to terms with the complexities of divine guidance. Shakespeare provides Julia Reinhard

280   *Literature and Religious Experience*

Lupton with a convenient way of investigating hope, healing, and benediction, while William Franke deftly triangulates Dante, *Hamlet*, and Mallarmé.

There is a branch of theology that deals specifically with the experience of God, which we know as mysticism. It is a motif to be found both in Kevin Hart's essay on A. R. Ammons and Jeffrey Sacks's consideration of unity and multiplicity in the poetry of Ibn 'Arabi. Yet, mysticism aside, it is debatable whether the idea of experience has much to do with Christianity, other than in the sense of being an essential dimension of all human affairs. Experience has, to be sure, a good deal to do with *religion*, as William James stylishly demonstrates; but it is doubtful that Christian faith is much illuminated by being dubbed "religious." If this is a risky claim, it is largely because there are so many contending definitions of religion, some of which, one might imagine, are likely to fit the Christian Gospel. Yet if religion, roughly speaking, is a matter of engaging in certain saving rituals and sacred practices marked off from everyday life, as well as conforming to certain divinely ordained codes, and if the point of all this is to establish contact with a rather fearful Deity, perhaps to placate him or win his favour, then it is highly doubtful whether Christianity falls into this category. In an astonishing passage, Jesus warns that the riff-raff of the back streets will take precedence in his kingdom over those pious types who obey the Mosaic Law. Pious types in the Gospel are the problem. Jesus is condemned to death by a committee of exceedingly religious men intent on not causing trouble for one of the cruelest imperial powers history has ever known.

In late capitalist times, religion has increasingly become a kind of therapy. It is more about crystals than crucifixion. The idea is to make you feel good about yourself, whereas the problem with a lot of people (Donald Trump, Tom Cruise, Rupert Murdoch) is that they don't feel bad enough about themselves. "Being yourself," that familiar piece of postmodern cant, was hardly a good idea in the case of Hermann Goering or the Boston Strangler. As far as religion-as-therapy is concerned, it is no accident that Hollywood is such an otherworldly place. It is home to every conceivable kind of spiritual gobbledegook, from necromancy to Scientology. (It is a sign of the intellectual profundity of the latter that even its name is a stupid tautology, meaning "the knowledge of knowledge." Some might make the same claim for the word "internet.") People who have too many butlers, minders, and swimming pools will naturally feel the need to take a break from this stifling materiality from time to time, and this is known as spirituality. Crystals are just the flip side of cocaine. Religion is there to soothe and comfort you, not (as for the Gospel) to get you killed. No Anglophone nation uses the word "comfortable" as much as the United States. The spiritual is the opposite of everyday life, so that from the standpoint of Madonna or John Travolta, Christianity is bound to look distastefully mundane. How can something as momentous as salvation depend on giving someone a drink of water?

Perhaps the most experiential aspect of the Christian faith today are such popular devotional practices as brooding on the five sacred wounds of the crucified Christ, or seeing in his death the most hideous torment ever inflicted. In fact, if Jesus really did only spend six hours on the cross, he got off remarkably lightly. A good many victims of the same form of execution, one reserved by the Romans almost entirely for political rebels and runaway slaves, thrashed around on their crosses for days. Perhaps the scourging Jesus is said to have received before his trek to Calvary helped him on his way. If you are about to be crucified, it is advisable to lose a lot of blood beforehand.

In his *Songs of Experience*, Martin Jay argues that the United States has always been a culture of experience, from the Puritans to the pragmatists. William James, for example, saw experience as the primary stuff of human existence. It was a foundation we could not dig beneath, since whatever we found there would still be a question of experience. Subjectivity, in short, goes all the way down, as it does for some German Idealists. Ludwig Wittgenstein, by contrast, who hailed from a Viennese high society with little time for petty-bourgeois Puritanism, argues that much of what we regard as experiential is not actually so. As he points out in his *Philosophical Investigations*, promising, expecting, intending, meaning, and a good many other everyday practices are not experiences. What experience accompanies the state of expecting her to return next Wednesday? Maybe none at all. I am describing a situation here, not reporting on an experience. It is not as though I feel a particular sensation throughout the period before she comes, which then vanishes the instant I clap eyes on her. Expecting may involve experience (keen anticipation, utter dread), but it is not an experience in itself. The images which come to mind when one reads *Middlemarch* are not part of the meaning of the work, and are of interest only to you and your psychoanalyst. When I ask "Is there a bus due?," no inner feeling need ghost my words for them to be sincere or comprehensible.

Christian Wiman writes well on prayer in this volume, and one might well ask what it feels like to pray. But what does saying "To be or not to be, that is the question" feel like? (It is, incidentally, the most difficult line in the world for an actor to deliver). What "experience" do the words convey? What does it feel like to promise? You may feel what you like, as long as you engage in the socially constituted performative known as promising. You have promised once you speak the words, even if you haven't the least intention of keeping them. Or take a custom like marriage. If a woman of reasonably sound mind stands beside a man before a cleric wearing a lacy veil and long white dress and pronounces certain sentences, then it won't do for her to turn round to her newly acquired father-in-law and say, "Sorry, I can't think what came over me. No disrespect to your son, mister, but what a damn silly thing to do." Marriage is a social institution, not an occurrence in your head. One might add that virtue is not an experience either, but a disposition. A generous-hearted person is one who is predisposed to act in a generous-hearted sort of way, not someone who walks around glowing and beaming with an inner condition known as generous-heartedness. In this sense, they are still generous-hearted even when they are asleep.

Meaning isn't an experience or mental process either. There is indeed a way of actually experiencing meaning, known as poetry, but this is a special case rather than the stuff of everyday life. If someone shouts "Fire!" in a theater, we do not generally pause to linger over the way the plosive "F" sound mimics the sudden outbreak of the blaze, while the rest of the word, with its long-drawn-out """ and rolling "r," captures something of its steady spreading. Poetry restores to language its full materiality, but it is not the best way to make oneself understood in Walmart. If one thinks of meaning as an experience, as opposed to thinking like Stendhal or Turgenev of the meaning of experience, it is easier to see it as one's private property, rather as one might feel oneself to be the proprietor of one's sensations. You can't, after all, have my pain, any more than you can have my back garden. But meaning is a way of using language, and language belongs to nobody. Even my most private experiences have to be interpreted—to myself as much as to other—and this involves using terms which others have used countless times before.

In a similar way, what is most scandalous about *agape*, as opposed to currently more fashionable forms of love (erotic, Romantic, familial, and the like) is that it is entirely impersonal. The Judaic culture of which Jesus is a product is not easily compatible with Romantic inwardness, any more than it is compatible with liberal individualism. *Agape* is a social practice, not a sentiment. I do not need to be personally acquainted with the person whose place I take in the queue for the gas chambers. I may find the vagrant to whom I chuck a piece of bread revolting, but that is no more relevant to the act of feeding him than finding him charming. This is why the paradigm of love in the Gospel is love of strangers and enemies, not friends. Anyone can love a friend.

Perhaps it is also why the so-called New Testament is so unswervingly hostile to the family, that great fetish of American society. Jesus seems to have precious little time for his closest relatives, giving the rough edge of his tongue to an

Afterword   283

overexcited fan who calls down blessings on the womb that bore him. There are several other examples in the text of how the family simply gets in the way of his mission. His celibacy does not betray a distaste for sexuality; in fact, unlike many of his devout acolytes today, he is remarkably laid-back about sex, as his encounter with the Samaritan woman would suggest. Celibacy of this kind is rather a way of freeing yourself from the business of diapers and mortgages in order to be available to anyone who needs your help.

For empiricists like John Locke and David Hume, experience is our only source of knowledge, yet it is a notoriously unreliable one. It is what assures us that our feet will still be there when we wake up, but it is the flimsiest of foundations on which to build. Like the media in Belarus, it is not really to be trusted, but it is all by way of information that we have. For a whole lineage of rationalists from René Descartes to Claude Lévi-Strauss, genuine knowledge means breaking with lived experience. It looks as though the sun is coming up, but actually the earth is going down. Putting a factory on stage, remarked Bertolt Brecht, will tell you nothing about capitalism. It is simply a fact about that system, Marx argues, that its fundamental mechanisms do not show up in the textures of everyday life, and not because anyone is trying to conceal them. It is a distinctively modern conception that our everyday experience is a matter of misrecognition. A rift opens up between how things are and how they appear to be—one which you can "resolve" *à la* Kant by claiming that things as they are are unintelligible to us. For Freud, the ego, which is the home of lived experience, can have no spontaneous knowledge of the unconscious (which in Freud's eyes constitutes the truth of our identities), since the ego exists only through the act of repressing these murky depths. The forces that shape our experience must inevitably be absent from it. We become human subjects only by virtue of a painful but necessary oblivion to much that goes into our making. Forgetting is good for you, and remembering is simply forgetting to forget.

In some contexts, the concept of experience is too cumbersome to be of much use. Instead of saying "I opened the door, put the tiger out for the night and closed the door again," I could always say "I had the experience of opening the door, experienced putting the tiger out for the night and experienced closing the door again." Has anything been gained by the manoeuvre? Doesn't the idea of experience simply cancel all the way through? "Experience" here is an empty signifier, a free-wheeling cog in the machine of language. This is not to say that the term is of no merit at all. "*That* was an experience!" is an indelible thing to say, even if only those who need to get a life would say it about opening the door. Similarly, "Does she have experience of operating on cataracts?" makes perfect

284 *Literature and Religious Experience*

sense. Experience can mean the flow of everyday sensations, or particularly memorable chunks of it, or the wisdom and know-how which come from having been in the game a long time. It is the first of these meanings which is peculiarly problematic, since it tends in empiricist style to reify the stuff of everyday life as "sense data." As Wittgenstein points out, however, my senses do not "inform" me of anything. They are not spies or counsellors.

The commodity form reifies experience as well. I happen to live on the northern coast of Ireland not far from Giant's Causeway, a UNESCO heritage site which attracts a large number of tourists. (When Samuel Johnson was asked whether the place was worth seeing, he replied, "Worth seeing, sir, not worth going to see"). For many years you could simply wander among the curiously shaped rocks of the Causeway, think of the mythical giant Finn McCool who stepped from there to the Scottish peninsula where Paul McCartney now has a house, and watch the Atlantic rumbling in.

Nowadays, however, things have greatly improved. You can have the Giant's Causeway Experience, which is a considerable advance on simply walking about the place peering at this and that. A whole battery of technological devices is now available, so that you can roam around the Causeway wired up like a suicide bomber. It is hard not to feel sorry for those millions of sorely deprived visitors in the past who explored the Causeway but didn't have the Experience. What we consume now is not objects and places but our sensations of them. Just as we never need to leave our cars, so we never need to leave our skulls. Since what all of these glossily packaged places have in common is the fact that they are experienced, they become, like commodities, interchangeable. Experience, a term which can mean something of exceptional value, ends up as a dead leveler. In a similar way, tourists are nowadays equipped with a device which allows them to see buildings without the fatiguing business of actually looking at them. This is known as a camera.

From Heidegger to Adorno, the warning went out that what is fading from the world is nothing less than experience itself. But this doesn't mean experience in the putting-out-the-tiger sense. It means something other than a flow of fleeting sensations which will have sunk into oblivion three minutes later. In the work of Walter Benjamin, it is closely bound up with recollection; and what is to be remembered above all is the tradition of the oppressed—of those obscure men and women, lost to history, who died in a struggle for justice but whose names will be mentioned in despatches on Judgement Day. It is not dreams of liberated grandchildren which drive men and women to revolt, Benjamin writes in his "Theses on the Philosophy of History," but memories of oppressed

Afterword

ancestors. The ambition of the enemy, he warns (he means the Nazis), is to wipe all alternatives to themselves from living memory. If they are victorious, not even the dead will be safe from their malignant power, since the dissidents amongst them will be written out of the record. For this to happen we must live off the top of our heads, existing only in the present. In a world of transient perceptions and instantly consumable objects, nothing stays still long enough to lay down the deep memory traces that Proust struggled to raise to consciousness. The eternal now of modern urban existence has eroded the kind of experience (*Erfahrung* rather than *Erlebnis*) which can enter the political unconscious and prove fruitful there.

One might argue that this side of Benjamin—the need to nurture deep subjectivity—is modernist, whereas the side of him that champions Brecht, Surrealism, and mechanical reproduction is avant-garde. Generally speaking, modernism turns from descriptions of things, which is the province of literary realism, to accounts of what they feel like. In this concern with individual consciousness, it offers an alternative to what it sees as the depthless anonymity of twentieth-century capitalism. The avant-garde opts for exactly the opposite strategy, turning that society's technology against itself by using it to scoop out the precious interiority of the bourgeoisie with shock, flatness, mechanism, fragmentation, impersonality, and montage, Meanwhile, science invades the inner sanctum of middle-class subjectivity in the form of psychoanalysis. Nothing could scandalize the Berlin and Parisian burghers more than a science of the human psyche.

At the center of Christianity lies an experiential void, otherwise known as the empty tomb. Yet it would have been no less void had one been able to look inside it a little earlier for a view of the Resurrection. Christians believe, by and large, that the Resurrection was a real event, but it was not an event in the sense that you could have taken a photograph of it had you been lurking around the tomb with a camera. This is not because it was unreal, but because it was too real for representation. If it defeats the image, it is because you cannot take a snapshot of ultimate reality, any more than you can of quarks or the unconscious. This is an event that transforms the whole notion of eventuality, including the distinction between the real and the symbolic, and thus falls through the net of language and over the edge of experience.

This, to be sure, is true of all things concerning God. Thomas Aquinas believes that theologians like himself do not know what they are talking about, one of the few beliefs they have in common with atheists. Take, for example, the doctrine that God is one. This is not an arithmetical proposition, since God transcends the language of accountancy. He is not one in the sense that Bruce Willis is thankfully one. God and the universe do not make two. He is not one in the sense of existing as a singular Being. In fact, he does not "exist" at all and is not best thought of as a Being. We have no idea of what it means to speak of him in such terms, even though it is essential to do so, since he is certainly not multiple either. Staying silent, as St. Augustine points out in the *Confessions*, is no help either. The theologian is in a Cordelia-like double-bind, able neither to speak nor to keep quiet. Yet of that of which we cannot speak, it is always possible to say a few words.

***

Terry Eagleton is a Distinguished Visiting Professor in English Literature at Lancaster University, UK. He is also a Fellow of the British Academy, an Emeritus Fellow of Wadham College, Oxford, and an Honorary Fellow of Jesus College, Cambridge.

Index

abolitionism(ists) 110, 112, 115, 118, 133, 137, 184, 185
Abrams, M. H. 167n21
absolute, the 32
absolute being 201, 202
absolute God 11, 206–7
absolute oneness 201
Abū al-'Alā' 'Afīfī 196
abundance 15
Achebe, Chinua 262
actualities 97, 98–9, 100, 101
Additiones 73
Adela Cathcart 167n25
Adelman, Janet 51
aesthetic magic 249, 250, 256
aesthetics 27, 156, 157
Agamben, Giorgio 45, 78, 79, 81, 147
agape 210, 214, 282
Ahmed, Sara 143n9
Alabaster, William 141
  breaking off his wedding engagement 153
  buying some books 153
  conjuring possible futures 152–3
  describes this interim 154
  encounter with Thomas Wright 148
  fidelity to the event of his conversion 155
  turning experience 141–57
  wager of 141, 151–2, 156–7
alienation
  from experiences 135
  experiences of 2
Allah *see* one (God)
All's Well That Ends Well 39, 222
All the Light We Cannot See 212
al-Qāshānī, 'Abd al-Razzāq 202
Althusser, Louis 93, 143–4, 150
  description of workings of ideology 151

Altizer, Thomas 3
  "death of God" theology 173n50
ambivalence 63
American Gods 243, 252–3, 255
Ammons, A. R. 280
anachronic critical approaches 102, 103
Anattapariyaya 218
ancient Israelites 178, 179–80, 185, 187
Ancient Near East (ANE), religious traditions of 178, 179, 189
aneconomic gift 228, 235, 236n34, 237
Anselm 62, 127
apocalypsis (revelation) 80
apophatically 235
Aquinas, Thomas 285
"Are you only my childhood?" 14–15
Arnold, Matthew 247, 265, 266
Arsic, Branka 237, 238
art as closed off vs openness 102
artistic magic 249, 250, 253, 255
Asad, Talal 165n15, 243, 247
atheism 11, 17, 127–8, 129, 154, 285
Atonement 60, 62
Attebery, Brian 243, 248, 253
At the Back of the North Wind 165, 167n25, 170–1
Auden, W. H. 1–2, 35
Augustine 2, 148, 263
Augustine conversion 145, 150
  compared with Pauline conversion 149–50, 151
Auschwitz 75
Austin, Lynn 183–5, 186, 187, 188
"Au tombeau d'Edgar Poe" 30
avant-garde 273, 285

Bacon, Francis 94
Badiou, Alain 77–8, 79, 86, 142, 142n8, 143, 144, 147, 151, 152, 153, 154
  on truth of an event 153
Baptist religiosity 14–15

Index

Barth, Karl 190, 259
"Bartleby, the Scrivener" 230, 232
Baudelaire, Charles 22
Beauty of Inflections, The 94n15
Beecher, Reverend Lyman 111
Begbie, Jeremy 171
belief 125, 131, 133, 134
  and atheism 127–8, 129
  conditions of and for 151–2
  emotional resources 130, 132, 135,
    136, 138
  flawed experience of 135
  and religious practice 151
Bell, Catherine 265, 266, 267
  on ritual 268
  on ritual and misrecognition 267
beloved 193–4, 195, 196,
  205, 206
Beloved 260
benedicere 52
benediction 39–40, 41, 42, 43, 46, 47–52,
  137, 239, 280
benevolence 227, 232, 233, 234
Benjamin, Walter 78, 284–5
Berger, Peter 3, 105n63
Bergson, Henri 31
Berry, Wendell 110, 119–22
Bible 178, 187 *see also* New Testament;
  Old Testament
  and sense of metanoia 117
  and slavery 184–5, 187
"Bidden Guest, The" 68–9
Bidgoli, Mehrdad 49–50
Billy Budd 227
"Bitter-Sweet" 15
#BlackLivesMatter 224
Blake, William 24–5
blessings
  and children 47, 51
  in Christian Scriptures 40–1, 51
  and curse 47
  of the deep 42, 48
  failed blessings 47
  greeting blessing 39–42
  heavenly blessings 42
  in Islam 41
  in Jewish Scriptures 40–1
  kneeling and falling for 49
  and phenomenological readings 41

and phenomenology of theatrical and
  religious experience 41
Priestly Blessing 39, 41, 46, 48
in Shakespeare's plays 39–40, 51 *see
  also King Lear*
as shields against danger and curses 46–7
Blood Meridian 189
blood myths 60
blood theology 62
Bloom, Harold 64
Bodhidharma 216
Boeve, Lieven 75–6, 77, 85
Book Against God, The 128, 129, 132–3,
  137, 139
Boston University 2
Brémond, Henri 31
Broken Estate, The 126
Buber, Martin 263
Buddha 213, 214, 218, 264
Buddhism 5, 7, 55, 214, 215, 216, 221,
  222–3, 264, 265
  connectedness concept 217
  enlightenment 265
  Heart Sutra chanting 217
  ignorance concept in 213
  impermanence concept 218
  interbeing worldview 214–15, 223
  interdependence concept 219
  karma concept 219
  kindness concept in 212–13
  lovingkindness concept in 210, 214
  mindfulness 211, 214
  name-and-form concept 218–19
  no-self concept 213, 217, 218, 222
  nothing/everything concept
    212–13, 222
  suffering concept in 218
Budick, Sanford 41, 47
Bultmann, Rudolf 60
Bunyan, John 166
Bush, Douglas 92
Butler, Judith 145n22
Byron 104n59

Cage, John 5
Calvin, John 62, 163, 259, 263
Calvinism 163–4
  Calvinist Congregationalism 111
  natural man concept 115

Index

Candle in the Darkness, A 183, 184–5, 186, 188, 189
Canterbury Tales, The 23
Canuel, Mark 103n55
Caputo, John 236, 236n34, 263, 265
Castiglia, Christopher 104n58
Cavell, Stanley 51
characterization, in novel versus in short story 109
charity 122, 212, 230, 231–2, 233, 238, 239
Chaucer, Geoffrey 22–3
Chesterton, G. K. 167–8n25
children 15, 17, 18, 45
    and blessing 47, 51
    and slavery 112, 113
China
    avoidance of fantasies 246
    mythology and folklore 253, 254–5
Christianity 1, 2, 280, 281, 285
    blessings in Christian Scriptures 40–1
    Christian faith 127
    conversions *see* conversions to Christianity
    and slavery 184–5, 187
chronos 80
Cicero 219
City of God 190
Civil War, as a theological crisis 186–7
Cole, Rachel 230, 232, 233, 235
Coleridge, Samuel Taylor 62, 166
Collected Poems 64n36
collective metanoia 118
collective unconscious 262
commination liturgy 45
commodity, and reifies experience 284
compassion 202, 210, 212, 219, 223
confession 261
Confessions 2, 148, 148n33, 151, 286
    "tolle lege" scene 149
Confidence Man, The 230, 231, 237
Conrad, Joseph 259, 269, 273, 274
contingent 150
contingent being 198, 202, 204, 205
conversions to Christianity 73, 81, 83, 116–17, 132, 151, 227 *see also* Augustine conversion; Pablo de Santa María; Pauline conversion
    Alabaster's experience 141, 155
    conversion-as-transformation 142

conversion narratives 82, 147
conversos 73
    dual mode of 75
    in the Epistles and Acts 79–83
    as interruption 85–6
    as *kairos* within a *chronos* 82–3
    and metanoia/metanoeo *see* metanoia/metanoeo
    and repentance 80
    and salvation 77
    as turning 80
cosmic order 244
Creation 59
creation 130, 198
creative fidelity 155
crucifixion/crucified 281
    as ultimate interruption of sacral violence 76
cultural objects, religiousness of 2
cultures 265–6
    cultural revolution 100
    and reaffirmation 98
Cur deus homo 62
curses 43
    and blessings 47

Dalí, Salvador 94
Dante Alighieri 21, 22, 25, 29, 33, 35–6, 119, 121, 166, 280
    on cultural politics 30
    on descent into hell 29
    negative theology 25–6, 32
    political position 36
    prophetic poetry 21, 22, 29, 30
    visio Dei 25
Dastur, Françoise 147, 150–1
Dearborn, Kerry 166n19
Deitweiler, Robert 3
Deleuze, Gilles 78
delusion 94
Demian 259, 262–3, 271–4
demonic Dao 255
demonic magic 244, 249–50, 252
de Moor, Johannes C. 178, 188
demystification 168, 169
depression, and religion 11
Derrida, Jacques 3, 147, 235, 236, 237
    on gift 228–9, 228n7
    on impossible gift 229n9

290 *Index*

despondent nihilism 104n58
destitution 15
determinism 133
Devil 64
devotional acts 8
De vulgari eloquentia 30
Dickinson, Emily 91
diffused suspicion 104n58
Dimock, Wai-Chee 179
discourse practices 271
disidentification 218, 222
Divine Comedy 119
divine grace 227, 233
divine guidance 279
divine hiddenness 177, 181, 182–3, 190
   as evidence for atheism and
      naturalism 190n54
   and free will 183
   and Israel's woes 178
   necessity of 182–3
   and suffering 177
divine inspiration 227
divine love 210
divine mercy 202
divine names 193, 196–200, 201,
   202–4, 205
divine revelation 21
Doctorow, E. L. 190
Doerr, Anthony 212
Donne, John 62
Dostoyevsky, Feodor 233
double predestination 163
Douglass, Ann 111
Douglass, Frederick 111, 184, 187
"Dover Beach" 266
Dubois, Martin 167
During, Simon 241n2
Durkheim, Emile 3
dynamic gifts 227–8, 235
   and interpretive frameworks 234–5
   and material gift, difference
      between 228–9
dynamogenics 227n1

Eagleton, Terry 101
"East Coker" 68
Eberhart, Richard 58
Eckhart, Meister 14, 15
economic exchange 235

economic gifts
   and dynamic gifts, experiential
      distinction between 233
economy of exchange 232
ecstatic experience 149
elevation 203–4, 205
Eliade, Mircea 3
Eliot, T. S. 1, 68, 120
Elisaeis, The 142
Elkins, James 102
emancipation 112
Emerson, Ralph Waldo 238, 279
emotional resources 130, 132, 135, 136, 138
Empson 61–2
Empson, William 61
emptiness doctrine 216, 219
enchantment 104
Endō, Shūsaku 260
Engels, Friedrich 97
Enlightenment 139
enlightenment 123
Epistles 80, 81, 82, 84
epistrephō 80
equanimity 214, 223
escapism 94, 96n24, 97, 104
essence, God as 196, 197, 198,
   199–204, 207
Ethos and worldview 265
evangelicalism 179–87, 189, 279
event 147, 149, 150–1
evil 279
evolution, and silence of God 183
existential hermeneutics 101–4
existential realism 116
experience 279
   and knowledge 283
   as sense data 284
   temporality of 141

Faërie 249–52, 253, 255
failed blessings 47
fairies 250–1
fairy stories 249–50, 251
faith 61–2, 125, 127, 130, 133, 263
   Christian faith 75, 127
   crisis of 133, 134
   as a definitive interruption of the past
      through the revelation of a new
      reality 74

Index

and experience 6
faith-versus-fiction dilemma 127
feminization of 139
religious faith 128
false consciousness 97, 99
and intimations of transcendence 92
fantasies 167–8, 172, 173, 174,
179–80, 182, 183–4, 185, 186,
188, 241
and aesthetic magic 249, 250, 256
affective aspect of 242
and artistic magic 249, 250, 253, 255
and demonic magic 244, 249–50, 252
and fairies/fairy stories 249–50, 250–1
literature of magic/superstition 246–52
non-realist fantasy 247
and superstition 241, 243, 244–6, 249,
253, 256
Farber, Leslie 151, 152
farewells 46
Father, the 171
Federici, Silvia 245
Felski, Rita 103, 103n55, 105, 168
Fergusson, David 162, 173, 173n46
Fessenden, Tracy 6, 235n30
Ficino, Marsilio 74
fideism 23
fidelity *see also* faith
to the event 153–4
grounded in doubt 155
as praxis 155
fides quaerens intellectum 127
Fifth Commandment 45
Fish, Stanley 4, 24
Fletcher, Caroline 184
flourishing 47
Floyd, George 223
*Foben shidao (The Buddha Belongs to the
Dao)* 243, 252, 253, 254–5
"For Isaac Rosenberg" 57
Foucault, Michel 3, 266
on power 267
free will 181, 182, 183
Freud, Sigmund 283
Friedrich, Hugo 32
Frye, Northrop 1
fundamentalism 127
Fuṣūṣ al-ḥikam 196, 197, 200, 202,
203, 205

Gadamer, Hans-Georg 229n9, 268
Gaiman, Neil 243
Gandhi, M. K. 224
Gardner, Helen 62
Geertz, Clifford 264, 265
generative lovingkindness 221
generous-heartedness 282
"Genesis: A Ballad of Christopher
Smart" 57, 59–61, 62, 63
genuine knowledge 283
Geoffrey Hill 57, 69
German Idealists 22
German Ideology, The 96
Ghibellinism 33, 36
Gift of Death, The 237
gifts
an economic gift 228, 235, 236n34, 237
and charity 230, 231–2, 233, 238, 239
dynamic gifts 227–8, 228–9, 234–5
and economy, immeasurable gap
between 236, 238
gift-economy 232
gift-exchange 230, 235, 237
immeasuring extent of 235
impossibility of 229n9, 230, 233, 236
material gifts 228–9
noneconomic gift 236
ontological gift 229n9
political rhetoric of 228n5
religious experience of 227–30
unappropriated gift 235–9
and vigilance 230–5
Gilead 184
Gilead novels 133–4, 135, 136–8, 139
Gilkey, Langdon 263
Girard, René 76–7, 127
God/gods 64
activity of 171, 172
and beings, relation between 197–8
dependent upon 200
essence as 196, 197, 198, 199–204, 207
hiddenness of *see* divine hiddenness
and human agency, relationship
with 180
interaction with humans 161–2
modesty of 66
multiplicity of 199, 200, 203, 204
names of 201
oneness 265

292 Index

oneness doctrine 285–6
system of 183, 186, 189, 190
unity of 200
unlimited distinction of 201
and world, distinction between 194,
196, 198–9, 200, 205
God and the Goddesses 4
"God's Grandeur" 266
"God's Little Mountain" 55–6, 57, 58,
63–4, 65, 67, 68–9
Gone to Earth 55–8, 63, 65, 69
Gospels 24, 80, 280
grace 279
Grand' Œuvre 27
Great War 272–3
Greco-Roman 244
Greenberg, Clement 1
Greenblatt, Stephen 4
greeting blessing 39–42
greetings 46
Guattari, Félix 78
guidance 161–74
guilt 8
Gunn, Giles 238

Habermas, Jürgen 268
Halevi, Solomon *see* Pablo de Santa María
Hamlet 23–4, 25, 26–8, 29–30, 33, 39,
40, 280
Hamlet in Purgatory 4
Hanegraaff, Wouter 245
Hanh, Thich Nhat 213
Harding, James 189
Harris, George 115
Hart, Kevin 7, 76
Hartman, Geoffrey 43
healing 280
Heart of Darkness 259–63, 272, 273
heaven 24–5
heavenly blessings 42
Hegel, Georg Wilhelm Friedrich 22
Heidegger, Martin 78, 268
Hellenic/Hellenistic sources 210–11
Heraclitus 272
Herbert, George 12, 14, 15, 26, 166
heresy 4
Heschel, Abraham Joshua 11
Hesse, Hermann 259, 269, 271–2,
273, 274

Hill, Geoffrey 57, 62–4, 64n36, 66–8
double nature of words 62–3
early stages of writing 58–9, 63
education of 61
and First World War 58
lateral writings 68
as a religious poet 59, 68–9
on his religious vision 65
view of poetry in visionary terms 64–5
Hillard, Molly Clark 168
historical criticism 103
Hoeller, Hildegard 230–2, 233, 235
Holy Scriptures 23, 25
Holy Spirit 169–70
"Holy Thursday of William Blake" 57–8
Home 136, 138
honor 45
hope 101, 280
Hopkins, Gerard Manley 266
Houellebecq, Michel 133
Housman, Alfred Edward 58
Howard-Snyder, Daniel 181n13
How Milton Works 4
Howson, Peter 94
Hugo, Victor 22, 212
human and divine agency, interaction
of 161–2
human experience, structuralist
views of 3
humankindness 211, 212, 224
humbling 47
Hume, David 283
Hungerford, Amy 4, 6, 235n30
Huxley, Aldous 3
hyper-specific historical moments 4

Iberia 73, 74, 84
Ibn 'Arabī 193, 280
Ibn Sīnā 197
icon 271
iconoclasm 4
identification 104
ideology 144, 168
and art and poetry 93
imaginaire operating as 98
idiosyncrasies, of doctrines 4
idolatry 259–74
idols 66
Igitur 27, 28

Index

Ilāhiyyāt (Metaphysics) 197
imaginaire, operating as an ideology 98
imagination 118
immortal joy 13
Imperial Masochism: British Fiction, Fantasy and Social Class 168
individuation 271–2
Ingersoll, Julie 188n41
Institutes of the Christian Religion 62
interbeing 213–14, 223
interdependence 209
interpenetration 209
interpretant 270
interpretive framework 238
interruption 73
  as a Christian faith 75
  and conversions to Christianity *see* conversions to Christianity
  and crucifixion 76
  enables a new freedom 76–7
  faith and reality 74
  and philosophy 78
  political interruption 79
  and religious experiences 77
  and resurrection 76, 80
  and rupture 76
  theology of 75–9
intersubjective experience 144
Isaac the Blind, Rabbi 64
Islam, blessings in 41
I will love you in the summertime 16

Jackson, Ken 4
Jackson, Rosemary 243, 247–8
Jacob, blessing of Joseph 42–3
Jacobs, Alan 228n7
Jaeger, Peter 5
James, William 3, 113, 227, 227n1, 233, 238, 263, 281
Jay, Martin 281
Jenson, Robert 171
Jesus Christ 17, 171, 279, 280, 281, 282–3
  blood of 60, 62
Jewish Scriptures
  blessings in 40–1
Josephson-Storm, Jason 245
Jung, Carl 262
justice 224

kairos 80–1
Kamienska, Anna 13–14
Kant, Immanuel 22, 247
karma 217, 219
kavod, honor or respect 51
Keats, John 91, 92, 98
Keen, Paul 93
Kenner, Hugh 62
kindness 212, 214, 215, 217, 220
King, Martin Luther 224
King Lear 41–2, 212–13, 279
  benedictional designs 47–52
  Culminations: Blessing, divided 48–50
  Epilogues: Blessing retold 50–2
  liturgy of curses 42–7
  Prologues: Beginning with blessings 47–8
King Log 68, 69
kneeling and falling, for blessings 49
Knight, Mark 7
Korpel, Marjo 178, 188
Kristeva, Julia 29
Kritik 265
Kucich, John 168
Kuntzler, James Howard 133
Kuzner, James 51

Lacan, Jacques 132
"Lachrimæ" 63, 69
"L'Action restreinte" 35
language 30, 173n46
Larsen, Timothy 164, 165
Lawrence, Sean 215
Lectures on Ideology and Utopia 96
légende des siècles, La 22
Leithart, Peter 229n10
Letourneau, Sara 212
"Letter from Oxford" 65
Levinas, Emmanuel 78
limit-of questions 264
Limits of Critique, The 103n55
limit-to questions 264
literature, transitive character of 104
"Little Gidding" section of *Four Quartets* 120
Locke, John 283
Logan, William 64n36
longing 55–69
lord/lordship 198, 201

294 *Index*

Lord of the Rings, The, series 243
lordship and essence, relation
 between 202
love 282
lover and beloved, indistinction
 between 193, 194, 205, 206
lovingkindness 210, 212, 214, 215, 221
Lowell, Robert 58
Luther
 1535 commentary on Galatians 62
Luther, Martin 74
Lynch, William 3

MacDonald, George 161, 164, 279
 awareness that the thread 172
 fantasy genre 167
 ideology 168n27
 propositional comments on
  providence 173
 realism and fantasy, division
  between 167
 reference to thread as guides 161–2,
  167, 169, 172–3
 reflections on suffering 166
 relationship with Calvinism 163
Macherey, Pierre 93
magic 241, 243, 250, 256
 aesthetic magic 249, 250, 256
 artistic magic 249, 250, 253, 255
 of commodity, competition, and
  capitalist expansion 255
 demonic magic 244, 249–50, 252
 genealogies of 244–6
 natural magic 244, 249, 250
 policing 245
 technical magic 249, 250
Mallarmé, Stephane 23, 26, 29, 33,
  35, 280
 and the event *Manqué* 33–5
 and *Hamlet* 26–7, 29, 30
 and incertitude 27
 and negative revelation 26, 31–3, 34
 œuvre 29, 30
 on poetic language 29–30, 33
 prophetic poetry 25, 27, 36
 syntax of 34
 tribute to Edgar Allen Poe 30
Mallarmé au tombeau 35
Manitongquat 210

"Man of Letters in the Modern World,
 The" 58–9
map, meaning of 269–70
Marcel, Gabriel 154, 155
 fidelity as praxis 154
Marotti, Arthur 4
marriage 282
Marvell, Andrew 62
Marx, Karl 97, 283
Marxism 93
Matt. 10:29 24
Mayan notion of unity 210
McCarthy, Cormac 133, 189
McClure, John 5, 235n30
McEvilley, Thomas 219
McGann, Jerome 92, 93, 99
meaning 282
 and power 269, 271, 274
Melville, Herman 227, 230, 237, 238, 239
 vigilance in keeping track of the way
  gift 230–5
"membership" 121–2
memories 284–5
Merchant of Venice, The 49
Mercian Hymns 69
Merton, Thomas 17
metanoia/metanoeo 80, 109, 110–11,
  113, 114, 115, 119–20, 122–3 *see also*
  conversions
 and Bible 117
 and change 110
 collective metanoia 118
 of faith and moral principle 115
 and penitence 115
 and reality 117
 recursive dimension of 122
 as sacrifice 110
 and *satori* 117
Metz, Johann Baptist 75, 77, 79
Midrash Tanhuma 66
Milbank, John 229n9
Miles, Jack 77n13
Milner, Jean-Claud 35
Milton, John 24, 119, 166
Miltonic fall 132
mimesis 95
mindfulness 211, 224
Miracles of Our Lord, The 164
Miserables, Les 212

Index 295

misunderstanding 267–8
modernism 285
modernity
  role of dynamic moral sources
    in 234n27
modernity, secular-religious
  opposition of 137
modus vivendi 155
Moltmann, Jürgen 77
moral sources 234–5
More, Tomas 74
Morrison, Karl 142n6
Morrison, Toni 183, 260
mortal sorrow 13
Moser, Paul 181n13
Moses 66
Moxey, Keith 102
Mt. Parnassus 66–7
Mt. Sinai 66, 67
Muḥī al-Dīn Ibn al-ʿArabī 193
Muir, John 211
multiplicity 280
music 165, 171–2, 173
Myriel, Monseigneur Bienvenu 212
"Mystery in Letters, The" 33
*Mystery of the Charity of Charles
  Péguy, The* 68
mysticism 280
  of Nothing 32
myths 28, 246–7, 248
  and fantasy, compared 248

Nagel, Alexander 102
name-and-form 219
narrative Paul 82
nasīb 193, 194, 195, 196
natural magic 244, 249, 250
natural man 115
nature 220
  in Stoic cosmology 220
necessarily existent 197
negative theology 25–6
"Neues Testament und Mythologie" 60
New Historicist criticism 4
Newman, Barbara 4
new spiritualities 5
New Testament 170, 282
  Matthew 24
  Acts 74, 80, 81–3, 84, 85, 110n1, 142

Romans 80, 81, 116, 187
1 Corinthians 80, 81, 83, 187
2 Corinthians 80
Galatians 62, 79–80, 84
Philippians 83, 84
Colossians 187
1 Timothy 187
Philemon 187
1 John 263
1 Peter 60
conception of time 80
Nicholas of Lyra 74
Niebuhr, Reinhold 2
Nietzsche, Friedrich 155, 233
Noll, Mark 186, 188
non-confessional confession of the
  postsecular 6
noneconomic gift 236
nones 5
non-realist fantasy 247
no-self 213–14, 217, 222
nothing 34, 47, 212, 215–16, 218, 221
  metaphysics 32
  and negative revelation 32, 33, 34, 35
  of the present and its political
    implications 35–6
  and revelation 25–8
Novalis 167, 271, 272
number "one" 204–5

"Ode to a Nightingale" 91–2, 94n16, 105
Old Testament
  Genesis 41, 42, 49, 170, 187
  Exodus 144
  Leviticus 50
  Numbers 46, 137
  Deuteronomy 39, 42, 43, 44–5, 46, 50,
    64, 187, 263
  Job 51, 179, 180, 182, 188, 189, 190
  Proverbs 169
  Isaiah 65, 184, 187
  Jeremiah 65
one (God) 197, 199–200, 201, 203, 204–5,
  206–7 *see also* divine names
  essence 196, 197, 198, 199–204, 207
  levels of unity 203
  lover and beloved, indistinction
    between 193, 194, 205, 206
  one not one 205

Oneness 209–10, 219
"On Fairy-Stories" 249
On Religion 3
ontological gift 229n9
originated being 205
otherness 75–6, 77
Otto, Rudolf 3, 263
Ozeki, Ruth 212

Pablo de Santa María 74, 83–5
  comments on Paul's epistles 84
  emphasis on repetition and
    return rather than rupture and
    revolution 84
Pablo de Santa María, conversion of
  conversion narrative 84
  description 73–4
  and Pauline conversion, compared 74–5
  returning 83–5
pain 164, 165n15
paradigms 268
Paradise Lost 119
Paradiso 25, 29, 36, 121
Paradiso VI 36
Parini, Jay 110
Parson's Tale, The 23
partial faiths 5
Partisan Review 2
Pascal, Blaise 60, 151
Paul 74, 76
  change 79–80
  conception of the resurrection as an
    "interruption" in history 80
  Damascus Road experience 83
  epistolary 80, 81, 82, 84
  existential realism 116
  faith of 79
  "messianic" time 81
  regaining of sight narratives 82
  as a thinker of "dialectic" 79
  as a thinker of "rupture" 79
  understanding of salvation 79
  view of time 79
Pauline conversion 74, 78, 81, 83,
  116, 145
  as a climactic moment in a coherent,
    diachronic history 74
  conversion narrative 74, 79–83
  dual reading of 77

immediacy 82, 149
  and Pablo's conversion, compared 74–5
  signified 74
Pauline Epistles 80
Peirce, Charles 269, 271
penal substitution, interpretation of 62
pensée 60
Pensées 151
"Pentecost Castle, The" 63
perennialist tradition 4
Perennial Philosophy, The 3
Pericles 44
Phantastes 161, 162n3, 165, 167–8, 168–9,
  170, 171, 173
phenomenological openness 234–5
phenomenology
  of "orientation" 143n9
  of the self 141
  of surprise 150–1
  of the "turn" is recognition 150
philology, and literature 61
Philosophical Investigations 281
philosophy, and interruption 78
physis 220
Picasso, Pablo 94
piety 263
Pionke, Albert D. 162n3
Plato
  eidos 273
Plotz, John 167
pneumatic sympatheia 220
Poe, Edgar Allan 112
Poe, Edgar Allen 30
Poésies 34
poetic love 206
poetics 5
poetry 282
  and faith 61
  as prophecy 26
  as a scala a Dio 67
"Poetry of Allen Tate, The" 58
poiesis 2, 9
political interruption 79
political theology 4
possibilities 94, 98–9, 101, 104–5
  and actuals 100
  critical openness to 104n59
  interpretive possibilities 93
post-critique 105

Index

post-historicist turn 103n55
Postmodern Belief 4
postmodern fiction 6
postsecularism 5–6, 235n30, 241, 243
power 266–7
 and meaning, links between 259
prayer 14, 281
 answer for 13–14
 benediction 39–40, 41, 42, 43, 46,
  47–52, 137, 239, 280
 honest prayer 15
Prayer That Will Be Answered,
 A 13, 13–14
"Prayer to Humankind, A: A Poem of the
 Heart" 210
praying, meaning of 12–13
prejudices 268
presentism 103n55
Priestly Blessing 39, 41, 46, 48
primary intuitions 17
Princess and the Goblin, The 161, 172
Prometheus Unbound 99–101
promising 281–2
prophecy 21
prophetic poetry 22
prophetic revelation 32
prostration 49
Protestant Reformation 147
Proudfoot, Wayne 3
providence 163, 164, 165–7, 169, 172–3,
  173n46, 174
 and Calvinism 163, 164
 definition of 162
 polyphonic approach to 173
 understanding of 165
pseudo-Dionysius 157
psychoanalysis 285
Pullman, Philip 127
pure poetry 31
Pyrrhonian Skeptics 214

Qur'an, God's unity in 265

Rahula, Walpola 213
Rainolds, William 148
Rashi 64
ratio-centric Man 245, 255
reaffirmation 98
real 104

realism 94, 133, 167
realist novel 247
reality 33, 198, 205
recognition 150
redemption 228, 279
religion 1, 144, 280
 as a cultural system of symbols 264
 institutional orthodoxy 4
 and interruption 78
 and social ethics 125
 as therapy 280
religious dimensionality 261
religious experiences 8, 144, 279
 conception as a perpetual form of
  interruption 77
 between participation and
  reception 228
religious materialisms 4
religious practice 151
religious sociology 3
Religious Studies 3
religious symbols systems 269
religious symbol systems 264
religious turn 4, 4–5
Remembering 110, 119, 123
remembering and forgetting 283
repentance for sin 110
representation 95–6
resurrection 285
 interrupts the world 80
 as ultimate interruption of sacral
  violence 76
retributive divine agency 180
revelation 21, 25
 negative revelation 25–8
 negativity, in Dante and Mallarmé 31–5
 and Nothing 25–8, 35–6
 of an other world 27
 prophetic 25, 27–8, 29, 30, 32, 33
 and prophetic poetry 21–2, 24,
  25, 29
 religious skepticism 23
 Word of 21
Ricard, Matthieu 215
Richardson, Robert 238n40
Ricoeur, Paul 50, 79, 86, 94, 271
 on literary visions 99
 work on ideology 96–7
Rimbaud, Arthur 22

rituals 228, 267, 280
power management 266
Road, The 133
Robinson, Marilynne 125–6, 127, 128,
133, 136, 137, 184, 260
Romantic Ideology, The 92
Romanticism 22, 91–2, 93, 166–7
enchanted imaginings 101
transcendent imaginings 99
and utopia 93–4
romantic racialism 114
Roxana 142
rupture 76
Ruskin, John 95

Sacks, Jeffrey 280
Sacred and the Profane, The 3
Sacred Canopy, The 3
sacrifice 62
St. Ambrose of Milan 59
St. Augustine 286
St. Basil of Caesarea 59
St. Bonaventure 59
St. Edmund Campion 63
St. Gregory of Nyssa 64n36
St. Jerome 110
St. Paul 65
salutation 40, 46
salvation 118–19, 123, 228
Salzberg, Sharon 222
Santideva 215, 217
Schaefer, Donovan 3, 242
schizophrenia 97
Schlegel brothers, Friedrich and August
Wilhelm 22
Schleiermacher, Friedrich 3, 263, 268
Schulz, Bruno 17
Schwartz, Regina 47
science 285
Scofield, Bruce 211
Scott, Nathan 2, 3, 4
Scrutiny of Scriptures 73, 83
secondary self 17
sectarianism 4
secular 243
and religious worldviews, contemporary
opposition between 75–6
Secular Age, A 128, 234n27
secular and secularizing 126–7

secularism 132
secularity
and dynamic gifts 228n3
hypothesis 5
movements of 4
secularization
history of 2
of masculinity 139
thesis 235n30
self 17, 218
self-reflection 22
self-seeking hunter of forms 69
self-transformation under grace 109
Senecan drama 219
sensationalism 133
sense of self 218–19
sensibility 4
sensibility, traditions of 3
Sentimental Designs 111n5
serial convert 157
Seven Types of Ambiguity 61
Shack, The 179–83, 189
Shakespeare, William 22, 24, 209, 279–80
acknowledgement of insecurity of
blessing 51
on hard truths of reality 224
scenes of blessings in plays 39–40
Shearman, John 104–5n60
Shelley, Percy Bysshe 96, 99–101
utopian vision of the world 100
shema (symbol and ritual) 265
Shenji, Mengru 243
Shifā' (The Healing) 197
Shiraz, Sadi 210
shiver 238
Shropshire Lad, A 58
sign and symbol 271
Sikka, Sonia 94n16
Silence 260
silence of God 279, 286
silence of gods 177, 178, 180, 181, 187–8,
189, 190
and evolution 183
in the face of human suffering 179,
186–7, 190–1
in the face of Israel's woes 178, 187
and free will 183
and human silence 178
methods for giving voice to 178

Index

necessity of 178, 182–3
and responsible partner concept 190
Silent God, The 177–8, 188, 190
slavery 111, 112, 118
  and children 112, 113
  and Christianity 113
  original sin of 113, 116, 118
  slaveholders 113, 114, 115, 118
  slave traders 114, 115
Smith, Matthew 26n11, 41, 50
"Snow Man, The" 68n54
social power 267
Song of Myself 14
Songs of Experience 281
Songs of Innocence and Experience 58
souls 17, 110
Sources of the Self 234n27
Southwell, St. Robert 63
Spellbound: The Fairy Tale and the
  Victorians 168
Spenser, Edmund 142
Spiewak, Jan 13
spiritual innocence 17
spirituality 280
Steiner, Rudolf 3
Stephen Prickett 166
Stevens, Wallace 67–8
Still, Colin 3
Stillinger, Jack 92–3n6
Stowe, Harriet Beecher 109–10, 111,
  112–13, 116, 117–18, 119, 122, 123
  and Calvinism 111
  depiction of North/South tensions 114
  divine inspiration 111
  on maternal love 115
  and *metanoia* 112, 113, 114–15, 117
  on metanoia and reality 117
  orders of personal conversion 113
  and romantic racialism 114
  on slavery as sin 113, 116, 118
Structure of Complex Words, The 61–2
Styers, Randall 244
subcreation 250, 251, 256
subhuman others 255
subjectivity 281
Submission 133
Sucitto, Ajahn 218–19
sufferings 77, 162, 164–5, 166, 173, 219,
  221, 273–4, 279

deserved human suffering 180
gods' silence on *see* silence of gods
sui generis 3, 4
superstition 241, 243, 249, 253, 256
  genealogies of 244–6
Suzuki, Daisetz 263–4
symbolical grotesque 95

"Take physic" 220–1
Tale for the Time Being, A 212
Tanakh 178, 179, 187
Tanner, Kathryn 265, 266
Tarjumān al-ashwāq 193, 205
Tate, Allen 58–9, 62
Taubes, Jacob 78
Taves, Ann 242
Taves, Anne 3
Taylor, Charles 128, 166–7n21, 227–8,
  229n9, 233, 234, 247
"Tea at the Palaz of Hoon" 67–8, 68n54
technical magic 249, 250
Tempest, The 39
Templeton, Arthur 212
Tenebræ 63, 68
Tertullian 62
theological language
  limitations of 173–4
theology of interruption 75–9
Thibaudet, Albert 31
Tibetan Buddhist monks 223
Tillich, Paul 2, 263, 269
TIME 2
Tóibín, Colm 127
Tolkien, J. R. R. 61, 243, 249–50, 256
"tombeau d'Edgar Poe, Le" 34
Tompkins, Jane P. 111, 111n5
Torah 64
To the Lighthouse 132
"to turn" *see* turning
tout court 94
"To William Dunbar" 57
Tracy, David 263, 264
transcendence 201
transcendental realism 95
transformation of social order 109
TRI 93, 101
Trinity 22
Troilus and Cressida 209, 219
true state 146

Truth 23
truth-event 141
Turner, Victor 268
turning 141–57 *see also* conversions to
    Christianity
Tuve, Rosemond 62
Two Gentlemen of Verona 49

unappropriated gift 235–9
unbelief 126, 127–8, 129, 130, 132, 133,
    134–5, 136, 137, 138
Uncle Tom's Cabin 109–10, 111, 112, 114,
    115, 119, 122, 123, 184
unconditional fidelity 155
Un Coup de dés 26, 31, 33
understanding 267–8
uninterrupted narcissism 236
unity[oneness] 210, 280
universal salvation 22
University of Chicago 2
unknowable 32
unknowing 24, 33
Upstate 133
utopia 93, 95, 96–100, 101

valediction 46
vale of tears 144
Varieties of Religious Experience, The 3
vernacular theology 4
Vetter, Tilmann 218
"vierge, le vivace, et le bel aujourd'hui,
    Le" 34–5
Vinaya 217–18
visio Dei 25
vision 91–105
visionary 22, 26, 69
visionary blindness 24
visionary imagination 93, 95, 104
von Schelling, Friedrich Wilhelm Josef 22

wagers 141, 151–2, 156
Webb, Mary 55–7
Weber, Max 3
Westermann, Claus 51
White, Vernon 174n51
Whitman, Walt 14
Wilde, Oscar 279
will
    limitations of 151, 152
Willibald, Sandler 76, 77
Wilson, Edmund 111
Wimsatt, W. K. 62
Winter's Tale, The 39, 51
wisdom 213
witch-hunting 245
Wittgenstein, Ludwig 281, 284
Wolff, Robert Lee 167n21
women, in *Gilead* novels 137–9
Wood, Christopher 102
Wood, Ellen 167
Wood, James 125, 126, 128, 130, 132, 133
    faith-versus-fiction dilemma 127
    loss of faith 126
    on purposelessness 128
    and secularization 127
    shadow of uncertainty 135
    unbelief 127–8, 134
    view on religion 127
World Made By Hand series 133
Wright, Daniel 167
Wright, Thomas 142
Wynter, Sylvia 245

Young, William Paul 179, 182

Zen koan 215–16
Zipes, Jack 168, 168n27

Printed in the USA
CPSIA information can be obtained
at www.ICGtesting.com
LVHW011644091223
766046LV00004B/70